Ethics from a Theocentric Perspective

ETHICS

EPT : PG 195-279

m: 195-210   Th: WRITE
T: 210-250   ABST#10
W: 250-279

James M. Gustafson

1. Theology and Ethics
2. Ethics and Theology
   (in preparation)

Ethics from a
Theocentric Perspective

Theology and Ethics

The University of Chicago Press

The University of Chicago Press, Chicago 60637

Library of Congress Cataloging in Publication Data

Gustafson, James M.
  Ethics from a theocentric perspective.

  Includes bibliographical references and index.
  Contents: v. 1. Theology and ethics.
  1. Christian ethics. 2. Ethics. I. Title.
BJ1251.G876   241   81–11603
ISBN 0–226–31110–4 (cloth) AACR2
      0–226–31111–2 (paper)

For Elmer W. Johnson

Contents

Preface

This book is the product of at least thirty years of "homework." The research done for it was not determined by the requirements of a highly specified project with a single issue, like *Christ and the Moral Life*, or *Can Ethics Be Christian?* It is not an effort to analyze the state of a discussion, like *Protestant and Roman Catholic Ethics*. Rather, I have drawn upon a broad range of scholarly and pedagogical interests, some of which have waxed and waned during this period and others of which have persisted throughout. I have, of course, been studying the major texts in the Christian tradition, particularly as they pertain to theological ethics. I have attempted to gain sufficient competence in the history of Western moral philosophy to know the issues, to see their relations to the ethics of Christianity, and to define myself in relation to some of the alternatives. From time to time I have concentrated on particular moral problems; early in my career when I taught social ethics I read intensively in various social and policy sciences; more recently I have been interested in science and technology, and particularly in biological and medical research and practice. Waxing and waning during this time have been interests in other sciences as well; it has become clear to me how much undergraduate interests in sociology and cultural anthropology, geology (particularly in earth history), and physical anthropology shaped some of my basic outlooks. For many years I have read *Science* each week, failing to comprehend far more than I have comprehended. While I have never studied literature and history with any particular professional intention in view, they have been part of my late night and weekend reading. For a few years I especially studied the Jewish ethical and legal traditions. In preparing to deliver the University of Chicago's Barrows Lectures in India in 1978, I studied the history, the culture, and the dominant religion of that great land for a year. I have never taught what is in this book in classes, except upon occasional provocations by students to spend a few minutes on these matters.

The footnotes and technical discussions could have been much more extended than they are. Before prudence captured my aspirations, I anticipated that almost as many pages as there are in the text would be given in the notes to more detailed discussion of things only touched on in the text and to extensive development of my agreements and disagreements with the writings of a great many persons whose work in one way or another impinges upon mine. After assurance by colleagues and friends that previous publications demonstrated my scholarly conscience, I reduced the scope of my intentions in this regard. I, of course, know better than they or anyone else how much there is that I do not know, and how many problems there are that require more intensive examination than I have given them.

This book is also the product of fifty-five years of living. It is the fruit not only of scholarly life but of reflection on events in which I have participated or which I have observed, on the lives of persons and communities that have been part of my own life, and on experiences of the worlds of nature and culture. Since my life has not been idiosyncratic, and the worlds of experience are those shared by many persons, I dare to believe that what is said is neither private nor narrowly sectarian.

Theologians are more verbose than analytical philosophers; their arguments are looser, and their rhetoric freer. As a class we write more like Josiah Royce and William James than we do like R. M. Hare and W. V. O. Quine. This book is not only in "professional character" in these regards but is also much longer, and in parts less tightly developed and more rhetorical, than my previous books. It is, as Rousseau says about his *Emile,* "too big, doubtless, for what it contains, but too small for the matter it treats."

If I had written only for systematic and moral theologians, the book could have been reduced by more than fifty percent. If I had the skills and talents to write for some of the contemporary philosophers whose work I admire, I might have gotten the basic argument down to the normal length of an article for a learned journal. I suppose a logician could reduce such logic as it has to a few symbols.

The size of the work is related to its scope. I have not undertaken anything of this scope before, and certainly will not again when both volumes are complete. But the size is also related to the readership I hope the book to have. Theologians are responsive to and responsible for a religious community that is much larger than the small cluster of their professional colleagues. While it is not our vocation to provide "snappy sermon-starters" for preachers, it is our vocation to help those who have the awesome responsibility of speaking for a religious tradition to a community of persons who are to some degree committed to it. We easily underestimate the interests of intelligent and learned laity who are concerned about theological and ethical issues that emerge in their experience; we should keep such persons in view. It is also our responsibility to speak to a community of persons who, while not identifiably Christian or even religious, have religious interests. These communities do not require that we be less learned, less careful, in the development of our discourse, but I believe it is fitting to be more discursive and to allow oneself a bit of passion in making crucial points. I was a pastor and preacher before I became a theologian; I hope some of the better traces of my first, and in many ways much more difficult, calling are in this work.

Among the many to whom I owe a great deal are the following.

Elmer W. Johnson, lawyer by profession, scholar and teacher by avocation, Christian churchman and responsible citizen by deep conviction, and friend, to whom this book is dedicated. Through his personal generosity and good offices I was able to write this book under ideal conditions. His confidence in my work, while inordinate, has sustained me; his interest in its development evoked numerous crucial and clarifying conversations; his concerns for ethical theory and for moral practice in corporate, professional, and public life stretch my mind and teach me a great deal.

Mary Ann Minelli, who efficiently and cheerfully rendered excellent copy from my own first draft, and in many other ways facilitated the completion of the manuscript.

Martin Cook, whose graduate studies enabled him by empathy to grasp my basic lines of thought, and who has challenged some of its basic positions and aided in making some formulations more precise. He also did much of the detailed bibliographical and editorial work.

David Tracy, with whom I have discussed in detail the spiritual and moral passions that in part generated this book, and conversed at length and in depth about its argument. We know where we differ.

Numerous nontheologians, who in conversations, seminars, jointly taught courses, interdisciplinary research groups, and in other ways have shaped my theology and ethics more than they ever intended.

The University of Chicago, for granting me an extended research leave of absence to write this volume.

President Fred Stair and the faculty of Union Theological Seminary, Richmond, who in 1978 invited me to deliver the Sprunt Lectures in February 1983, and thus hastened the concentrated pursuit of the goal of bringing out a coherent interpretation of theology and ethics. The second volume of this work, *Ethics and Theology*, will be the basis for the Sprunt Lectures.

The faculties of the Pacific School of Religion and of the Phillips University Graduate Seminary for invitations to deliver the Earl and Scott lectures, respectively. These occasions were the first public airing of themes of this volume.

Stephen S. Bowen, a lawyer with a theological mind, whose critical reading of the penultimate draft noted both editorial and substantive matters to which I have attended.

Larry L. Greenfield and Robin W. Lovin, who in different ways freed me from many institutional cares and responsibilities by adding to their own.

Louise. "Then the Lord God said, 'It is not good that the man should be alone; I will make him a helper fit for him'" (Gen. 2:18). He did, for me.

1

An Interpretation of Our Circumstances

Every effort to develop a coherent theology is shaped to some extent by the author's perceptions of the circumstances in his or her culture and in the churches. A theologian can have a view of what features of disobedience or unbelief within the church are threatening the historic integrity of the tradition and the faith, and thus can address his or her work to overcoming those threats. It might be that an author has some vision of the "dominant mentality" of the age, one that permeates not only members of the religious community but members of a given culture. To this he or she might attempt to provide a theological critique or, more ambitiously, an alternative way of construing the world. In its most ambitious form this alternative defines the "question" that is raised by the culture, and then in turn provides the theological "answer." Or, the theologian might have a sophisticated interpretation of the intellectual milieu which renders traditional religious beliefs and practices incredible, odd, or archaic. He or she might attempt to show that theology is a worthy enterprise for intelligent persons, and seek to counter the arguments made against it by its secular critics.[1]

Theological ethics is no different in this respect from systematic theology. Protestant theological ethics in various of its historic phases, and certainly in many of its recent forms, seems to have postulated that legalism is the archenemy of Christian faith and of Christian morality. Legalism, it is claimed, is rationalistic, overly simple in the provision of answers to complex problems; it becomes repressive and thus is counter to the freedom of the Christian. It invites an effort to attain salvation by good works, issues in a static rather than dynamic morality, is more concerned to issue prohibitions than to stimulate aspirations to do good, and so forth. The issues of Christian ethics at a given time and place are viewed as analogous to St. Paul's concern that conformity to the Jewish law was being required of the Gentile Christians in the primitive church. Between the risks of antinomianism and legalism, the latter is judged to be more perilous to Christian integrity, if not to Christian morality. Others come along to find Christian ethics wallowing in relativism, or are deeply disturbed by the decline of traditional standards of Christian morality,

---

1. I have in mind here the following: Martin Luther, "The Pagan Servitude of the Church," in *Martin Luther: Selections from His Writing*, ed. John Dillenberger (Garden City, N.Y.: Doubleday, 1961), pp. 249–359. Herbert Richardson, *Toward an American Theology* (New York: Harper and Row, 1967). A "sociotechnic intellectus" dominates our culture (p. 20). "Theology must develop a conception of God which can undergird the primary realities of the cybernetic world, viz., systems" (p. 23). Paul Tillich, *Systematic Theology*, 3 vols. (Chicago: University of Chicago Press, 1951–63), 1:59–66. F. D. E. Schleiermacher, *On Religion: Speeches to Its Cultured Despisers,* trans. John Oman (New York: Harper and Brothers, 1962).

and in turn see that the risk of antinomianism is more perilous than that of legalism.[2]

Like other efforts to write theology and theological ethics, this one is also guided by certain perceptions of both historic and highly contemporary circumstances in society, culture, and religion. One does not come to a perception of circumstances by simply adding up a variety of statistics, piling up information from the relevant works by historians, scientists, social scientists, and cultural commentators. One's perception is informed, but not limited, by the wealth of materials and an open-minded study of them, and by personal involvement in human life. This leaves one with mixed impressions: sometimes more with the cacophony of Gunther Schuller or John Cage than with the harmonious completions of melody that one enjoys in Brahms, Beethoven, and Schubert. It sometimes leaves one with the impressions of the mature Jackson Pollock rather than with the subtle but formed totality of Monet, not to mention the integration his tremendous figures that Michelangelo provides in the Sistine Chapel ceiling. No doubt even the modern movements in art, foreign as they seem to an earlier Western tradition, are informed by a perspective. It may be a technical perspective on what constitutes a musical idea and its expression, or it may be something as deep and perhaps implicit as attempting to resonate with a general view of the world, or the spirit of the times.

Any theological response to a perception of the issues of life in the world invites the charge of circularity: no theologian adds up impressions, stores images and sounds as if mechanically recorded on film and tape, reads all relevant historical, scientific, and social studies before forming a cumulative impression. No one else does either, as is amply demonstrated by social scientific studies of poverty and nutrition, from proposals by physicists about the risks involved in nuclear energy, or from various historians' efforts to state what have been the dominant forces in determining the character of a particular epoch, including their own.[3] Intellectual interests predispose us to see some things and ignore others; intellectual and moral concerns predispose us to order what we see in certain ways so that certain features are judged to be more salient than others; symbols, metaphors, and beliefs assist us in providing some coherent interpretation to all the impressions and information that we gather.

2. Among our contemporaries, for an antilegalist view, see Paul Lehmann, *Ethics in a Christian Context* (New York: Harper and Row, 1963), especially pp. 124 ff. A response to Christian relativism motivates much of Paul Ramsey's work; see his *Deeds and Rules in Christian Ethics* (New York: Scribner's, 1967), for example, pp. 145–225.

3. For example, on the nutrition issue, compare the famous essay by Garrett Hardin, "The Tragedy of the Commons," *Science* 162 (13 December 1968): 1243–48, with the essays on food in *Science* 188 (9 May 1975).

Likewise, there are religious concerns that inform the theologian's efforts to state the meaning and significance of what he or she perceives and responds to in the world.

The extent to which "perspective" informs perceptions has long been discussed. What one sees and does not see is related to where one stands. Surely there is, in any self-critical observer, an interaction between what is seen and the concepts, metaphors, and the like used to describe and evaluate what is seen. A mutually corrective process occurs in ordinary experience that is not different from what occurs in the development of a modern science. Beliefs, metaphors, and theories presumed to be adequate to explain or interpret the meaning of what is experienced prove to be inadequate, and must be revised.[4] The notion of the mind, the human spirit, as a tabula rasa certainly is not true, and has long been discarded, though important and necessary efforts are made by philosophers and others to show how we can minimize distortions that come from our perspectives—whether in physics, in economics, in ethics, or in theology.

All this is by way of indicating that the evaluative description of relevant circumstances for theological ethics that this chapter develops is shaped in part by some deep religious convictions. Yet in many portions of the chapter, evaluative descriptions similar to mine can be offered by persons who have no articulated religious beliefs. Much of what I say is relatively commonplace; the ways in which I construe some more general significance for what I say comes from a theological perspective.[5] I clearly do not mean that I can view the world from God's perspective, that my theological construing of the world is the way in which God construes the world. Rather, my interpretation of the significance of what I describe is theological in that its critical reference point is what for the moment can be called an Other, an ultimate power, and thus is construed in relation to that.

Some Aspects of Our Culture

One of the persistent characteristics of human beings since the dawn of consciousness is that our species extends the range of its domination

4. See the historically oriented philosophy of science in such works as Stephen Toulmin, *Foresight and Understanding: An Inquiry into the Aims of Science* (New York: Harper Torchbooks, 1963); *Human Understanding*, vol. 1 (Princeton: Princeton University Press, 1972); Norwood R. Hanson, *Patterns of Discovery: An Inquiry into the Conceptual Foundations of Science* (Cambridge: The University Press, 1958); Thomas Kuhn, *The Structure of Scientific Revolutions*, 2d ed. (Chicago: University of Chicago Press, 1970).

5. For a discussion of theology as a way of construing the world, see Julian N. Hartt, "Encounter and Inference in Our Awareness of God," in *The God Experience*, ed. Joseph P. Whalen, S.J. (New York: Newman Press, 1971), pp. 51–54.

over forces and powers deemed at first beyond its control, for the sake of greater security to individuals and communities. Hans Jonas has richly developed the significance of a major difference between plants and animals, namely, the motility of animal life.[6] Through the development of the capacities to move, animals extend the range of their purposive activity in a way that plants cannot. Time also becomes significant; desires can be met only by taking time to exercise the powers of locomotion to find that which fulfills them. Plants, by their immobility, are far more susceptible to their immediate environments. In the predecessors of our species there was a further increase in the use of locomotion and space, of the capacity to articulate desires, and of time to extend the range of domination over the natural environment in order to secure fulfillment of human purposes. Cultures are dependent upon the growth of capacities for this control; cultures are the environments of artifacts and meanings which are shaped to render the life of the human community more immune to the uncertainties of natural conditions, human feelings, and historical events.

With the development of cultures and social arrangements a network of dependencies grows so that humans are not only dependent upon "raw" nature but also upon those artifacts, myths, and symbols, and patterns of persistent social arrangements that develop in interaction with nature. The scope of human intervention in the natural processes is increased with the domestication of grain grasses and animals, the making of tools for hunting, and other activities. Yet nature continues to pose threats to the survival of individuals and communities, and to these are added the threats of the cultural and social creations themselves: the threats of other human communities which have developed their own means to secure life for themselves; the threats of failure due to the inadequacies of the artifacts; the clashes between the myths and symbols which interpret the natural world and the world of experience they are supposed to explain; and increasing susceptibility to disasters resulting from excessive reliance upon human creations which can be drastically harmed by natural and human forces. Surely the history of our species is one of increasing extension of human control over the forces of nature, of the creation of second natures in culture, of the development of human artifacts culminating in modern technology, of the establishment of controls over human behavior itself by means that vary from the most raw forms of physical coercion to the most subtle forms of indoctrination and education. This has liberated us from many of the causes of the insecurity and anxiety that in former times preoccupied our ancestors. The mastery of fire makes

6. Hans Jonas, *The Phenomenon of Life: Toward a Philosophical Biology* (New York: Dell, 1966), pp. 104–6.

controlled warmth possible; the knowledge of the causes of smallpox and the development of inoculations to immunize us to it apparently have eradicated this ravaging disease from the face of our planet. There is less famine in the world now than in the nineteenth century, in spite of the population growth.

Thoughtful persons need not be told that this increase in mastery has not eliminated insecurity and anxiety: these feelings simply are evoked by different objects, by other contingencies, including new ones that are the unintended and unanticipated consequences of the extension of human mastery itself.[7] Our own period of history and of technological development is replete with examples of this. Faced with countless deaths due to malaria and countless more restrictions of healthy functioning in those who are diseased but continue to live, we successfully develop DDT to eliminate the carrier mosquitoes. Then we find that the DDT has harmful consequences to human and other forms of natural life, and that mosquitoes can develop resistance to the DDT. With the spread of public health measures, such as better disposal of human waste and the purification of water supplies, we are able to expand the life expectancy of human beings in many societies by significant measures, only to find that population grows at an alarming rate. We then must be occupied not only with attempting to diminish the rate of population growth but also with developing sufficient nutritional resources and the political and economic means to distribute them to avoid massive malnutrition and starvation in many parts of this planet. Human mobility generally is increased with the development of means of rapid transportation, as is our individual mobility with the private automobile, but we find that we face grave shortages of the fossil fuel to sustain these means of transportation. An understanding of human genetics and the concurrent development of medical technology enables the medical profession to detect in utero not only the sex of the fetus but also an increasing number of indications of genetic "defects." We are left with the problem of deciding what constitutes a sufficiently significant aberration from a statistical norm to warrant the anticipation of a "defective child" and thus, for many parents, the consideration of securing an abortion. The functioning of the human brain remains a great mystery, but our knowledge of its processes and functions grows with comparatively great rapidity. This opens the possibilities of increasing

7. Theodosius Dobzhansky describes the interesting case of efforts to restrain the growth of the European rabbit population in Australia. It had been brought to the continent a century previously by European settlers and became "a pest of major proportions." In 1950 a viral disease, mysomatosis, was introduced into the rabbit population to control its rate of growth. Rabbits died of the infection. In five years the disease had become less severe, more rabbits were recovering from it, and when it was still fatal the length of time between the infection and death lengthened. Theodosius Dobzhansky, *Mankind Evolving* (New Haven: Yale University Press, 1962), pp. 302–3.

control of its functions, and thus of human behavior, human thought, and human purposes.

Each of these sorts of research and the interventions that follow them have been laudable achievements. Increased knowledge has increased the capacities to control certain known threats to human well-being. Malaria was reduced for a considerable length of time in most parts of the world; parasites that debilitate human functioning were reduced, to the benefit of millions of persons; the development of rapid transportation has vastly increased that motility of the human species, which Jonas perceptively calls a necessary condition for the extension of human purposive activities. The progress in human genetics has enabled investigators to explain a large number of health problems, and has opened the possibility not only for the abortion of fetuses that are radically defective but also of therapy for individuals who have been unlucky in the genetic lottery. Many ill patients have been aided by pharmaceutical therapies that function in the brain, even when an accurate explanation of why and how they function remains unknown. These and many other achievements have reduced human suffering, extended the life span, and enlarged the realm of satisfaction that comes with human achievements. This progress has occurred at a rapid rate. To be sure, there are the counterproductive consequences which new research, new technology, and new public policies and individual therapies must now pursue. My intention is not to elaborate such next steps but rather to indicate that both the achievements and the less than happy consequences raise some ancient and difficult issues in the mind of a theological interpreter.

All such achievements have been motivated by human valuations; they express human desires directed toward certain specific ends, such as particular genetic research and subsequent therapies, and more general ends, such as relief of suffering, betterment of health, and enrichment of human experience. Each of these achievements has expressed some things that are valued about human life. We are in a deep way moved by the suffering of our fellow human beings; when the causes of that suffering can be controlled, or even eliminated, we strongly desire to develop the knowledge, the technical means, the social policies, and the other resources necessary to that end. Malaria is debilitating; the control of its effects through the use of quinine and its derivatives in large populations is not feasible, especially in conditions of poverty and ignorance. It is surely more efficient to eliminate the carrier of the disease than to engage in a symptomatic therapy for those to whom it has been carried or is likely to be carried. We value not only the elimination of suffering from the disease but also the most efficient means by which the cause can be eliminated.

When large populations are debilitated as the result of parasites that are spread by the lack of sanitation facilities and by impure water supplies, we are moved to act as effectively as possible on the point in the "causal chain" of disease at which the maximum beneficial results can occur. There can be no question that this is a better way to relieve health problems than through the distribution of therapeutic palliatives, whether sulfa-derived drugs to eliminate one cause of diarrhea, or Pepto-Bismol to remove the immediate discomfort. We value relief from suffering for individuals, and for human communities as small as a family and as large as a nation; we value the greater productivity in human work that freedom from disease makes possible. We work so that coming generations will not have to suffer from the same diseases that have afflicted countless generations in the past.

It is not necessary to engage in similar reflection on the rest of the illustrations. Increase in knowledge is a purposive human activity; it stems from the valuations of individuals and communities; it is directed towards ends that human beings value. We can reason inductively from these and other human activities to a somewhat empirical verification of what we do value about human life. We value many things. While one might attempt, as philosophers and theologians have done for centuries, to bring all of them under a single term or concept such as happiness or pleasure, that level of generalization usually obfuscates rather than clarifies not only our practical choices but also a rigorous examination of the range of objects of human valuation. It turns out that the achievement of certain ends brings unintended and often unanticipated consequences that counter the desired effects and makes us less certain of our ability to plan rationally. Public health measures have increased the life span in many societies, but in the absence of the control of births, the development of larger resources for the production of food, the establishment of the necessary conditions for energy production and other things which make the increased productivity of food possible, events move toward tragic consequences. Good intentions successfully fulfilled create conditions in which beneficial and deleterious consequences come about inexorably and together. The range of human foreknowledge, while expanding in certain areas as a result of our progress in the sciences, nonetheless is incomplete, and undesirable consequences for which the innovator cannot be held causally and morally accountable follow in the course of events. The limits of human capacities to control all consequences of our interventions into the natural and historical processes of life, while being decreased in some arenas, nonetheless remain, and as a result action involves risks.

These observations, however, do not indicate what we ought to value about human life. To be sure, general answers are available: we ought to value human well-being, or happiness. In the practical order of our modern society, however, it is probably harder than in some simpler societies to avoid virtual antinomies as we specify various aspects of well-being, and even more as we specify the necessary conditions for fulfilling them. Physical life is valued, if not as an end in itself, as the necessary condition for the possibility of any other values for human beings. We value not merely physical life but the sustenance of certain qualities that are necessary for various aspects of human well-being. What are the necessary qualities? What aspects of human well-being ought we to value? Why do we value what we value? If we value the capacity for normal intelligence and in the light of this begin to abort all fetuses that can be diagnosed to have chromosomal aberrations that destine them to sub-normal intelligence, do these ends and means need to be justified? Persons of superior or normal intelligence are not destined to be happy, to make contributions to the well-being of others, or to contribute to the common good of the human communities to which they naturally belong. Many things we value about human life are not subjected to sufficient critical scrutiny; in circumstances of scarcity, persons and societies are forced to choose among the things properly valued, and between persons who will have access to what is valued. Also our valuations, whether as in-dividuals, as small social units like the family, or as societies that are institutionalized as nation states, are curved in upon our immediate self-interests. Whether we choose to explain this by a natural principle of a struggle for survival (not merely physical survival at a minimal state, as in conditions of starvation, but survival at a certain level of human com-forts), or as a human defect which can be remedied in some way, indi-viduals and communities are in most cases curved in upon their own immediate interests.

These illustrations indicate that modern societies and cultures, as well as individual persons, are gifted with capacities and possibilities that are naturally and properly exercised to increase control over what were formerly contingencies, accidents, matters subject to fate or to the irra-tional determination of the gods—to necessity, however it has been sym-bolized. They also indicate that to be human, in spite of the vastness of human achievements, is to be limited. Knowledge and foreknowledge are expanded; capacities for control of future events are extended; finitude, however, is not overcome. Capacities to value even what is necessary for the sustenance of other existing persons, not to mention future ones, are restrained by preoccupation with more immediate self-interests. We are tempted to sloth, to a self-satisfaction with conditions as they now exist for us, and to their preservation. We are tempted to pride, to overweening confidence in our knowledge, foreknowledge, and capacities to control the future consequences of our interventions. We may not be sure what the ultimate purpose of life is, but we can be certain that we are finite, limited. We may not be sure that there is an ultimately sovereign and purposive power governing all things, but we can be sure that we are creatures, and that we are not God.

The limitations of foreknowledge and control of consequences that are discernible in the areas of intervention into the physical processes of life are even clearer when one observes human efforts to control social, political, and economic processes in individual societies, and in the relations between societies and states. Some of the differences between the two areas of investigation and action were highlighted in a very sharp way in the *Methodenstreit* at the turn of the century, especially in the German literature. A sharp antithesis was drawn between the *Naturwissenschaften* and the *Geisteswissenschaften* in the face of the ascendency of the methods and objectives of the natural sciences.[8] The questions debated and the distinctions made were many. Could one with confidence transfer the assumption that events were controlled by natural laws to the realms of human action? Or was the subjective meaning of human action, its intention or motive, a "causal" factor which was not subject to the determinations of laws?[9] (The same question in more sophisticated form continues to be debated in contemporary philosophical action theory.)[10] If human actions, individual and collective, are not governed by natural laws in the sense that the physical world is, what is the status of generalizations in the studies of human activities? Is sociology a nomothetic science, that is, a science that can develop laws of social processes which make predictions of subsequent developments possible? Is history an ideographic science that deals with the particular characteristics of individual events or sequences of events, and thus is not susceptible to the formulation of laws? In dealing with social realities and with "historical individualities," is the formulation of ideal-types the only reasonable way to make generalizations? If so, is their function to be the classification of historical and social data, or is it to provide heuristic devices by which the particularities of events and movements could be elucidated in light of exaggerated ideal constructs called ideal-types?[11]

8. Some of the major contributors to this discussion were Wilhelm Dilthey, Heinrich Rickert, and Max Weber. For a recent discussion of the issues which focuses on Dilthey, see Michael Ermarth, *Wilhelm Dilthey: The Critique of Historical Reason* (Chicago: University of Chicago Press, 1978).

9. See *Max Weber: The Theory of Social and Economic Organization*, trans. A. M. Henderson and Talcott Parsons (New York: Oxford University Press, 1947), pp. 87–115.

10. The literature is vast. For one trenchant example, see the famous article by Donald Davidson, "Actions, Reasons, and Causes," *Journal of Philosophy* 60 (1963): 685–700.

11. See Max Weber, *Methodology of the Social Sciences,* trans. and ed. by Edward A. Shils and Henry A. Finch (Glencoe, Ill.: The Free Press, 1949), pp. 89 ff.

Like most efforts to polarize possibilities, these turn out in the long run to be too simple. We have vast amounts of data, some terribly important and some terribly trivial, from the investigations of individual and collective human actions. Many more activities have proved to be subject to forms of quantification than novelists, philosophers, and theologians believed to be possible.[12] Both common sense and the fortifications of quantifiable data have led not to attempts at predicting certainty but to the development of more precise probabilities which eschew certainty but give us favorable odds for the predictions of particular events. Vast knowledge industries have grown, using all of the most highly developed kinds of technology to move from crude observation, individual insight, and geniuslike intuition to calculation of probable consequences that would result from alternative courses of action in the complexities of human societies. Some of these studies have, with some justification, merited ridicule for their triviality; many more have confirmed, disconfirmed, or led to the revision of insightful observations. The volume of information gathered has reached the point not only of choking the investigators with excessive data but of duplication of efforts. Yet few persons would seriously defend the view that it is better to be ignorant about society, to engage in interventions in various of its processes by a blind trial and error, than to have information that is as accurate as possible.

The perspective of the investigator has a bearing on the development of the natural and biological sciences; this is even more the case in the social, behavioral, and policy sciences. At the time of this writing economics is the social science to which the American public is being most exposed due to the seemingly intractable problem of the combination of rapidly increasing inflation on the one hand and a high rate of unemployment on the other hand. The wider philosophical convictions, the moral beliefs, and the social interests of various economists who recommend policy, respond to questions by reporters, and write articles for mass-circulation papers and magazines are not hidden from the perceptive observer. Like every scientist, the economist must choose what data are relevant to the processes under study. What seem retrospectively to be the most significant factors that caused changes? What data need to be taken into consideration to provide an adequate, if not complete, explanation of the changes that are occurring? The debate about whether the monetarist party is correct is partially over accuracy of scientific assessment and judgment. Is its interpretation of the significance of money supply in the economy an accurate one? Among the many "causal" factors that play upon the production of goods and services in a modern

12. Economists excel in this effort. See, for example, Gary Becker, *The Economic Approach to Human Behavior* (Chicago: University of Chicago Press, 1976).

technological society, is the ready availability of money at relatively low interest-rates a factor of such importance that the restriction of that supply by higher rates will have the desired effects of reducing the rate of inflation? If various parties can agree to that, another question must be asked. What consequences are probable when a decisive increase in interest rates is put into effect? This is a matter of prediction, and is subject to careful quantifiable analysis. The choices get moved to how one ought to decide which probable consequences are acceptable and laudable, and which are judged to be deleterious, and to whom, and how might they be avoided. Or if they cannot be avoided, who is to bear the burden of the desired stability in the economy? And, if it is agreed on the best of scientifically informed probabilities that some groups will suffer, how are the economic needs of these groups to be met? Or are they simply to be ignored?

It is likely that some economists, at least when they recommend policy, begin with answers to the latter questions rather than the earlier, more scientifically verifiable ones. Scholarly judgments and moral beliefs are entwined in the perspectives of the observers.[13] A deep sensitivity to the plight of the poor in the society, whether rationally defended by a sophisticated theory of distributive justice or not, is likely to affect not only the judgments about what risks are worth taking, and who is to be subject to serious risks, but also the judgments about the salience of certain data, certain institutional features of economic life, and perhaps even the worth of the monetarists themselves as economists. Yet no recommender of economic policies on a national level will defend his or her views in terms of moral sympathy or a theory of distributive justice alone. To be persuasive, such a person must indicate that there are economic interpretations of events that are, if not true, at least as plausible as those of his or her antagonists. He or she must show that the fulfillment of moral sympathies and moral doctrines is workable in terms of the economic processes of a given society, or in terms of the reformer's proposed alterations in economic processes and institutions. These proposals never move far from basic convictions; they may be about the extent to which individual liberty is to be restricted in a society, and what the permissible limits on it are; they may be about the extent to which efficiency is an economic value to be prized and at what points it is permissible to tolerate inefficiencies and for what ends; they may be about whether individuals and families are to be held accountable for their own economic well-being, what conditions excuse them if some adjustment is to be made to meet their unfavorable circumstances, and what these adjustments should be.

13. See, for example, Arthur Okun, *Equality and Efficiency: The Great Trade-Off* (Washington, D.C.: The Brookings Institution, 1975).

Yet, for all the increase in knowledge, all the public and sophisticated discussion of economics and of policy, the limits of foreknowledge and even more the limits of control of consequences become apparent. This can best be seen in extreme types. Pure free-market economics ought to work; that is, it ought to achieve the goals valued (those criteria of what works and is good) by economists of that persuasion. But it does not work unless a large number of conditions are present, and all never are present. Classic texts in free-market economics did not fully foresee, for example, the developments of the kinds of corporations that are so visible in technological societies. The alteration of the society from one basically of production to one more characterized by services was not foreseeable. The responses of various groups whose unfavorable living conditions were a result of the vicissitudes of a free market were not controllable by the owners of vast wealth. Resentment against vast discrepancies in income and standards of living was not manageable. The sense of the injustice of distribution of power in a society, expressed through the organization of labor and in many political reforms, was not controllable. Whether motivated by a primitive resentment against being at the mercy of an economic system in which one had no significant self-determination, or by a clearly worked-out view of what justice requires in a society, the responses of vast populations could not be managed by those who had economic power. Limits of foreknowledge and limits of capacities to control events are not eliminated by the vast increase in the amount of data, by an explanation of the processes of economic life, or by awareness of the points at which human choice and economic power can intervene to have some measure of decisive effect on forthcoming events. Some recognition of the limits of human capacities must inexorably be faced. They must be faced in societies with concentrations of power in central governments and deep confidence in centralized planning as well as in those more oriented to the market.

Reflections on economics, and on other social, behavioral, and policy sciences that provide data, moves one to issues much broader than those of policy formation. Some are argued by philosophers and by the social scientists themselves, such as the extent to which human choices and human actions in the complex processes of interaction are themselves "caused." If they are "caused," can the knowledge of such causes ever lead to accurate predictions? Many social experiments have been made on the basis of confidence in knowledge about what "causes" human behavior, only to have it found out that the remedies for the presumed causes not only do not eliminate the problems but create some that were not anticipated. One thinks of the variety of community experiments in nineteenth-century America, of the enlightened paternalism that constructed Pullman Village in Chicago, and of many other instances. While progress has been made in explaining human behavior and social developments since the time when demons were personified as causes, the philosophical arguments about explanations of human actions and of historical and social events have not been resolved. The limits of foreknowledge and of control of consequences have been moved but not eliminated.

In the face of the ambiguities of the consequences of many intentional human interventions into social processes, some persons believe that in some areas it is better to let events take their course than it is to interfere in them. This may be the the the case in dealing with social phenomena as well as with biological processes. No reasonable person argues that it is better not to intervene in the biological processes of a human body that are destroying or impairing its healthy functioning when therapeutic action is available, though there are occasions when patients ought to be permitted to die. And certain social "disorders" are remediable. In medical care there is a kind of Augustinian assumption, namely, that good is prior to evil, that there are natural processes that make for health which can be sustained if threats to them are eliminated. The medical profession does not create health; it removes threats to it and sustains it. Where the interactions in human situations are very complex, where knowledge is limited and control of consequences fragile, an argument can be made that in certain conditions it is better not to intervene. Radical free-market economics would be an example of this; the assumption is that without certain kinds of interventions the prior "health" of an economy can be trusted and that the benefits latent there will be forthcoming.

These sorts of reflections cannot be permitted only on a highly generalized level, as if the limits of knowledge and control were the same with reference to removal of a decayed tooth and the elimination of discrepancies in human educational achievement. Even if one were disposed to do so a forceful general argument of a romantic sort cannot be made that all of modern knowledge and all of technological development ought to be restrained. It is not the intention here to consider that possibility. The limits of knowledge and foreknowledge are significantly different in various areas of intentional interventions (or noninterventions); consequences are more predictable in some areas than in others. But there are limits, especially in our knowledge and control of social processes and human action. While we may not be certain that God exists, it is clear that human life does not have attributes that God was judged to have in certain theologies—accurate foreknowledge of all events and sovereign power to determine their outcome.

Dramatists, novelists, theologians, philosophers, and ordinary persons have had ways of speaking about the grandeur and the limits of human beings for centuries. The development of our species, from the simple beginnings of greater motility in our animal ancestors to the evolution of our marvelous and still not fully understood nervous system, has given us advantages and capacities that other animals do not have. The biological conditions necessary for the development of art and literature, of myth and symbol, of humanistic learning and science, are distinctively present in the human species. The capacity to be (to some extent) self-determining agents, to have purposes and intentions and to be able to direct the capacities of our bodies in accord with our purposes is a remarkable and still not fully explained gift. The overcoming of many limits of "necessity" which are so severe for plants, and less severe for many animals, is the marvelous characteristic of our species.

Yet it is clear that we have not overcome finitude, the most fundamental limitations of constituting a biological species, of being dependent upon and interdependent with other persons, institutions, and culture, and the natural environment around us. Individually we are subject to disease and death, and as we eliminate the instances of death due to one cause, more persons will have to die from another; as we decrease deaths due to cancer, we do not eliminate death but simply put the burden of causing death on other factors.

The Greeks made similar observations in much more primitive cultural conditions, and did not hesitate to accuse one another of hubris. The biblically based religious traditions have been ever alert to the signs of excessive pride. These terms have many references to particular forms of behavior, and to particular motives for action. They are evaluative descriptions of persons and of actions. It is not the point of this book to develop these matters in detail. But certainly one general notion can be stated: such traditions point to what is judged to be an unacceptable transgression of limits of a proper range of assertiveness and activity. Those limits are culturally variable and historically shifting. But the sense, at least, of some proper limits is present.

More generally, for all the achievements that our biological capacities and our cultural developments make possible, there is no overcoming fundamental human conditions of finitude: biological conditions and historical and cultural conditions. In beautiful irony, Pascal has made the point.

> Cromwell was about to ravage all Christendom; the royal family
> was undone, and his own forever established, save for a little
> grain of sand which formed in his ureter. Rome herself was trem-
> bling under him; but this small piece of gravel having formed
> there, he is dead, his family cast down, all is peaceful, and the
> king is restored.[14]

14. Blaise Pascal, *Pensées* (New York: Random House, 1941), no. 176, p. 62.

To be sure, this *Pensée* does not take into account the many causal factors that were involved in the demise of the Puritan Revolution; it is much too simple. To be sure, where modern medicine is available, that "little grain of sand" is seldom the cause of death. But the thought calls attention to a necessary condition upon which all human activity is dependent, a body that is functioning in close to a normal way.

Some of the issues which the religious traditions have responded to in myth and legend, in historical narrative and doctrine, are still pertinent, even under different historical and cultural conditions. Are humans seeking to overcome their natural finitude? What are the purposes that drive them to increase their mastery over the forces to which, in even highly developed technological cultures, they still remain subject? What benefits are being sought? And for whom are they sought? What are the harms or evils that we are attempting to eliminate or avoid? Why do we judge the desired consequences to be beneficial or harmful? Whose interests do they serve? What future time-span do we have in mind when we consider the consequences of our interventions in natural and social processes? Do we conduct our affairs with illusions about our capacities to foreknow and to control? Do we conduct them with illusions about our rational autonomy, our independence as individuals and as a species from a whole and complex network of relations to other persons, other societies, other cultures, and to animal life, plant life, and even the inanimate features of the natural world? Are we as freed from determinations by all sorts of natural and social forces as we assume when we extend the realm of human mastery? Or do we need to take more into account the factors of human interdependence with other persons, other societies, and nature? In our proper human drive to limit our susceptibility to what the ancients call fates or necessities, do we live with an illusion that we can control the destiny of the world? If we do not, how do we take human finitude into account in our activities? Has man become not only the measurer but, as Protagoras asserted, the measure of all things? Do the effects of that long course of human evolution that brought to our species these remarkable and distinctive capacities warrant the inference that all other things exist for our benefit?

These are, I suppose, "global questions." I have attempted, however, not to raise them in a "global" fashion but to indicate with a few brief illustrations that they are reasonable questions raised by many particular events in modern life. To be sure, a theologian might frame them in a certain way because he construes the world in the light of certain deep religious and moral convictions. But one can come to these questions from other perspectives, with other fundamental convictions. They are reasonable questions and are raised in various ways by many persons who are disturbed by many events in our times. Ancient religious questions are not rendered silly by modern developments; they are present in different conditions of human development. One does not need religious interests or sensibilities to ask them; the fact that they are being asked by many persons without declared religious interests may even warrant the hypothesis that something like religious sensibilities are latent in a vast number of thoughtful human beings who consider themselves indifferent if not hostile to historic religious traditions. Though we may not agree on how best to describe human uniqueness, I take it to be unassailable that man is not God.

Some Aspects of Religion

Religion has a utility value to persons and cultures; it always has and, as long as it exists, it always will. When historic religions lose their adherents, functional equivalents develop to meet the needs that those religions met. The religious construal of the world that this book elucidates is also presumably useful, even though, as this section shall indicate, it is grounded in part on a criticism of utilitarian religion. The question at issue is not whether religion has some value for persons and cultures; it is whether religions ought to be justified almost exclusively, or exclusively, by their benefits to their adherents. Religions have always provided myths for indicating the meanings of human experiences in a very broad context of the limits of human life. They have provided cultic rites which, like cultural achievements in other areas, remove some of the threats to human well-being, enable persons and groups to cope with contingencies in natural and historical events, and help them to celebrate the benefits they have received in childbirth, in culture, and in many other areas. But the issues that divide persons who think about religion in any evaluative or normative way are the criteria for adequate religion—the criteria for better or worse religion—and indeed, in that very difficult realm, the criteria for "true" religion.

Even the most theocentric views of Christianity have appealed to the benefits for persons and societies from adherence to their views. Augustine, in that great theological interpretation of historical events, *The City of God,* leaves his readers with a sense that Rome would have benefited more from adherence to his powerful Deity than it did from fidelity to the pagan deities of popular and sophisticated Roman religion. Indeed, one conclusion is that the presumably false religions were a significant factor in the demise of Rome. Calvin, who is frequently pictured as having one of the most austere views of the Deity in the tradition, nonetheless hastened to assure his readers that this power was intended for the benefit of human beings, particularly those chosen by divine election. Jonathan Edwards, that erudite and powerful pastor and preacher in Northampton,

Massachusetts, in the eighteenth century, while he gave one of the most theocentric views of the meaning of the whole of the creation, nonetheless was certain that religious faith was deeply beneficial to the interests of his parishoners. Indeed, many of his revival sermons appeal to the immediate spiritual self-interests of persons as he understood them in both his dull, logical prose and in his flights of evocative rhetoric.

One could cite examples from the various non-Western religions to show that the salvation of the individual is the long-range objective of most religions. Or, one could cite examples from many religions to show that the interests of a group are what religion ensures. The biblical accounts from the first to the last books offer examples of the benefits promised to persons and communities if they adhere to the cultic and moral laws, if they repent of their wrong-doing and rectify their bad conduct, if they have confidence in God to sustain and restore spiritual life, if they have certain beliefs, and if they have certain basic human qualities like purity of heart. Given the warrants from the biblical materials for assuring benefits to those who are conscientious in their religious attitudes and practices, it is no wonder that the same or similar benefits were used throughout the centuries to entice, cajole, invite, convince, or persuade persons to adhere to the Christian faith.

Religion functions as an aspect of culture to assure persons and communities that even in the events which most threaten their individual and corporate lives there is some ultimate purpose at work. One does not need sophisticated theories from anthropology, sociology, psychology, history, or other human studies to recognize that various "functional" theories of religion can be supported by a considerable amount of evidence. And the certainty with which some persons have believed that proper religious life leads to one or many benefits for persons provokes the painful and rich discourse of the counterexamples: those instances in which there is every reason to believe that persons or communities have been faithful to the expectations of the Deity, and yet suffer. These pose sharply that traditional problem of theodicy. Jeremiah's lamentations and Job's resistances, we know, are matched in other religions by equally forceful comments on the apparent injustice of deities who do not reward moral virtue or cultic purity. Indeed, doctrines of life in the next world, or of eternal life, in part function to resolve the problem of assuring believers that religious piety finally is beneficial. Hell is the place where God's retributive justice is worked out on those, among others, who have had happy prosperous lives in this world which from moral and religious standpoints they did not deserve. Heaven is the place where God's compensatory justice is exercised on, among others, those who deserved more benefits in their earthly lives than they received, given the probity of their conduct and the fervor of their religious faiths.

What human needs religious activities meet and what human desires they tend to fulfill are matters about which various interpreters continue to argue. What "mechanisms" operate to make religions socially and individually useful is also a matter of debate. One's opinion regarding that depends in part on what theories or hypotheses about social and individual behavior one finds most adequate. These matters need not to be taken up at this point.

My contention is that, as certainty about a life after death erodes, and as agnosticism increases about what kind of life that could be even among those who continue to adhere to belief in it, religion is increasingly advanced as instrumental to subjective temporal human ends: desires for happiness, for success, for freedom from guilt and anxiety, for the certainty that there are some unchanging realities in the midst of rapid change, or even chaos, and some grounds for hope in the midst of a sense of being fated. The large question that I have to deal with in this book as a whole is whether there are any other grounds for religious piety and discipline than those that assure its benefits for various phases or occasions of the human condition, including death. My contention is that in our own time, as much as in any other, religion is propagated for its utility value to individuals and communities. Religious belief, trust, and practice, are offered as useful instruments for getting on well in the business of living, for resolving those dilemmas that tear individuals and communities apart, and for sustaining moral causes, whether they be to the right, the left, or in the middle. Both individual pieties and social pieties become instrumental not to gratitude to God, the honor of God, or service of God, but to sustaining purposes to which the Deity is incidental, if not something of an encumbrance. And as the secular alternatives to religious instruments increase in number, as the products on the salvation and moral markets increase in variety, there develops, in practice, less and less distinctiveness to the religious alternative.

Paul Tillich preached and then published one of the most famous and moving sermons of the mid-twentieth century, entitled "You are accepted."[15] It is grounded in biblical materials; it echoes central themes of the Reformation; it moves deeply many persons who are burdened with guilt and anxiety. It is ultimately assuring that nothing can separate us from the grace and the love of God. The authenticity of this sermon within the biblical and Protestant traditions cannot be radically challenged; of course it does not say all that the tradition has affirmed, but no one sermon can. It expresses in an extraordinarily powerful way one deep strand of Christian piety.

15. Paul Tillich, "You are Accepted," in *The Shaking of the Foundations* (New York: Scribner's, 1948), pp. 153–63. Tillich's text is Romans 5:20.

Echoed more faintly in countless sermons, in hundreds of hours of pastoral care, and in small groups, this assurance becomes very cheap grace, indeed. It becomes a warrant for not being burdened by the moral guilt of broken vows, of moral obligations rationally undertaken but then ignored, of violation of natural duties in family or community, of venting one's passions to the detriment of other persons. Very easily the Pauline rhetorical question "If God is for us, who can be against us?" (Romans 8:31b) loses its theological proposition and becomes the rhetorical question "Can there be any serious threats to our sense of well-being if we simply do what we think is in our immediate self-interest?" The question "Who shall separate us from the love of Christ?" loses its scandalous reference to the particularity of the work of Christ which warranted the assurance for the apostle (Romans 8:35a). The grand assurances of Romans 8:37-38 are theologically castrated to assure people that whatever seems to bring them happiness is what they ought to do, and whatever impediments there are to that aspiration, be they natural duties, moral obligations, control of the passions, or rules of moral behavior, have no significantly binding force. God, if he is even remotely present in the thought of either the assuring preacher or pastor, or in the thought of the anxious parishioner or "counselee," is generally not invoked. And even more certainly, it does not occur to such persons to ask whether God is honored by the immediate individualistic self-fulfillment that one is assured is all right, or whether there are any patterns of social and interpersonal moral obligations that must be adhered to if life is to be ordered according to the purpose of the Deity. The cheap grace against which Dietrich Bonhoeffer reacted so strongly in the 1930s has become even cheaper, for it is available now without one having to decide whether or not it required a costly transaction between God and man, the crucifixion—a matter that the churches against which Bonhoeffer was reacting held at least as dogma.[16] Even a piety that has some biblical warrants, remote as they often are in the practical transactions of life, becomes purely instrumental; indeed, with the erosion of the theological framework that made such pieties at least a reasonable option within the Christian tradition, there is little to distinguish the instruments of reassurance that come from religion from those that are available from other entrepreneurs in the huge salvation market that characterizes American and other parts of Western society and culture in our times.

Personal repression and oppression seem to have replaced the traditional problem of sin and guilt. One should become liberated from whatever represses or oppresses. The therapeutic has triumphed, as Philip

16. Dietrich Bonhoeffer, *The Cost of Discipleship* (London: SCM Press, 1959), pp. 35–47.

Rieff has so brilliantly lined out for us; Erich Fromm and Eric Berne and countless others have grasped the heart of the gospel, it seems, and happily do not encumber it with any references to an awesome Deity in whose hands are the destinies of the world, or with embarrassing beliefs about the very scandalous event on the basis of which St. Paul could proclaim Christian freedom.[17] Sin and guilt used to require contrition and repentance, but now assurance comes without such acts; religion is instrumental to individual happiness and social success, and even to more satisfactory sexual functioning. Not only liberal Protestantism has taken this turn; it is that continuation of "New Thought" tendencies from the nineteenth century in the preaching of Norman Vincent Peale, it is a message of some of the preachers of the new evangelicalism, it is amply present in Roman Catholicism. Religion helps us to be free and happy; if God is somehow involved in that, we do not hear much about it. If Jesus is involved, he certainly is not beckoning people to the costly obedience of self-sacrificial love. Certainly one does not wish to talk about the restraining moral will of God, for persons already have a load of guilt; to add obligations imposed by a deity would simply increase the burden from which they are to be relieved. To live for others rather than for self is, in modern interpretation, a cause of the problem rather than an answer to it; "We must love God only and hate self only" sounds like a prescription for mental illness rather than a proper moral commandment, a proper way to fulfill the human vocation.[18] To have a powerful sense of obligation and duty, whether in one's interpersonal relationships, one's work, or elsewhere, is believed to be counterproductive to happiness and self-fulfillment. There is some merit to such charges, but whether the primary spiritual and moral problem of our time is to be seen in them is debatable.

Certainly there are "consolations of religion." There are also inspirations of religion. The critical issue with reference to contemporary pieties is whether there is any justification for the consolations and inspirations other than the subjective feeling-states that they evoke in individuals. My argument is that such consolations as religion offers come from a deep spiritual consent to the divine governance; that that old defect of hubris or pride is the problem that correlates with the failure to give that consent; and that much of contemporary instrumental religion is wrong theologically as well as pastorally because it does not set human life within the appropriate limits, not only of finitude, but of ordered relationships in institutions and between persons. The argument is not so thoroughly

17. Philip Rieff, *The Triumph of the Therapeutic* (New York: Harper and Row, 1966); Erich Fromm, *Man for Himself* (New York: Rinehart and Co., 1947); Eric Berne, *Games People Play* (New York: Grove Press, 1964).

18. Pascal, *Pensées*, no. 476, p. 156.

"negative" as this suggests, however. It is also that proper religion evokes and requires a response to possibilities of human action in interpersonal and institutional relationships; that the old defect of sloth deters us from making the efforts to respond as we ought; and that one of the problems of contemporary instrumental pieties is that the response is not made with reference to what can be discerned about the possibilities and requirements of the ordering power of the world, but with reference to immediate self-gratification which demands little that our superficial desires do not naturally lead us to secure.

One could cite many more illustrations of pieties; one could evaluate them more precisely in terms of the extent to which each would be susceptible to the charges of superficial utility that the most offensive merit. The struggles of Job and of Jeremiah, and of their counterparts in the literature of other cultures, the agony of Christ's passion, the replicas of those struggles, unnoted in any literary form, that countless conscientious persons go through year after year: these are *in extremis* not only manifestations of honest and proper human quarrels with a deity whose purposes do not coincide with immediate human self-interests or rational arguments based on certain principles of God's goodness and human justice. They also vividly indicate the trivialities of cheap pieties, and the necessity in a theocentric view of life for coming to terms with the fact that the destiny of human life is not in human hands. The "Long Friday," as the Scandinavians call what we call "Good Friday," is truer to human experience than the superficial Easters to which instrumental pieties of the present age seem to point.

If there are instrumental individual and personal pieties, there are also instrumental social and moral pieties. Like the personal ones, these have deep roots in the Western religious tradition. As I noted, St. Augustine seems to have believed that the peace and prosperity of the Roman Empire would have been better ensured had the God of the Bible been the God of Rome; his long and, to the modern reader, somewhat tedious interpretations of Roman and biblical history move toward such a conclusion. Certainly there is biblical warrant for this sort of interpretation of history. The Pentateuch itself promises the success of the ancient people of Israel if they follow the laws and commandments of Yahweh. The agony of that event which was so terrible that it alone now is used as referent for the word "holocaust" has many of its puzzles established by a frame of reference from the biblical materials. The burden of the problem is even larger because some of the most fervently pious of twentieth-century Jews apparently faced their extermination with some assurance that it was in accord with that biblical faith. Religious faith is supposed to be instrumental to the survival and prosperity of historical communities.

Politically and socially liberal Christians readily recognize utilitarian religion when piety is put into the service of nationalism, or of anticommunism. When German Lutheran theologians earlier in our century established on theological grounds that *Das Volk* was a *Schöpfungsordnung,* an order of creation, and when this intensified the fervor of German nationalism, clearly religion was a sustaining force for what became a demonic state.[19] When American fundamentalists have divided the world between the good and the evil, those who are with Christ and those who represent the anti-Christ, and with certainty identify the anti-Christ with communism, it is not hard for liberals to see that piety and tradition are put uncritically into the service of a political cause. In the writings of the earliest generations of Puritans in America, with their sense of the destiny of this pilgrim people to expand into the wilderness in order to establish on this continent the New Jerusalem, we see how Puritan piety served well the interests of the immigrants, and could easily provide incentives for the industriousness of the merchants in the Connecticut Valley and those farther to the west.[20] It seems inevitable that wherever persons interpret their own history as an analogy to the history of the people of ancient Israel, God is on one side and not the other; religion is in the service of the political, social, and economic interests of those who can identify themselves with the ancient people who had a special vocation under Yahweh. It is true of many Calvinists in the Republic of South Africa; it was true of some British imperialists in India. It is also true (something liberals would like to avoid) for much of contemporary liberation theology, whether written in the interests of the oppressed poor of Latin America, of blacks in the United States, of women, or of any other group—whether a minority or a majority in number. Intellectually delicate and complex issues are involved in this matter, to which I shall return.

There are trivial utilitarian forms of individual piety, and there are those forms of piety which, while they are of benefit to individuals, have more complex criteria for evaluation of their propriety. There is cheap grace, and there is grace which still is grace even if it does not come pleasingly packaged and at a low cost. So there are trivial forms of social and moral pieties that are useful for moral purposes, and there are moral pieties that are more complex, inherently more ambiguous morally, and recognized as such. Of the most trivial sort have been those occasions when what is ostensibly a cultic act, prayer, has become a tactic in the

19. See, for examples, Paul Althaus, *Theologie der Ordnungen* (Gutersloh: C. Bertelsmann, 1935), and Werner Elert, *The Christian Ethos,* trans. Carl J. Schindler (Philadelphia: Muhlenberg Press, 1957), pp. 96–101.
20. See, for example, Sacvan Bercovitch's interesting study, *The Puritan Origins of the American Self* (New Haven: Yale University Press, 1975).

course of a moral protest. I refer to that weird phenomenon in America called the "pray-in." In at least some of its forms it was nothing more than a "sit-in" with an odor of sanctity, and it is not hard to believe that the shift from sitting to kneeling position was made so that any disruption of the protest would appear somewhat scandalous. I refer to the development of "liturgies" such as were used in church meetings in the late 1960s, in which statements such as "God is an unwed mother on the West Side of Chicago" appeared. The only warrant for what is, in the most technical theological sense, blasphemy in a statement like this is that it might shock insensitive persons into awareness of a deep and proper moral concern. It is hardly theologically adequate, not to mention sound or true. The authors of such statements would surely have been very properly offended if some one had written that God is the president of Standard Oil of Indiana, or the secretary of the Department of Health, Education, and Welfare. These blatantly trivial uses of piety for moral ends were not subjected to many critical principles of evaluation other than that they would have a tactical effect in the service of a moral cause. They are pure sophistry, in the historically technical sense. My point is that, no matter what the moral cause, this sort of instrumental use of cultic activity and religious language is simply wrong.

The matter becomes more delicate and complex as the religious arguments, pieties, and disciplines are justified on other than tactical grounds, and are warranted by a variety of purposes. That is surely the case with liberation theologies. I hasten to note that my own social and moral sympathies and arguments would sustain in most instances the intentions of the theologians and church leaders interested in a more equitable distribution of access to opportunities and of the resources to meet fundamental human needs. The issues pertinent to this discussion can be highlighted by suggesting two ideal-typical (and thus oversimplified) forms of argument about social involvement; these would pertain with equal force to defenders of any political and social position, from far right to far left.

The first extreme type would argue that religious and theological activity is legitimately determined by the perceived critical social issues of the time and place of the religious community. This is, in oversimplified form, the method of correlation alluded to in the opening paragraph of this chapter. What is the moral and social question? When we have a clear view of the question, then we can turn to the resources of theology and religious practice to establish the theological and religious "answer." The critical point, in this extreme type, is that the question is determined by current moral and social interests, and thus shapes the selection and interpretation of the resources from the tradition that are used to answer it. Sharp religious and theological divisions turn not on more purely the-

ological or historical religious grounds, but on the moral or social issue
at stake. Differences in religious practice and theology occur as a result
of different interpretations of the moral and social milieu. Where different
religious groups agree that a question is critical, their different moral
answers to the question become all the more striking. In the contemporary
United States the debate among religious groups on abortion comes close
to exemplifying the ideal-type. Abortion is a critical question. It became
critical for Protestants, who had largely accepted without much self-consciousness the traditional Christian prohibitions against it, only when it
came to their attention as a result of other groups' activities. The Roman
Catholic antiabortion position has a solidly argued backing, given certain
fundamental assumptions in Catholic moral theology. The current vitu-
perative debate, however, is largely a matter of taking sides on the moral
issue, and then finding moral, religious, and political arguments that can
sustain the moral position that has been taken. An alternative procedure
might be a radically contrasting type of argument.

Such an argument would take more purely a theological starting
point. What knowledge of God is available to us? What can we affirm,
with the best arguments we can marshall, about God's purposes for life
in the world? What beliefs about God pertain to the moral issues we
confront in the time and place, in the social locations, of contemporary
life? How do we draw proper inferences from these beliefs to interpret
the moral circumstances in their light? What principles for the ordering
of society and interpersonal life are backed by the religious beliefs which,
if they do not provide precise rules of conduct, at least set the serious
points for consideration in coming to a moral judgment? In this ideal-type
the religious beliefs and outlooks would shape the question, and not
merely provide an answer to a question shaped by purely moral and social
interests. One would come to the current issue of abortion with a clear
understanding of the religious and theological principles, and the attitudes
toward human life, that are evoked and sustained by the religious affections directed to the Deity. From that one would begin to think about
whether induced abortions are permissible or not, and under what conditions one might argue that they are. Theology and religion would not
be instrumental to the moral argument but would have a greater role in
shaping the moral question, in describing the circumstances in which the
moral issue emerges.

Most actual use of religious ideas, principles, and attitudes in moral
matters is a mixture of the ideal-types. Clearly this is the case with the
sophisticated arguments of the liberation theologians. It is not for me to
judge whether the sequence of development of that theology began with
the properly intense sense of injustice, and then moved to develop theological arguments in favor of certain forms of social change. There are

ample grounds in the biblical materials for being concerned about the poor and the oppressed; indeed, one cannot argue against that with solid evidences from the biblical materials themselves. It is not the case that Latin American social conditions, the positions of blacks in America, the subordination of women in almost all societies, became moral questions for Christians without being informed by deep and perduring strands of the biblical materials and theological developments since biblical times. A process of confirmation of the adequacy of a religious moral view develops on the basis of a variety of items: biblically based beliefs about at least some of God's purposes; the resentment of those who are oppressed in any society; the justifications for a paternalistic view of the responsibilities of the rich to the poor when love of neighbor gets transposed into a kind of pious Victorian charity; the disproportionality between actual social conditions and those principles of justice that can be given powerful theological backing; the potential for violence that occurs if some amending procedures are not undertaken to develop a fairer society; the new alertness of the churches all over the world as a result of activities in councils and synods; the social conditions of societies; and many more. Legitimate questions can still be raised; but they become basically theological questions, questions about our knowledge of God from wherever that is derived. Has there been too narrow a selection from the richness of the biblical materials and the tradition, so that we now have a unitarian God of liberation, and a unitarian liberation of particular groups? Is the Deity solely on one side of the issue? Can God's power be understood to be more sovereign, thus ruling nature as well as social experience, and thus qualifying the certainty of his identification with one cause or one course of action? The temptation, even in sophisticated and morally legitimate ventures, is to put the Deity and religious people in the service of moral ventures, and to seek the support of theology and religion for what are, finally, morally rather than theologically determined causes.

The temptation of religion is always to put the Deity and the forces of religious piety in the service of the immediate needs and desires of individuals, small groups, and societies. I admit that this has, alas, always and everywhere been the case, and that there are deep roots for this flowering within the biblical tradition itself. Religion is put into the service not of gratitude, reverence, and service to God but of human interests, morally both trivial and serious. Religion—its theologies, its cultic practices, its rhetoric, its symbols, its devotions, becomes unwittingly justified for its utility value. God is denied as God; God becomes an instrument in the service of human beings rather than human beings instruments in the service of God. The fact that this has almost always been the case, and that it is the case at the present time, is no warrant for accepting it as normative.

Religious Studies

We have become very knowledgeable about the instrumental character of religious beliefs and practices in the past decades as a result of
the research and teaching that come under the title of "religious studies"
in American universities and colleges. Psychology of religion, sociology
of religion, anthropology, history of religions, phenomenology of religions,
and philosophy of religion all have contributed to the more detailed and
precise analysis of the uses of religion in the human community. The
principal effect of these studies should not surprise any theologian, however, for surely the Reformation of the sixteenth century was prompted
in part by Martin Luther's recognition that the selling of indulgences by
the corrupt church of the time was a human activity meant to ensure the
felicitous state of souls after death. Normative theological critiques of
religious practices have often, in the history of Western religions, been
based on observations that they are manipulations by humans to ensure
humanly desirable ends. While it is not the stated intention of the various
approaches to the scientific or scholarly study of religion to unmask the
pretensions of various traditional religious beliefs (though personal motives of this sort might contribute to scholarly zeal), nonetheless the effect
of many investigations is just that. Religion is explained in terms of the
human needs that it meets; its institutional forms, myths, symbols, cultic
activities, and morals are shown to be constructions of reality that assist
persons and societies to cope with their limits, to celebrate their successes,
to order their lives in accordance with what are judged finally to be matters
of individual and social self-interest.

There is nothing improper at all about such investigations. Indeed,
I made a modest contribution of my own to this sort of enterprise.[21]
Ecclesiology was high on the list of theological priorities at that time,
largely due, I believe, to the preoccupation with the unity of the church
of the World Council of Churches' Commission on Faith and Order. In
my reading of much of the literature of the forties and fifties, and in my
participation in the work of the commission, I was joined by scholars of
sociology of religion in an effort to deflate some of the theological rhetoric
that dominated those discussions. It was an effort to say to theologians
that they ought to take into account more explicitly the very "earthen"
character of the Christian church, the aspects of its life that could be
explained in great part by social theories. Surely this was not a new
insight; historians and others had been aware of the social, political, and
other nontheological determinations of the life of churches for a long time.

21. James M. Gustafson, *Treasure in Earthen Vessels: The Church as a Human
Community* (New York: Harper and Brothers, 1961).

No deep skepticism was required to see that throughout the history of the churches grand theological reasons were offered as the sufficient principles of explanation of events and developments that could be more economically explained without recourse to theology. At least theologians had to take into account these other explanations in their loftiest discourse. F. D. E. Schleiermacher provided a marvelous example for this enterprise in his own exposition of *The Christian Faith,* in his efforts to avoid "magical" interpretations of the efficacy of religious beliefs and practices.[22]

"Religious studies" need not intend to purge religious beliefs and practices of unwarranted pretensions. They have their own legitimate motivations. Freud's contributions clearly were motivated both by his clinical interests and by his broader interests in explaining historic cultural developments; a negative evaluation of religious beliefs and activities developed as a result. The contributions of Marx, directly and indirectly, to the explanation of religion, based on the philosophical critique of his mentor, Ludwig Feuerbach, were motivated by his own social and moral interests, but they also yield interesting and important studies of the sociology and the history of Christianity. Cultural anthropologists of various theoretical persuasions have developed principles of interpretation which have applicability wider than to the cultures which generated them. Phenomenologists of religion, who with great intuitive powers offer insights into the essential aspects of religious life through their observations of religion in many cultures, add to the measure of our understanding of the nature of the human reality of religion. American community studies from the Lynds' *Middletown* forward help us to comprehend the role of religion and religious institutions in North American social settings. The more historical sociological contributions of Max Weber, both in the formation of illuminative concepts and types, and in the ambitious and majestic interpretations of several world religions, help to explain various aspects of the development of cultures in a way that the exclusive use of theological principles of explanation does not.

In these studies and in many more there is always an implicit if not explicit theory of the nature of religion itself, of that to which its beliefs and activities ultimately refer. Philosophies of religion are implicit or explicit in the studies of scientists and historians of religion. And the evidences adduced by the humanistic and scientific scholars of religion surely need to be taken into account in the development of normative views of religion. A normative view, however, will never be fully sub-

22. Friedrich Schleiermacher, *The Christian Faith,* ed. H. R. Macintosh and J. S. Stewart (Edinburgh: T. and T. Clark, 1928). For his discussion of the contrast between "the magical" and "the empirical" ways to explain the Christian doctrine of reconciliation, see pp. 429 ff.

stantiated by the results of the scientific studies of religion, or by a combination of one or more of the theories of religion that underlie such
studies. This is particularly the case if these studies claim to offer a
sufficient explanation of religion, and not simply an explanation of some
of the historical, social, and psychological conditions necessary for religion to be meaningful.

These matters are brought into account here because there is evidence to indicate that normative practitioners of religion, from theologians
to local functionaries, frequently accept the general results of these studies, or selections from them, to provide an adequate basis for the justification of religious life and thought. It cannot be denied that common
acceptance of certain religious beliefs and practices reinforces social identity with particular communities. It is questionable that the need for social
identity with particular communities in our culture and period of history
is a sufficient basis for defending religious beliefs and practices. Indeed,
insofar as religious beliefs and practices are justified because they fill this
need, certain basic assumptions and evidences from scientific studies of
religion have become the normative basis for religion. The simple question
can be asked, Why religious beliefs and practices? Why not the beliefs
of a social class and its practices? Why not beliefs about athletics and its
practices? Why not political beliefs and their practices? A problem even
from a descriptive point of view arises. What distinguishes religious beliefs
and practices from other beliefs and practices that fulfill the same, or at
least a similar, social and individual need? There is a simple, practical
question to the leaders of religious institutions: If other beliefs and practices fulfill the need equally well or better, on what basis does one appeal
to any particular significance for religion?

My casual observations of what takes place in much that goes under
the name of pastoral counseling in North America Protestantism provide
an example. If the heuristic principles used to understand the plight of
the parishioner (or "client," now that pastoral counseling has spun off
from ecclesiastical auspices to join the market for those who need some
kind of psychological help) are indistinguishable from the principles used
by one or another school of psychotherapy, what distinguishes pastoral
counseling from any other kind? And if what finally distinguishes it is that
the pastor is one sympathetic to religious factors as possible therapeutic
benefits to the parishioner, and those religious factors are justified solely
because they have these benefits, has not the pastor simply accepted as
normative certain conclusions and assumptions from scientific studies of
religion?

Theology itself can drift or deliberately leap into the same position.
If theology cannot be sustained on better evidences than those used by
astrologers and alchemists, to take extreme examples, and if one continues

to believe it is worthy of being sustained, on what grounds can it be defended? Or, if theology refers only to the symbols and myths which provide a coherent meaning of human experience in a given culture, what is to distinguish Christian theology from a Homeric view of the world? To be sure, the myths and symbols used are different, but if the justification for their use is that they provide a coherent way of interpreting the meaning of human experience, cannot any myths and symbols do as well within a given culture and a given historical period? If the argument is that one's own religious myths and symbols provide a more adequate way to interpret the meaning of human experience, what are the criteria for adequacy? Is it that they enable one, for example, to take into account a wider meaning and a final resolution for human suffering? What are the references of the meaning and the resolution? Highly "confessional" theologies can be sustained, up to a point, on the basis of theories and evidences from the scientific studies of religion.

A current example, here cast in a simpler and more extreme form than its most sophisticated defenders make, is the interest in narrative and story as way of "doing theology." Narrative and story certainly can be supported by biblical tradition; there is little speculative theology in the Old Testament and little in the synoptic gospels. The stories grip the reader; they have a power that the arguments against the Arians or the Origenists do not have. Not only stories, but the use of metaphors and similes is clearly present in the biblical material. It is surely to be admitted that persons are more affected by the poignancy and detail of character, plot, and events as they are portrayed in brief parables or long narrative accounts than by dogmatic assertions of the truth of a religion, or philosophical defenses of it. There is something both intellectually and practically cogent about the recovery of the more direct and less abstract forms of religious discourse. Biography and autobiography come into play: we know ourselves in relation to the story of our lives; we often understand ourselves better in response to stories than to ethical and theological principles. Novels, drama, poetry, music, and graphic arts have powers of illumination for many people that the abstractions of philosophers and theologians do not have. Certainly, then, such aesthetic representations have a religious significance. One can be affected by undisturbed concentration on, and absorption of, Bach's *St. Matthew Passion* in a way that is not only aesthetic but deeply religious, and certainly one can be more moved in this way than by reading a theological treatise on the atonement. For all of its anthropomorphism, Michelangelo's depiction of the creation on the ceiling of the Sistine Chapel can evoke a deeper religious as well as aesthetic response than a rehearsal of the arguments about creation out of nothing. Stories, narratives, metaphors, similes, and other aesthetic presentations of life, no doubt have formative powers in the development of coherent and meaningful outlooks on life, and in the interpretation of the significance of events—interpersonal, institutional, historical, and natural. In a sense not to be denied, these things have religious importance. And the Christian story can be a powerful defining source for persons even in our time, as it has been for centuries. Stories function to form the normative moral culture of a community; they function to shape and sustain moral character; they function to elucidate the significance of the limit experiences of human life such as death or natural and historical calamities. Theology can be done as a story, and it can function reasonably well in many such cases, powerfully in others, and not at all in still others.

But why the Christian story? Or why the Jewish story? Or why the *Ramayana*? Or why the Homeric stories? If one is confessionally religious in a sense that can be both simple and intellectually sophisticated, that is, if one belongs to a community for whom certain stories are normative, and if one cannot provide a more generalized justification for one's religious outlook than that, then in effect one's defense of a religious belief and practice is on grounds that can be explained by any one of a number of the theories of religion that come forth from "religious studies." The Gilgamesh epic, the biblical narratives and myths, the Homeric stories, my own ancestors' accounts of Odin and Thor: these have all functioned as the stories of people's lives; they have all functioned to sustain certain virtues in certain cultures during aspects of their histories. In effect, theologians can accept the reduction of religion that is the conclusion of a number of its philosophical and scientific accounts, and proceed to do theology on that basis.

I indicated that "religious studies" are worthy of support in their own right; religion has no privileged position among human phenomena that isolates it from being interpreted and explained by principles that are not its own historically privileged ones, any more than do athletic contests (the sociology, philosophy, and psychology of sports), warfare, political leadership, or any others. A healthy complication of human understanding of religious phenomena comes from such studies, compared to the understanding of the uncritical "simple believer." There has been a very healthy unmasking effect; the pretensions of religious leaders and theologians can be exposed to their own benefit when they see themselves and their work in the mirrors provided by religious studies. The point raised here is quite another. The view that religion is instrumental to various human needs, that it is of utility value to its adherents, becomes a very accurate description of religious beliefs and activities; it has, through different theories, a wide and deep explanatory power when applied to religion. What comes naturally to religion—its human benefits—is now substantiated by vast amounts of data from various cultures and by various (and competing) theories about which needs it meets and how they are filled. Either wittingly or willy-nilly, the descriptive and explanatory powers of religious studies can be, and often do become, accepted as the adequate (and only defensible) normative basis for religious beliefs and practices.

That leaves no strong principles for critical interpretations of the instrumental and utilitarian character of religion. If and when religious leaders and thinkers accept a thoroughgoing instrumental view of religion as its normative basis, the only principle on which religion can be defended, sustained, and propagated is its instrumental, utilitarian significance. To be sure, degrees of relative adequacy of various religions in meeting various human needs can be evaluated. But the final reference is to the subjective meaning and significance of beliefs and practices. God (or the gods) is put in the service of human beings, and it is asserted that that is why a god is created. Whatever God, gods, myths, rituals, beliefs, and cultic activities best serve human needs are the ones to be sustained.

The Theological Scene

The contemporary options in theological literature pertaining to the doctrine of God, or at least ways of speaking about God, are part of our circumstances. My alternative to these will be further developed in a subsequent chapter. I will offer no further comment on work that calls itself theology but omits any significant reference to the Deity.

Certainly in theology, as in other areas of research and thinking, one of the best ways to understand a position that has been developed is to ascertain the critical problems in competing views that the work in hand is trying to solve, or to avoid. Theologians, the present writer included, are much more able to see the difficulties in other positions than they are in offering a final resolution to them. This ought not to embarrass us, for it is clear that theological reflection is not in a position to provide the same kind of evidences in support of its theories as are genetics or physics. Progress in theology is not possible in the same way that progress in the natural sciences is; while there are new evidences about the world that have to be taken into account, and confirmed theories about the development, for example, of the human species that cannot be ignored, these do not provide a sufficient basis for theology unless one should claim that theology is simply a process of deducing generalizations from the theories of the sciences. Thus one can deeply appreciate the efforts of one's contemporaries to overcome certain perceived problems in the theological positions of others, and one can, I believe, show in a fair minded way how various theologians defend their systematic positions on the Deity in order to avoid problems that others have gotten into. The present work will be no exception to this. In this chapter, however, the purpose is to give the reader some bearings from the way in which I interpret the significance not only of modern culture and religion, but also of the theological enterprise itself.

Many contemporary theologians believe that in the past too much was said about God with too much certainty; most of contemporary theology is marked by a modesty of intention that has not always held sway in the past. Yet it needs to be recognized that many theologians from early times forward have been very cognizant of the limitations of speculative discourse about God, of the mystery that marks the limits of human capacities to speak about God. Indeed, the impression of a near paradox is unavoidable when one reads Augustine and Calvin; they press the limits of human thought about God and his will as far as they can go, while at the same time warning that some things cannot be fully stated in rational terms.

Even if the mystery of God is emphasized, theologians attempt to make a case for the appreciation of what is ultimately mysterious. When a theologian characterizes the Deity over and over as an ultimate mystery, what problems is he attempting to overcome, or to avoid? And why are these perceived to be problems?

One problem the theologian is trying to solve or to avoid is epistemological. God is not susceptible to the same kinds of investigations that phenomena are subject to; God is not an object like the planet Saturn toward which space vehicles can be sent, of which photographs can be taken, and from which a whole range of data can be collected. God is not an object like DNA so that he can be patterned by a double helix with a "genetic alphabet" of four nucleotides. God is not an object like a modern corporation that can be investigated to discern the structures of prestige and authority, the flow of communications, the decision-making process, the relations to other corporations, to the government, and to the public. God is not an object like the human brain, which, while still far from fully understood, yields its "secrets" to increasingly refined investigative techniques and can be therapeutically experimented upon with certain drugs even when it is not fully known why and how the drugs work.

Because God is not an object like phenomena subject to scientific investigation, how he is known necessarily is different. And since he cannot be known in the same way that phenomena can, not only must the theologian be circumspect but he must also find those modes of expression which are appropriate both to that which is known and to the circumstances of the knowers. Attempts to exhaust the mystery, the unknowable, the hidden Deity, are not only subject to the charge of intellectual pride; there are simply limits of possibilities of knowledge which must be acknowledged by any critical theologian. The operations of the human mind do not neatly correspond with the structure and processes of ultimate reality. The language of theology has to be at best analogical, and perhaps only metaphorical.

Yet the theological enterprise is not given up. There is some basic conviction of being sustained in the world, of being limited by all sorts of conditions, or being given new possibilities for life, which cries for some form of expression beyond those given to us by the less and the more exact sciences. There are hard limits to what can be said with certainty about our "natural knowledge of God," or from the "natural piety" that many persons have. The sense of the mystery of God is not simply the opaqueness of his reality that cannot be fully penetrated by the human mind but the ineffability of his presence even when he is "known." The mystery of God is not just that there are secrets which people cannot know, that there is something toward which a whole series of investigations point with increasing accuracy as they overcome ignorance, as in the case of knowledge of Saturn or of genes. It is that the reality that is "known" or experienced does not yield the precise formulations that phenomena do. Mystery is not equivalent to unknown or unknowable but rather to known (in the sense of experienced) but not fully describable and explainable.

Thus, recourse to the language of mystery is undertaken to avoid the kinds of claims that a few theologians have made in the past, and to answer the expectations of claims that many nonreligious persons have of the theologian. Theologians often speak of the meaning rather than the truth of religious language, particularly if truth necessarily implies verifiability in the same way that the double helix structure of DNA can be verified. To speak of the mystery of God is meaningful.

Not only the practitioners of natural theology have claimed too much certainty for the knowledge of God; the practitioners of biblical theology, or of "revelational" theology, have also overstepped the bounds. Literalism in biblical interpretation has not been as historically long or widespread a movement in Christian history as is sometimes thought, at least not the kind of literalism that has characterized the fundamentalist movements of the past hundred years. There is little point in describing once again those simplistic views of the writing of the Bible that have led to certainty about the texts as utterances of the Deity, and to a certainty about their meaning that sophisticated persons cannot achieve even with contemporary texts. But, in the eyes of many, the biblical theologies that have confidence in the sufficiency of the Bible as a basis for theology, without being literalistic in their interpretations, also transgress the bounds of mystery. The Bible for these theologians becomes, with great certitude, the source of our knowledge of God. God in his freedom chose to make himself known in the events recorded there, in the lives of persons narrated and discussed there, and in the outlooks toward the past and the future that the people of the Bible held. I suppose that the claim that all theology begins with exegesis of the biblical texts is as sharp a way to point to this confidence as any. The epistemological problem is overcome or avoided at one major juncture of the discussion of theology: for various reasons theologians have confidence in the biblical record as the place to begin their theology. The problem is not overcome fully, for there are still the remaining difficulties about the persuasive warrants for thinking within the biblical materials and from them to some generalizations about the Deity. Also within this confidence in the Bible one still has to face questions about the kinds of language the text itself uses when it speaks of the Deity: its similes, metaphors, analogies, and symbols. And certainly the sense of the mystery of the Deity is expressed in many biblical passages together with more precise statements about him (if analogies, metaphors, and symbols can be said to be precise). Biblical language about God varies from the profound but obscure "I am who I am" to the plainest sorts of anthropomorphic language. The varieties of biblical language, the absence of the speculative type of theological construction that seems to make greater claims for literal truth, and the unclear status of the nature of the revelation that is in the Bible, make some theologians accent the mystery of God.

Among contemporary theologians, Karl Rahner writes most prolifically about God as mystery. In Chapter 2 of *Foundations of Christian Faith,* entitled "Man in the Presence of Absolute Mystery," the reader finds a dense, but rich, summary of Rahner's many other writings on this subject.[23] Rahner is clear about what he is seeking to overcome or avoid in writing about God. Those who argue from various observations about nature tend to think they have captured the essence of the Deity in their concepts. They make God an object alongside of other objects in the world. Pantheism, while it bears a measure of truth in its sensitivity to the transcendental experience of God as the absolute reality or the original ground, does not properly understand and articulate the difference between God and the world. Dualism understands that there is a difference, but it makes the difference to be similar to differences between "categorical realities," like the difference between trees and rocks.[24] Other benchmarks which Rahner uses to indicate what he is avoiding are also established in this chapter.

23. Karl Rahner, S.J., *Foundations of Christian Faith,* trans. William V. Dych (New York: The Seabury Press, 1978), pp. 44–89.
24. Ibid., pp. 62–63.

With deliberate self-consciousness Rahner over and over uses the language of mystery as the most appropriate for writing about God. Persons have transcendental experiences in "the presence of the absolute mystery we call 'God,' an experience which is more primary than reflection and cannot be recaptured completely by reflection." Man's "orientation towards the absolute mystery always continues to be offered to him by this mystery as the ground and content of his being."[25] The word God refers to

> "the ineffable one," "the nameless one" who does not enter into
> the world we can name as part of it. It means the "silent one"
> who is always there, and yet can always be overlooked, unheard,
> and, because it expresses the whole in its unity and totality, can
> be passed over as meaningless. It means that which is really
> wordless, because every word receives its limits, its own sound
> and hence its intelligible sense only within a field of words. . . .
> For it is the final word before we become silent, the word which
> allows all the individual things we can name to disappear into the
> background, the word in which we are dealing with the totality
> which grounds them all.[26]

It is "the final word before wordless and worshipful silence in the face of the ineffable mystery."[27]

Silence before mystery: this, with deep religious power, expresses the human experience of God. Clearly then, a theology has to be careful to avoid making excessive claims for the knowledge it proposes; it must be worded in such a way that this fundamental character of the human experience of God is not oversimplified or essentially violated. Whether the language of philosophical reflection or the biblical language is used, this language can never be taken as a literal correspondence with the reality to which it refers. But religion itself, not to mention the intellectual enterprise of theology, requires that persons not only say "the final word before wordless and worshipful silence in the face of the ineffable mystery" but also explicate it conceptually. There is at least the practical requirement of an "explicit, conceptual and thematic knowledge" of God; such language is "a reflection upon man's transcendental orientation toward mystery," and is necessary.[28] But the limits are clear: "the meaning of all explicit knowledge of God in religion and in metaphysics is intelligible and can really be understood only when all the words we use there

25. Ibid., p. 44.
26. Ibid., pp. 46–47.
27. Ibid., p. 51.
28. Ibid., p. 52.

point to the unthematic experience of our orientation towards the ineffable mystery.''[29]

How can this process be undertaken? What are its possibilities as well as its limits? The process can be undertaken through the use of analogies. But analogies, for Rahner, are not the same as they were in what he calls the ''school philosophy'' with its analogy of being. There analogies functioned as a ''midpoint between univocation and equivocation.''[30] Happily, for Rahner, his basic philosophical views (which I shall not begin to explicate here) make it possible to establish a stronger sense of analogy. Transcendental experience (the experience of the ineffable and nameless) ''is the condition which makes possible all categorical knowledge of individual objects.'' This assertion points to the relationship between knowledge of particularities on the one hand, and knowledge of the ineffable on the other. One is grounded in the other; neither is a midpoint between univocation and equivocation about the other. It is on this basis that analogous statements signify what is ''most basic and original [experience of the ineffable] in all our knowledge.''[31] This provides a basis for saying quite a lot about God, with a relatively high degree of certitude.

> We ourselves, as we can put it, exist analogously in and through our being grounded in this holy mystery which always surpasses us. But it always constitutes us by surpassing us and by pointing towards the concrete, individual, categorical realities which confront us within the realm of our experience. Conversely, then, these realities are the mediation of and the point of departure for our knowledge of God.[32]

The relation of the categorical to the transcendental—of the particularities and individualities we can name and know in the many realms of experience to the ineffable, nameless holy mystery—warrants all that Rahner can proceed to say about God. The mediation of the presence of the transcendental in the particular warrants moving from the particularities of experience to knowledge of God. And it is God's self-communication in Jesus Christ that warrants a great deal of traditional Christian theological reflection on the ineffable. A philosophical position, as I indicated, undergirds these possibilities. It even undergirds his view of the nature and authority of the Roman Catholic church, and thus he can defend a good deal of that authority in matters of doctrine and morals. But even in passages in which the most is made of the access route to the

29. Ibid., p. 53.
30. Ibid., p. 72.
31. Ibid.
32. Ibid., p. 73.

ineffable, in which a lot is said about God, one is reminded over and over that one has come to the last word before moving to worshipful silence in the face of a holy mystery.

A theology that is based upon the senses of dependence, gratitude, and obligation to a deity, a theology based on these as aspects of religious affections (such as the theology developed in this book) cannot but resonate with Rahner's powerful sense of the primal religious consciousness, what he calls transcendental experience. It will take cognizance of this, and will be acutely conscious of the fact that our reflections only point to the reality of what Rahner calls holy mystery. The fact that the approach to theology is basically from morality will make some difference in what is said about the Deity, and different risks than Rahner takes will be taken here. The philosophical conviction which enables him to move by his way of analogical thinking is not one I share, and thus, while I sometimes say more and different things about God than Rahner says, I cannot say them with the same certitude. Indeed, there will be points at which Rahner opts for mystery much sooner than I, and other points at which I have less confidence in the mediations of the "holy mystery" in particularities. The former will occur in ways in which I will use theories and evidences from some sciences for both theological and moral purposes; the latter will show in what I say and do not say about Christology. The perplexing and persisting question for any theology is raised sharply by this contemporary theologian: at what points in one's reflection on the primal experience of the reality of God does one take recourse to the language of "mystery"? How does one, in a prudent effort not to say too much too specifically and with excessive certitude, say enough about God to develop a theological ethics? Does too early a recourse to mystery impoverish theological ethics? Does taking recourse too late run the risks of that sort of objectification of the Deity that Rahner and many other contemporary theologians rightly attempt to avoid?

Karl Rahner is by no means the only modern theologian who is concerned to avoid making God an object like phenomena in the world. Nor is he the only one seeking to avoid modern forms of pantheism or of radical dualism. Tillich, like Rahner, is concerned to be rather careful in the choice of words and concepts that are used in theology and, while he has no aversion to the language of mystery, it is not used as frequently as it is in the writings of the German Jesuit. Indeed, in my judgment, Tillich is readier than Rahner to develop a very abstract system of concepts for speaking about God once he has the basic lines of method worked out. After clearing much philosophical error or misconception out of the way, Tillich comes to two sentences which are marked in the memories of all students of his theology: "The statement that God is being-itself is a non-symbolic statement. It does not point beyond itself."[33]

"God is being-itself" seems to me to be a step beyond what Rahner is ready to take, or if he takes it he is more concerned quickly to assure us that this would be a statement in a secular form of the "last word" that can be expressed before we are silent before the holy mystery. Tillich has his own theological and philosophical reasons for making the statement as directly as he does, which I shall not explore here. Certainly he is trying to avoid the anthropomorphic language that has often characterized Christian religion; certainly he is establishing a basis on which God cannot become what Rahner calls an object of categorical knowledge, a thing differentiated from other things by its concrete particularities. The statement that God is being-itself carries in Tillich's theology a heavy load of philosophical-theological freight, and he moves quickly to say a good bit more about God in symbolic language. Indeed, once one has it clear that God is being-itself, "nothing else can be said about God as God which is not symbolic."[34] There are warrants in the relations of being to human beings, however, for then proceeding to say quite a bit about God in symbolic language. Just as Rahner has a way of moving analogically to spell out a good deal about the Deity and his relations to life in the world, so does Tillich. There is at least a formal similarity between the two theologians. Tillich asks what he calls "the crucial question. Can a segment of finite reality become the basis for an assertion about that which is infinite? The answer is that it can, because that which is infinite is being-itself and because everything participates in being-itself."[35] With greater ease and comfort than Rahner, Tillich lays claim to the traditional view of *analogia entis*. All sorts of aspects of reality can then provide access to symbolic language about God, and symbolic language is by no means weak and trivial language, for symbols participate in the reality of that for which they stand (to recall another famous statement by Tillich). Indeed, he writes, "If a segment of reality is used as a symbol for God, the realm of reality from which it is taken is, so to speak, elevated into the realm of the holy. It is no longer secular. It is theonomous."[36] His example is the term "king"; when God is called king, one not only says something about God symbolically but also about "the holy character of kinghood."

The idea of the participation of the finite in the infinite, of particular beings in being-itself, provides a warrant for drawing many analogies between that which is not God and God; a great deal can be said about

33. Tillich, *Systematic Theology,* 1:238.
34. Ibid., p. 239.
35. Ibid.
36. Ibid., p. 241.

being-itself though it is said symbolically. There is, of course, an alteration in the reference of the symbol in the process of using it theologically. For example, the symbol of a personal God is derived from the deep human existential person-to-person relationship. This might lead the careless person to judge that God is an individual just as one calls another person to whom one is related an individual, or even call God the absolute individual. But one cannot do this unless one also calls God the absolute participant, for both individualization and participation (one of many key polarities in Tillich's thought) are "rooted in the ground of the divine life" and "God is equally 'near' to each of them while transcending them both."[37] What, then, is warranted by beginning with existential person-to-person relations? Not that "personal God" means that God is a person. "It means that God is the ground of everything personal and that he carries within himself the ontological power of personality. He is not a person, but he is not less than personal."[38]

This example illustrates briefly, but cryptically, the procedure by which Tillich can proceed to use a large number of polarities drawn from experience and especially from person-to-person relationships, to write a great deal about God symbolically. Indeed, given at one stage the impression that not much can be said about God, and the clear statement that "God is being-itself" is the only thing nonsymbolic that can be said about God, the reader is a bit surprised by how many traditional concepts and ideas that have flourished in the history of Christian theology can be incorporated into the theological system. To be sure, there is a transformation, or at least an alteration, going on so that many of the traditional meanings given to these ideas turn out to be distorted or incomplete. But the central theme of much of Tillich's theology is a central theme of traditional Christianity, namely, the "salvation" of individual persons and, I believe one can fairly say, of culture as well. The human situation is redescribed in the light of concepts drawn from existential thought and other contemporary ideas; the redescription, however, is meant to unveil the deeper truth that the ideas and concepts referred to in the past. As in the case of Rahner, so here there is a vast philosophical undergirding to what is said more specifically about the human situation, and it is not germane to elucidate all of that at this point. Whether individual persons or culture are under discussion, the ideal is a kind of spiritual ideal; culture is to be theonomous; individuals are to have a centeredness and wholeness.

This point can be illustrated by attending to one of Tillich's discussions of theonomy; in such discussions one begins to see what is to some

37. Ibid., pp. 244–45.
38. Ibid., p. 245.

persons a spiritual and theological richness, but is to others vagueness and mystery in the worst sense. The vocabulary is esoteric to the uninitiated, and perhaps in the end it is most meaningful to those who have a kind of deep empathy with Tillich, and with the Spiritual Presence about which he speaks. One cannot be certain that one expounds him fairly when one chooses terms other than his to express what one thinks is being said. Being-itself, the nonsymbolic expression of God, is symbolized as Divine Spirit, or as Spiritual Presence. This Spirit is not something strange that is imposed on persons or cultural activity from the "outside." Rather, it determines and directs from "within." "Theonomous culture is Spirit-determined and Spirit-directed culture, and Spirit fulfills spirit [human spirit] instead of breaking it."[39] Human individuals and human cultures are grounded in being-itself; the Spiritual Presence is that to which human life is to be open; it is the source of creativity and flourishing in persons and cultures; it is the source of the healing that reunites what has been estranged. While being-itself has both form and *dynamis,* or spiritual power, in my judgment it is the *dynamis* that is most emphasized in Tillich's thinking. This is a crucial point, I believe, for Tillich's theological ethics. If there is anything that appears over and over which is antagonistic to the Spiritual Presence in Tillich's thought, it is those forms of life, whether moral rules or subjection to social institutions, which he judges to be heteronomous, or subjected to a strange extrinsic law imposed from "outside." For reasons I shall not discuss here, what is imposed from the outside does not participate in being-itself properly; it is opaque to the Spiritual Presence. It cannot communicate "the experience of holiness, of something ultimate in being and meaning" as theonomous culture does.[40]

Like culture, morality is to be theonomous. It is clear by now that this cannot mean for Tillich that it is to be based on a divine law that is, for example, given in the Decalogue, or upon rules of human conduct that are inferred or deduced from an objective order of creation. Rather, it is the fulfillment of the law of our being as human, as that (and I can only put it this way) wells up from within us when we are motivated and directed by the Divine Presence, the *dynamis* of being. Love makes this theonomous morality possible, but "love is not a law; it is a reality. It is not a matter of ought-to-be—even if expressed in imperative form—but a matter of being. Theonomous morals are morals of love as a creation of the Spirit."[41] I, at least, cannot avoid the strong impression that, like much of traditional Christian thought, Tillich's is anthropocentric; the

39. Ibid., 3:250.
40. Ibid., p. 25.
41. Ibid., p. 272.

significance of the Christian faith is its reference to a process by which human life, individually, interpersonally, and culturally, is to be "saved." Nor can I avoid the strong impression that its salvation is to come from the proper "inner" relation between persons and culture on the one hand and the Spiritual Presence on the other.

This makes it very difficult, if not impossible, to develop theological ethics in the sense of seeking to derive some notions about how life is to be governed in relation to norms of human conduct that are external to the self, that are at least consonant with our reasonable perceptions of what is required to sustain the proper order of human communities and their relations to the natural world of which they are a part. Clearly Tillich, like Rahner, is seeking to avoid making God a phenomenon like things that can be named and distinguished from each other by their particularities. More so than Rahner, of course, he is heir to the Protestant tradition, stemming from Luther, in which the problem of sin is the central one, though sin is redescribed in contemporary terms. The answer to the moral questions of modern life is not to be sought primarily in establishing those indicators of right moral action, or right moral ends, that can be inferred from the ordering of nature. One must qualify this statement in a special way, for Tillich can affirm it in the sense that there is an orientation of individuals toward their self-fulfillment which ought to be realized. It is to be realized, however, not by conforming actions to externally binding obligations and principles but by an inner process that is nothing short of a kind of conversion. The "inner quality" (my term) of the lives of persons is of more concern by far than their actions; the spiritual quality of a culture is more important than the ways in which it orders life. The *dynamis* of the Spiritual Presence is what makes culture and morality authentic.

This is a very un-Calvinistic theology. While in the Reformed tradition religion also serves as a means for salvation, more than in Tillich's theology the end of life is to celebrate and glorify God. It is hard not to come to the conclusion in reading Tillich that the almost exclusive purpose of God is the enrichment and fulfillment of human life. There is a sense in which Tillich's theology, like most modern theology, has made the Deity a utility device for the fulfillment of human aims. To make the point more dramatically, one can point out how remarkable it is that Tillich, like most modern theologians, still has not come to grips with the significance of what many developments in modern science have made clear: the minuscule place of human life in the order of nature. Or, what Herbert Butterfield, in a generalization about scientific thought in the seventeenth century (three centuries ago!) calls "the assertion that it is absurd to suppose that the whole of this new colossal universe was created by God

purely for the sake of men, purely to serve the purposes of the earth."[42]
Not only is the language of Spiritual Presence vague; not only does Tillich
embellish it primarily in terms of its *dynamis* rather than by any ordering
form, but also in the end the human relation to being-itself serves only
human ends—the enrichment and fulfillment of human life.

Both Rahner and Tillich develop their systematic theologies with
the substance and backing of explicit ontologies. Both are philosophical
theologians, not only in the sense that every theologian is philosophical
by virtue of implicit or explicit commitments on epistemological and other
basic questions, but also in the sense that each argues analogically about
what can be said about the holy mystery, or being-itself. Neither is a
biblical theologian in the distinctive Protestant sense which frequently
asserts that all theology must begin with the exegesis of Scripture. Both
of them, of course, desire to be biblical; they certainly claim a deep
congruity between what they write and some of the basic messages and
ideas of the Bible. Surely they differ on the question of the authority of
the Bible for theology—but that is not my interest here. It is clear, however, that for neither of them is exegesis of biblical materials the principal
point at which they begin to develop their particular utterances about God
and his relations to the world.

Two strands of recent Protestant theology are much more biblical
in significant respects than are the theologies of Rahner and Tillich. These
two are eschatological theology and the theology of the acts of God in
history. Certainly both are also familiar in some Roman Catholic writings
as well, particularly since the Second Vatican Council. Like other theologies, these are also seeking to solve certain problems and to avoid
others. One problem they wish to solve is the tendency of more speculative
philosophical theologies to lose the religious concreteness and particularity of the biblical imagery and language; "Spiritual Presence" may
resonate with more religious passion than "being-itself," but neither
seems as evocative of a relationship to the Deity as "Father." Another
distinguishing feature is the concern to hold the biblical materials dearer
as the body of faith and tradition which carries the historic particularity
of the witness of the Israelite and Christian communities through cultures
and through histories. Of course, as I noted, more speculative Christian
theologies do claim a congruence with biblical themes and doctrines, but
they move a greater distance from the primary texts than many other
persons believe is theologically or religiously legitimate. The more immediately biblically grounded theologies clearly have greater confidence
in the biblical materials as the sufficient, or nearly sufficient, source of

42. Herbert Butterfield, *The Origins of Modern Science*, rev. ed. (New York: The
Free Press, 1965), p. 69.

theological truth. It is characteristic of them to contrast the biblical theological principles with those established on more independent philosophical grounds. The distinctiveness of Christian theological reflection
as biblical reflection is a point such writers greatly stress.

I have selected the first very influential book by Jürgen Moltmann,
his *Theology of Hope*, as the basis for observations about eschatological
theology.[43] Its worldwide impact in both Protestant and Roman Catholic
circles was very great; indeed, its influence on the churches of the Third
World was probably at least as great as on those in Europe and North
America. If I do not radically misunderstand the argument of this book,
there are four crucial steps in its development. The first is an argument
about how biblical theology itself is to be most accurately interpreted. As
against other prevailing views, Moltmann argues for the centrality of
eschatology to proper interpretation of the biblical message. He enters
a caveat which is important to note: "The term 'eschatology' is wrong."[44]
There is no *logos* of the future; thus it is more appropriate to talk about
promise (a notably more personal term). The second step isolates the key
event in the biblical material for understanding the meaning of the promise,
the resurrection of Jesus Christ. But the possibility of this and its significance relies on another biblical principle, the contingency of creation.
"Only when the world can be understood as contingent creation out of
the freedom of God and *ex nihilo*—only on the basis of this *contingentia
mundi*—does the raising of Christ become intelligible as *novo creatio*."[45]
The third step is that on the basis of this we can know some critically
significant things about the nature of the world, and particularly about the
characteristic of human history. Reality has a "historic character." In the
light of the resurrection of Jesus this historic character does not mean
merely that there are contingencies in history. "To expand the historical
approach to the extent of taking account of the contingent does not as
yet bring the reality of the resurrection itself into view."[46] What is involved
in understanding "reality" from the standpoint of the resurrection is the
possibility of new creation. It becomes an analogy of "what is to come."

> [T]he resurrection of Christ does not offer itself as an analogy to
> that which can be experienced any time and anywhere, but as an
> analogy of what is to come at all. The expectation of what is to
> come on the ground of the resurrection of Christ, must then turn
> all reality that can be experienced and all real experience into an

43. Jürgen Moltmann, *Theology of Hope,* trans. James W. Leitch (New York: Harper
and Row, 1967).
44. Ibid., p. 17.
45. Ibid., p. 179.
46. Ibid.

experience that is provisional and a reality that does not yet contain within it what is held in prospect for it.[47]

The fourth step is simply the implication of these beliefs for our attitude toward reality: it is one of hope because of the assurance of the possibility and actuality of a new creation. One might think that a new creation would produce more dread than hope, for the creation in which we live provides at least a basis for some measure of confidence. New creation does not produce dread, of course, because the content of the resurrection assures us that it is beneficial to the human species.

From these steps a number of practical inferences can be and are drawn. What is now present will pass away; what is now repressive to human aspirations can be altered as human beings are both motivated and directed by hope; what is apparently explicable by more deterministic views of cause and effect is not really so determined, and can be altered. Indeed, the "revelation of the risen Lord . . . stands as a sort of *primum movens* at the head of the process of history. It is in virtue of this revelation that the reality of man and his world becomes 'historic,' and it is the hope set upon this revelation that makes all reality inadequate and as such transient and surpassable."[48]

In good faith with the author of a scholarly theological treatise one cannot treat this last quotation as homiletical hyperbole, or as unintelligible. All reality is surpassable. To be sure, one would like to know what this sort of statement means for the interpretation of nature. While there is no serious development of that point, it appears that Moltmann desires to fly in the face of centuries of development in the natural sciences. "It is not possible to speak of believing existence in hope and in radical openness, and at the same time consider the 'world' to be a mechanism or self-contained system of cause and effect in objectified antithesis to man."[49] Of course, it is not clear in this theology, as it is not clear in much other recent theology, just what "world" refers to, but it seems, among other things, to refer to what we learn from the natural and social sciences. "In view of what is meant and what is promised when we speak of the raising of Christ, it is therefore necessary to expose the profound irrationality of the rational cosmos of the modern, technico-scientific world."[50] It is hard to avoid drawing the inference that the interpretation of "reality" that is based upon the resurrection of Jesus Christ implies that the limitations of human activity, the dependencies of the human species on the ordered processes of nature with their causes and effects, as well as the

47. Ibid., p. 180.
48. Ibid. , p. 88.
49. Ibid., p. 69.
50. Ibid., p. 179.

forms and possibilities of human action are all open not only to contingency but even to a more radical new creation. If this inference is not ill founded, then we can see how a theologian can move from the statement of a doctrine based on an interpretation of a central event in the Bible to interpretations of the "world" without taking serious account not only of the lived experience of persons but also of the well-established explanations of the natural world of which we are part. Not only the historical life of the species, in which actions of persons do have a range of intentional discretion, and consequences have a range of contingency, is presumably illuminated by the implications of the resurrection of Christ, but also the courses of the heavens, the earthquakes and hurricanes, and the genetic code. Perhaps Moltmann does not intend to say this; perhaps he wants his theology, like most modern Protestant theology, to pertain solely to the human spiritual condition. Perhaps he still believes that the whole of this universe was created solely for the sake of man. Or perhaps he thinks that if one can believe what he proposes to be faithful Christian theology, then one can better deal with the repressions, the sense of limitations, and the determinations that seem to oppress so many persons. If it is the latter, what he offers is a remarkably elaborate framework, subject to more critical analysis than is given here, to evoke and nourish hope in the hearts of people. Theology is justified, then, by its presumed beneficial effects on human attitudes.

One is told that this theology not only motivates but directs human activity. Life is to be open to the future; present institutions and arrangements do not have absolute and eternal validity; one can be freed from the bondage that the absolutization of present arrangements creates. This theology sustains a basic future orientation to all human action. There is a *telos*—indeed there is something like a final cause toward which all is oriented: the future, God, which causes the present. But it is difficult to derive much particular guidance for present moral activity from a *telos* that is as empty as the future (especially when we are told that there is no *logos* of the future), even the future that guarantees new creation which is beneficial to human beings. Nature, and the explanations of it that are given by the natural sciences, certainly are not theologically significant sources for guidance for moral activity; the only significant reference to creation in the *Theology of Hope* is to the biblical doctrine of *creatio ex nihilo* as a necessary presupposition to Moltmann's use of the resurrection of Jesus as the critical revelatory event for understanding reality. The contingency of the creation rather than its orderliness is stressed here. It is difficult to get much particular moral guidance from contingency.

Moltmann, like many theologians interested in ethics, is in part occupied with a theological political tradition of the orders of creation which has backed very conservative views of human society. Not only were family, economy, and state ordained by God in that tradition, but particular historical forms of family life (like patriarchalism), economy, and state received theological and moral sanctions that resisted all forms of social change. Certainly his God of the future undercuts any absolutization of particular historic forms of human institutions and society. In a collection of essays published as *Hope and Planning*, one finds ethical inferences, meager as they are, drawn from his escathological theology.[51] "This fundamental eschatological openness and unfinished quality of reality makes relative those ordinances in which human behavior becomes habitual, so that they become open processes of the integration of God's history."[52] "Man and human society must acquire an eschatologically determined historicity rather than a lasting nature."[53] In the presence of views that would resist all social change, as well as the basic theology that Moltmann develops, the motivation for these statements is understandable. It is remarkable, however, to read that, "The recognition that man does not have nature but history means an overcoming of all naturalistic or quasi-naturalistic ways of thinking."[54] What inferences are to be drawn from this assertion? To be sure, there are no laws governing social developments in the same way that laws govern the orbiting of the planets or that Mendelian laws govern genes, but does this mean that generalizations with high degrees of probability about the course of events in human society have to be overcome? That human activity is not explainable at all by investigations of the human brain? Does it mean that Moltmann's eschatological theology makes all evidences of ordering processes in human life, individual and social, both theologically and ethically irrelevant? Does it lead to an "individualistic decisionism" in ethics?

Moltmann perceives the problem. His views might lead to the extreme position in which "there is no fixed order, no lasting relationship, no institutional foundation under man's feet."[55] This extreme is to be avoided. So what is the alternative? "[O]ne only does justice to the disclosure of reality as history . . . if one designs an *ethic of moral process* and if Christian ethics understands itself . . . as a *science of history*."[56] One can fairly interpret this to mean that ethics must be designed in such a way that it takes into account historical changes and the processes by which moral choices are made. Certainly such a view is coherent with Moltmann's theology, and it can be supported on other grounds as

51. Jürgen Moltmann, *Hope and Planning,* trans. Margaret Clarkson (New York: Harper and Row, 1971).
52. Ibid., p. 107.
53. Ibid., p. 112.
54. Ibid., p. 118.
55. Ibid.
56. Ibid., p. 122.

well. But the question remains: In the light of what criteria, what ends and principles, does one find one's way in the process? There has to be some point of continuity, if not stability. Moltmann acknowledges this as well. "The ethical decision is always related to the instant and yet still points beyond it in hope, in self-surrender to and belief in a certain future." If that future "is not to be made unreal as empty openness for the arbitrary character of every new plan, one must talk about a concrete future. Only in terms of a concrete future do ethical instants acquire continuity, does history become a process within the context of its events."[57] And here we come to what that is: "Promise and commandment destine the community for an eschatological fellowship, i.e., for the assembly of those who live from the hope in that future which is determined by the historical event of Jesus Christ." This eschatological community "cannot be absorbed or fitted into a social structure." It is to find its place as "light of the world, salt of the earth." What is the moral significance of this "concrete future"? It is simply and only the relativization of all present things. It provides "a source of eschatological unrest within a society which attempts to save itself from history through a dream of technological perfection."[58] The idea of a directive still has to be included, but the directive amounts to a specification of the unrest. Social institutions are to be questioned "about their final purpose and their eschatological justification." It gives hope and courage—basic attitudes—for, "In the expectation of the *shalom,* of the kingdom of God which comes to earth, of the new heaven and the new earth, one can find and give hope and courage for a life which is now, for the most part, determined only by functions."[59]

The main point simply returns to the basic theological convictions: from the perspective of eschatological theology, both culture and nature would be decisively historicized. These "ethical" conclusions are coherent with the basic theology. Obviously one can come to similar conclusions on the basis of other theologies or of nontheological principles; one need not have Moltmann's theology to understand the relativities of history, though one would need something like his theology to establish even the remote possibility that nature can be historicized. (Whether nature can be historicized is a matter of scientific, not theological, investigation.) The crux of the whole pattern is his understanding of the Deity. If he was seeking a doctrine of God that would support an interpretation of life in the world that understood its contingencies and its possibilities, he certainly found one. If his doctrine of God is to be justified on the grounds of its adequacy to the biblical materials alone, there are matters that are

57. Ibid.
58. Ibid., p. 124.
59. Ibid., p. 125.

very arguable. If it is to be tested by modern understandings of nature (if this is relevant, and since he thinks such understandings are too deterministic, they seem to be relevant) the doctrine of God is exceedingly deficient. His God, to be sure, is lord over nature and history, but if the contingency of nature is the principal thing to be said about it, and the evidence for that is the Genesis creation account and the resurrection of Jesus, vast amounts of evidence about the determinations that are present in nature simply have to be ignored to make the argument at all. In the end, I believe, the relevant point for this discussion is that his view of God is primarily significant for human persons, to create conditions in them of hope and courage by interpreting "the world" in such a way that it and they are not fated. That is the maximum of "ethics" that is derivable from this theology; it is a theological interpretation of "the world" from which a basic orientation toward life can be derived but which provides no significant bases theologically, historically, or naturally for the guidance of human action. I invite the reader to see how far he or she would get making a choice about an induced abortion, about issues of justice and liberty in the establishment of monetary and fiscal policies, about how to conduct modern warfare (if warfare can be justified at all) in light of this theology and ethics. Things are not immutable; they can be changed. God, the future, makes possible hope and courage. That, I believe, is all Moltmann can tell us.

"God acting in history" is the principal theme of the other biblical theological alternative for ethics. Its recent forms are not unprecedented in theological history or in biblical religion. Indeed, the principal authorization for its recent revival was its biblical character. Who has read theology in the past four decades and cannot recall seeing one place or another the citation of "Assyria, rod of mine anger" as an illustration of the way in which prophetic writers saw historical events as the medium of the divine purposes and the divine agency? One can read histories of Western Europe or of North America, and find that major events in the lives of human communities were interpreted as marks of the wrath or the calling of God. The great black plague of the mid-fourteenth century, inexplicable on the basis of what was known about disease at that time, engendered numerous speculations about why this visitation of the wrath of God was to come on to the world at that time. From John Winthrop to Cotton Mather to Jonathan Edwards the Puritans interpreted not only their opportunities on this continent as a calling of God, but also the deleterious experiences they endured as visitations of the judgment of God. The whole genre of sermons, called with some appropriateness "jeremiads," was developed to warn the people of the religious significance of the signs of the times. In the sixteenth century Luther interpreted social roles and functions, or offices, as "masks of God" through which

God acted to preserve human society; to be a father was to be a mask of God, doing God's work in the world; to be a magistrate was another mask.

"God simply *is* what God manifestly *does*," wrote Joseph Sittler in his creative little book, *The Structure of Christian Ethics*.[60] The warrants for such an assertion are not philosophical, or at least not for most of the theologians who write in this manner. The recent concentration on this notion arose in part out of the work of biblical scholars with theological interests. Many of them were interested not only in establishing the idea of God to be found particularly in the Old Testament material; they were also interested in the life of the churches. Among them was the late G. Ernest Wright. His book, *The God Who Acts: Biblical Theology as Recital*, both summed up and further developed its theme.[61] The argument is on the one hand about what the Bible says, and on the other about what the theology of Christian churches ought to be. Biblical theology is distinguished from the theologies of paganism and from later speculative Christian theologies by being "first and foremost a theology of recital. The worshipper listens to the recital and by means of historical memory and identification he participates, so to speak, in the original events."[62] Biblical theology is consonant with biblical language, which "will always be the despair of the precise and exact theologian who above all desires a simple, coherent system."[63] It is not a system of ideas but a recital of the formative events of the history of members of the community, events "as the redemptive handiwork of God."[64] What could be said about the knowledge of God "was an inference from what actually happened in human history." History was far more important than nature; it was in historical events that the "Israelite eye" saw "more clearly than anywhere else what God willed and what he was about."[65] History was the mediation of God's activity. "The language of nature is distinctly secondary."[66] God is both known and addressed in terms that relate him to society and to history. If, as Wright and others believed, the theology of the churches must be biblical, then there is the warrant for using this biblical theme as central to constructive theology.

60. Joseph Sittler, *The Structure of Christian Ethics* (Baton Rouge: Louisiana State University Press, 1958), p. 4.
61. G. Ernest Wright, *God Who Acts: Biblical Theology as Recital* (London: SCM Press, 1952). In 1962 I heard Wright describe himself as "an Old Testament scholar of the Albright School, and a biblical theologian of Calvinistic persuasion."
62. Ibid., p. 28.
63. Ibid., p. 32.
64. Ibid., p. 38.
65. Ibid., p. 44.
66. Ibid., p. 49. The point has become widely accepted. "Other religions think in terms of cosmos and nature. Christianity, rooted in Biblical sources, thinks in terms of history." Gustavo Gutierrez, *A Theology of Liberation*, trans. and ed. Caridad Inda and John Eagleson (Maryknoll, N.Y.: Orbis Books, 1973), p. 174.

This approach necessarily comes to three questions. What has God done? What is God doing? And, what ought we to do? Theologians, predictably, do not answer the three questions in the same way. Formally, the most prevalent procedure for moving from an answer to the first question to one to the third is by way of historical analogies. What has God done? Here one "recites" biblical narratives selected, of course, according to some contemporary interest or theological principle, and on the basis of some explicit or inchoate answer to the second or third questions. What is God doing? One begins to answer that by finding sufficient similarities between the circumstances of the passages recited and present circumstances to warrant a historical analogy. In the circumstances theologically described and interpreted in Exodus 5-14, God was actively leading his people out of bondage in Egypt to the promised land. Present circumstances for many people are socially and historically similar to those of the ancient Hebrew people in Egypt; God does similar things in similar circumstances; therefore what God is doing now is leading people from bondage to liberation. What ought we to do? The hidden premise is that we ought to be doing the sort of things that God does; if God is leading people out of bondage, we ought to be engaged in activities consonant with his action, indeed, we ought to be the means of his action. And so one moves from recital of the past to an evaluative description of the present in the light of that recital, to a religious moral imperative whose content is derived in part from the answers to the first two questions. The first ethical question is never, "What ought we to do?" It is, "What is God doing?"

Ethics done in this way is theocentric in principle. That it is faithful to the theocentricity of the biblical materials is not only commendable but establishes (however it is criticized or amended) the legitimacy for theocentric ethics in the Jewish and Christian traditions. How recent theologians have used this procedure I have discussed in previous publications, principally in *Can Ethics Be Christian?*, and thus I shall not give a detailed analysis here.[67] One must note, however, that there are more or less critically sophisticated ways in which it has been done. And some of its salient principles are worthy of some attention.

Paul Lehmann has held the theme of the divine action and presence in the world to be central for ethics throughout his career as a writer of theological ethics. Not only is the Bible the source of legitimation for developing ethics based on what God is doing, it is also to the Bible that one turns to find the content and intention of what God does. Lehmann's basic position is that God is doing humanizing work in the world. This

---

67. James M. Gustafson, *Can Ethics be Christian?* (Chicago: University of Chicago Press, 1975) pp. 117–44.

idea, so central to his *Ethics in a Christian Context*, continues in his *The Transfiguration of Politics*.[68] The more recent book, forged during the events of the late 1960s, ties the humanization theme to the theme of revolution. The link between them is freedom; freedom is the central feature of being human for Lehmann, and revolutions obviously occur in the name of freedom.

> Revolution and humanization have to do with passion, process, and promise through which happenings in history make room for freedom, i.e., for what is human in man and in society, and for what it takes to make and keep human life human in the world. Revolutions happen when the burden of unfreedom becomes unbearable and explodes into a new beginning, with a story all its own.[69] . . . The bond between revolution and humanization is freedom.[70]

Because revolutions are freighted with ambiguity, they must be "transfigured" by Jesus Christ. This is stated clearly in the book's purpose, which is

> to show *that the pertinence of Jesus Christ to an age of revolution is the power of his presence to shape the passion for humanization that generates revolution, and thus to preserve revolution from its own undoing. All revolutions aspire to give human shape to the freedom that being and staying human take; and all revolutions end by devouring their own children.*[71]

The presence of Jesus Christ in the midst of revolutions provides the transfiguring power and direction that keeps them from their own undoing.

Lehmann's work on revolutions is impressive for its boldness. Just as the kind of recital of God's actions in history that Wright indicates is central to theology of the Bible requires attention to some of the details of particular historic events, so also Lehmann is bold to interpret the meaning of particular revolutions of our time, and the writings of those who have led them, from his theological perspective. His question is not an abstract question typical of the history of Christian theology: When and under what conditions is it morally licit to disobey or overthrow established authority? Rather, he has plumbed the current literature about recent revolutions and interprets it in the light of his biblical theological themes. This requires, as he finally indicates on p. 231, that one return to reading the Bible tropologically, as Augustine recommended. This

68. Paul Lehmann, *Ethics in a Christian Context; The Transfiguration of Politics* (New York: Harper and Row, 1975).
69. Lehmann, *Transfiguration*, p. 23.
70. Ibid., pp. 4–5.
71. Ibid., p. xiii.

warrants what he calls "incarnational hermeneutics," a process which seeks "to discern the word and will of God in, with, and under the discernment of the times in which we live, and in turn to discern 'the meaning of this time' in, with, and under the word and will of God.'"[72] The doing of this makes it possible, in his judgment, to establish "a correspondence between the biblical and the human meaning of politics."[73] As I understand his procedure in practice, it reads an account or interpretation of a current political event in the light of selected biblical passages, and the biblical passages in the light of the current event or interpretation of it. It is important to stress that very particular events and very particular biblical passages are used; no very generalized framework of theology functions to mediate between the two as, for example, in H. Richard Niebuhr's interpretation of what God was doing in World War II. Often the reasons for the selection of the current event and of the biblical passage are apparently self-evident for Lehmann; there is no wider justification for the selection of either. The method, it seems to me, is not significantly different from that of fundamentalist "prophets" who read the biblical materials in light of the struggles between the Soviet Union and the United States, and those struggles in the light of selected biblical materials. Lehmann clearly believes such fundamentalist understanding of the biblical materials is wrong; for him the transfiguration of Jesus is the paradigmatic event which offers the clue to understanding revolutions and what is required to save them from devouring their own children. It is still, however, as if one has the *New York Times* in one hand and the Bible in the other, and correspondences between selections from each give one the political meaning of the gospel and the gospel meaning of politics—and not in generalizations of a high order but in detailed particularities. Only something like that would provide the warrants for an extended quotation from Ché Guevara followed by, "In the Gospel of Matthew, it is written that. . . ."[74] Or, in another discussion of Guevara, the following:

> His own guerilla activities in Bolivia were a casualty to multiple blunders. As a sympathetic critic has remarked: "Guevara had too much iron will and too little political sophistication.". . . At the same time, "his death represents a great paradox: the failure of his political strategy is also the victory of his example. His military defeat gave him an existential victory." . . . One thinks, almost without thinking, of the confrontation between Jesus and Pilate (John 18, 19). There was no military defeat, of course; but there was an obvious failure of political strategy and a victory of Jesus' example. Yet it was precisely the obvious that was being

72. Ibid., p. 232.
73. Ibid., p. 233.
74. Ibid., pp. 225–26.

transfigured. The quickening pace connecting an earlier transfiguration with an earlier and more literal crucifixion echoes strangely in the capture and assassination of a contemporary and committed revolutionary.[75]

H. Richard Niebuhr's celebrated phrase from the posthumously published *The Responsible Self*, "God is acting in all actions upon you. So respond to all actions upon you as to respond to his action," is a warrant for the same general enterprise as that which engaged the attention of Paul Lehmann.[76] If persons are to respond to God's action in all actions upon them, they must know something of the characteristics of God's intentions. For Niebuhr as well, the Christian turns to the biblical materials to gain some knowledge those intentions. In his three articles on the Second World War, published in *The Christian Century*, one sees quite a different procedure from Lehmann's.[77] It is not a tropological reading of the Scriptures, finding apparently clear correspondences between very particular current events on the one hand and very particular biblical texts on the other, though Niebuhr is confident that the biblical message and symbols have disclosed something of the reality of life in the world under God's rule, and thus can be used to interpret the meaning of general events. Like the interpretation of the significance of war in the Calhoun Commission report of the Federal Council of Churches (in my judgment the most remarkable document to come out of an American ecclesiastical commission in the twentieth century, and worthy of far more attention than it has received),[78] Niebuhr's interpretation is built on the basis of theological generalizations, developed from the biblical materials, about God's actions. God as judge is one such idea. What can the meaning of this be in the midst of a world war? It cannot mean the action of a Being who executes vengeance, for God's judgment is not separable from redemption. It is not merely punishment for sins, as though God were restoring the balance between those who inflict suffering and those who suffer, and as if the pains of war were inflicted on those most guilty rather than on the innocent. It cannot mean that God is discriminating about the relative morality of various groups involved, so that one is completely pure and the other totally evil. The truth of judgment cuts both ways.

75. Ibid., pp. 148–49.
76. H. Richard Niebuhr, *The Responsible Self* (New York: Harper and Row, 1963), p. 126.
77. H. Richard Niebuhr, "War as the Judgment of God," *The Christian Century* 59 (1942): 630–33; "Is God in the War?" ibid. 59 (1942): 953–55; and "War as Crucifixion," ibid. 60 (1943): 513–15.
78. "The Relation of the Church to the War in the Light of Christian Faith," in John Leith, ed., *Creeds of the Churches* (Garden City, N.Y.: Doubleday, 1963) pp. 522–54.

It means that if a Hitler is seen to be the rod of God's anger he is not thereby justified relatively or absolutely; for he does not intend what God intends, "but it is in his heart to destroy and to cut off nations not a few." It means, also, that if the United Nations are the instruments of God's judgment on Germany, Italy and Japan, they are not thereby justified, as though their intentions were relatively or absolutely right. God does not act save through finite instruments but none of the instruments can take the place of God even for a moment. . . .[79]

This is a very theocentric interpretation of the war; the whole account, of course, is more subtle and thorough than a few citations indicate. What is the significance for human conduct of the interpretation of war as God's judgment? Niebuhr indicates three consequences. First, we must abandon "the habit of passing judgments of our own on ourselves and on our enemies or opponents." "Instead of asking whether we are right people or wrong people we shall simply inquire what duty we have to perform in view of what we have done amiss and in view of what God is doing." This duty involves resistance to those who are "abusing our neighbors" but does not mean that we judge our neighbors who are being abused to be more worthy morally than their abusers. Second, we must abandon "all self-defensiveness, all self-aggrandizement, all thinking in terms of self as central."

It is a judgment on our nation which in its actions, sentiments and omissions has demonstrated its profound preoccupation with its own prosperity, safety and righteousness, so that in its withdrawal from international political responsibilities, in its tariff, monetary and neutrality legislation, it has acted always with a single eye to its own interests rather than to those of its neighbors in the commonwealth of nations.

Third, "response to God's action in war is hopeful and trusting response. It never gives up the one whom we oppose, as though he were too depraved for redemption or for restoration to full rights within the human community." Nothing is beyond the scope of redemption, and that must be remembered even when fighting against the abusers of humanity. The judgment of God in the war is the judgment of God the redeemer; war is not only crucifixion, but it is to be conducted in faith in resurrection.[80]

H. Richard Niebuhr's way of using the biblical material is significantly different from Lehmann's. It appears that the meaning of the "presence of Jesus Christ" for Lehmann is morally significant because it stimulates and shapes freedom, in the sense of freedom from bondage.

79. Niebuhr, "War as the Judgment of God," p. 631.
80. Ibid., p. 632.

Niebuhr, in these articles and elsewhere, wrote about God's creative, judging and governing, and redeeming work; the theology, in my opinion, is more complex. Also, rather than use particular biblical passages in correspondence with particular current events, Niebuhr has developed theological generalizations on the basis of biblical evidences, and in turn uses them to interpret more general current events. This makes it impossible for him to identify completely the activity of God in events with the causes of one party in a conflict; his Deity is the universal judge of all sides in a conflict. All sides come under the judgment of God; all sides both need to and can be "redeemed"; all sides are called to fulfill their duties to God rather than to their immediate self-interests.

Niebuhr's theocentricity, developed as it is from the biblical idea of God acting in history, is as thoroughgoing as any in recent Protestant theology. Philosophically, it can be stated in the following way: the universal is present in every particular.[81] Niebuhr, however, never developed his views in the philosophically abstract way that Rahner and Tillich did. Although Niebuhr's Deity, who is the creator, governor, and redeemer, specifies more theological foundation than does Moltmann's God, who is future, it is more difficult to establish precise indications, principles, and rules for conduct from this foundation than it is from some other theologies, such as the tradition of the natural law in Catholic thought. Like most Protestant theology, Niebuhr's backs certain fundamental attitudes of persons and communities, rather than providing bases for precise moral judgments about particular cases. In one way, the three consequences for human action that he indicates in the article on war as God's judgment are (1) do not assume that all the morally right is on your side, (2) do not make your moral judgments on the basis of individual or corporate self-interest, and (3) do not be vengeful, but seek to bring good out of what is relatively more evil. These consequences do correlate with the theology but have more to do with stance, or attitude, than with precise rules of conduct.

H. Richard Niebuhr was also faithful to what G. Ernest Wright noted as the weight of the biblical understanding of God, a God who acts in history. Of course, for Niebuhr one would have to respond to natural events, or to events in the natural world caused by human action (such as ecological crises), in terms of "God's action" on human beings in and through these events. If God is judging all sides in World War II, he is surely judging human beings in any calamities which have deleterious consequences for human life and for the whole of the natural world. And even natural catastrophes such as earthquakes could be interpreted theologically in terms of their meanings for human life, though probably not

81. Niebuhr, "Is God in the War?" p. 954.

in terms of theological explanations of their causes. Yet, history as the arena of human choice and action received more attention than nature from Niebuhr as data for theological interpretation.[82]

What most Christian moralists (and moral philosophers as well, if they read his work) would find most objectionable in Niebuhr's theology and the consequent ethics is the incapacity of this view to come to indisputable moral certainty about the rightness or wrongness of human actions. With Niebuhr's theology one cannot say that God is unambiguously on the side of the oppressed in human society; he is judging the oppressors but also the oppressed. Even when historical events force choices, as in the case of war or in the case of the civil rights activities in the United States in the decade of the 1960s, while one makes firm judgments about participating on one side, one cannot participate with the wholehearted zeal of a valiant crusader, nor can one act in such a way that the possibilities of some "redemption" of the other side are wiped out. One can come to certitude but not to objective certainty about one's choice. And lying beyond this is a theological belief I have not articulated here, the biblical and Augustinian one that everything that is, is basically good by virtue of its creation by God. This raises other theological and ethical problems that I shall not discuss here. It is clear, however, that this theology and its consequent ethics is highly theocentric and has to be seen as continuous with aspects of the biblical tradition, with Augustine, Calvin, and the Reformed tradition. Ethics does not find its answers simply in valuing what is good for human beings, or at least not in valuing what is the perceived good for particular persons and their communities in a given time; ethics, if it is now ethics at all in a recognizable Western sense, finds its answers in what individuals, making finite judgments, can determine about what God is doing in the world.

The last theological movement from which I shall take my bearings in this book is process theology. This movement, with its very abstract and, in my view, speculative developments, has some affinities with this present book, and it is for that reason that I comment on it.

Process theology is seeking to solve or avoid several distinctive problems. First, its practitioners believe that the deep gulf which is claimed to exist between subject (man) and object (God) and which is a warrant for much theology of revelation and radical skepticism can be bridged, if not filled in. John Cobb makes the epistemological point very simply in the introduction to Whitehead's philosophy that opens his own Christian natural theology. "At any rate, Whitehead launched boldly forth on the speculative possibility that human experience as such is a clue to

82. That we know less about Niebuhr's interpretation of God's action in nature than in history is a function of the literary evidences of his thought.

the ultimate nature of things."[83] That either human experience or the knowledge of the natural world developed by the sciences is at least a "clue" to knowledge of God is, of course, a necessary supposition of all natural theology. Getting out of what Charles Hartshorne calls the egocentric predicament requires a basically realistic theory of knowledge, whatever qualifications might accompany it.[84]

On the basis of such a view of knowledge, as with medieval theologians, arguments for the existence of God can be made on those general criteria on which rational persons presumably can agree. The doctrine of God, as central to theology, is not sealed in the limits of a historically relative book (the Bible) and a particularistic historical tradition that developed from that book. One can do a very "public theology." For some process theologians this puts the question of God in the same framework of criteria as the question of the truth of any other assertions.[85] For others the "natural knowledge of God" serves more to explicate the religious life and the theological doctrines of the Christian community; it is a confirmation of what persons usually call "revelation."[86] In both cases, however, God is explicable to those who have not had particularly religious experiences, who do not relate to the world in an attitude of piety, and certainly who are not committed to the historic Christian community.

Certainly one of the things that process theologians correctly criticize is the anthropocentrism, or the homocentrism, of traditional theology.[87] There is a genuinely prophetic aspect to their enterprise. Hartshorne makes the point in a way that those seventeenth-century thinkers studied by Herbert Butterfield would well understand and applaud. "There has been a secret poison long working in religious thought and feeling, the

83. John B. Cobb, Jr., *A Christian Natural Theology: Based on the Thought of Alfred North Whitehead* (Philadelphia: Westminster Press, 1965), p. 27.

84. Charles Hartshorne, *The Divine Relativity* (New Haven: Yale University Press, 1948), p. x.

85. This is how I understand the intention of Schubert Ogden. See, for example, his *The Reality of God* (New York: Harper and Row, 1966), pp. 1–70.

86. This is how I understand Daniel Day Williams's use of it. See his *The Spirit and the Forms of Love* (New York: Harper and Row, 1968).

87. In his critique of liberation theology Schubert Ogden says, "I refer to the exaggerated humanism, or homocentrism, for which the larger world of nature is, in effect, the common enemy of the most varied human groups, advantaged or disadvantaged alike. If such homocentrism, with its presupposed dualism of history and nature, has been a defining characteristic of modern Western culture generally, it has also been typical of the whole movement of liberal theology that has sought to come to terms with modern culture in reflecting critically on the traditional forms of Christian witness. . . . Whatever the form of bondage to which they may be oriented—political, economic, cultural, racial, or sexual—it is solely with *human* liberation that they are typically concerned, and if they regard nonhuman nature as having any value at all, it is the strictly instrumental value it has for realizing *human* potentialities." Ogden, *Faith and Freedom: Toward a Theology of Liberation* (Nashville: Abingdon, 1979), pp. 103–4.

poison of man's self-service, not genuinely his service of God."[88] The
Deity described and explained by process theologians is not only the God
who acts in history, the recital of whose deeds is the starting point for
further theological investigation. God is related to the natural world as
well as to the world of human intentions and actions. Surely it is this
which made theologians like Cobb more sensitive to problems of ecology
earlier than many other Christian thinkers.[89]

One of the clues to the inclusion of nature in theology is the fundamentally relational view of the world and of God that pervades process
theology. Human beings are understood primarily in social terms; they
are social beings. It is not only that human experience is a clue to the
ultimate nature of things but also that human experience is understood
in social and relational terms, and thus social and relational concepts are
clues to what can be said about God. While it would be excessive to claim
that the process theologians have an organismic view of reality (if that
implies that not only are all aspects internally related to each other but
also that the laws of cause and effect determine the consequences of the
interrelations for individual persons), nonetheless, the organic metaphor
for interpreting the whole of life (nature and society) is more apt than a
mechanistic one, that is, one that sees the whole as made up primarily
of individual parts, but parts related to each other to make the whole
function.

Every theology has to deal with the relation of God to the world.
As I understand process theology, its quarrel with more traditional theologies is over *how* God is related to the world, and whether these relations
in any significant measure are internal to God and thus must be taken into
account in the description and explanation of the Deity. Daniel Williams,
in his study of love, provides an example of the importance of this quarrel.
One of the legacies of the Greek metaphysics to Christian thought was
funneled through the theology of St. Augustine. It is the idea that God
is immutable and eternal (i.e., nontemporal). This is a persistent theme
in Augustine. One finds it, for example, in the opening words of "The
Nature of the Good: Against the Manichees": "The Supreme Good beyond all others is God. It is thereby unchangeable good, truly eternal,
truly immortal."[90] It is a theme repeated over and over in "On the Trinity";
for example, "For the essence of God, whereby He is, has altogether
nothing changeable, neither in eternity, nor in truth, nor in will; since
there truth is eternal, love eternal; and there love is true, eternity true;

88. Hartshorne, *The Divine Relativity*, p. 58.
89. See John B. Cobb, Jr., *Is It Too Late? A Theology of Ecology* (Beverly Hills,
Calif.: Bruce, 1972).
90. *Augustine: Earlier Writings,* ed. and trans. John H. S. Burleigh (Philadelphia:
Westminster, 1953), p. 326.

and there eternity is loved, and truth is loved.''[91] The notion of perfection required that what is perfect must be nontemporal and must be immutable; what is changeable is less perfect than what is unchangeable; what is independent and self-contained is better than what is dependent or inter-dependent. Williams's argument is that this view of God is really not Christian, and that process theology can better expound the significance of God's love.[92] But the concern goes deeper than that. It is that God has social relations. Hartshorne makes this point clear: "A personal God is one who has social relations, really has them, and thus is constituted by relationships and hence is relative—in a sense not provided for by the traditional doctrine of a divine Substance wholly nonrelative toward the world, though allegedly containing loving relations between the 'persons' of the Trinity.''[93] It is not only that God is in relation to the world but that "internally" God is affected by these relations to the world. One aspect of God is "maximally relative.''[94]

The problems perceived to be central to what is often now called classical theism, with its notion of immutable substance, are solved, in the eyes of the process theologians, by stressing the interrelations of God and the world. What happens in the world has effects upon God. The Deity of the process theologians, however, is not pure duration, an *elan* flowing and pulsing through and totally within life processes themselves. There is also an "utter abstractness" of the essence of God. God is not pure contingency; there is an "abstract feature" of the supreme reality which is God.[95] Thus one has a view nicely composed of the titles of the first two chapters of Hartshorne's Terry Lectures, "God as Supreme, Yet Indebted to All," and "God as Absolute, Yet Related to All." The most distinctive point, as I view it, is that God's participation in the world is influenced by human actions and fortunes; how God thinks and feels about the world will reflect what is going on in the world.[96]

To the best of my knowledge no one has published a systematic, inclusive theory of ethics based on process theology. John Cobb does include a chapter on ethics in his *Christian Natural Theology*. While it is couched in the esoteric language characteristic of highly systematic Whiteheadean philosophy, it does provide clues to how a theologian would use a form of process philosophy in ethics. On the basis of far less intensive study of this movement, I have come to the judgment that is at least

91. Augustine, *On the Trinity*, trans. A. W. Hadden, bk. 4, 1, in *The Nicene and Post-Nicene Fathers*, ed. Philip Schaff (Grand Rapids: Eerdmans, 1956 reprint), first series, vol. 3, p. 70, col. 1.
92. Williams, *The Spirit and the Forms*, pp. 90–110.
93. Hartshorne, *The Divine Relativity*, p. viii.
94. Ibid., p. 95.
95. Ibid., pp. 79–88.
96. Ibid., p. 44.

implicit in Cobb's discussion, namely, that the dominant view of ethics is one of the realization of values. It is a value-centered ethics, not an obligation-centered ethics. Cobb writes, "In Whitehead's view, there is a definite oughtness in life. We may speak of this oughtness in terms of moral obligation." The last term is given a footnote which reads, "This is not a characteristic term for Whitehead."[97] Although Cobb seeks to engraft a strong theory of moral obligation on to the Whiteheadean view in his own construction of ethics, it is instructive to ponder why the term is not characteristic of his master. Cobb's own exposition suggests why. My reading both of the master and of the Christian theologian can be briefly summarized. First, given the relational or process character to reality, there is an immediacy to the realization of values which are related always to the context in which they are emerging and apprehended. Prior to any obligation to actualize or realize values is their emergence; prior to any action to realize them is the appreciation of them. Thus what process theology gives us is an ethics of the appreciation of emergent values in the context of the joining of past to future, in the context of the interrelations with other things of what can be designated as a particular value. Second, in Whitehead's thought it is clear that aesthetic language is more appropriate to moral experience than is the language of the civil or natural law. It is not only that beauty gives value to actual occasions of experience but also that beauty is an aspect of the experience of values.[98] Aesthetic modes of thought do not lend themselves readily to legal modes of thought. Evil is basically a condition of disharmony or discord; it is the occasion for "negative value." Cobb notes quite properly that "Whitehead was far more interested in propositions about beauty than in propositions about goodness." Right conduct "must be directed toward the realization of high values."[99]

Since process theology is a lively option in North America at this time, some bearings must be taken from it. If I understand its principal aims, it provides a view of "reality" or of God which is congenial to perception of process and development not only in the course of human civilizations but also in the course of nature itself. A "static world-view" such as revisionist Roman Catholics charge the Aristotelian principles of neo-Thomist theologies with having, is cast out; theology is no longer weighted down with such metaphysics. My own perceptions of nature and history at least move in this same direction. Process theology is also not totally dissonant with some of the dominant themes of the apprehensions of the God in the biblical tradition; while a "recital" of God's actions

97. Cobb, *A Christian Natural Theology*, p. 98.

98. Ibid., p. 101. Alfred North Whitehead, *Adventures of Ideas* (New York: Macmillan, 1933), pp. 324–40.

99. Cobb, *A Christian Natural Theology*, p. 108.

in history appears highly anthropomorphic in the light of the highly generalized and abstract concepts of process thought, there is an affinity between them. But process theology does not describe the Deity as pure flux and duration immanent in life; it is not purely vitalistic. It can, again in highly abstract ways, account for perduring and persisting aspects of reality as well. It provides a strong basis for understanding, as Hartshorne indicates, that the actions of human beings make a difference to God; that events in nature and history make a difference in reality generally conceived.

There are, however, points which are not congenial to the present work. As I will indicate in subsequent chapters, I am persuaded that the primary moment in a religious view of the world, and therefore an assumption in theology, is the affection of piety: a sense of dependence on, and respect and gratitude for, what is given. Process theology explicates in metaphysical terms the dependence and interdependence of all things, but this position is established as a purely rational one, demonstrable from human experience, that finally grounds true knowledge of God. For most process theologians, it seems to me, the steps from our knowledge of human experience and the world to knowledge of God are necessary and continuous. For exposition of the significance of the sense of dependence, both Rahner and Tillich are more profound in my judgment. The realistic epistemology of process theologies makes recourse to this sort of datum of a religious orientation to the world relatively insignificant. Finally, metaphysics is necessarily abstract; it formulates even its concepts about the most specific and concrete realities of experience in highly abstract language or symbols. While it tests the adequacy of these formulations with reference to general experience and various forms of knowledge about the world, my impression is that its illumination of "the whole" sheds little light on the particulars of human life in the world. It has the strength of turning religion from preoccupations with benefits for human beings; in this sense it is highly theocentric. But its level of generalization goes beyond what I find to be very illuminating. If Rahner takes recourse to the language of "holy mystery" too frequently and too soon, the process theologians have with excessive confidence explicated it.

All that can be gleaned from these brief evaluations of some of the major contemporary options for thinking about God and his relations to the world are some bearings for the further development of this book. To elucidate them exhaustively at this point risks premature foreclosure, for there is more terrain to be covered. I suggest only the most crucial ones. A theological construing of the world certainly has to view in some guarded and critical way the Deity as "objective" to ourselves and to the world. Whether this can be done without running into the problems that so concerned Rahner and Tillich, namely, making God a categorical reality like the phenomena that can be named and differentiated, is not perfectly clear; but religious and theological orientations which refer only to subjective ways of viewing the world are more problematic. The Deity toward which we are oriented must be a deity related to the natural world, the world described and explained by the natural sciences as much as one related to historical experience, and to the realms of human action and their consequences. Whether one can sufficiently back what is said about the Deity on the basis of a variety of evidences adduced from nature and experience remains an open question; efforts to do so, however, are worth the risk, for a vacuous God provides no bearings whatsoever for the conduct of life in the world. The "God acting in history" and the process theologians at least mark efforts to have an objective reference to our words about God, and to describe with some meaningful detail or concepts his relations to the world; in one case it verges on excessive specification, and in the other on excessive abstraction. While there are bearings of lesser significance than the ones indicated here, these indicate the basic directions in which I believe an adequate theology must go.

Preoccupation with Theological Method

"That the contemporary theological scene has become chaotic is evident to everyone who attempts to work in theology. There appears to be no consensus on what the task of theology is or how theology is to be pursued." So writes Gordon D. Kaufman, the author of a systematic theology and of a book appropriately entitled, *God The Problem*.[100] The sentences are dramatic. They appropriately reflect a very contemporary situation. Whether the lack of consensus is as novel as the sentences taken in themselves might lead one to believe is a historical question. Consensus in the strongest sense has never existed in the history of Christian theology, though probably the present circumstances are more chaotic than before. Among the options there are clearly those, for example, of evangelical Protestants, who are certain about the correct way to pursue theology and thus need not worry about the liberal theologians' perceptions of chaos. Whether the absence of consensus is greater by a significant order of magnitude in theology than it is in literary criticism, philosophy of science, history, and other fields is also a matter that could be debated; surely theology's plight is not unique.

100. Gordon D. Kaufman, *An Essay on Theological Method* (Missoula, Mont.: Scholars Press, 1975), p. ix. For his earlier extensive discussion, see Kaufman, *God The Problem* (Cambridge, Mass.: Harvard University Press, 1972).

A perception of chaos is as significant as the evidences that it exists. If chaos is perceived, and if there is a continuing interest in overcoming it, theologians are thrown back to some very significant questions and issues. As in some other fields of humanistic investigation, so in theology there emerges the question of method. Certainly the fairly widespread sharing of Kaufman's perception has led to a considerable preoccupation among very important scholars of theology with the question of method. "If theology is to survive as a distinctive and significant form of intellectual activity, it is essential that some order be brought into this confusion and the proper work of theology be clarified."[101]

Bernard Lonergan, S.J., like Kaufman, also perceives a historic shift of the methods of theology. He writes, "When the classicist notion of culture prevails, theology is conceived as a permanent achievement, and then one discourses on its nature. When culture is conceived empirically, theology is known to be an ongoing process, and then one writes on its method." Clearly, for Lonergan, culture is now conceived empirically, and thus it is necessary to establish the framework "for collaborative creativity" that will generate significant work in the ongoing process of theology.[102] Kaufman's confusion is clearly not just a Protestant phenomenon; Roman Catholicism is also driven back to concerns about method in theology. My impression is that there have been far more books and essays on theological method, and far more dissertations on the methods of various theologians, in the past fifteen years than in many decades previous to them, and maybe even in the history of theology. For my purpose, it is the phenomenon of the interest in method in theology that is important to note, and to reflect upon, more than the discussions of method themselves.

To explain the development of this preoccupation is a historical task, and one to which a number of authors have devoted themselves indirectly if not directly. The secularization of culture over the past several centuries has raised radical doubts about the significance of religion, and thus about the importance of theology. Epistemological issues have increasingly divided theologians and certainly continue to be central to the discussions of method. Confidence in biblical revelation has eroded as a result of several centuries of historical and critical scholarship and other cultural developments. The triumphs of eighteenth-century Deism were followed by the radical criticisms of Feuerbach and others in the nineteenth century. Modern sciences have raised questions not only about some of the substantive assertions that theologians have made but also about how we come to know reality. Metaphysics was eclipsed by positivism, and it is

101. Ibid.
102. Bernard Lonergan, S.J., *Method in Theology* (New York: Seabury, 1972) p. xi.

hard to think of God without being metaphysical, covertly and implicitly if not openly and explicitly. A theological problem present in the New Testament itself, namely, how a historically particular person and set of events can have the universal meaning claimed for them, has gotten more complex through the centuries in which the provincialism of Western culture has been eroded by more and deeper knowledge of other cultures.

The concern for method can be called, I believe, the philosophy of theology. It is not philosophical theology in the sense that process theology is; it is not an effort to develop rational arguments for the existence of God, and for the truth of particular characteristics of God. Nor is it philosophy of religion; this enterprise necessarily begins with the datum of religion and proceeds to analyze what its references are, how its language and symbols function, and so forth. Just as philosophy of science is a different enterprise from scientific investigation itself, so philosophy of theology has become a different enterprise from theological investigations of any substantive sort. No one has established that an investigator does better science as a result of his knowledge of the philosophy of science, though self-criticism of one's method and procedures is a merit. But it seems to be asserted that investigations of substantive matters of theology cannot be properly engaged in until one has established the proper methods for investigation. If this assertion is an exaggeration, it is an exaggeration in the right direction. It is as if one had to write a full-scale propaedeutic to a substantive project of thinking about man and nature in relation to an ultimate ordering power, and of how one would go about writing in a way that would cover all the problems one would get into once one began to write it. And then, of course, one needs a propaedeutic to one's propaedeutic. It is as if one had to resolve the methods of science before one engaged in any scientific investigation, as if the correction of method did not take place in the process of dealing with the substance of the problems under investigation. In fairness to Kaufman, we need to note that a big problem is central—*God The Problem*.

There are very good reasons for this preoccupation with problems of method in theology. Not only are there the historical developments that I briefly enumerated; there is also the current academic situation, in which departments of religious studies are as often the context in which thinking about theology is done as is a body of Christian believers. Theology has been done in the past largely as a vocation to speak for the substance of the faith, the material of the tradition, in ways that explicated it and accounted for the reasons why a new formulation needed to be made. The theologian spoke for the faith and to the church. At present, simply because of the academic location of much study of theology, the scholar does not feel the same accountability to the religious community. There are, of course, exceptions to this.

To assume that even the recently received traditions in theology did not take cognizance of the problems of method, not to mention many earlier traditions, is an error. Tillich's long "Introduction" to his *Systematic Theology* is followed by a chapter on "Reason and Revelation."[103] These chapters are an exposition and defense of the author's method, and of the procedures that are required to fulfill his purpose. Karl Barth was not philosophically or methodologically uninformed or naive; he was quite clear about the critical first choices he made to establish the grounds for his biblical theology; he takes into account over and over the alternate methods used to resolve problems he resolved in his own way.[104] H. Richard Niebuhr's *The Meaning of Revelation* can clearly be read as an essay in theological method.[105] Schleiermacher's "Introduction" to *The Christian Faith* carefully lines out the basic methods and procedures and propositions on which rest the subsequent development of a system of doctrine.[106] In all of these works and in others, the philosopher of theology was also the investigator of the substance of theology. It is apparent to the reader of such works that the two tasks deeply inform each other, that something in intention like an experiment is taking place in which there are alterations in methods and procedures as a result of attempting to deal with substantive theological problems. Just as the most instructive work in literary criticism includes the discussion of texts in the light of the methods that are being espoused, so also instructive work in theology shapes method not only in relation to general philosophical questions but also in relation to the texts or the ideas to which the method is to be applied.

One has to inquire about the expected audience of the more independent discussions of theological method. To whose criticisms are the philosophers of theology seeking to respond? Who do they think is interested in their essays? Who is to be instructed by them? The best of this sort of work has in mind at least three possible groups. Since it is done by high-powered intellectuals, often in the context of secular universities, this work generally reflects the kind of criticisms that theologians think their colleagues in philosophy and other disciplines would make of the theological enterprise. There is merit in having such persons looking over one's shoulder; the criteria for adequate work generally become more rigorous, and the sophistication of the philosopher of theology gives

---

103. Tillich, *Systematic Theology*, 1:3–68, 71–105.
104. For example, Barth's consciousness of the method of his theological ethics in his *Church Dogmatics*, II/2 (Edinburgh: T. and T. Clark, 1957), pp. 512 ff.
105. H. Richard Niebuhr, *The Meaning of Revelation* (New York: Macmillan, 1941).
106. Schleiermacher, *The Christian Faith*, pp. 1–128.

him or her a sense of intellectual confidence. The second group is other
theologians; these either share the quandaries of the philosopher of theology or need to share them because they have not faced the critical
issues. In this respect there is specialization of a discipline whose social
perimeters are established not by religious communities but by the colleagues whose possible criticisms one has in mind. This is proper, for
theology is a scholarly and intellectually demanding enterprise, and the
community of scholars of theology is an appropriate community of discourse. The third group are ministers of religion and persons training to
become such, with a few of the laity added to them. These persons have
to take responsibility not only to be critics of theology but primarily to
speak for and act in the light of what theology is all about. For the person
called upon to preach each Sunday, to conduct public worship, and to
engage in the "cure of souls," the academic license to reserve judgment
on substantive issues until one's method for dealing with them is worked
out is not a possibility. To be sure, many ministers of religion and laity
participate in the quandaries about which theologians puzzle, though not
with the same degree of intellectual finesse, and thus this is a proper group
to be concerned about.

Among the first group there are not very many persons who really
care about theology, and those that care most tend to have already determined that Christianity is like astrology at its worst, and like Marxism
and Freudianism at its best, all of which, to Alasdair MacIntyre for example, are insufficient in many ways as a basis for human living.[107] Indeed,
MacIntyre ends up respecting orthodox Christianity more than liberal
Christianity, orthodox theology more than liberal theology, while vehe-
mently rejecting both. The orthodox are at least theists; the liberals are
really atheists who want to continue to use traditional religious language.
Thus in a review in which he seeks to demolish J. A. T. Robinson and his
principal sources, he closes with an example of his rhetorical powers:
"The creed of the English is that there is no God and that it is wise to
pray to him from time to time."[108] If we theologians have other academic
colleagues who are seriously interested in religion, the common ground
on which to start a conversation is, in my judgment, the common religious
interest; such persons will not be as interested in the methodological
purity and rigor if those questions have to be resolved before the substance
of the religious interest is expounded.

The propriety of the academic community of fellow theologians is
at least as soundly grounded as the propriety of other groups of scholars

107. Alasdair MacIntyre, *Against the Self-Images of the Age* (Notre Dame, Ind.:
University of Notre Dame Press, 1978), pp. 3–87.
108. Ibid., p. 26.

who write mainly for each other. If one has followed, for example, the literature on moral philosophy in the major books and articles over the past four decades, it is clear that moral philosophers were more interested in the ideas of others about moral philosophy than they were in morality itself. My perception of the current interest in hermeneutics is that there is more reference to the literature and arguments of other hermeneutical philosophers than there is to texts which the principles of interpretation ought to help us to understand. All of this is not to be demeaned, though the breadth of the range of its consequences should not be overestimated. Preachers will continue to preach and believers to believe; agents will continue to engage in moral actions; readers will continue to interpret the texts that they read. The gulf between the specialized and sometimes arcane interests of the academician and those who engage in the activities about which academics want to think properly exists in large measure as a result of the necessary specialization of vocabulary and symbol, but also because of the lack of interest in a wider readership.[109]

The third group, made up of ministers of religion and a number of laity, is, I believe, a proper group to be concerned about. Its members do have theological quandaries, and face them not only when they have to preach but when they experience the limits of human satisfactions, the issue of the basis for personal integrity, the need for some meaningful objects of confidence and for orientations toward their activities. For such persons the substantive theological questions arise first in the course of human experience and professional responsibilities. In many instances the questions that preoccupy the philosophers of theology are real but inchoate. To be sure, there are many persons who are properly judged to be so simple and naive that the theologian has a prophetic function to force them to face questions. In the order of experience, however, those questions probably come alive when the religious framework these persons have begins to totter and crumble as a result of its insufficiency to bear the weight of experience they have been led to believe it can bear. Among recent theologians, Tillich's influence is understandable in this context; the experiences which he interprets, to be sure in his own concepts and symbols, are shared by many persons in modern culture—estrangement, guilt, and so forth. He has provided for many preachers, and through them some laity, a plausible response which is grounded in a fundamental religious interest.

109. In these remarks I criticize myself as well as others. I spent six years working on *Can Ethics Be Christian?* with the haunting feeling that those whose answer was negative on philosophical grounds would not be interested in my efforts to develop a careful affirmative; that those whose answer was affirmative were so certain of their convictions that the question was not worth entertaining; and that a few persons primarily from this second group might take the argument seriously.

Perhaps I have exaggerated this preoccupation with method in theology. I certainly have not indicated fully the extent to which this concern has positively informed my own work. But MacIntyre's recent jibe at Roman Catholic theologians is quite appropriate to others as well; theologians are often more interested in other theologians than they are in God.[110] There are and always have been substantive issues in theology and religion that require abstract and sophisticated deliberation and thus generate the propaedeutic literature on method. I believe the central issue is that Christianity has always claimed its historical particularity—the biblical events and their records—to have universal significance and import. Certainly a substantive enterprise in theology from the biblical times forward has been to overcome and sustain that particularity at one and the same time, to stand with and for that historic particularity while insisting that its significance is universal. Concentration on this central issue alone would no doubt illuminate the issues of theological method historically, generate all of the possible options for dealing with them, and provide a set of ideal-types by which all theologians in Christian history could be illumined. In addition to this issue, there are many others. There will never be the consensus that Kaufman seems to aspire to in his honest and devastating description; nevertheless a greater ordering of the priorities of substantive theological issues is possible. But the best development of method will take place as theologians deal with the substance of theology. Philosophers of theology are also needed, and theologians need to have that thinking cap in their wardrobes, but the enterprise is derivative from actual investigations. After two millennia of Christian theology, and more in other traditions, it is clear that even the best method is not going to provide the empirical evidence and explanatory theories to give theology the same security that the paleontologist can have as a result of establishing the order of development of species fossilized in different but successive strata of sedimentary rocks. The subject matter of theology does not permit perfection of method, though some methods are more adequate than others *for specific purposes*. The *purpose* of theology is the prior and more important question. All methods of investigation, including theological ones, are instruments of purposes.

Christian Ethics

The literature in the field of Christian ethics is as varied as that in other fields of study of Christianity. On the whole it has had a very clear

110. Alasdair MacIntyre, "Theology, Ethics, and the Ethics of Medicine and Health Care: Comments on Papers by Novak, Mouw, Roach, Cahill, and Hartt," *The Journal of Medicine and Philosophy* 4 (1979): 440.

practical purpose: to assist morally serious Christian people to make proper moral judgments and engage in right moral actions, and to stimulate Christian people to reform (or in some cases defend) the social arrangements of their societies and of the human community as a whole. Much of the literature, particularly the Protestant literature, has sought to be prophetic, to establish a sound moral indictment of current practices or orders of life in light of the claims of biblical faith. Roman Catholic literature has in the past more characteristically sought to prescribe and proscribe specific acts. The variety of literature is great, and I shall comment only on certain strands or trends from which I take my bearings in this book. I shall not analyze and survey it in the same way that I have in previous publications.[111]

One characteristic of recent literature has been the already mentioned preoccupation with questions of method; a great deal of my own work has been of this sort. The best reason for this concentration is the intellectual dissatisfaction with the theological and philosophical rigor of Protestant moral exhortation and argumentation. As Paul Ramsey and others have pointed out, much of Protestant ethics was in the "wastelands of utility" without much clear justification for being there.[112] Ecclestiastical and other documents were poorly argued; they frequently went from interpretations of circumstances to a moral indictment to a prescription or recommendation of a course of action without critical awareness of how the connections between these steps could be defended. Even the most brilliant authors were much better in their particular assessments and recommendations than they were in the strength of the arguments they made for them. The dissatisfaction, however, has been more than intellectual; there has been a conviction that, with philosophically solid reasoning, Christian ethics will be more likely to guide persons to the right action than more intuitive approaches will. Ethics is a process of giving reasons for action; the establishment of good reasons both prior to action and in the justifications of actions after the fact is likely to develop more appropriate actions and evaluations. The influence of the general interests of recent Anglo-American moral philosophy also affected this work seriously. Openness to this influence was warranted for the reasons I have just given, but also by the desire to make the ethical enterprise of Christianity more academically respectable. The ethicians imagined they had, or actually did have, the philosophers looking over their shoulders, just as other theologians did. And given the development of religious studies in the recent decades, the concern for method provided

111. Most recently in James M. Gustafson, *Protestant and Roman Catholic Ethics* (Chicago: University of Chicago Press, 1978).
112. Paul Ramsey, *War and the Christian Conscience* (Durham, N.C.: Duke University Press, 1961), p. 6.

a program for critical analytical work on texts written over many centuries that was not in the service of a particular religious tradition or religious moral point of view.

The laudable features of this characteristic have drifted off somewhat into a preoccupation with the formal questions of Christian ethics. Many of the best American scholars in the field became the analysts and critics of the argument of others; for a number of reasons they have tended not to make proposals of a substantive sort themselves.[113] There has been a tendency for scholars of Christian ethics to become philosophers of Christian ethics, comparable to the philosophers of theology I described above. Even when they direct attention to very particular moral questions, this penchant tends to hold sway. The theological aspects of ethics become merely a set of data for analysis; one does not make judgments of a substantive theological sort. The desire to be able to converse with secular colleagues about moral matters or about ethics as a discipline leads to the bracketing of theology itself. Personal religious convictions are held in abeyance, or perhaps wither away; certainly for many the primary community of their identity is not the church. The problems noted above in the preoccupation with method in theology proper occur here as well; in the light of whose potential criticisms are essays and books being written? Who is to be instructed by them? What is the purpose of the enterprise of Christian ethics?

The formal questions have not been so much those that pertain to theology, per se, or even to the relation of theological beliefs, principles, and outlooks to moral matters. They have basically been those that arise out of moral reasoning about particular acts and circumstances. The procedures for dealing with cases, whether the war in Vietnam or a particular patient in an intensive-care unit, have always been attended to in Roman Catholic moral theology. The application of principles to cases in that tradition had clear procedures, and was worked out within established distinctions. Protestant ethics had not developed the casuistic tradition, but in light of the preoccupation with certain practical moral questions it became necessary to do so. One of the historically fortuitous circumstances that fostered the return to casuistry was the emergence of great interest in medical ethical problems at the same time that Protestant moralists were also learning quickly from Anglo-American moral philosophy.

This focus of attention has led to the ignoring of some general issues of theological ethics. Many Protestant and Catholic casuists assume there is no necessary relationship between what one asserts and believes about God and the answers to particular moral questions, or if there is such it

113. A colleague for whom I have the very highest respect read my early notes for this book. He opened our conversation with, "What are the criteria for theological ethics?"

is divisive to engage in discussion of those matters when there is an urgency to come to conclusions acceptable to non-Christians and to secular people. But practical moral questions, if driven by a process of inquiry to their borders, require some reflection that is theological, or at least is the secular equivalent to theology. There are, for example in the medical area, issues of why we value human life, and why we value some aspects of it more than others, when forced to make choices that are difficult. There is the question of our beliefs, our larger vindicating reasons, about human life, and about human life in broader social and historical perspectives. These matters can be left tacit and unexplored; they can be examined in order to drive conflicts to more general levels of basic beliefs or orientations toward the world; or proponents can make a case for the beliefs that fundamentally orient their attitudes and actions in a whole arena of human affairs. To be sure, practical persons of affairs, whether physicians or makers of public policy, on the whole are not interested in "global questions," and it is they who have set the agenda to which a great deal of the work of Christian moralists attends.

In contrast to the trend toward concentration on refined practical moral reasoning is the trend toward magnifying the importance of the "global questions." The questions of importance for theological ethics are questions of the ethos of modern culture, with its preoccupation with technical rationality, its relatively uncritical approval of all advances in technology, its "thingification" of persons so that they become means and functions and not ends in themselves, the triumph in it of scientific ways of thinking, its quantifications of qualities in cost-benefit analysis and technology assessment, and so forth. Historical precedent exists for this concentration on the big questions, for ethics quite properly is the study of ethos. And ethos, though hardly something that can be limited in the way that the relevant data of a medical case can, has its effects on the ways in which persons perceive circumstances, the relevant aspects of cases, and the ends to be achieved. Ethos is part of that tacit knowledge that affects basic value-orientations, which in turn warrant priorities of ends in both social and personal life. Certainly it is a legitimate function of the Christian ethician to engage in a critique of ethos—to make prophetic evaluations of what he or she conceives the current ethos is in the light of some beliefs garnered from the religious tradition or from contemporary philosophical movements which are more appropriate to these matters than analytic moral philosophy.

More so than those who are occupied with the formal questions of method and the procedures of practical moral reasoning, the critics of ethos are passionate reformers. The enterprise of Christian ethics for them, as for earlier and contemporary versions of the "social gospel," is to instigate change. And the change that is to be instigated obviously is that which is susceptible to the analysis that has been made. Change in ethos becomes a primary practical purpose of Christian morality. Change in fundamental orientation toward the world, in attitudes toward persons, society, and nature, and in the order of priority of values in culture and society is what is required. Such a concern is quite congenial with some of the basic directions that the constructive sections of this book take; indeed, previously in this chapter I have noted the anthropocentric preoccupations of culture and religion, and hinted that a theocentric perspective would require a radical shift in thinking and attitude, and consequently in action. The difficulty with such a theocentricity is that a process of conversion, of transformation of perspective, is required, and that practically (if one is concerned about change) this is hard to achieve. Indeed, given the socialization processes of culture and society, it is difficult to apprehend what the points of explicit activity would be to which one could turn one's reforming zeal. If those preoccupied with methodological questions and with practical moral reasoning accept uncritically too many conditions of modern culture and society, they at least have more precisely defined and definable issues to address. But surely what is correct about the critics of ethos is their perception that basic beliefs, or merely tacit acceptance of the drift of the culture, need to be examined. The interests of the casuists and those of the critics of ethos, however, need not be antithetical. By pushing the casuists to theological margins one comes to questions of ethos; by pushing the ethos to its practical consequences one comes to casuistry. And, it may be that changes in ethos come about more as the result of "necessity" (that is, of the required responses to breakdowns of prevailing ethos) than as a result of intentional efforts to alter it.[114]

There is a movement in Christian thought and life, however, which is more explicitly theological and biblical than much of the criticism of ethos, and this is the liberation theology movement.[115] Its major scholarly proponents are certainly in keeping with the fundamental lines of the "God acting in history" theology, as I have indicated. As a generalization about this movement, the following will suffice. The authors have a theological, social, or moral principle which is used to establish the appropriateness of their biblical interpretation, their interpretation of the central message of both the Old and New Testaments, of what God is doing in history, and of the historical and social circumstances in which we live. There is a strong tendency in this movement to eschew the precision of political ethical concepts. Instead they tend, as H. Richard Niebuhr did

114. I made many of these points in a piece of journalism: "Theology Confronts Technology and The Life Sciences," *Commonweal* 105 (1978): 386–92.
115. The literature is vast and growing monthly. The most famous book is Gustavo Guttierez, *Theology of Liberation*. Orbis Books is the major publisher of liberation theology.

in his articles on World War II, to move from a theological interpretation of historical processes and events to the consequences of this interpretation for human action. They move from theology to politics without passing through ethics. In my judgment, the bypassing of clear concepts from political ethical thought as that has been developed in the West is not necessary. It is done because some of these concepts and procedures have been used in the past to justify precisely those social repressions that the liberationists are seeking to overcome. Their criticism is correct if a formal concept of justice, for example, has been so wedded to certain material content that justice became a rationalization for what is now perceived (quite rightly) to be injustice. If, for example, "equals shall be treated equally" has been wedded not to those who have equal needs for the fundamental requirements of physical and other dimensions of human life but to status such as sex (males shall be treated equally, but males and females shall not), or such as social-class ascriptions, there is some justification for worrying about using the concept of justice in present circumstances. It is clearly the case, however, that the judgment of the material content is a different one from the judgment about the use of the formal principle. From their own theological perspective, these authors can establish solid arguments for a different rating of who the equals are who are to be treated equally; need can clearly come higher than it is in the societies to which this theology is addressed. My point is that with clearer and more precise use of traditional political ethical concepts, the liberation theologians could make more precise indictments of present social conditions and clearer prescriptions about the social conditions that ought to prevail as a result of the social changes they seek to foster. Prophetic indictment can be very precise; it need not be vague and general. Proposals for more desirable states of affairs can be quite precise; they need not await a revolution out of which it is hoped some new birth of humanization will come. The conditions for humanization, to use a favorite word from this literature, can be stated quite precisely; the word need not be left as vague as it frequently is.

Liberation theology is a theologically serious movement. Whether it has a unitarian theology is a theological question of great ethical significance.[116] This opens another line of critical analysis of the movement. Whether its creative, liberating deity is sufficient for an adequate understanding of the ordering power that ultimately limits and directs history and nature is a serious theological question. Whether its deity is confined in his actions too exclusively to the realm of history and not sufficiently

116. See H. Richard Niebuhr's famous article, "The Doctrine of the Trinity and the Unity of the Church," *Theology Today* 3 (1946): 371–84, for the forms of theological unitarianism in Christianity.

to the ordering of nature is a serious question. Whether the moral interests of this deity are too closely identified with one group of persons in society is surely a question that H. Richard Niebuhr's interpretation of God's activity in a war warrants raising.

Alasdair MacIntyre constructs a hypothesis about contemporary moral theology: "Either it will remain within the theological closed circle: in which case it will have no access to the public and shared moral criteria of our society. Or it will accept those criteria: in which case it may well have important things to say, but these will not be distinctively Christian."[117] Most moral theologians would argue that the dichotomy is not necessary; nonetheless the challenge is one that has been met, most cogently and consistently, I believe, by John Howard Yoder.[118] Since I have discussed his work in previous publications, I shall not engage in a lengthy analysis here. Yoder himself articulates his position in relation to those writers of Christian ethics who in effect transform the specifically Christian into the generally agreeable principles of morality in one theological way or another. What makes Yoder's work important is precisely that he centers his ethical writings not on the second person of the Trinity, that device by which ethicians as well as theologians find a way to make a universal claim for the historical particularity of Jesus, but on the teachings of Jesus in the gospels, and on the call to discipleship to Jesus. This position Yoder calls "biblical realism." A coherent view of the teachings of Jesus and of the meaning of Christ as example must be developed, of course, on the basis of certain principles which highlight certain texts from the synoptic gospels, and which bring a kind of sharp focus to what this ethics is. Yoder selects, in *The Politics of Jesus*, the Lukan account, and develops his ethics of nonviolent resistance to evil in basic accord with his Anabaptist tradition.[119] As such he remains within MacIntyre's closed theological circle, though MacIntyre's dichotomy exaggerates the notion that this circle is unintelligible to one who does not share it. What is important to note is that Yoder (and, in a different way, a great deal of the Protestant liberal tradition as well) is not ashamed to be distinctively Christian, and in effect claims that Christian morality is the morality of Christian persons. The particularities of this morality are precisely what are to mark Christian behavior. Of course not all action of Christians bears that distinctive mark, but there is a historic particularity not only to the reasons for being moral but also to certain features of morality

117. MacIntyre, *Against the Self-Images*, p. 23.
118. The best-known work is John Howard Yoder, *The Politics of Jesus* (Grand Rapids: Eerdmans, 1972).
119. For a study of Luke by a biblical scholar with similar interests, see Richard J. Cassidy, *Jesus, Politics and Society: A Study of Luke's Gospel* (Maryknoll, N.Y.: Orbis Books, 1978).

itself. Christians have a particular vocation; they are called to a particular obedience to a particular person who is known through texts written at a particular time long ago. Their community has a distinctive vocation in the world; it is neither expected to assume nor ought to assume the full responsibilities for the whole of the moral life of the human race, to find reasons for action that will be applicable to secularists, Hindus, Muslims, and Eskimos. Its morality expresses its faith; its faith forms a community with clear boundaries.

It is patronizing to say that it is useful, in the mix of Christian communities and views of morality, to have this stringent tradition alive, just as it might be seen to be useful to have Marxists around to remind the exponents of the free market that there are some matters that seem lost in the outlook of the capitalist. Such a view assumes that the value of a position is its contribution to discourse on a moral plane, that the reason for interest in the position is that it represents a moral ideal which wiser persons know is "unrealistic" but nonetheless need to be reminded of from time to time. The issue that has to be joined is theological, not simply ethical. Theological integrity more than moral distinctiveness is the challenge of the traditional radical Protestant view. That challenge has been taken up from time to time since the sixteenth century, and most dramatically in that century when the major Reformers were threatened by the effectiveness of the Anabaptist witnesses. My conviction is that all constructive theology in the Christian tradition needs to be defined to some extent in relation to this radical option. I note it here not because in subsequent chapters I shall in detail engage in a differentiation of my position from this, but because it represents the sharpest challenge to any theology and theological ethics that desires to claim some backing from the particularities of the Christian tradition while moving in quite another direction. There are historical warrants for this radical position in the early Christian church; there are biblical warrants for it; there are sociological and moral warrants for it. The theology and ethics of the radical Protestant tradition cannot be as easily dismissed as most theologians believe. I note Yoder's option here because it is the one most dramatically different from the option I shall pursue.

My subsequent argument will not take up precisely and in detail the benchmarks I have indicated in this brief commentary on contemporary work in Christian ethics. The benchmarks, however, are important. Ethics concerned only with the formal aspects of argumentation avoids making substantive theological judgments; such work is great for analysis and for criticism but it leads to no proposals. Concentration on practical moral reasoning limits the area of consideration; it needs to be pushed to its theological boundaries. Ethos criticism has the merit of asking the big questions that casuistry avoids, but its own stance must be pressed to some practical conclusions on specific areas of human activity. Liberation theology bears examination both theologically and ethically. And the radical Christian ethics of Yoder mark a substantive position for which there are many sound defenses; to opt against it is to opt against some fundamental claims of traditional Christianity.

Philosophical Ethics

Among the moral philosophers whose works have been taken seriously in the past decades, there are none who would base their ethics on theological principles, whether derived from "natural reason" or from a historical religious tradition. Given the basic assumptions of the philosophical enterprise in the modern Western world, this is as it should be. Even that next of kin to theology, metaphysics, is eschewed by most contemporary moral philosophers, and it has been argued that there are no necessary relations between what one adheres to metaphysically and one's ethics. The relations between "philosophical ethics" and theological ethics in Western culture are long and involved. From the religious side one aspiration has been to find a universal, or at least more general, justification for the moral views of a particular religious tradition; thus early Christians were influenced by Stoicism, Augustine by neo-Platonism, the medieval theologians by Aristotelianism, nineteenth- and twentieth-century Protestants by Kantianism, and so forth. Jewish law and ethics have a somewhat similar history.[120] With the more radical secularization of Western culture in recent centuries, and with the growing knowledge of cultural pluralism and various vital religious traditions, it has not been unreasonable to seek a basis for morality that transcends religious beliefs, one that can be held to by persons holding different religious beliefs and that would appeal to all "rational" and "autonomous" agents.

The laudable purpose of much moral philosophy is to find a common basis for morality to which all persons from all historical communities might adhere. (Defenders of relativism, of course, still exist.) This purpose then has to overcome "nonrational" assumptions that are present in religious beliefs that can be a foundation for morality. Beliefs about a deity are not susceptible to purely rational justification; the evidences adduced to support such beliefs are such that not all persons can agree upon their merit. Particularly, if a religious ethical view is based upon a belief that God has revealed himself, or has revealed a moral code in the Bible or in the Koran, the validity of that morality is grounded in communal re-

120. I obviously have in mind Maimonides but also the influence of Kant in Moritz Lazarus, *The Ethics of Judaism*, 2 vols., trans. Henrietta Szold (Philadelphia: Jewish Publication Society of America, 1900, 1901), and in Herman Cohen, *Reason and Hope,* trans. Eva Jospe (New York: Norton, 1971).

ligious convictions which not everyone shares. There is something called "faith" which for centuries has been contrasted with "reason," something called "revelation" which is contrasted with "natural" sources of knowledge. And faith is something one either has or does not have; revelation is something in which one either believes or does not. If these things are not absurd, they are at least private (belonging to particular communities which share them), and appeals to them exclude persons who are not persuaded of their truth. Religious moral views traditionally have taken quite seriously the particular historical events that have given birth to a religious tradition, such as the receiving of the Decalogue by Moses, or the coming of Jesus Christ, or the revelations to Mohammed. Or they have been built up from myths about the creation and ordering of the world that have been carried in narratives and cultic activity, as in Hinduism. These myths are also relative to particular histories and to particular cultures. To be sure, the particular histories and myths can be thought about in such a way that from them are gleaned bases for morality that are not finally dependent upon their historical origins. And at least within Western culture there are certain principles that historic religious traditions have sustained which are justifiable on grounds that do not make appeals to these traditions. But historical particularity is to be overcome, for it is both partial and divisive. These are not issues that contemporary moral philosophers discuss very much. It is assumed that the positive claims made for historic religious moralities are beyond the pale of discussion; the issues debated are within the boundaries set by the rejection of "nonrationality" and historical particularity. Cultural relativism is assumed to be something to be overcome.

Within those boundaries the debates, of course, flourish. Commonsense observations about human actions have always taken seriously the point that human action is engaged in for the sake of realizing certain purposes and producing certain effects. This is true about the development of agriculture, in the development of banking and finance, the passing and enforcement of laws, and the cultivation of the medical arts. It has seemed that it is also true with reference to moral action: action is directed to purposes of achieving what are deemed to be desirable (good—for someone or something) results. "Moral" action seems simply to be a species of the genus "action," and has in common with other actions the purpose of achieving desired and desirable effects. Rudimentary critical reflection leads to many problems in the commonsense view. What are the criteria for determining whether a consequence is desirable, whether it is "good"? And good for whom or for what? For how many persons? For what communities? The judgment that certain consequences have occurred as a result of certain purposive actions is a factual judgment; the judgment that the consequences are good or bad seems not to be. At least it is arguable whether all persons can agree on the valuation of consequences. Or if one can gain significant consensus about what consequences are good, the consensus is so general as to be relatively meaningless in particular cases. "Happiness" is a case in point. And so we have extensive debates about teleological ethics in general, and more recently about utilitarian ethics. Not all rational agents can agree on what ends are good or on what consequences are beneficial; it may be, then, that ethics based on rationality needs to omit or reduce the significance of consequences in order to avoid this problem. Further, while rational persons can agree that certain things such as health are beneficial, it is not clear that the human value of health is a "moral" value. So one must distinguish moral values from nonmoral values in order to determine what constitutes a moral evaluation of consequences.

These sorts of questions have not deterred adherents to the classic natural-law tradition from insisting that ethical theory based upon a "natural" understanding of the order of nature, including human nature, is possible. Their basic convictions have a history which antedates the rise of modern moral philosophy. In this tradition there is a confidence that there is a moral order imbedded in nature, and in human life as part of the natural order; that things are naturally inclined toward the fulfillment of their inherent final end, or *telos*; and that there is a correspondence between the operations of the human mind and this order of the universe. It is on this basis that "natural theology" has been developed, and is defended now by those who argue that the successes of modern science confirm this supposition.[121] On the same basis the morality of the natural moral law can be developed. If there is a correspondence between the natural moral order and the operations of the human mind, then there can be a rational basis for morality on which all reasonable people can agree. One need not make appeals to biblical texts to authorize moral principles and values on the basis of "revelation," though happily the morality of the biblical people is, on the whole, a positive expression of the natural moral law. One can claim that there are some moral ideals that go beyond what the natural moral law requires, such as those that can be derived from the synoptic gospels, but adherence to these is for persons who have special vocations.

The historical and contemporary evidence, however, is clear. Not all rational persons agree with the basic assumption that the operations of the mind correspond with the moral order of the universe; not all agree that there is a moral order of the universe; certainly not all agree with the moral conclusions that are authorized by the adherents to this rational

---

121. See Stanley L. Jaki, *The Road of Science and the Ways to God* (Chicago: University of Chicago Press, 1978).

moral theory. The first principle of natural law—seek good and avoid evil—is hardly debatable, but it is also so general that it solves few particular dilemmas that occur in human life. Procedures have been developed both to put some substantive content into the good and to control the processes of reasoning from first principles to particular occasions, but it is clear that not all reasonable persons can agree on either of those matters. We end up with an ironic situation in North America; the community that is probably perceived to have the most distinctive moral outlook on certain questions such as abortion, the Roman Catholic church, has this natural-law foundation for its ethics, a foundation intended to overcome serious disagreements on moral questions without recourse to historic particularities.

If the options of traditional natural-law theory and utilitarianism are unsatisfactory to achieve that goal of a moral theory, and a practical morality on which all rational persons can agree, then the moral philosophers have to look elsewhere. One place to which they have gone is to human action, and not to the characteristics of human nature, which suggest that there are inherent ends to human activity which can guide persons to the good by inclination. Human beings are agents; they have the capacity to act. Action is purposive; intentions are determinants of the exercise of other human capacities. Indeed, moral accountability requires that persons be agents; other species cannot be held accountable for their behavior in the same way that human beings can because they have not developed the necessary biological conditions for intentional activity. They have purposive activity (they seek food, for example) but they do not have consciousness of intentions and accountability for them in the way that human beings do. So some view of human agency is a presupposition of all moral theory; human action cannot be explained in the same determined cause-effect way as other events can. If one insists on causal language, it can be said that one's reason for acting is a "cause." Utilitarians and classic natural-law thinkers would not disagree on this basic point, made in a general way. But some moral theorists seek to build their normative ethical theories upon the necessary conditions for action.

The basic lines for a normative moral theory based upon a theory of human action run like this.[122] There are certain necessary conditions for human action: rationality and autonomy. These conditions are necessary for intentions to be formed and for control over one's various "powers" to determine the consequences of actions. The merit of positing these two primary conditions is clear when one sets them against their

122. The formidable and distinguished works of two of my University of Chicago colleagues build their moral theories from theories of human action. See Alan Donagan, *The Theory of Morality* (Chicago: University of Chicago Press, 1977), and Alan Gewirth, *Reason and Morality* (Chicago: University of Chicago Press, 1978).

opposites. An insane person is not rational; he or she suffers conditions which excuse actions and make it licit for others to act on his or her behalf. The person under duress is not autonomous; he or she is coerced by various external factors which force the doing of things against his or her "will." Certainly even the most deterministic theologian, one such as Jonathan Edwards, has to safeguard at least a small measure of rationality and autonomy in order to hold persons to be morally accountable. This description of the conditions for action, for some moral theorists, becomes the basis for a normative theory in the following way. Since these conditions are necessary for moral action, and since we all need to have them respected by others in order to act morally, we have an obligation to respect the same conditions in other moral actors. Thus one can develop a series of proscriptions which indicate what we ought not to do to others, and what others ought not to do to us. It is easier to delineate what we and others are to be protected against than it is to indicate in a more positive way what we ought to do to actualize or realize some measure of the good. Obligations to refrain from intervention are quite clear; there is a respect for, and seemingly a confidence in, the other's capacity to know what purposes he or she should pursue. The effect of this sort of argument is to restrict the considerations that are pertinent to morality. The features relevant to morality are described in a way that is much more limited than that of a classic teleologist or a utilitarian. On the basis of this limited description, and the further condition that it is necessary to have our autonomy and rationality respected (which is a hinge from the descriptive to the normative), one develops a normative view of ethics. Indeed, in Alan Gewirth's powerful book, he argues that it is possible to move from his Principle of Generic Consistency by processes of strict deductive logic to the right moral choice in particular circumstances.[123] A very rationalistic view of morality is proposed on which all rational persons ought to be able to agree.

Gewirth's book builds upon his comprehensive scholarship not only in the literature of recent moral philosophy but of the Western tradition as a whole. He carefully indicates how his argument differs from efforts by other philosophers to solve the same problems. He defines his position in relation, for example, to the "prescriptivism" of Richard Hare, against the ideal observer theories of Richard Brandt and Roderick Firth, and against many other options in the historical and contemporary marketplace of ethical theories. I do not need to develop these matters further to make my general point that those most rational of thinkers about ethics, the moral philosophers, share a common purpose of finding a rational basis for morality on which all rational persons can agree. Yet the ful-

123. See Gewirth, *Reason*, pp. 129–98.

fillment of that purpose has eluded them; one need only read in a cursory manner the countless pages of discussion in the last four decades in philosophical journals and books to be overwhelmed with the detailed attention they give to each other's work in order to show where it is in error.

A theologian working in ethics is much informed by these discussions, and certainly cannot discount the importance of finding a basis for morality that is more general than the authorizations for tribal customs, whether the tribe of the Kachins of Northern Burma, or the tribe of Christians scattered across our planet. He certainly cannot hope to persuade the moral philosophers that proper moral theory must be theocentric, and that evidences can be adduced to support a theocentric view in such a way that there is no "nonrational" move or moment in the development of it. Depending on his views on other matters, he will enlarge the area of consideration for ethics at the cost of not being able to make the clear and precise distinctions that are possible on some philosophical grounds. He will not be satisfied to define the relevant features of morality within those limitations that a narrow concept of ethics can manage and to leave what is beyond those margins to other things, like political theory or economics. Ethics delineated theocentrically might not even be recognizable as ethics in the sense that has been largely accepted throughout Western cultural history and certainly in recent moral philosophy.

The general direction of moral philosophy is to make man the measure of all things.[124] Indeed, as one moves from utilitarianism in which the consequences of human action are measured—to be sure in terms of their benefits to human beings—to ethics developed from recent action theory, man as the measure becomes even more restricted in scope. Certainly there is nothing like the "will of God" against which to test the propriety of human intentions and actions; certainly there is no longer anything like the moral order of the universe to which human actions are to be conformed. One cannot help but wonder whether this trend of moral philosophy does not itself rest on certain assumptions about the nature of human persons, their liberty and their individual isolation, which might not be factually accurate. One wonders about the extent to which this direction was historically set by intellectual and cultural movements of the Enlightenment that have their own historical relativity and partiality. One wonders if morality does not have more to do with the affections and inclinations, not merely as premoral conditions for action but also in other important ways. And one certainly wonders whether, since the most rational of thinkers about ethics have not yet achieved their aspiration

124. "All traditional ethics is anthropocentric": Hans Jonas, *Philosophical Essays: From Ancient Creed to Technological Man* (Englewood Cliffs, N. J.: Prentice-Hall, 1974), pp. 6–7. My debt to Hans Jonas's writings far exceeds what is apparent from the few citations to them in this book.

for a moral theory that would be persuasive to all rational agents, attention is not still worth giving to the historical traditions out of which have come a great deal of the motives and goals for action among humankind. To wonder about these things is not to dismiss or ignore the issues raised by moral philosophers in the modern period or in the past. From such wondering it is clearly not sufficient to lay hold dogmatically on a particular historical text about particular historical persons and events and build from that a moral theory by itself. Certain polarities that have characterized discussions for centuries need radical modification. It is not as if "faith" is unreasonable, though evidences adduced for it will not satisfy most philosophers; indeed, faith is not the leap into the incredible that the stereotype often held in the radically secularized academic communities portrays. "Revelation" is not a magical way to knowledge about reality; what has been claimed for it has always been mediated through human experience and events and always reflects their significance. The theologian can and must reflect upon human experience in its moral and other dimensions in such a way that an alternative view of the ethical can at least be intelligible to the moral philosopher, though the theologian does not expect to persuade. There are other than theological reasons for asking whether recent moral philosophy is adequate to human experience and to the relations of human beings to the rest of nature. But this is to get ahead of my account.

Conclusions

This account of my perceptions and interpretations of the circumstances of the culture, religion, theology, and ethics is, in spite of its length, cursory. Yet it does give the main lines of the issues that I respond to in the remainder of this volume and in the next. A general direction of investigation has been delineated, and many particular items on the agenda have been stated explicitly or implied in my critical evaluations. To develop a list of items at this point would not be profitable, but the major lines of criticism can be drawn out to indicate the major thrust of the forthcoming chapters.

Culturally, religiously, theologically, and ethically, man, the human species, has become the measure of all things; all things have been put in the service of man. Man is always the *measurer* of all things; among the millions of forms of life only our species has developed the biological capacities to know, measure, evaluate, intend, experiment, and test perceptions. This is the glory of the human species; this is the distinctiveness that can be described and is to be valued. But to be the measurer of all things does not necessarily imply that all things are to be in service of man.

There are many reasons, not only theological ones, for raising questions about this drift of modern culture, religion, and morality. To be sure, it is present in all cultures, in one degree or another, and in all times; I am not concerned to develop a historical argument that our culture and our religious activity is more homocentric or anthropocentric by specific orders of magnitude. One reason for questioning the implications of this drift is that focus on man, and on man within very limited time-spans of life, leads to a distortion of the place of man in the universe. As physicists and astronomers have developed explanations of the origin of the universe, we see that even the most rudimentary preconditions for the evolution of the most primitive forms of life took millions of years to develop. There were contingencies of natural events that made development of life possible on our planet in a way that it has not developed elsewhere even in our solar system. As paleontologists and chemists and biologists have developed explanations of life on this planet, we know that there have been critical junctures at which the happy association of natural events made possible the rudimentary biological developments from which our species has developed. As astrophysicists and others assess the possibilities for the long-range future of our planet and its place in the universe, it becomes clear that in one way or another there shall be a *finis*, a temporal end, to life as we know it. If it were not for that knowledge, one might live contentedly with the traditional Western assurance that everything has taken place for the sake of man; that man is the crown of the creation. Since that assurance is not possible in the light of the coming *finis*, it is appropriate to take these evidences and hypotheses into account in thinking about the place of man in the universe and the dependence of man on processes past, present, and future for existence. Culture, based upon the capacities of our species, has injected radically new factors into the processes of the history of nature. Their impact on biological evolution is to some degree measurable; their impact upon the wider natural world on which we depend for our existence is to some degree predictable.

Man has become the measure in religion, theology, and ethics. Religion has turned from the celebrations of the glories of the natural order (and for some good reasons, such as awareness that it is a threat as well as a sustainer and thing of beauty) to preoccupation with subjective problems of individuals. Religion and God have been put in the service of human needs. Theology continues to assure human beings that the Deity serves to fulfill particular human desires. In the case of eschatological theology, such as that of Moltmann, it appears that theologians can ignore what can be known about the universe and the place of man in it; the resurrection of Christ from the dead seems necessarily to imply that nature is open to a new creation. Ethical thought in Western culture, whether under Christian or secular auspices, has with great persistence been concerned with what is good for man and all too frequently has failed to take into account the interrelations of individuals with other persons, the constraints necessary for the corporate or common good of specific human communities and the whole of the human community, and the well-being of future generations. Man is the subject and the object of the good.

Considerations such as these direct attention to a theological tradition which turns from man to that which is objective in relation to human subjects. Put in first-order religious language, this anthropocentrism implies a denial of God as God—as the power and ordering of life in nature and history which sustains and limits human activity, which "demands" recognition of principles and boundaries of activities for the sake of man and of the whole of life. It seems to imply a denial of the need for humans to *consent* to "being," to recognize not only that conditions for human action and the development of culture are present but also the dependence upon basic resources of life that are ignored at the peril of human and other life. It seems to imply that tragedy can be overcome, or if it cannot be overcome, it has a purpose which is realizable in benefits to individual persons and to the species. But this is to get ahead of my story.

In one important respect the theological direction of this work bears similarities to the turn taken by many of the theologians earlier in the present century. Liberal Protestant theology, like evangelical Protestant religion, had become preoccupied with the significance of religion for human subjects and for human culture and morality. Whether one reads Karl Barth, Henry Nelson Wieman, H. Richard Niebuhr, or others, one finds that the generation of these theologians had various reasons for turning attention from religion as a human phenomenon to God as its proper object. "From subjectivity to objectivity" is not a bad way of indicating their basic intention. They worked this out in different ways, and the differences are important. I shall not work out the implications of the turn in the same way that any one of these men did. There is, however, sufficient similarity in the interpretation of the religious and cultural circumstances to warrant the same basic insistence on theocentricity. My arguments on behalf of theocentricity will not develop simply from a retrieval of the biblical theology, as did some of theirs, but will take into account other sources as well. It will turn toward a selective retrieval of basic aspects of the highly theocentric tradition which focuses on the thought of John Calvin and moves backward toward those who deeply influenced him and forward toward those who were deeply influenced by him. Ethics in this perspective becomes something quite different from its traditional meaning; indeed, it may not be recognizable as ethics in the traditional Western sense at all. It is important to suggest some of the aspects which this alteration of perspective brings to the enterprise of ethics in order to foresee the importance of the steps that are taken in subsequent chapters. To the question of what happens to ethics in a theocentric perspective, then, I now turn.

2

Theocentric Ethics
Is It Ethics in the Traditional Sense?

The distinctive thrust of this book is toward the development of a theocentric ethics. Some features of this thrust need to be indicated at this point in order to give the reader an orientation to a pattern of thought that may be strange and unfamiliar.

What is the discipline of ethics all about? What are the major characteristics of both its substance and its method in the history of human thought and experience? Answers to these questions can be found in many textbooks and articles, and thus it is not necessary to give a full account here.[1]

The discipline of ethics is concerned with what is morally right and wrong about human actions and what is morally good and bad about the consequences of actions. It is also often concerned about what characterizes morally good or bad persons, that is, about human character. Ethical issues occur when the answer to the question "What ought I (or we) to do?" is not obvious. Since that question could pertain to whether we ought to plant our potatoes today or wait a few days until the ground is dryer, as well as to whether we ought to break a promise we have made in light of certain conditions that have arisen which we did not anticipate, it is clear that ethicians have to determine what distinguishes the "moral" from the "nonmoral." Unfortunately there is no universal agreement on the precise boundaries between the moral and the nonmoral. Thinking about these boundaries leads one to the classic distinction between two forms of ethical theory in the West: teleological and deontological. If one's characteristic language about morality uses the terms good and evil (value terms) one is very likely to fall primarily under the teleological type. One is likely to make judgments about the actions of others, or about one's own proposed actions, in light of the intentions of the agent, or in light of the consequences of actions, that is, in light of the value judgments about the intended and/or actual ends or consequences (their "goodness" or their "badness"). If one's characteristic language about morality uses the terms right and wrong, one is very likely to fall primarily under the deontological type. One is likely to make judgments about what persons *ought* to have done or ought to do. Some rule or principle that ought to be obeyed is likely to be on one's mind. The types are distinguished by the primacy of the language of goodness and value on the one hand, and of oughtness and rightness on the other. The distinction becomes very sharp when one asks whether the consequences or intentions of an action are what makes it right, or whether certain actions are right even though the consequences are deleterious to certain things that we properly value. That justice is to be done, though the heavens fall, is a classic deonto-

1. For a clear and learned brief account, see Alan Gewirth, "Ethics," *Encyclopaedia Britannica,* 15th ed. (1974).

logical statement. Further distinctions made by moral philosophers about the issues of moral theory need not be developed here.

The material considerations (in contrast to the formal ones) that enter into moral judgments are the main issue on which the distinctions made in this chapter turn. What are the sources that persons turn to, what sources should they turn to, in deciding what they ought to do, whether that is formally decided in the deontological or the teleological manner? In normative ethics (distinguished from "meta-ethics") what is the content of the principles or values that ought to determine conduct? It is not necessary to delineate all the options for answering this question in order to bring the interests of the present chapter into focus.

The Central Reference Point: Man or God?

The thesis of this chapter is that the dominant strand of Western ethics, whether religious or secular, argues that the material considerations for morality are to be derived from purely human points of reference. In terms of good or value the question is, usually, What is good for man? or What is of value to human beings? In terms of right or wrong it is, usually, What are the right relations between persons? Alternatives are these: What is good for the whole creation? What is good not only for man but for the natural world of which man is part? What conduct is right for man not only in relation to other human beings but also in relation to the ordering of the natural and the social worlds?

The human-centered strand is dominant, but there have been strands of traditional ethics which are more in accord with the alternatives. They have been stated in purely religious terms: God, rather than man, ought to be the measure of all things. Jowett, for example, translates a speech of the Athenian in Plato's *Laws,* "Now God ought to be to us the measure of all things, and not man as men commonly say (Protagoras). . . ."[2] In a later section the following speech occurs.

> Let us say to the youth:—The ruler of the universe has ordered all things with a view to the excellence and preservation of the whole, and each part, as far as may be, has action and passion appropriate to it. . . . And one of these portions of the universe is thine own, unhappy man, which, however little, contributes to the whole; and you do not seem to be aware that this and every other creation is for the sake of the whole, and in order that the life of the whole may be blessed; and that you are created for the sake of the whole, and not the whole for the sake of you.[3]

2. Plato, *Laws,* 716C, in *The Dialogues of Plato,* trans. Benjamin Jowett, 2 vols. (New York: Random House, 1937), 2:488.
3. Plato, *Laws,* 903CD, ibid., 2:645.

This is a secular version of the more religious language used in the first quotation. Certainly in Stoic morality, the right or fitting relationships were not only between persons but between persons and the natural order as that was then understood. The references of right conduct were to an order of life that was objective to persons.

Many authors have indicated that one of the decisive differences between the dominant tendency of Western ethics and that of the ethics of Hindu culture is that in Indian culture human life is set within a cosmic and natural context in such a way that the cosmic is supreme and that, in a sense, man is made for the cosmos rather than the cosmos for man. Betty Heimann makes this point dramatically by choosing two quotations which she believes are typical of Western and of Hindu philosophical thought. From the West she chooses Protagoras: "Man is the measure of all things." From Hindu thought she chooses the following: "This Atman (the vital essence in Man) is the same in the ant, the same in the gnat, the same in the elephant, the same in these three words. . . . The same in the whole universe."[4] While single quotations cannot capture the complex cultures they are meant to typify, the aptness of Heimann's choices reflects her long and serious consideration of the differences between these two cultures. For my purposes it is not that the Upanishads are to be praised and Protagoras condemned, but that the quotation from Protagoras sustains the observation that the normative material criterion for ethics in the West is not the cosmos but man.

Certainly biblical morality had a clear objective referent for the material considerations of morality. Morality was to be governed by God's will, not by man's will; it was to be governed by the law of the Deity, not by the customs of man. The long history of commentary on the story of Abraham and the sacrifice of Isaac that is part of the religious moral lore of our culture indicates that we are deeply disturbed when a divine command is not in accord with the precepts of common human morality, when the will of God seems to run counter to one of the moral principles on which persons from almost all cultures agree, namely, "Thou shalt not murder."[5] The human quarrel with Yahweh that this narrative quite properly evokes testifies to doubt whether any rule of conduct, or any particular precept or command that violates the fundamental conditions for human well-being, is truly moral. We are morally offended when the will of God runs counter to our human understanding of what is right and

4. The second quotation is from *Brhadaranyaka Upanishad,* 1, 3, 11, in Betty Heimann, *Indian and Western Philosophy: A Study in Contrasts* (London: G. Allen and Unwin, 1937), n.p.

5. For a collection of rabbinic commentary, see Shalom Spiegel, *The Last Trial,* trans. Judah Goldin (New York: Schocken Books, 1969). Kierkegaard's account is most familiar. See his *Fear and Trembling,* trans. Walter Lowrie (Garden City, N.Y.: Doubleday Anchor, 1954). For Woody Allen's "midrash," see "The Scrolls" in *Without Feathers* (New York: Warner Books, 1976), pp. 26–27.

good for man, and in this case for a particular innocent human child, Isaac.

We are on familiar terrain in the discussions of ethics in the West. Are God's commands right because he commands them, or does he command them because they are right? The dichotomy forces an either/or choice, it seems; at least the ways in which it has been developed face us with the forced choice. Socrates, with his dialectical skills, drove Euthyphro into this dilemma. In a discussion of piety, he asks Euthyphro, "It is loved because it is holy, not holy because it is loved?" Euthyphro admits that the gods love piety because it is holy. Socrates' declaration is forthright, "I mean to say that the holy has been acknowledged by us to be loved of God because it is holy, not to be holy because it is loved."[6] The answer saves the moral character of the gods, but on the basis of what principle? On the basis of the principle that human judgment determines what is right and what is holy. This is necessarily the case since it is not ours to know precisely what the divine judgment is. But the character of the gods is also saved on the basis that what is judged to be right for man must be right for them. That old quarrel, going behind Job in time in Near Eastern culture, appearing in Greek culture, and recurring throughout the history of Western culture, is resolved in Socrates' assertion. God approves only what is right for man; man's good is the principal consideration in determining what God wills. It is morally offensive to have a god who would not will what is good for man. Man's good is the moral measure of all things.

Dichotomies are interesting devices to force issues; they drive matters to the extremes of an either/or choice: either a precept is right because God commands it or God commands it because it is right. Either man was made for the cosmos or the cosmos was made for man. Either man was made for God or God was made for man. Either God is the measure of all things or man is the measure of all things. Some observations which pertain to the central thrust of this book are germane at this point. From what we know about the development of our universe, the development of the preconditions for the evolution of life on our planet, the development of various species and the extinction of many, the contingencies (unless one is sure of a divine providence) that occurred which made possible the evolution of mammals, and the forecasts for the future demise of our universe (to be sure, in billions of years), it is very difficult to sustain the belief that the cosmos was made for man. If there is an ordering power behind, within, and through all these natural processes out of which human beings have developed, it is difficult to say that God was made for man or even that God developed the universe for the sake of man. Indeed,

6. Plato, *Euthyphro*, 10, in Jowett, *Dialogues*, 1:392.

to traditional Western religious ears it is as offensive to say that God was made for man as it has been to Western moral ears to say that a command is right because God commanded it. But if, both on traditional Western religious grounds and on the grounds of an understanding of the development of life sustained by the relevant sciences, we cannot say that God was made for man, or that the universe developed for the sake of the human species, then do we not have to wonder whether the view that man is the moral measure of all things can be sustained?

Of course, much more needs to be said about what man is, about man's place in the universe, about what the human good is and over what time span it is to be considered, and about what right conduct for human beings, in relation to whom and to what, is. These critical matters are deferred at this point; here I am concerned to indicate that there are some good reasons for asking in our time and in the light of the Western religious tradition whether the apparent assumption that man is the moral measure of all things can be sustained. Certainly the only way in which one can have theocentric ethics which finally sustains and supports the idea that what God wills is what is good for man is to argue that the good for human beings coincides with the ultimate divine purpose. Historically, most of Christian ethics has assumed this to be the case. Even the grand and living tradition of Christian natural-law ethics has made this assumption. While there are Stoic influences in the development of the natural-law tradition within Christian thought, the notion that the fitting action of persons required a resignation to an objective order of life was altered. Rather than the "cosmos" being the object of divine governance, with human beings as a part of that, the well-being of man is understood to be the supreme object of divine governance, and the order of nature is understood to exist for the sake of man. To be sure, there are limits to proper human actions: the belief that the order of nature exists for the sake of man does not warrant license for human beings to do what they please with nature. They are not, for example, to intervene artificially in the process of human sexual intercourse so that the possibility for the transmission of life is obstructed. On this point it appears that the moral order and the biological order are one and the same. The qualification of that assertion is that it is permissible to restrain sexual activity to a wife's infertile periods; here the moral order refers to the human capacities of choice and volition. Readers of Catholic moral theology are well acquainted with other precepts of human conduct that can be derived from the moral order. Basically, human beings are naturally oriented toward what fulfills human well-being, both in our natural temporal existence and in our ultimate eternal end. Happily, for this tradition, as for almost all Christian thought, the rest of the creation was understood to be in the service of our species. With our natural orientation toward our fulfillment, and with the coincidence of the "hierarchy of being" with a hierarchy of value, human beings are supreme in both. The rest of the natural order is purposively directed toward the fulfillment of human life. God has so ordered the world that by man's conforming to the natural order the greatest human good will be fulfilled. God is not morally arbitrary; he has created an order of life which has a moral direction built into it. Only on rare occasions, such as the command to Abraham to sacrifice Isaac, has he gone counter to that natural moral order, by giving a secret command to an agent.

What is in line with the argument of this book from this Catholic tradition is that the material considerations for a normative ethics are to be derived not only with reference to man but with reference to the place of human beings in a larger ordering of life in nature and in history. What is not well established, in my judgment, is that the ordering of nature is as inherently moral as it appears to be in this tradition, that there is a purpose inherent in nature which makes man the chief aspect of the creation in whose service all other aspects are properly placed, that the happy coincidence of the ordering of nature and what is beneficial to man can be sustained, and that the assessment of the meaning of natural events has to be made with reference to their benefits to man. There are material considerations of ethics objective to human beings: this is correct. It is at least plausible to acknowledge that there is a power and orderer governing nature, and man as part of nature: this I shall argue. But that the Deity has so designed all things for man as the chief end of his creation there is good reason to doubt. The issues between the position being developed here and the Catholic natural-law tradition are several. One is whether we can be certain from what we know about the ordering of the natural world that it has the deep moral direction, the inherent service to man, that is assumed in natural-law tradition. Another is whether, whatever we say about God's power and order, they are so clearly oriented toward the well-being of individual persons and even toward our species as seems to be assumed. Another is whether we can know the significance of that order for morality with sufficient clarity to make the judgments about many particular acts that Catholic moral theology makes with a high degree of certainty. Surely no Roman Catholic would say that God was made for man; that would be blasphemy of a high order. Yet the tradition assumes, as does most of the Christian tradition, that the purposes of God are finally for the benefit of human beings. That might be a way of saying many of the same things that one could say if God were made for man.

There is a long history in human cultures of attempting to interpret the significance of all sorts of natural events, particularly natural calamities, in terms of some deep significance in them for man and man's relations to God or the gods. The focus is on their significance for human individuals and communities. What is right about this is that human beings have the capacity to respond to events, including calamities, in a way that other creatures cannot. But in Western religion, this response has generally been in terms of an assumption of a divine providence directed to what is beneficial to those persons most intimately involved.

Not untypical of this tendency is an account of the collapse of the gallery in the church building in Northampton, Massachusetts, in March 1737, written by the congregation's minister, Jonathan Edwards. Edwards gives a very plausible description of the causes of the collapse. "Our meeting house is old and decayed, . . . the cells and walls giving way, especially in the foreside, by reason of the weight of timber at top pressing on the braces that are inserted into the posts and beams of the house." He indicates that the heaving frosts after an unusually cold winter had been especially hard on the building. It seems that there was a high degree of probability that the gallery would collapse from the weight of the members of the congregation. It did, shortly after a sermon began. "But so mysteriously and wonderfully did it come to pass, that every life was preserved; and though many were greatly bruised, and their flesh torn, yet there is not, as I can understand, one bone broken or so much as put out of joint, among them all." How does one account for this? "It seems unreasonable to ascribe it to anything else but the care of Providence, in disposing the motions of every piece of timber, and the precise place of safety where everyone should sit, and fall, when one were in any capacity to care for their own preservation." "Such an event may be sufficient argument of a divine Providence over the lives of men."[7] The natural causes of the event were well understood by Edwards; no doubt an adequate building code adequately enforced would have required the building to be closed. The significance of the event had to be judged in terms of providence. As the editors of the works of Edwards indicate, the event might be seen "by the unthinking world to be a signal token of God's displeasure against the town";[8] instead, by its effects (the conversion of many persons) it is seen to be a token of God's goodness. The explanation of the collapse is given in good commonsense terms. The explanation of the absence of deaths and many serious injuries is given in purely theological terms; God disposed the motions of every piece of timber and where each person should sit or fall. This redescription of the event must find its significance in terms of what is beneficial to human beings. One

7. Letter dated 19 March 1737, quoted by Isaac Watts and John Guyse in their Preface to Edwards, *A Faithful Narrative of the Surprising Works of God. . . . ,* in *The Works of Jonathan Edwards,* 2 vols. (Worcester, Mass., 1834, 1:345–46; reprinted, Edinburgh: The Banner of Truth Trust, 1974).

8. Ibid., p. 345.

can safely say that if many deaths had occurred that another redescription would have been given, equally beneficial to human beings in the long run.

It is not only Catholic natural-law theories and Calvinistic theories of special providence that are certain that the purposes of God are for the well-being of man. All the social reform movements that have sought justification in theological principles have been based on this same certainty, as have movements which have sought to restrain radical social change in the name of the divine orders of creation. The social gospel movement in North America is but one example. The assumption was most clearly stated by Walter Rauschenbusch when he wrote that "the will of God is identical with the good of mankind."[9] One can find biblical backing for such a view. Rauschenbusch read the prophets of the eighth century B.C. in this way, and not without evidence from the texts. The Kingdom of God was interpreted in ways radically criticized by biblical scholars who recaptured a more radical eschatological vision of its coming, but, as interpreted, it served as a symbol of the realization of moral ideals and aspirations for greater equity in the distribution of the good things of the earth, for greater participation by all members of the human community in the determination of their destinies, for the measure of tranquillity that seems desirable in the relations between groups within a society and between nations. The idea of the Kingdom of God was moralized in terms that could be defended on the basis of human moral values, and on the basis of ethical principles that would, if followed, ensure human well-being. The ultimate power and reality were seen to be clearly and unambiguously on the side of man; morally right-thinking persons, reflecting on the biblical messages and on the social evils of the times, could know with some precision just what it was that God willed in human society. God was clearly for man, and human values determined the terms.

Even the ethics of the neoorthodox theologies, which developed in part as a revolt against the humanistic emphasis of the social gospel and other liberal theologies, were certain in the end that the Deity, though high and lifted up, was for man. He could not be otherwise for a theology that sought to get its material norms from the biblical materials, and particularly for a theology that centered the knowledge of God in Jesus Christ interpreted as the manifestation of the presence of the grace of God. In Karl Barth's theology and ethics the witness of the Scriptures is to a gracious God, whose commands are affirmative of human values,

9. Walter Rauschenbusch, *The Social Principles of Jesus* (New York: Association Press, 1916), p. 128.

whose purposes are for the well-being of humans.[10] Barth's ethics are as theocentric as any in this century; they require that persons hear and obey the commands of God. They are backed by the assurance, revealed in the Scriptures, that the God who commands is a gracious God, and therefore that his first word to man is permission for, and affirmation of, life and its flourishing. To be sure, Barth, more than some others, was cognizant that the gracious Creator cared for the world of nature as well as the worlds of history, culture, and man. Barth more than most of his contemporaries understood that the uses that our species made of other forms of life, particularly of animal life, required recognition that in many instances life was "sacrificed" for human benefit.[11] While the rest of life exists for the service of man, the fact that human beings must sacrifice other forms of life for their own well-being is not a matter to be taken callously. Nonetheless, the commands of God are primarily in the service of the needs of man.

The history of ethics in Christianity could be rehearsed in extensive detail to establish further evidences of this dominant trend, but this is unnecessary. It is necessary, however, to return to the dichotomy that has forced the basic issue of theological ethics in the West: Are God's commands right because he commands them or does he command them because they are right? Are God's ends good because he chooses them or does he choose them because they are good? The dichotomy needs to be examined to see whether the choice is a necessary one, and whether an oversimplification has not been developed in the dialectical process. One sort of examination, which will be engaged in with greater attention subsequently, is "Right for whom?" and "Right for what?"; "Good for whom?" and "Good for what?" It is better to make one's interpretation of the right and the good primarily in relational terms than in substantive ones.[12] Historically the dichotomy has always been assumed to refer to what is right for man, what is good for man and what is right for man primarily in relation to other persons. The right is determined finally with reference to the *telos,* or the good, for man. The traditional way of setting up the problem assumes that man is of ultimate value, that God's reign and rule are almost exclusively oriented toward the sphere of human activities, and that all other things exist for the sake of man.

For now, we can ask rhetorical questions. What happens if what is right for man requires that we see that man is rightly related not only to

10. See, for example, how Barth makes the case that the law is the form of the gospel, that command is permission, etc., in his *Church Dogmatics,* II/2, pp. 583–630.

11. Karl Barth, *Church Dogmatics,* III/4, (Edinburgh: T. and T. Clark, 1961) pp. 351–56.

12. See H. Richard Niebuhr, "The Center of Value," in *Radical Monotheism and Western Culture* (New York: Harper and Row, 1960), pp. 100–113.

other persons, not only to social institutions and their relations to each other, but to the elements of nitrogen, oxygen, and carbon so necessary as conditions for life itself, to worlds of plants and animals, and even to the inanimate features of our planet? What happens if right conduct has to take into account human dependence on things which are not ultimately objects of human creation and are beyond human control? We can still say that God commands certain things because they are right, but the context is enlarged in which the rightness of human activity is assessed. The enlargement is theologically significant, for it assumes that God's rule is not as exclusively focused on the actions of man and on the events of history in which human exercises of power are so determinative, but that it also governs nature, the natural ordering of life within which our species lives and from which it has established a distinctive degree of independence. One might still say that God values what is good because of its goodness; it is not good because he values it. But the arena of goodness, of value, is expanded. Good for whom? For individuals living in a given time and place? For our generation more than for future generations? For man, rather than for the world of plants and animals? If one's basic theological perception is of a Deity who rules all of creation, and one's basic perception of life in history and nature is one of patterns of interdependence, then the good that God values must be more inclusive than one's normal perceptions of what is good for me, what is good for my community, and even what is good for the human species.

As I have shown, it is possible to have theological ethics which confines the right and the good to anthropocentric terms. The history of the Western religious traditions is replete with examples of such ethics. Such views can be readily explained: they arise certainly, in part, out of the fact that we are the species that has capacities even to wonder about what is right and good, and quite naturally we are concerned about what is right and good for us. They arise out of the embarrassment that comes from the possibility that the Deity is not moral, or not moral in the terms by which we judge morality. They arise out of the egocentric predicament that creates the problem of theodicy; for the theodicy question arises only on the assumption that God necessarily wills the good of a particular person or community as that good is humanly understood.

On the whole, neither theology proper, nor theological ethics, has attended sufficiently to strands in the biblical and Christian traditions which indicate that the purposes of God are not necessarily coincident with our perceptions of them; which take seriously those intimations of a sovereign power that not only sustains human life and well-being but sets the limits of human pursuits; which tell of a God who not only has enabled human achievements and actions but requires "consent to being," to what is right and good for human beings as they confront their awesome possibilities and their inexorable limitations. It cannot be denied that the basic trend of the Christian tradition has always viewed God's grace and goodness primarily in terms of his grace and goodness for man. The history of man since "the Fall" for Jonathan Edwards, for one example, is the "history of redemption," the history of the redemption of human souls.[13] The theological concentration has been on history—"salvation history"—and "salvation" has pertained to human individuals or to (at most) human communities. Even the great and admirable Edwards, whose philosophical theology and ethics provide the significant idea of "consent to being," had to assert for religious reasons that God's purpose for human beings (not, however, the chief end of the creation) was their redemption. Even God's righteousness, a term which could have an awesome sense of otherness, means for Edwards, his faithfulness in fulfilling his covenant promises to his church, or his faithfulness towards his church and people, in bestowing benefits of the covenant of grace upon them.[14] To be sure, redemption is of persons, for it necessarily involves accountability for the faults from which they are to be redeemed. But nonetheless, as Clyde Holbrook has carefully indicated, the "utilitarian" strand in Edward's thought is not easily squared with the great theme of consent to being.[15] As we shall see in Chapter 4, even the strand of Christian theology that has most highlighted the sovereignty of God has always found ways to ensure that its exercise was just in relation to man (retribution for sinners and compensation for the redeemed in the next life) and that it was ultimately for human benefit.

Theologians and ethicians have shown remarkable myopia in not taking into account the inferences that can be reasonably drawn from some of the most secure knowledge we have of the creation of the universe, the evolution of species, and the likely end of our planet as we now know it. Ernst Troeltsch in effect laid down the gauntlet to theologians on this point decades ago in a passage which, while not fully accurate in terms of recent science, nonetheless makes the valid point.

> We obviously cannot lock out the consequences of a Copernican system. We may not shrink from the immensity of the All, in which we, together with our whole solar system, are swept upon paths which defy thought. In view of the uniformity of the entire universe opened up by spectral analysis, the geocentric and anthropocentric view of things must vanish. Man has to adapt himself to no longer being able to establish a physical centre of the universe. . . . We know that the formation of our earth arose by

13. Jonathan Edwards, *A History of the Work of Redemption*, in *Works*, 1:533–619.
14. Ibid., p. 533, col. 1.
15. Clyde A. Holbrook, *The Ethics of Jonathan Edwards* (Ann Arbor: University of Michigan Press, 1973), pp. 24 ff.

detachment from another heavenly body, and our entire organic life on this earth seems, in comparison to the duration of the world, like breath on cold window panes, which disappears the next moment. But what the world is without organic life, we do not know. At a certain point we emerged from the development, at a certain point we will disappear again. More science does not say. As the beginning was without us, so will the end also be without us. Transferred to religion, this in sight means: the end is not that of the Apocalypse.[16]

One need not take recourse to the traditional religious rhetoric that man is a "worm" before God to see that theology and theological ethics need to reconsider the place of man in the universe in light both of some neglected aspects of the religious tradition and some well-established principles of explanation in modern sciences. I have previously quoted from Herbert Butterfield's observations about seventeenth-century science, to the effect that scientists had to recognize "that it is absurd to suppose that this colossal universe was created by God purely for the sake of men, purely to serve the purposes of the earth."[17] Loren Eiseley, in his gracefully written *Darwin's Century,* indicates at many points how the naive anthropocentrism of Christian culture often blinded brilliant men from grasping the significance of their principal empirical observations of the geological strata of the earth, or left them unable to assess the possibility of the extinction of many species, because of a belief that a divine plan brought everything progressively to the apex of man. With reference to literature that certainly was coherent with patterns of evolutionary thought, for example, he writes, "Many passages reveal that this type of anthropocentric concentration made the assumption inevitable that with the appearance of man the geological story was complete."[18] In order to see the larger significance of a massive accumulation of data from many sources, "it was necessary to break out of a particular, man-centered way

16. Ernst Troeltsch, *Glaubenslehre*, p. 64. Translated and quoted by B. A. Gerrish, in "Ernst Troeltsch and the Possibility of a Historical Theology," in John Powell Clayton, ed., *Ernst Troeltsch and the Future of Theology* (Cambridge: Cambridge University Press, 1976), p. 117. "Man's age upon earth amounts to several hundred thousand years or more. His future may come to still more. It is hard to imagine a single point of history along this line, and that the centre-point of our own religious history, as the sole centre of humanity. That looks far too much like . . . absolutizing our own contingent area of life. That is in religion what geocentricism and anthropocentricism are in cosmology and metaphysics." From "The Significance of the Historical Existence of Jesus for Faith," in Robert Morgan and Michael Pye, eds., *Ernst Troeltsch: Writings on Theology and Religion* (Atlanta: John Knox, 1977), p. 189. Troeltsch's critique here is of Christocentrism, but the relevance of his words is even larger.

17. Butterfield, *Origins,* p. 69.

18. Loren Eiseley, *Darwin's Century* (Garden City, N.Y : Doubleday Anchor, 1961), pp. 96–97.

of looking at the world.''[19] Anthropocentrism kept scientists from seeing and understanding the significance of data. A break in the focus of concentration was required; if man is the measure (and not only the measurer) of all things, it is difficult to assess accurately the place of the human species in the long temporal scheme of things, and in the intricate web of the interdependence of things. The anthropocentric focus might even keep us from grasping some significant things about the ultimate power and ordering of life, about the majesty and glory of all that sustains us, about the threats to life over which we have no definite control. The ultimate power is not the guarantor of human benefits; there are many benefits which are ours, but ''all things'' simply do not work together for the good of individuals and of the human community.

Theocentric ethics could defend the view that the material considerations of moral life are almost totally related to what is good for us, what is right in person-to-person relations. One would be able so to restrict the considerations of ethics if the Deity were for man above all other things. But if the Deity is not bound to our judgments about what is in our interests, then theological ethics is radically altered. It may no longer be ethics at all in the traditional sense of Western culture and Christianity. Other questions then are raised. What can be discerned about the purposes of that power on which all of creation depends for its sustenance and for its possibilities of development? What actions are right for man in relation to the sustaining, ordering, limiting, and creative power of God? If God's purposes are for the well-being of the whole of ''the creation,'' what is the place of human well-being in relation to the ''whole of creation''? Man, the measurer, can no longer be the measure of the value of all things. What is right for man has to be determined in relation to man's place in the universe and, indeed, in relation to the will of God for all things as that might dimly be discerned.

A Moral Pause

There are good moral reasons to pause before moving headlong in the direction this book is taking. If, to play with the dichotomies, the cosmos was not made for man, the ''whole'' was not made for our part, and God was not made for man, then some worrisome matters arise. If man is seen more in continuity with the ordering of nature, and less in terms of the ''grandeur'' that is his as a result of his freedom, then it is easy to demean his value and significance. We need to be forthright about the moral perils that can result from going in this direction; to observe what concentration on the human good and human interest has preserved

19. Ibid., p. 136.

and protected in the life of the human community. These values might be put at risk by shifting to a strong theocentric perspective, particularly one that does not see the purposes of the ultimate power to coincide perfectly with our interpretations of what constitutes human well-being.

The anthropocentric concentration has protected the dignity of the human species and the dignity of individuals. The dignity of the species is protected by those precepts which require that we favor man over animals in all instances in which human life is threatened. It is protected by those precepts which make it clear that the natural world can and ought to be put in the service of human aspirations for health and reasonable material comfort, for development of culture, and for fulfillment of individual well-being. Any interpretation of life which excessively accents the similarities rather than the distinctive differences between man and the rest of the creation is likely to be more ready to find reasons in certain circumstances to curb human activities that enhance human dignity and the possibilities of human achievement. Any interpretation which highlights the modest place of man in the whole of the natural world and takes account of the consequences of the development of human culture and particular human acts on "the whole" of creation is likely to find reasons for restraint of cultural development and human actions. The very imposition of restraints can be viewed as an insult to, or a violation of, human dignity.

The biblical and Christian traditions have provided deep and strong backing for the value of human dignity. The Genesis account of the creation gives us, from a religious perspective, the most solid grounds for human dignity. Calvin, like most theologians who have attended to that account, finds it an assurance of the special dignity of our species, and a record of the divine benevolence that is directed toward us. "We ought," he wrote, "in the very order of things diligently to contemplate God's fatherly love toward mankind, in that he did not create Adam until he had lavished upon the universe all manner of good things."[20] If God had put Adam on the earth while it was still "sterile and empty" he would not have provided sufficiently for human welfare. "Let us make man in our image, after our likeness; and let him have dominion over the fish of the sea, and over the birds of the air, and over the cattle, and over all the earth, and over every creeping thing that creeps upon the earth," says God.[21] While theologians have disputed through the ages about which human capacity makes man in the image of God, they have not disputed the notion that the passage warrants that high dignity which we claim for

20. John Calvin, *Institutes of the Christian Religion,* I, 14, 3; 2 vols., trans. Ford Lewis Battles, ed. John T. McNeill (Philadelphia: Westminster, 1955), 1:161–62.
21. Gen. 1:26, R.S.V.

our species. Nor have they disputed that all the rest of the creation exists for our service. What higher claim for dignity can be made, from a religious perspective, than that man is made in the image and likeness of God? Interestingly, few theologians have read the passage to be an account of the dependence of human life on light and water, on seeds and plants, on animal life, all of which God saw was good (and not, I take it, only good for man). There certainly are moral perils in any interpretation of life that in any way weakens our beliefs in the distinctive dignity of human life or that weakens the religious backing for it which is so forcefully made in the notion that man is made in the image and likeness of God. Even scientists who relish interpreting the development of our solar system and the evolution of life to show how dependent man has been on all that has gone before, how brief his history is, and how it will come to a termination, often pause to remember that our species is the only one we know that has the capacities to investigate all these matters and to acquire information regarding them.

There is no denying human distinctiveness, or denying that it is a warrant for according special dignity not only to the species but to human individuals. Indeed, for many interpreters of the development of societies and cultures the move from the primacy of the social unit to the primacy of the individual has been a clue to human progress. In the biblical tradition itself there are traces of such development; Yahweh was concerned earlier for the "people," that is, for the social historical unit of the ancient Hebrew community. Both his compensations and his retributions were to be visited upon the nation, not upon individuals; accountability was that of a group more than that of an individual. Similar developments have been traced in other cultures. In one period of Greek culture the virtues served the well-being of the city-state, the organized community; only through a process of development did the moral virtues we attach to individuals come to be seen as superior to the warrior strengths that contributed to the welfare of a community.[22] The caste system of Hindu society identifies individuals by their social locations; their rights and responsibilities are determined by their ascribed social status; the dignity or lack of dignity of individuals is due not to their worth as human individuals, not to the rational natures they have as a result of being human, but to the fact that they were born in certain families belonging to certain castes. That this is repressive of individual human dignity is apparent.

When the group, the city-state, or the caste is of higher significance than individual members there is clearer warrant for denying life or limiting the range of activities of individuals than there is when the individual is

22. For an account of this change, see Arthur W. H. Adkins, *Merit and Responsibility* (Oxford: Oxford University Press, 1960).

prior. Modern Western democratic states continue to recognize the validity of such a view in emergencies when the well-being of the nation is threatened either by external foes or by certain forms of socially disruptive behavior within. It is the normal priority of the dignity of the individual, however, that sustains individual "rights." It warrants the requirements of "informed consent" by patients before physicians can intervene in their bodily process. It warrants free speech and the free exercise of religion. It warrants legal measures to break down discrimination against individuals because of accidents of birth in one race or another, or as female rather than as male. It warrants resistance to arbitrary exercise of power by the state or by individuals over others, and resistance to tyranny, whether of an individual ruler or of a community. It is the first defense against a Thrasymachus, against any view that makes the holding of power a legitimation for its use against others without sufficient reason. It is the priority of the dignity of the individual over that of the community that requires that restraints of individuals rather than exercise of individual capacities be justified. One does well to pause to consider these benefits of an anthropocentric ethics when proposing an interpretation which might in some way undermine them.

Although the Enlightenment was a significant movement in justifying and developing the dignity of the individual, there are biblical roots which also led to it and sustained it. Within the moral codes of the Jewish people in biblical times there are clear safeguards against infringements of individual rights. Certainly a deity who knows the very number of the hairs on our heads, and provides for our needs, as is portrayed in the teachings of Jesus, cares about individual persons. To be sure, the dignity of the individual was frequently violated in the life of the institutional church; any number of threats to its presumed corporate well-being were sufficient to remove persons by excommunications, interdictions, and death. The deplorable aspects of the history, however, do not mitigate the fact that there are teachings in the tradition which support the dignity of the individual. To be sure, the institution and its participants had a long history of persecution of those who did not adhere to their judgments about the truth; again, however, the seeds of respect for individual dignity within the tradition cannot be denied. And certainly on the point of salvation, the individual has been of central importance throughout the history of the Christian churches. These matters must be recalled when one begins to propose any religious interpretation which might lead to a weakening of support for individual dignity.

Many evidences from human experience attest to the fact that individuals prize their freedom, their capacities to be self-determining agents. At least in Western societies there is a large body of literature that indicates how in the development from childhood to adulthood persons enlarge the range of their self-determination, emancipate themselves from the bonds of family, and develop automony. The notion of resentment, so forcefully developed by Nietzsche and refined by Max Scheler, indicates the power of the desire for autonomy against personal and social forces that restrict the realm of self-determination in individuals and in groups. [23] The concept of alienation refers in part to the sense of resentment that occurs when any meaningful self-determination of the destiny of persons or groups is destroyed by the ways in which the economic and social orders are developed. Despair occurs when persons feel trapped by forces that apparently are beyond their control, when they feel fated, when they foresee no possibilities of exercising their capacities in their own best interests. Moral accountability itself assumes the capacity for agency, the capacity to develop purposes and to exercise powers in accordance with them. It is only when persons are judged unable to be self-determining agents due to illness or other restraints that they are excused from accountability for their actions, or that other persons have a right to act on their behalf. Any interpretation of life that seriously qualifies this valuation of human capacities for agency can run counter to some of the deepest of human sentiments and to the fundamental conditions for the moral ordering of human life. These human sentiments and these conditions are strongly protected by anthropocentric ethics.

Political and social arrangements which protect a wide range of individual choices are based on the assumptions of this capacity for agency and the dignity of individuals. Duress and coercion, torture and terrorism, run counter to cherished freedom and dignity. Arrangements are made in the political, economic, and social orders for the participation of individuals in the decisions which have significant effects on their lives. Political democracy ensures the participation of individuals in the selection of those who will exercise power over them and on their behalf. The market economy offers a range of choices to persons not only in terms of selection of what they choose to consume but also in determination of how their productive capacities will be engaged. The reward systems of meritocracies are adjusted to the achievements of individuals utilizing their capacities; persons are not determined by the accident of birth to be sweepers or farmers but can aspire to achieve what is in their interests, within the constraints of a given economic order. Individuals choose their marriage partners; they are not subject to arranged marriages or to selection of mates within a given ethnic or religious group.

23. F. Nietzsche, *On the Genealogy of Morals*, trans. Walter Kaufman and R. J. Hollingdale (New York: Vintage Books, 1969), pp. 73–76. Max Scheler, *Ressentiment*, trans. William W. Holdheim, ed. Lewis A. Coser (New York: Schocken Books, 1972).

Indeed, forceful critics of existing social orders frequently base their judgments on the failure of existing societies to fulfill the principles of freedom and human dignity. Ethnic identification is not a politically significant feature for a citizen; whether one is black or white, a Swede or a Latin, one has a right to participate in the electoral process. Race and other forms of social identification are not economically significant; all persons have rights of access to employment and promotion on the basis of their qualifications. If social and economic arrangements make it impossible for some individuals and groups to fulfill their basic needs for sustenance, the system is judged to be unfair to them, for they have not chosen to be in their predicaments. Compensation of one kind or another is due them. Any interpretation of life that would provide the slightest warrant for an alteration of such social, political, and economic arrangements must be espoused only with the greatest care and forethought.

Perilous consequences of an extreme anthropocentrism, however, have been recognized by individuals, communities, and institutions. If the dignity of the human species is presumed to warrant its exploitation of nature for the sake of not only human survival and a modicum of comfort but also for the sake of satisfying whimsical desires, humanity is in trouble. The conditions of dependency of man on the rest of nature are such that violation of them leads to threats to human well-being and, in extreme instances, in threats to human survival. People in our time are acutely conscious of this. With the expansion of human population, with the decline of new frontiers of undisturbed nature, and with the consumption of natural resources necessary to maintain the standards of living known in the wealthier parts of the world, there is a new recognition of this dependence, and a qualification of the penchant to exploit nature heedlessly for the sake of uncurbed human desires. The discussion in recent times of the "limits to growth" points to a consciousness of human dependence upon nature, whether or not one is persuaded by the arguments for or against specific proposals. The capacities of a technological culture to resolve many problems that the rapid development of this culture has created cannot be denied; one of the wonders of our species is its ingenuity in exploring, developing, and using new resources. But limits must be faced; no one has argued that there is an automatic assurance that our planet can support American standards of living for all the human beings that can be born. Human distinctiveness is a warrant for special dignity, but people must be seen in their interrelations with the rest of the natural order for the sake of human well-being itself. If one is to wait for "natural correctives" to exploitation there will be vast costs of human misery and suffering due to malnutrition, starvation, and other disasters.

The high value placed on individual human dignity, if this warrants unlimited individual rights and liberties, is also, in the extreme, self-destructive. Restraints on individual claims to fulfillment of desires are present in natural communities such as the family; there is a recognition of natural duties to others which require the curbing of individual desires by parents and children, and by siblings in relation to each other. Restraints are present in the legal system of the nation, though the limits of tolerable dissent, tolerable exercise of individuality, tolerable aggrandizement of individually controlled wealth and power are not always clear. At the very least we are not permitted to exercise our self-determination in such a way that we violate the rights of others to exercise their self-determination; yet even in this regard the lines of permissibility are not precise. In extreme cases in which the survival of the nation-state is threatened there is little dissent to the right of the state to conscript persons for military duty and to subject them to extreme threats to their lives for the sake of the well-being of the nation as a whole. The very conditions necessary for the sustenance of individual dignity and individual rights require restraints upon the range of choice and the scope of activities of individuals. Anarchy is intolerable; the perils of extreme individualism are recognized.

The hard questions come up in the particular circumstances of uncertainty where the claims based on an extreme anthropocentrism must be curbed by recognition of the order of relationships between human beings and nature, between individuals and other individuals, between individuals and groups, and between groups. The point to be made here is a general one. Anthropocentrism has sustained the dignity and the rights of humans, collectively and individually. This cannot be denied. But even from a view that gives highest value to the human species, limits must be recognized. While an interpretation of life that runs counter to the anthropocentric perspective raises serious questions about how such dignity and rights can be protected, an interpretation of life from a perspective of extreme anthropocentrism raises other questions of at least equal moral importance.

One must look carefully at the perils of an ethics which is based upon "objective" material norms derived from social needs, from nature, or from God. The direction taken in this chapter is susceptible to grave difficulties in terms of how it might excessively curb human activity.

In the current turn toward "ecological ethics," one peril is already perceptible: a romanticism about nature. It is foolhardy at our stage of cultural development to think that we can return to a primitive "natural order"; it is also morally shortsighted. The history of human culture is in part the history of the development of human defenses against the threats of nature. An undue reverence for the processes of nature puts the existence of individual human lives and of groups at high risk. The mosquitoes that carry malaria, parasites that thrive in polluted water and human waste, severe winters in vast regions of the globe, earthquakes, droughts in Africa and elsewhere, and rats that carry bubonic plague are all parts of the natural order. The catalogue of items from nature that threaten and debilitate human well-being could be extended almost indefinitely. If a turn toward a theocentric ethics implied an uncritical turn toward nature as indubitably beneficial to our species (or to other species), one would clearly have an intolerably romantic basis for the conduct of human life. Reverence for nature of this sort can be criticized from many standpoints, including theological ones.[24] Respect for nature can be distinguished from reverence. It does not involve a romantic sacralization or moralization of nature, but it does involve a recognition of human interdependence with nature, some limits to human exploitation of it, and some guidance in how it is to be used.

The turn toward theocentric ethics requires that consideration be given to the "larger good," and even to the "good of the whole." This could, if not carefully developed, lead to the suppression of the well-being of the species, or of individuals, for the sake of a "whole." Grave issues have to be acknowledged. How is the "larger good" to be defined? What "whole" does one define as the "totality" whose good is to be the objective of human activity? And, who is to define that good? Answers to such questions are susceptible to deep influence by the immediate self-interests of individuals or communities in power. History is replete with occasions in which persons in power have defined what is the good of a "whole" in such a way that tyranny has been justified and the overriding of individual rights and liberties has been warranted, and the net effects have been an increment of human evil in the world. In the name of "national interest," infringements of the rights of individuals and groups have occurred; in the name of threats to "national security," the FBI has harassed Martin Luther King and others; in the name of the "manifest destiny," imperialistic activities have been authorized; in the name of the "unity of the church," heretics have been burned. If, in the name of a theocentric ethics, one must begin to define a larger good, or a good of the whole, extreme care must be taken to ensure that proper individual and group interests are protected. The processes and procedures for determining such larger goods have to be carefully delineated.

Probably every effort to define a collective or larger good has been costly to the interests of certain individuals or groups. This, I take it, is inevitable. For the sake of the security of Western democratic societies, and the defense of the values that sustain them, thousands of individual lives were sacrificed in World War II. For the sake of economic stability,

---

24. A theological point is made in a joke my father always told in Swedish. The pastor calls on Farmer Lindstrom. Pastor: "That surely is a beautiful cornfield the Lord has given you, Lindstrom." Lindstrom: "Ya, Pastor, but you should have seen it when the Lord had it alone."

the United States has tolerated an unemployment rate of six or seven percent. For the sake of flood control and the provision of recreational resources, farmers have been evicted from their productive land. For the sake of developing better medical care, experimentation on human beings is necessary, and lives have been put at risk. For the sake of providing electric power in the face of the depletion of other sources, persons are put at risk from nuclear accidents. For the sake of the well-being of future generations it appears that some restrictions of the activities of the present generation are required. Voluntary sacrifice of individual or group interest, while it clearly is a virtue commended by Christianity, is hardly an un-ambiguous moral obligation. Nor does one find thousands of persons, including devout Christians, lining up to demonstrate that no greater love hath man than this, that he risk his interests for the sake of the community. The question necessarily emerges: Which interests of individuals or groups will be sacrificed for the sake of a larger good? Is there a fair, or just, way to distribute the required sacrifices? Is there a way to compensate those who must sacrifice for the sake of a larger good? What potential benefits for "society" or for future generations are sufficient to warrant sacrifices by individuals or groups? What is a defensible "risk/benefit ratio," as current terminology states this issue?

Perhaps the most awesome prospect of a turn toward a theocentric ethics is the possibility of a religious fanaticism about particular moral solutions. Perhaps no one is to be feared more than a devout Christian or a Muslim behind a gun (or nuclear weapon) who is absolutely certain that his cause is God's cause. Certainly belief that a cause is the will of God can vastly raise the motivation of persons to fulfill it. For the sake of the liberation of Jerusalem from the infidels (supplemented by many other motives on the part of the participants), crusades were carried on through several centuries of the history of the church. With the same certainty men took arms against the pagan tribes of northern and eastern Europe and against Jews; the truth of the church had to be accepted, even if by forced conversions. Slavery was defended in the United States on the basis of the notion that blacks were ordained by God to be slaves. The ancient Hebrew people conquered the Canaanites in the certainty that Yahweh had promised them the land; with similar certainty Calvinists in South Africa conquered black tribes in the nineteenth century. If every act of human sexual intercourse is to be open to the transmission of life because the biological order is the divine order, then regardless of consequences there is no adequate reason to use artificial means of conception control. If abortion is described as murder, and murder is clearly against God's law, then there can be no occasions on which induced abortions can be justified. Because the use of alcoholic beverages was believed to be contrary to the moral law of God, Protestants, with the passion of crusaders, supported the prohibition amendment to the Constitution of the United States.

Moral certainty grounded in the will of God, for religious persons, provides the greatest possible authorization for either refraining from or engaging in certain actions and causes. The authorization is no longer simply human rationality, social custom, or civil law: It is the highest authorization; it is Divine. For devoutly religious persons, obligations to God supersede obligations to oneself, to the community, and to the state; the sense of obligation is intensified immeasurably. There is no stronger possibility of moral fanaticism than this, though there are clearly the secular equivalents to it in modern cultures. Any argument for theocentric ethics must take this into account. What can be claimed about "God's will," and the degree of certitude with which the claim can be made, are serious concerns in the light of the possibilities of religious moral fanaticism. Substantive theological issues are involved. How we can know what the ultimate power and orderer wills must be specified. The always present possibilities of self-deception and corruption of will and purpose have to be taken seriously.

This "moral pause" is necessary in the development of the direction of this book. To omit it would be to ignore critical objections. The resolutions proposed, however, are matters for subsequent development.

A Religious and Theological Pause

Previous sections of this chapter have indicated points at which this present work takes somewhat different directions from those of some aspects of traditional Christianity. The quotation from Ernst Troeltsch in many respects covers the major shift. Theology and religion remain "Ptolemaic" in basic outlook. Obviously this does not imply that theologians defend a geocentric view of the universe against a scientific point of view. For theologians, however, the focus of the divine reality remains very much on our planet and on man. This strikes me as odd and wrong, not only in light of what we know about the world of nature of which we are a part but also as a distortion of some of the basic intuitions of Western religious experience (as well as aspects of Eastern religious experience), intuitions that human life is part of and depends upon realities grander, more majestic, more awesome than humanity itself. While there is ample evidence that the Western religious traditions are deeply concerned for the salvation and well-being of man, there is evidence also that they have perceived the power, the glory, the majesty, and the "excellence" of God. While Western theology might have been Ptolemaic until modern centuries on scientific grounds, Western religion has also contained a significant "Copernican" element from biblical times forward. One needs only to recall that while Moses was assured that Yahweh had a special mission and concern for the ancient Hebrew people, he was told that the answer to the question "What is his name?" was "I am who I am."[25] One recalls the words of Solomon at the dedication of the temple, "But will God indeed dwell on the earth? Behold heaven and the highest heaven cannot contain thee; how much less this house which I have built."[26] One recalls the great ascription of glory in the first letter to Timothy, "To the King of ages, immortal, invisible, the only God, be honor and glory for ever and ever."[27]

The dominant strand of piety and theology, however, has focused on the grandeur of man, on the purposes of the Deity for man, and primarily on the salvation and the well-being of man. From those perceptions of the distinctiveness of our species that are recognized in the accounts of the creation has come a tendency to assume that the intentions and activities of the Deity are primarily oriented toward human benefits. Indeed, in some cases the divine purposes seem to be exclusively oriented toward human benefits: the salvation of man is claimed to be the ultimate intention of God. I have noted the tendency to assume that, because man seems to be at the top of the hierarchy of being, the well-being of man necessarily is the primary purpose of all other aspects of creation and of the Deity. To alter the primacy of this focus, I hasten to say, does not necessarily lead to the equating of the significance of man with the significance of animals, plants and trees, or the significance of hydrogen, oxygen, carbon, and the other essential elements of life. But it does require that man as a species, individuals as persons, and human communities be redescribed in relation to other aspects of nature, to powers beyond their control, to a destiny which is not in human hands, and to a termination which, as Troeltsch vividly describes, will be without us. This shift does not imply that human well-being is not sustained by the ultimate power and orderer of life, that human capacities (developed through evolution, for which we can take no credit) are not distinctive and to be valued, or that the forces and powers beyond our control are antihuman. But it does require a perception of the human species in relation to the vast ordering of life which also must, religiously speaking, have some meaning in the purposes of God. While man, by virtue of human capacities, has a special dominion, nonetheless *all* things are "good," and not just good for us. Special dominion implies special accountability as much as special value.

25. Ex. 3:13-14. R.S.V.
26. I Kings 8:27. R S.V.
27. I Tim. 1:17. R.S.V.

Surely those distinctive human capacities to know, to reason, and to act are grounds for the human preoccupation with the human condition. Self-consciousness is, to be purposely tautological, consciousness of self. Attention to self comes naturally. The biblical and Western religious traditions grew in part out of the consciousness of selves as accountable beings, and as accountable ultimately in the presence of the Creator. The experiences of shame and guilt arise out of this consciousness. The predicament of man is the ego; the external powers are not pleased with human conduct; the gods must be placated or appeased. Thus it is understandable that the preoccupation with the human condition leads to a preoccupation with the means of liberation from guilt, redemption from a sinful condition, release from the conditions of finitude—in short, salvation. The anthropocentric, indeed egocentric, turn of religion is no deep mystery and requires little explanation. But man becomes excessively preoccupied with his own situation, and with his own situation in relation to God. The chief purpose of religious life becomes a resolution of the human predicament, not a turning toward the sustaining and threatening powers of life or, ultimately, toward God. To play on the words of Solomon, in the dominant tradition not only will God dwell with man on earth but the primary purpose of his activity will be to provide a satisfactory solution to man's religious and moral predicaments. It becomes easy to ignore, in this preoccupation, that heaven and the highest heavens cannot contain the Deity. Religion itself becomes excessively anthropocentric, Ptolemaic; God is thought to exist and act almost exclusively for the benefit of man. The Christian story, beginning with the Apostle Paul, has intensified this concentration. Indeed, one of the consequences of the direction taken in this book is to propose an alteration of the egocentric, anthropocentric concern of Christian piety and Christian theology. The salvation of man is not the chief end of God; certainly it is not the exclusive end of God. Concern for human salvation must be placed in a wider context than that of Ptolemaic religion. The preoccupation with self has to be altered; the proper orientation is not primarily toward self but toward God—to the honoring of God, and to the ordering of life in relation to what can be discerned of the divine ordering.

Other points at which the direction of this book requires alteration of some traditional themes of Christian piety and theology will be taken up in subsequent chapters. But there are continuities with the tradition as well as alterations of it. Much of what the idea of the sovereignty of God has traditionally referred to is encompassed by this direction. The sense of the dependence of man upon sustaining powers and events beyond human control points toward that. The awareness that the destiny of the world is not in human hands, that the beginning of creation was an event unimaginably beyond the powers of man, and that its termination will inexorably occur, points to that. A great deal of what the Christian tradition has understood about human life is included. Human finitude, not merely with reference to the finality of death, but also to the many constraints imposed on life and action is retained and emphasized. The possibilities of development of culture and capacities for human action, and the sense of accountability to the larger order and ultimate orderer of life is included. The tradition's perceptions of human faults of sloth and pride, of "idolatry" understood as fixation on objects not worthy of our full confidence, and of man's disordering of life, are included. These and other aspects of continuity with the Christian tradition are developed in subsequent chapters.

As I have already indicated, modern scientific accounts of the origins of the universe, of our planetary system, of life and its evolution, of the evolution of human life, of the interrelatedness of aspects of nature and culture, and of the termination of our planetary system are brought to bear upon the theological position that is taken, and in turn upon the theological ethics that are developed.

Just as it was important to take a "moral pause" in order to assess some of the consequences that are likely to occur as a result of the direction taken in this book, so a "religious and theological pause" is important. Every more or less systematic theology or theological ethics is selective from within the rich variety of strands, concepts, images, and even purposes that are present in the Christian tradition. Thus the necessity of selecting certain strands, and of a reinterpretation of the place and significance of various strands, is not novel. It always takes place in theology; it has taken place throughout the history of theology. Nor is it novel to develop a religious and theological perspective in such a way that it takes into account concepts and theories of man, nature, and society that have their origins in other bodies of intellectual endeavor such as natural and human sciences or philosophy. Historians of theology demonstrate over and over how constructive or systematic positions rely upon these sources, often more than the theologian is aware.

Nonetheless, some projection of the turns that I am taking with reference to some rather central themes of traditional Christianity is worthwhile. Just as one must pause before endorsing an interpretation of life that could undermine certain traditional moral values, so one must pause before developing a theological position which significantly alters themes or strands of piety and theology that have been rather central to the tradition for centuries. Writers of theology have taken account of the points at which critical objections to their views can be made. This procedure was a central feature of the method of disputation that shaped medieval theology, as any reader of Thomas Aquinas knows; one finds it present with less formal clarity in Calvin, Edwards, Barth, and many more. One point at which I have turned from a central aspect of the tradition is the displacement of the salvation of persons as the principal point of reference for religious piety and for the ordering of theological principles. To many readers this might well make the position taken unrecognizable as authentically Christian. The warm and friendly deity of a great deal of contemporary piety is displaced; the assurance that regardless of how difficult and tragic human life is, God will make it right, at least for persons who trust in him, is brought under serious questions. So also is that notion of the retributive justice of God on which has hung so much of the fervor of Christian preaching and practice, whether in the revival sermons of Jonathan Edwards or in the sacrament of penance in the Roman Catholic church. These are matters not to be altered or discarded lightly; any displacement of them or radical reinterpretation of them must be undertaken with care.

There is nothing novel about the important theological-ethical issues that come to the fore here. The question of the justice of God or the gods has occupied the human community in the ancient Near East, in the literature of the Greek tradition from Homer through the tragedians and forward,[28] and in Hinduism and Islam. The statement of the issue has, I believe, always assumed that God or the gods had to be moral as the "moral" was defined by human beings. The problem of theodicy itself assumes this principle. To interpret the justice of God differently does not make one indifferent to human suffering and flourishing, but it does set these concerns within a different and wider theological context.

Conclusions

I have in this chapter further developed some of the indications of the central thrust of this work. The continuity is principally in the turn from anthropocentrism to a more theocentric focus of attention. Here I have foreshadowed further developments of the argument by indicating that ethics set in a theocentric context, where the *theos* is not the guarantor of human benefits, may not be recognizable as ethics in terms of the most common understandings of it in the secular and religious traditions of the West. I have foreshadowed further developments in the argument by indicating that some substantive matters of traditional Christian piety and theology come under question in light of the views developed. I have opened the way to some uncomfortable conclusions. If God is "for man," he may not be for man as the chief end of creation . The chief end of God may not be the salvation of man. Man's place in relation to the universe

28. See Marvin H. Pope, ed. and trans., *Job,* 3d ed. (Garden City, N.Y.: Doubleday Anchor Bible, 1973), pp. lvi–lxxi.

has to be rethought, as does man's relation to God. The moral imperative that I shall develop in due course is this: we are to conduct life so as to relate to all things in a manner appropriate to their relations to God. If the relating of all things in a manner appropriate to their relations to God does not guarantee benefits to man as we traditionally perceive such benefits, the consequences can be both religiously and morally uncomfortable. What we judge to be good for man, or for a human person, or some human group, may not be in accord with the ordering purposes of God, insofar as they can be discerned. The chief end of man may not be salvation in a traditional Christian sense; it may be to honor, to serve, and to glorify (celebrate) God (as the Calvinists have always said but not always believed and practiced). Human purposes and human conduct have to be evaluated not simply on the basis of considerations derived from reflection about what is good for man. Rather, reflection is needed on how human life is to be related to a moral ordering objective to our species. It may be that the task of ethics is to discern the will of God— a will larger and more comprehensive than an intention for the salvation and well-being of our species, and certainly of individual members of our species. Yet the conditions for this discernment are not such as to provide absolute certainty about God's purposes. And thus, moral life will continue to have its risks. It will have its "necessities," and in many circumstances it will be tragic from human points of view. I have opened the way to the possibility of such conclusions.

3

Convictions and Procedures
An Interlude

I have indicated my interpretation of various cultural and religious circumstances to which I am responding, and the basic direction or thrust of my response. The reader has been alerted to some of the critical objections that can be taken. Now an interlude is in order to expose and develop the basic convictions and procedures that inform and direct this work: the priority of experience, its highly social character, and the historically conditioned character of theological development. This chapter does not further the substance of the argument but briefly defends some of the convictions on which it is based.

Convictions: The Priority of Human Experience

Human experience is prior to reflection. We reflect on human experience itself, and on objects perceived, interpreted, and known through our experiences of them and through the experiences of others. Religion and morality are aspects of human experience; theology and ethics are not only articulations of ideas in relation to the ideas others have expressed but are ideas about aspects of experience. Experience is social; it is a process of interaction between persons, between persons and natural events, and between persons and historical events. Its significance is explained and its meanings assessed in communities that share common objects of interest and attention and share some common concepts, symbols, and theories. Experience is not only socially generated; it is socially tested. And it is experience of others, of "things" objective to human persons. This is the case in the sciences, in ethics, and in theology; it is the case in all ways of knowing and understanding.

Our primary concern is with religion and morality. Theology and ethics are reflections on religion and morality; they are the constructs, concepts, theories, and principles which are tendered both to explain and to justify religion and morality. An experiential priority, however, requires attention. Whatever might be said about theology and ethics necessarily refers to human experiences. Indeed, there is no way in which a certain kind of anthropocentrism can be avoided. If there is knowledge of God it is human knowledge of God; it is knowledge of God mediated through human experiences, either of one's own, of a community in which one participates, or of another person (and particularly those "paradigmatic" persons whose experience and teaching is deemed to give authentic knowledge of God). Knowledge of what is right and what is good for human beings is gained from reflection on experiences, on what constitutes right actions and right relationships, and on what constitutes human flourishing and human evil. Neither theology nor ethics has fulfilled its intellectual purpose if it merely describes religious and moral experiences, or religious and moral dimensions and aspects of experience. Reflections move from

115

experience and properly take on a degree of abstraction; judgments are made not only about the adequacy of what is said with reference to more primary experiences but also to the "objects" experienced and the claims that are made about them. As theologians have long recognized, we have knowledge of God in relation to man; indeed, even such knowledge of God in relation to the natural order as we might have is derived from human knowledge of that order. There is no avoiding the truism that man is the knower, and that the known comes through human experiences of one or many sorts. There is no avoiding the truism that man is the measurer: language, concepts, percepts, quantifications, theories, and tests of truth and adequacy are all human activities, and thus aspects of human experience.

The force and implications of these truisms, however, needs to be felt. Experience is prior to reflection. This is not to deny that there are reflective elements present in the ordering of even very primary experiences; the human mind or brain is not an unorganized and unorganizing receptor of all the sensations that it can possibly receive. For theology particularly, I believe it is necessary to stress this priority of experience. When doctrines become dogmas, they seem to take on an authority of their own, or one conferred upon them by ecclesiastical authorities. It is all too easily forgotten that doctrines and dogmas arose out of the experiences of persons and communities in the past, and thus are conditioned by the individual, natural, and historical circumstances in which those persons and communities lived. The doctrine of "creation out of nothing," for example, cannot be explained without understanding that it stems from human experience of the mystery of life and efforts to provide a way of thinking about, relating to, and accounting for that mystery.

In order to be clear, thinkers distinguish particular kinds of experience. One can think about what distinguishes aesthetic from moral or religious experiences; one can think about what distinguishes aesthetic expressions in human culture from religious expressions. This effort to be clear has great merit. In its absence unnecessary confusion reigns. An enthusiastic response to the beauty of the sun setting behind the Lofoten Islands in arctic Norway clearly does not involve a moral judgment. The judgment that murder is wrong is not an aesthetic judgment (murder may be aesthetically ugly, but it is not morally wrong on that account).

The differentiations, however, can be exaggerated. If one, for example, thinks about the objects experienced, it is possible to have aesthetic, religious, and moral responses to the same object not only at the same time but commingled with each other. An experience of the reality of God would be, on the face of it, a religious experience. Yet there is a tradition which perceives beauty in God; the human response to God then has aesthetic aspects or dimensions. There is a tradition which speaks of

God as the moral commander, or as the ultimate moral orderer of life, and thus a moral aspect or dimension is central to the religious experience. For analytical purposes we might distinguish between the beautiful, the holy, and the moral aspects of the object, God; we might attempt to distinguish between the aesthetic, religious, and moral aspects of the experience of God. But the complexities of experience resist the divisions which analysis makes for purposes of clear thinking.

Various persons listen to performances of Bach's *St. Matthew Passion,* or Haydn's oratorio *The Creation.* From the point of view of religious interest, each celebrates, both in the text and in the music, central themes in the Christian religious heritage. In each case text and music refer to events that are interpreted to have deep religious significance. "O, Sacred Head Now Wounded" can evoke a depth of piety in Christians that has extraordinary richness and power. "The Heavens declare the Glory of God" can raise the spirits of the devout believer to heights of joy far beyond what the silent reading of a Psalm with the same theme can do. It is difficult from the perspective of religious piety to distinguish the aesthetic from the religious aspects both of the compositions and of the experience of hearing them. Yet surely each can be viewed as basically an aesthetic object, and the experience of many listeners is primarily, if not exclusively, an aesthetic one. From an aesthetic perspective it is purely a matter of convention that the *Passion* is performed during Lent; it could just as well be performed during Advent. From the perspective of Christian piety it would be as odd, if not shocking, to hear the *Passion* during Advent as it would be to hear Bach's *Christmas Oratorio* during Holy Week. While distinctions can be made between aesthetic and religious aspects of objects of experience, and of the human experience of the objects, they are distinctions made in part in relation to individual and group perceptions. Experience is prior to the distinctions, and except in the extreme instances such as the aesthetic response to a sunset and the moral response to murder, one ought not draw them too sharply. Experience resists, to some extent, our concepts and our analyses.

Not only are distinctions made between the religious, the moral, and the aesthetic. In the analysis of human subjects distinctions have traditionally been made between affections or passions, intellect or cognition, and volition. In moral analysis, for example, many scholars seek to confine the morally relevant features of agents to the cognitive and volitional aspects. This is done, it seems to me, in order to delineate sharply between the moral and the nonmoral, the moral and the premoral. Since morality pertains to human action, and human action relies upon human agency, and human agency requires both the formation of purposes or intentions and the direction of the "will" by those purposes, the key features of human subjects are asserted to be cognitive-intellective and volitional. Passions and affections are judged to be nonmoral, or premoral; they pertain to inclinations which seem not to be fully subject to purposive direction and volitional constraints. Or they are the preconditions of capacities to act which are to be directed by purpose and will. Certainly another reason for either excluding or diminishing the importance of affections and passions in moral theory is that they can be very unreliable guides to the right and the good. Indeed, untamed by constraints of will, and untutored by intellectually formed moral purposes, they are instinctual, erratic, and volatile. They are judged to be those aspects of human nature that are most continuous with other animals, whereas the capacities for intellectual determination of purposes and for determination of will" distinguish human beings.

Prescriptive moral theories all rest upon descriptive accounts of human life, particularly of the features of human agency that are relevant to morality. There is an inevitable circularity to moral theory, though it can be a large and nonvicious circle. The circle can be drawn from different starting points. A theory of the nature of morality, or a prescriptive theory of ethics, can begin the circle, and from it human capacities and actions are interpreted, selected, and developed as the distinctly morally relevant features. Or, a theory of the nature and characteristics of human beings can begin the circle; what is said to distinguish morality is governed by that theory. Kant's ethical theory and Kant's account of human action are consistent with each other. Thomas Aquinas's account of the nature of human acts is consistent with his moral theory. Freud's account of human persons and their behavior is determinative of a Freudian "theory of morality." Reinhold Niebuhr's account of the nature of man determines to a considerable extent his views of ethics and the recommendations he makes for action. One cannot have an ethics of virtue if one's account of the morally relevant features of persons excludes the capacities for habituation of morally approvable characteristics. One cannot have a prescriptive ethical theory based on persons as rational, autonomous agents if one's account of human nature and human activities seriously qualifies either rationality or autonomy. The distinctions between affections, intellect, will, and appetite are useful to aid our understanding of the descriptive accounts of human life on which various moral theories rely, and our understanding of the strengths and weaknesses of various prescriptive ethical theories. No contemporary writer claims that these terms refer to separate human faculties, as if each named a self-subsistent entity existing somewhere in the human mind or body. Yet the distinctions can, and in my judgment often do, falsify the unity of the human self, and lead to an underestimation of the interrelations and interpenetrations of the capacities conceptually distinguished. Experience is prior to the distinctions; morality as an aspect of human experience might not be as neatly divisible into aspects of the person as some moral theorists hold. Indeed, morality can be viewed as an aspect of experiences that can be described primarily in "nonmoral" terms, and not as a distinct kind of experience. It is, for example, an aspect of political behavior. Similarly, religion as an aspect of human experience might not be as neatly divisible between the affective, the volitional, and the cognitive as is often claimed.

In morality and in religion there are affective as well as cognitive and volitional aspects of experience. To be sure, there are theories of ethics that are rationalistic, that posit a capacity to detach oneself from affective inclinations toward certain values and certain moral beliefs in order to find those that are rationally universalizable. There are also theories that relegate morality to the realm of the purely emotive and understand morality as a matter of pro- or con- attitudes. There are theories which defend the view that there is a natural inclination of the affections and the will toward the good. The good, however, is not merely inclined toward or felt; it is also known, and thus there is a cognitive aspect as well. If one begins with human experience, it seems to me that in the rawest moments of moral concern these aspects of the self are commingled. For example, in the perception of an event in which a person is clearly being taken advantage of, one is affectively moved by a sense of injustice being done; one implicitly if not rationally has made a judgment that what is being done is unjust or unfair, and one is normally motivated to rectify the unfairness if one can. The order of experience is not the order of justification. One does not have a theory of justice by which to evaluate what is occurring in the event, and then to determine on the basis of this that justice is being violated. One does not make a rational assessment of how the principle of justice pertains to the facts of the matter, in the light of that make a judgment and subsequently "signal" the will in some way to do something about it. I do not intend to demean these time-honored distinctions as analytical tools; we cannot get along without them. But all three aspects are present in the ordinary course of moral experience, and a theory of morality has to take all three into account.

Religion, it has been argued, is a matter of the affections or the emotions. This I shall defend. It is not merely a matter of emotions in terms of some "high" that occurs in a response to a liturgy or to a sermon; it is more settled than that, and thus one needs to speak about the relations of affections to settled dispositions. And, as Jonathan Edwards—that fine assessor and grader of religious affections—well knew, religious affections can be deceptive unless they are examined in relation to some cognitive and some more volitional aspects of life. There are those who have espoused theories of religion "within the limits of reason alone." Kant is the most famous of such persons, but there are contemporary versions of such theories.[1] Such views surely are insufficient with reference to the religious aspects of experience as these have been described by phenomenologists of religion, as well as to actual experiences of piety in all religions. It is, of course, correct to take the cognitive into account. St. Augustine, for whom love (not merely an emotion but an orientation of the self toward objects) was the primary source of motivation, understood that you cannot love what you do not know. That is, there is some inchoate if not elaborated awareness of what it is that evokes an affective religious response. Whether that "object" is "real" in the same sense that phenomena are is a theological question; but surely it has reality in the perception of the person whose affectivity is evoked. Myths, religious traditions, and concepts are provided by cultures and give "knowledge" of that which is loved or feared, that which inspires. Just as in morality the work of the intellect assesses the reliability of more affective orientations toward values, so in religion it is the work of the intellect to examine, clarify, and conceptualize the object of affections. Religion is also a matter of the will; it is a matter of an attitude or volition, a directedness toward an object, or toward objects, which motivates worship and moral activity.

In dealing with morality and religion as aspects of human experience it is best to consider seriously the interconnections between the affective, volitional, and cognitive features of each, and of their relations to each other in experience before excessively distinguishing and separating religion from morality, or the aspects of the person from each other. Distinctions can be drawn and for purposes of understanding are necessary, but experience is prior to refined distinctions and to some extent resists the imposition of categories we develop. This assertion of the "unity" of experience, prior to our imposition of sharp distinctions on it, is a conviction which informs the present work, though it is not adequately defended here.

Another such conviction is that human experience has a deeply social character. To stress the social character of experience is not to deny that there are private moments of experience, that there are significant differences between individuals in what they experience and in the ways in which they explain and understand the meanings of their experiences. Our experiences occur in the processes of interaction, or in the processes of responding to the natural world and to events. This is no doubt a truism, but it is a truism that is easily ignored.

1. I. Kant, *Religion within the Limits of Reason Alone,* trans. T. M. Green, Hoyt H. Hudson (New York: Harper, 1960). Ronald M. Green, *Religious Reason: The Rational and Moral Basis of Religious Belief* (New York: Oxford University Press, 1978).

Evidences to support this truism are ample. We know that infants develop their mental capacities in a process of interaction with their mothers and other persons, and that in the absence of sufficient stimulation in social contacts even certain capacities for brain development do not occur. The human organism is dependent upon social interaction for its normal development. We know that communication is basic to human experience, and that communication takes place through gestures, language, and symbols that have some common references within a given group. We know that survival itself requires interaction with other persons as well as the use of the natural world of which we are a part. Certainly most of the very critical and most deeply meaningful experiences persons have are in their relationships with others: love is social, hate is social; our self-respect is socially sustained or undermined; our profoundest joy and our deepest grief come into being in human relationships; our moral obligations involve the human community and other individuals; our guilt and shame have social references; our possibilities for individual flourishing are dependent upon the relationships that we have; our sense of alienation, frustration, and despair is often caused by social arrangements. Further rough evidences of the profoundly social character of experience are unnecessary. Their importance for this work is evident in my conviction that, regardless of the commonplace character of these things, they must not be lost sight of in the development of a religious morality and of a theological ethics.

Experiences are articulated, explained, and given their human meanings through cultures, and cultures are the products of societies and social experience. Language, the phenomenon that attracts such a concentration of the interest of many investigations in our time, is the most common evidence of this. Language is a social phenomenon, just as gestures are. Some commonly accepted references of gestures, words, and sentences are required for meaningful communication. The development of language is one of the achievements of our species, and it facilitates the range of things about which we can communicate with one another. The specialization of "languages" is important not only in the creation and preservation of identifiable national communities and cultures, but also of groups with special competencies and interests within nations and across national boundaries.

Language and symbols that are socially meaningful are necessary for shared explanations of events in the world. Anyone without competence in higher mathematics reaches the limits of his or her capacities to comprehend explanations of biological or physical processes in articles in *Science,* for example, when the words have highly technical references and mathematical symbols and formulas are used to provide efficient and accurate explanations. In a similar way, while a scientist might well com-

prehend the meaning of the words in Jonathan Edwards's explanation of
how and why no one was killed in the collapse of the gallery of the
Northampton meeting house in terms of divine providence, the plausibility
of the explanation requires a set of shared beliefs about the special providence of a sovereign deity that governs all events. Differences in the
explanation of actions and events express differences in communities; a
behaviorist construes and explains human conduct in a way different from
an orthodox Freudian, and a believer in the reality of demons sharply
differs from both of them. Symbols, concepts, and theories of explanation
are adequate or inadequate relative to communities that share certain
convictions, whether tested by experiments or merely accepted on the
basis of traditional authority.

The meaning of events and actions, and the explanations of them,
by which individuals and communities understand their larger and more
general significance are also products of societies and cultures. Acceptable
explanations of events largely determine their more general meaning and
significance. The history of the impact of scientific investigations on the
religious interpretation and understanding of nature, and of our human
interrelationships with it, is a good case in point. A religious interpretation
of special providence was undercut by the developments of science in the
seventeenth century; it was replaced by a religious interpretation of the
Deity as the clockmaker. The Deity as the clockmaker had an agonizing
death during the nineteenth century when evidences from geology, biology, and other sciences pointed toward the importance of processes of
development in nature and when no static standard of "perfection" could
any longer be defended. As one set of acceptable explanations displaces
another, the religious and human meanings are either displaced by different meanings or are revised to take account of the newly acceptable
explanations. These are all social events; they are all processes in which
the boundaries of communities that share common symbols are changed.
If one, for example, accepts E. O. Wilson's comprehensive explanations
of human activity, social organization, morality, and religion given in his
secular version of a systematic theology, *On Human Nature,* certain
meanings of human life that have developed in richly textured religious
symbols or in theological concepts and arguments no longer hold.[2] Sociobiological explanations have a totality, or if one accepts them as limited,
they define in part what kinds of other symbols and beliefs about human
life and about historical and natural events are warranted. Or, one can

2. Edward O. Wilson, *On Human Nature* (Cambridge: Harvard University Press,
1978). I reviewed it as a secular systematic theology in *The Hastings Center Report* 9 (1979):
44–45.

choose to live a radically disjointed life in which scientific language has no bearing on religious symbols and explanations.

An example of how explanations drawn from two communities are believed to coincide is Sir John Eccles's first course of Gifford Lectures, *The Human Mystery*.[3] Eccles's scientific investigations of the brain, for which he received a Nobel Prize, and investigations of others are interpreted in such a way that the philosophical judgment of a "dualist-interactionist" theory of the mind-brain relation is defended. This is to be sharply distinguished from a purely materialistic cause-effect accounting of the functions of mind on the basis of biochemical and other physical processes in that remarkable organ protected by our skulls. Eccles's view warrants for him a traditional religious belief that a superior intelligence creates the soul. "It is my thesis that we have to recognize the unique selfhood as being the result of a supernatural creation of what in the religious sense is called a soul."[4] His view also provides a warrant for a political and moral outlook. "I repudiate philosophies and political systems which recognize human beings as mere things with a material existence of value only as cogs in the great bureaucratic machine of the state, which thus becomes a slave state."[5] There is, for this distinguished scientist, a happy coherence between his explanation of the relation of mind to brain and his religious and moral views. A purely materialist view of the operations of mind would not accommodate, or at least not in the same way, the moral and religious meanings of life to which Eccles adheres. Eccles can, in a sense, belong to communities of both explanation and meaning that for others are mutually exclusive.

Meanings and explanations are carried by communities, and their adequacy or validity to persons depends upon the degree to which individuals adhere to the basic beliefs of particular communities. This is clear in Arthur Danto's *Mysticism and Morality*.[6] This study of Eastern morality and religion, concentrating on Hinduism, provides an interesting case of culture conflict. If certain theories about human life held in India are true, for example, the theories of Karma and reincarnation, then morality in the sense in which Western culture understands it is false. The understanding of the meaning and causes of human actions that are supported not only by metaphysical beliefs in Hinduism but also in its religious myths and rituals and its social practices, simply do not sustain the views of human accountability, rational autonomy, and respect for individuals qua persons that ground Western conceptions of morality. The traditional

3. John Eccles, *The Human Mystery* (New York: Springer International, 1979).
4. Ibid., p. 144.
5. Ibid., p. 237.
6. Arthur Danto, *Mysticism and Morality* (New York: Harper Torch Books, 1973). See, for example, pp. 3–45.

Hindu beliefs about human action are, from a Western point of view, simply false. Discourse about the truth or falsity of these beliefs can take place more vigorously now than it could have in the sixteenth century. This opens the possibility for cultural interaction (at least among intellectuals), and thus for testing the adequacy of traditional beliefs. Hindus will be converted to membership in a (loosely defined) Western community, Westerners will be converted to Hindu beliefs, some hybrid communities will arise, or a process of alteration in the symbols and their references will occur in the development of either or both traditions.

Human experiences and their explanations and meanings are seldom completely individualistic. They are shared socially; they have their significance for groups, some of which are sharply defined by tests of membership and others of which are only vaguely delineated. Explanations and meanings are socially interpreted and socially tested. This is no less the case for scientific explanations than it is for religious and moral symbols and theories. To affirm that explanations and meanings are socially tested does not imply that their validity or adequacy is relative to the number of individuals who adhere to them. It is not to argue that there are no more objective references that transcend particular communities by which they can be tested. But even such tests develop as communities interact with each other, as they alter their received traditions and views, and as they evolve into new communities.

Because of the social and historical character of symbols, explanations, and beliefs, any organized community that freezes its requirements for membership according to the symbols and explanations adequate at a particular time is bound to have difficulties, especially in the modern world. At this writing, Pope John Paul II is increasingly exercising institutional authority over the theologians of the Roman Catholic church even when he is also acknowledging that the church erred in the condemnation of Galileo in the seventeenth century. It is undeniable that some of the basic tenets of traditional Roman Catholic morality rested on outmoded Aristotelian biology; if more modern scientific biology provides different factual and theoretical bases for understanding the human organism, then a morality built on errant biology will not stand the test of time. This is not to say that morality is determined by biology, but that morality has to be developed with reference to the most accurate body of facts about that to which it pertains. The communities in which beliefs, symbols, and explanations are tested are several; the process is still social, but the boundaries are extended. Just as theological development has to accept a heliocentric view of our universe, so a religious moral view has to take into account relevant data from biology for some moral purposes; and its moral view might change.

There is no way in which we can be totally relieved of the boundaries of the particular communities to which we belong and the particular periods of culture in which we live and work. Surely there is a proper aspiration to overcome the narrowness of the communal and cultural boundaries, the time- and space-boxes in which we are confined. Development in thought and life occurs as we surpass the achievements of those from whom we have received, as we overcome the biases we recognize in other times and other places, and as we come to an assurance that we have resolved problems that others have not. Surely it is a laudatory accomplishment when descriptions and explanations of human or other aspects of reality achieve a measure of consensus on the part of persons from different cultures and of different political and religious beliefs. We see this in the development of the natural sciences. There might be those who would still audaciously claim that their ideas will not be improved upon, that they have established the universal truth in science, in religion, or in philosophy. The historical record, of course, teaches us to be wary of such claims. To be sure, there are different tests of universalizability in different fields of cultural achievement. There is, no doubt, a progression in natural scientific work that is not matched in the social sciences, in philosophy, and in theology. In the realms of aesthetic life there is change and development but hardly a universal test for "progress." The detailed work of the historians of science has demonstrated that even in science, the least culturally bound arena of modern cultural activity, progress occurs within and between communities. And, even in this area, it is difficult to be emancipated from prior understandings of reality or from cultural biases. The remnants of Aristotelianism impeded progress in science in the seventeenth century; some of the most significant developments in the understanding of evolution in the nineteenth century were marred by the assumption that Caucasians must be at the top of the progressive development of the human species.

Dorothy Sayers, in her reflections on Dante's *The Divine Comedy* and the criticism of it, makes this general point both gracefully and poignantly.

> Our successors will speak of the "Neo-Elizabethans" precisely as we speak of the "Victorians," and in the same tone of voice; "depth-psychology" will take its place in their museums alongside of "faculty-psychology"; "faith in the future" will seem to them as reprehensible as "nostalgia for the past" does to us; and their journalists will use "twentieth century," as ours use "medieval," by way of a handy term of abuse for such crudities, cruelties, and superstitions as they may happen to disapprove. If all truths are period products, then our own standards offer no secure basis for passing judgment on those of former ages; if any

truths have claims on universality, then every claim, old or new, requires to be examined on its merits.[7]

Of course, in certain critical areas of culture and investigation we do not need to argue against all old claims to truth; the contemporary astronomer does not have to take on Ptolemy, or the contemporary biologist Aristotle. But he or she does have to take on the received tradition of theory and observation within the scientific community to demonstrate its inadequacies, point out its errors, and improve the relevant principles of explanation. And the rate of change differs in different enterprises; the literary "Neo-Elizabethans" have had several generations of descendants since 1955. Even where "our own standards" offer a far more secure basis for passing judgment on former ages, they function within communities of shared concepts, procedures, criteria of investigation, and modes of expression.

In ethics and theology the aspirations for universality have their own cultural and communal contexts. In both, strong claims for the universality of particular historical contributions have been made. When "nature" referred primarily to the immutable and eternal, whether in the nature of man, the nature of society, the nature of what we call "nature," or the nature of God, principles of morality or religion that could claim to rest on nature were thought, simply, to be universally true. They were presumed to be free from bounds of time and culture. That apparent coincidence of the operations of the human mind with some of the operations of objective realities which seems a presupposition of some of the startling developments of science was believed to be the case with a whole range of human perceptions. Aristotle's ethics is grounded in his understanding of human nature. Those who would radically reject his ethics, or aspects of them, must reject that understanding in part at least, or the way in which it is relevant to morality, or the notion that there is a "human nature" that is as fixed as he thought. Efforts to achieve knowledge of God naturally, without recourse to a special status for a particular historical tradition or historical figure, have aspired to establish the eternally true principles of ultimate reality. But the "nature" of that reality was understood differently; the emanationism of the Neoplatonists was different from the view of the Stoics; the Deity as process is, we are assured over and over again in the literature, different from "classical theism." It turns out that one has different traditions of natural theology, and different traditions of universalizable ethics. This becomes even clearer in the cross-cultural comparisons between, for example, forms of Hindu philosophy and dominant forms of the West. More superficially and iron-

7. Dorothy L. Sayers, Introduction to Dante, *The Divine Comedy,* vol. 2., *Purgatory* (Baltimore: Penguin Books, 1955), pp. 45–46.

ically, the perception comes to attention when Roman Catholics defend natural-law ethics because it is the tradition of their church.

Efforts to overcome the boundaries of our communities, or to extend the membership in them, cannot and ought not to be demeaned. Practical issues in contemporary culture sustain the motivation for such efforts, as well as that ancient and honorable desire to arrive at Truth. "Pluralism" is the catchall word used to cover the reality of the presence of different moral ideals, different ways of moral life, different approved ends of human action, and different principles of conduct. Any given society in our time has competing values, and as soon as an isolated culture is discovered in the Philippine Islands or in the jungles of the Amazon it becomes the object of curiosity, ethnographic study, and "outside" influence. Where the differences in morality lead to civil strife, to unbearable confusion in the lives of individuals, and to disorders between states, there is a proper motivation to find those beliefs, values, and principles by which disputes can be rationally and peaceably moderated, if not overcome. Significant differences in morality have not been overcome by the general secularization of Western societies, nor by the formation of ethical theories on which all rational persons can presumably agree but philosophers cannot. Lack of success, however, ought not to deter effort, for the effort at least challenges those who adhere to historical and communal particularities to make clear their reasons for their beliefs. It forces them to locate those points at which commonality is possible and those points at which deep differences in judgments continue.

There are those who dream of a unified world culture. They see, with a touch of realism, that a universally acceptable morality cannot be created or sustained without cultural sustenance and nurture. If the present prospect of a more universal culture rests primarily on the worldwide acceptance of science and technology, it has become clear that these features do not eliminate deep differences in moral and religious beliefs. At this writing the Western world is astonished by the vitality of Islam in its vast geographic spread from Morocco to the Philippine Islands. Scientific medicine and folk medicine exist side by side in many parts of the world. The users of modern technology can be believers in astrology. That portion of American Protestantism that is growing at the fastest rate is the least affected by critical examination of religious beliefs. Oral Roberts, the successful television evangelist, is assured that God told him to build his medical school in Tulsa, Oklahoma, even when a variety of evidences indicate that it is not needed. Communities are bounded, and persons can belong to several without even inquiring whether major aspects of each are abrasive to each other.

At the end of this chapter I indicate in three ideal-types what choices I believe a theologian has to make in regard to communal and historical boundedness. Suffice it to say here, I cannot remove myself from a religious perspective informed by a Western religious tradition any more than I can eliminate my membership in a community that is informed by many aspects of modern knowledge. No claim for a simplistic universality can be made. That, however, does not require resignation to the limits of one's communal and historical legacies. Within communities, one's convictions and thoughts are testable; between communities, one's convictions and thoughts are testable so long as they have some references to common realities. But there is no point at which one leaps to a fictive community of persons and ideas that are not in part determined by any community. To that we must all give consent.

Experience is of persons and things that are objective to the self, at least for normal human experience. (Persons may experience the reality of pink elephants during hallucinations, but this experience is not normal.) We react to stimuli at the most elementary physiological level; we respond to other persons and to events. Even when we respond to "ourselves" there is some objectification of an ideal self, the memory of the self in the past, or some aspect of our personal lives on which we focus special attention.

Our thought is frequently prompted by stimulating books and articles that we read, or by events that have a significant impact upon our affections or on the course of our lives. Our actions always have a moment of response to something that is occurring or that we believe is occurring. We put on gloves in response to the cold; we eat in response to pangs of hunger or the desire for an aesthetic experience; we purchase in response to advertising; we laugh in response to acts of comedy; and so forth. Collectively we act in response to events external to ourselves. The nation increases its arms budget in response to a perceived threat from the Warsaw Bloc nations; we give money in response to the presence of starvation in Cambodia or Nigeria; we boycott grapes in response to our understanding of the status of workers in the vineyards of California.

This is all so obvious it appears trite to recall it. Yet it is additional evidence not only of the social character of experience but of the presence of that which is objective to individuals or to communities and which elicits or evokes reactions, responses, and deliberate actions. No matter how much the characteristics of our responses and actions are determined by our communities, or by individual interests and biases, they are nonetheless responses to "other than self," or to objectifications of "self as other." Because there is this objective pole we can engage in "reality checks." We can assess the accuracy and the adequacy of our knowledge and understanding of that to which we are responding. We can make judgments about the significance of what evokes responses in light of the seriousness of consequences and the effectiveness of means of action. We can act collectively because there is a common "other" to which we respond, and a common evaluation of it. We can communicate with each other because our words and symbols refer to a common reality to which we are attending. We can investigate, test our findings, and make judgments about our theories in relation to the work of others because there is a common object of our studies. This is the case for our moral actions as well as our scholarly investigations, for our religious ideas as well as our scientific theories.

Human experience is prior to reflection. We reflect on human experience itself, and on objects perceived, interpreted, and known through our experiences of them and through the experiences of others. Religion and morality are aspects of human experience; theology and ethics are not only articulations of ideas in relation to the ideas others have expressed but are ideas about aspects of experience. Experience is social; it is a process of interaction between persons and other persons, persons and natural and historical events. Its significance is explained and its meanings assessed in communities that share common objects of interest and attention and share some common concepts, symbols, and theories. Experience is not only socially generated; it is socially tested. And it is experience of others, of "things" objective to human persons. This is the case in the sciences, in ethics, and in theology; it is the case in all ways of knowing and understanding.

Convictions: Religion, "Others," and the "Other"

Religion is part of human experience; it takes place within communities, and historic communities have traditions. What is least persuasive to the radically secularized mind is that religious activity is in any way a response to an "Other." What is debated among theologians, and probably also is uncertain to many persons with religious interests, is just what the "Other" is, and how it can be symbolized and conceptualized. Chapter 5 contains proposals pertaining to the latter; at this juncture a case will be made that religious affections and activity are generated in response to "others" and, for the theistic religious consciousness, to an "Other."

Religious affections and activity are evoked in human relationships to "others." This suggests that I shall develop fully an account of the genesis of religion; I shall not. It is important, without attempting to state a fully adequate theory of the genesis of religion, nonetheless to reiterate some observations and convictions that pertain to it. Elsewhere I indicated that there are aspects of experience which evoke and sustain certain senses or sensibilities and on the basis of which theological inferences are drawn.[8] These senses can be called aspects of piety, or aspects of religious affections. I shall only briefly state them here.

One of the most primal of all "senses" that is central to religion is the sense of dependence. It arises out of a whole range of basic human experiences. For our individual existence we are dependent upon the sexual activity of our parents, on the process of fertilization of an ovum by a sperm, and on the care we receive in infancy. For our continued sustenance we are dependent upon certain reliabilities of the natural order: on the basic elements that make life possible, on rain and sunshine, on the growth of plants and animals. Our daily life requires the existence of orderly social arrangements and the fulfillment of social roles by countless persons. We trust drivers to stop at red lights; we assume, unless we are paranoid, that persons we meet casually during the day will not harm us; we have a measure of confidence that legislators will protect our legitimate interests through law; we assume that institutions and persons will function to provide for our economic needs. The breakdown of customary expectations accents this sense of dependence; we are startled to find how much we have assumed the reliability of others when we find that the services they provided suddenly are not available.

Theologians have generally recognized the importance of this sense of dependence as a primal moment in religious life. Beginning with the creation account in Genesis, and continuing through the teachings of Jesus and the New Testament, it is in one way or another adduced as a basis for religious affections and activities. It is invoked in the tradition in the notion of faith or trust; it is highlighted in Edwards' famous Boston sermon, "God glorified in man's dependence." The sense of dependence becomes a basic principle for a theological system in Schleiermacher's *The Christian Faith,* and it is adduced by recent theologians as different as H. Richard Niebuhr and Karl Rahner.[9]

The sense of dependence is usually accompanied by a sense of gratitude. The sense of gratitude, however, does not rest on the same rather substantial evidence as the sense of dependence. The sense of gratitude is evoked by the experience of goodness or benefits that are

8. Gustafson, *Can Ethics be Christian?* pp. 82–116. In that book I indicate the contributions of the writings of John E. Smith of Yale to my thinking about experience and religion. See, for example, his *Experience and God* (New York: Oxford University Press, 1968).

9. Edwards's sermon is found in *Works,* 2:3–7. "The Common element in all howsoever diverse expressions of piety, by which these are conjointly distinguished from all other feelings, or, in other words, the self-identical essence of piety, is this: the consciousness of being absolutely dependent, or, which is the same thing, of being in relation with God" (Schleiermacher, *The Christian Faith,* p. 12). For H. Richard Niebuhr's views, see "Responsibility in Absolute Dependence," in *The Responsible Self,* pp. 108–26. For Karl Rahner's discussion, see *The Foundations,* pp. 77–79.

ours as a result of the objects on which we rely. We fully understand when persons curse as a result of the absence of the sustaining and necessary supports for life—for survival, for the fulfillment of legitimate human aspirations, for fair shares of what is available in life. We understand the enmity that can arise with the onset of debilitating diseases, with loss of means of livelihood as a result of accidents or destructive forces of nature, and with the powerlessness that forms of social organization bequeath to large numbers of persons. We understand why some persons commit suicide, deciding that it is better not to be than to be. But the primal experience of most persons most of the time is that it is better to be than not to be, whether this is explained as the desire to survive or more grandly as a heartfelt response to the wonder of one's own existence and of the marvels of the world of which we are a part. And except in the most desperate of human circumstances there are indications of reasons for gratitude along with reasons for enmity and despair. As trite as it may seem to say so, most persons, even in unpleasant circumstances, can find some modest reasons for gratitude—the silent affection of a friend, a moment of opportunity to improve one's lot, a memory of a better time.

In the biblical religious traditions the sense of gratitude has been central both to piety and to the reasons for being moral. Prayers, psalms, hymns, and whole liturgies have been developed to express thanks for those things which have been given to us, those things that are enjoyed for which individuals and groups can take no credit. No traditional service of Christian worship omits thanks to God in its prayers and in its hymns. Gratitude to God is a fundamental reason for being moral in Judaism and Christianity. It is one of the hinges by means of which the community turns from what it understands God has done to what it understands it is responsible to do. The law is the prescriptive code that in part expresses the thanks of the ancient Hebrew people for their liberation from bondage in Egypt. In the New Testament the deeds of love commanded of the church are said to be motivated by gratitude for the love of God that has been shown in Jesus Christ.

A sense of obligation is as prevalent as a sense of gratitude. To be sustained by the care of others, to acknowledge our dependence upon orderly processes, to have others in our care, to know that orderly processes require our participation and cooperation—these are aspects of the experience out of which a sense of obligation emerges. We have natural duties as parents and as children for which we do not contract; they are part of the social fabric and must be fulfilled even if we consider only our individual self-interest. We recognize that, to accomplish certain purposes that are beneficial to us as individuals or to groups, it is important to acknowledge mutual obligations in the forms of covenants and contracts. Social roles, job descriptions, and voluntary commitments of the use of our time and energy all involve obligations, and are all occasions which evoke a sense of obligation. There is no human community, whether of thieves or of self-sacrificing servants of the poor, that is not sustained by a defined or implicit set of duties and obligations. In organized communities there are sanctions against those who do not comply with the rules, job descriptions, and expectations of other individuals or of the group.

There are no significant religious movements in the history of culture that have not stipulated religious or theological sanctions for certain forms of behavior. The morality of the four varnas of Hinduism is grounded in a religious perception of what is proper in the cosmic ordering of all of life. The Decalogue and the priestly codes in the Pentateuch stipulate principles and rules of conduct, both cultic and moral, as the proper way for people to express their obligations to Yahweh. Islamic law, the Sharia, like the Halakhah of the orthodox Jewish tradition, develops the duties which are incumbent upon those who are faithful to the Deity. Even a salvation-centered religion like Pauline Christianity, which stresses the grace of God which frees persons from guilt, also indicates certain moral expectations to those who are free. "'All things are lawful, but not all things are helpful,'" writes the Apostle Paul.[10]

Where one has a sense of dependence, of gratitude, and of obligation, there follows for conscientious persons a sense of remorse and repentance (a matter strangely undiscussed by moral philosophers). Few, if any, persons live free of a sense of remorse, of guilt, or a sense of repentance. Failure to acknowledge dependence takes the form of an assertion of self-sufficiency; self-sufficiency not only irritates those on whom one relies but also can be self-destructive. The line may be faint between legitimate self-confidence and excessive self-sufficiency, but it is generally perceived to be there. Failure to acknowledge gratitude not only offends those who have given what we cannot give and do for ourselves; it can issue in the meanness of brutal self-aggrandizement. Failure to acknowledge obligations drives the wedge of distrust into human relationships, and when it issues in failure to fulfill legitimate expectations of behavior it disrupts the necessary functions of human communities. A sense of remorse or guilt and a sense of repentance, are natural aspects of human experience.

Certainly most, if not all, religions prescribe principles and rules of conduct or ideals of life that are not always or fully met by their adherents. Nurtured in those beliefs, the adherents generally acknowledge their own failures to comply with the rules or to fulfill the ideals. Whether they are matters of the pollution of a Brahmin temple by Indian Harijans or an act of murder which is against a divine commandment, not only is acknowledgment of culpability expected but some inner alteration of the "heart"

10. 1 Cor. 10:23. R.S.V.

is engendered. To be sure, the alteration might come more from fear of the sanctioned reprisals than from a sense of genuine repentance. To be sure, religions have sustained trivial rules of conduct, both cultic and moral, against which rebellion is legitimate. But the experiences of accountability, guilt, and repentance become religiously significant when set in certain contexts. Both psychologically and cultically, religions have defined the steps and stages of true repentance. In Christianity the Catholic sacrament of penance traditionally provided proper cultic form to these steps and stages. The root experience, however, on which this is built is part of common human experience—the sense of having done some wrong, of not fulfilling some ideal.

Except for those who are in the blackest nights of despair, human beings see, or seek for, some possibilities for altering those conditions which oppress them, or for sustaining those conditions which support them. To be human is to have some sense of such possibilities. This is traditionally talked about in terms of human freedom, in terms of the human spirit; I choose more modest language. But certainly our capacities for human agency, whether large or meager in scope, are the natural basis for this sense of possibilities. Within limits, persons can become other than what they are; they can alter some of the external conditions of life; they can see opportunities to alter the course of affairs by their intentional interventions. Frustration and despair are the consequences of limitations put on our capacities to act by external or internal forces beyond our control; but we not only live in hope, we seek those great or modest ways in which our aspirations can find some measure of fulfillment. Whether investigators will eventually prove that even our hopes and our choices are determined by biochemical processes in the brain or not, experience will sustain the sense of possibilities.

There are religious views, both Western and Eastern, which are developed on the basis of a metaphysical determinism. If the determinism is not absolute, if the systems leave some small places and times for human accountability for actions (as all the major ones do), they also acknowledge a sense of possibility. The sense of possibility is not only a fact of human experience that must be accepted. There are religious views that see the ground of these possibilities in the conditions of life provided by its Creator and Sustainer. The sense of possibility is a human phenomenon; it is seen to have a religious significance in religious traditions.

Many commentators and observers of human life have been persuaded that persons are oriented toward some supreme end; that life, while in particulars confused and confusing, has direction toward a goal. That goal may be as general as human flourishing, or happiness, or it may have specifically religious qualities such as communion with God, the vision of God, *moksha,* or *Nirvana.* Certainly others who are not persuaded by such a single supreme end have often lived by a similar pattern, though one less grandiose in its objectives. To be human is to have purposes; to have purposes is to intend ends; to intend ends is to have a sense of direction. Persons differ; there are those who seem to integrate their activities in such a way that all specific actions direct them toward their ultimate end, or are means to it. There are those who seem to have the "rational life-plans" that John Rawls and other philosophers describe or prescribe. There are those who, if they have a sense of direction, have not reflected on it but simply follow dominant impulses and drives. And, clearly, there are many without a dominant sense of direction, whose lives are impulsive, wandering, self-contradictory, reactive, and in other ways aimless.

To some extent communities have a sense of direction. The development of the fathers of our country, imbedded in the charter documents of the state, was toward a social and political goal; while historical changes have occurred and the society has become more complex than they could anticipate, we continue vaguely to define our national unity by a direction toward certain ends or values. Demonic and tyrannical states have had a sense of direction: who can forget the Nazi government of Germany in our century?

Religions build upon human senses of direction, and incorporate them into their ritual, cultic, and moral activities. Both Augustine and Thomas Aquinas assumed that to be human was to have a natural orientation toward an end; most human activities were explainable to these great fathers of the church in terms of the ends that persons sought, the desires that they had. They shared with many other Christians through the centuries the notion that this natural directedness was toward the supernatural end of communion with God, the vision of God. Human experience, interpreted in terms of a sense of direction, is incorporated into a religious and theological vision. The eschaton, the coming of the reign of God, has been for many Christians not merely the mark of the *finis,* the temporal end of history, but also of the *telos,* the final goal of life. Christians have been counseled to create "foretastes" of that end in their present lives, whether individual or corporate; they have been exhorted to organize human societies so that that Kingdom is actualized as much as possible in particular historical conditions. To have a sense of direction is part of human experience; it is brought into religious visions of life.

Religion is not unnatural; it is grounded in these senses, and in many other aspects of human experience. Theology is not reflection upon something supernatural, as if we could reflect on something that is not in any way related to human experiences. But religion is grounded in experiences of "others": of nature, of human communities, of human creativity and action. Religions as aspects of human cultures provide myths, symbols, and analogies which interpret the meaning and significance of various aspects of human experience in the light of convictions that life is not a human creation, that its destiny is not fully in human control, that there are requirements of human action and relations that have to be met for the sake of survival and flourishing, and that absolute fatedness is not the human lot. Theology tenders concepts and symbols which have attempted to explain these realities and experiences of persons; it has tendered explanations of the existence of these experiences and of their meaning and significance. Religion is grounded in experiences of self: self in relation to other selves, self in relation to memories and aspirations of self, and present self in relation to past self. It is grounded in communities that have common experiences and that have sought in concert the meanings of these experiences—experiences of good crops and failed crops, of earthquakes and the starry skies above, of wars and peace, of injustice and manifestations of justice, and of health and disease. Religion arises out of experiences of "others"; it is not idiosyncratic projection of human imaginations untested by experience or by assessments of those gifted in the realm of ideas and concepts. Theology construes these experiences: it provides principles of explanation of their meaning and suggests ways in which life needs to be conducted in the light of that meaning.

Religions vary; we have monotheisms and polytheisms, and we have religions with saints and heroes but no recognizable deity. They all share several things. They share some common recognitions of the human circumstance in relation to that which is beyond human control. They share certain affections and dispositions toward whatever is—moments of awe, reverence, fear, gratitude, guilt, and liberation. However they articulate that which is beyond the means of scientific investigation and proof, they nonetheless sense the reality of its presence. This is the moment, the time, and the point at which the religious consciousness moves beyond what radically secular persons feel. This is the step or the leap which distinguishes the religious consciousness from the secular. The step or the leap, I believe, is also taken by many who for various reasons are bored with or offended by traditional religious symbols and concepts. There are many who respond to another "dimension" in their affective lives and in their dispositions who do not name "gods" or "God." But for those who are identified with particular communities, the step is overt, acknowledged, and articulated in the symbols and concepts that construe the world of experience theologically and religiously. The step of monotheism is distinctive. From experiences of others or of otherness it, for reasons of heart and mind, respects and reveres *an* Other; it acknowledges dependence upon and expresses gratitude to *an* Other; it develops a sense of obligation to *an* Other, and a sense of repentance in the face of its failure to relate properly to *the* Other. This theological construal of "others" is not given in the experiences themselves, and cannot be argued in such a way as to persuade all rational persons. It flows from the conditioning of hearts and minds nurtured in the language of monotheistic piety which empowers capacities to attribute, and finally, simply *to see* experiences of diverse others as various manifestations of the *Other*. These capacities enable one to respond to the occasions which provide human possibilities as occasions ultimately provided by *an* Other; to see life as being directed toward *the* Other—in human moral activity and in worship. From experiences that are shared in common, to experience of others, or of otherness, to experience of the reality of an Other; these are the steps, phases, aspects, of monotheistic religious faith and life.

Procedures: Theological Tradition and Development

Religions are historical phenomena. Even primitive religions, apparently relatively free from the winds of change, are subject to alteration as a consequence of contacts with other cultures and the impact of significant persons within them. The great "historic religions" of our planet, those that have sacred scriptures, written and artistic records of development, and oral histories, have all changed throughout the course of the centuries of their existence. Their institutional forms develop: in some cases through the "routinization of charisma," as Weber noted; in others through the institutionalization of the processes by which the beliefs and activities characteristic of a given religion can be passed on from generation to generation. In some it is through interaction with forms of social organization in the cultures and states in which the religion lives or through the formation of new institutions to meet newly perceived needs and requirements. Their beliefs develop. Speculations occur and issue in metaphysical and other doctrines unthought of by early adherents; certain features of sacred texts are highlighted by adherents and scholars with particular religious interests, and other features by others. Both conscious and unintended processes of "indigenization" occur as religions are planted in cultures foreign to their original locations. Their cultic lives develop. While there are continuities, the "outward forms" change with different cultural milieus in time and space; reformers deliberately change them either to retrieve the primitive forms or to make them more readily acceptable to modern people. It is unarguable that changes occur through time in the great historic religions.

How development and changes are to be evaluated is a question on which there are sharp differences among adherents to any religion. Development does not necessarily imply improvement; change is viewed by some as a degeneration of the authentic truth and identity of a religion, and by others as a process necessary to its vitality and, under certain conditions, its survival. For some, authentic development of a religious tradition occurs only insofar as the changes can be justified as the unfolding and growth of something implicit in the origins and sacred texts that mark the clearest differentia of the faith. The ways in which scholars and other religious leaders attempt to demonstrate that developments in institutional forms and cult have been implicitly present in the documents and rites of the early phases of a religion are remarkable. For some, a basically sophistic justification is given for change and development: what determines the proper forms of a religion is what appeals to the largest number of persons in a particular time; questions of tests of truth diminish in importance. For some, historical changes are inevitable; they feel no need to secure a warrant for them in the fruitful seed of the beginnings, though they might well be concerned to mark clear lines of continuity as well as of change. For such persons, the marks of change are not necessarily occasions for embarrassment.

Our attention here is given to theology, one aspect of the Christian religious tradition. There are those who would acknowledge and defend the development of theological ideas insofar as they can assure themselves that the process only unfolds what is implicit in some canonical books or in institutionally accepted creeds. The formula of Chalcedon must be implicit in the New Testament; the bodily assumption of Mary must be implicit in the accounts of the most primitive beliefs. The sixteenth-century reformers' return to the New Testament with their criterion of *sola scriptura* is another case in point: it is not the unfolding and development of truth implicit in the Bible, but a return to the Bible as the standard of truth in the light of which developments are to be judged. For some, development of theological ideas can be justified as long as there is some rough and general coherence between the traditional ideas and those that are advanced. Traditional notions of sin, for example, are seen to be generally coherent with contemporary notions of estrangement, alienation, exploitation, and repression. Others, more radical, have less hesitation about discarding beliefs and concepts which they consider outmoded in the light of various forms of contemporary knowledge. The eighteenth-century Deists are a case in point. The weight of the evidence that is admitted to theological construction changes from that which is given by the tradition to that which has contemporary cultural authority. The presumption has shifted from one in favor of preserving the tradition insofar as possible to one in favor of contemporary criteria for assessing the viability and truth of tradition.

Vocal and visible persons within and outside the Christian community have taken the position that Christianity is authentic only when there are clear statements of belief that mark its identity, and to which its members are required to adhere. Precisely at this writing, Pope John Paul II has approved the censure of the Swiss liberal Catholic theologian, Hans Küng. Surely cheers are ascending from the lips of many Roman Catholic theologians and church leaders in various parts of the world. And, oddly from my point of view, there are secularists who are cheering with them, for while they cannot accept Christianity, they want Christianity to be something stable, unaltered, and dogmatic. What is grossly in error and reprehensible about such views is the failure fully to acknowledge changes in religious ideas in the Bible itself, and changes in religious ideas in the history of the Christian theological tradition. What is dishonest is that the historical points at which the advocates of these views wish to freeze truth and which become tests of subsequent changes are themselves palpably different from the charter canonical document, the Bible.

The principle behind the difficulty in accepting changes in religious ideas is the belief that truth in Christianity was given once and for all time in a given person and set of historical events, and in the record of these events and the early articulations of their meaning (that is, in the Bible). Religious truth is supposed to be "objectively true," devoid of the relativity of some other intellectual enterprises. The historic particularities of the moment of religious truth are not only accepted but become part of the content of that truth itself. God presumably chose to reveal the eternal and immutable truth about himself through the events in the history of a particular historic people, and in the events and life of one man who came to a particular place in a particular time with its particular religious and political conditions, and its particular mode of execution of criminals. A historically relative tradition, institutionally delimited by judgments of the canonicity of certain texts, is the source and test of eternal truth. What is acknowledged to be historically particular is the point and content of eternal and immutable truth. And, for the most orthodox, it is the only point and content of any religious truth.

There is another cultural movement that has aspired to immutable and eternal truth about reality, modern science. The aspirations and claims of some of its devotees are remarkably similar to those of many in the Christian tradition. Yet we know from the detailed work of historians and philosophers of science such as Norwood Hanson, Stephen Toulmin, and others that scientific concepts and explanations have developed in relation not only to new means of knowing the objective realities to which they refer but also to changes in received ideas, many of which retained remarkable hold on brilliant persons. Science is a historical cultural movement. Linnaeus could gather an extraordinary amount of information about the species of plants in the world, and provide a taxonomy for ordering it largely on the basis of the belief, not radically challenged in the eighteeth century, that there seemed to be virtually a Platonic ideal, a form, for each species. This presupposition could only inhibit him and his collaborators from grasping what was so essential to developments in geology and biology in the nineteenth century, the idea that species have developed from prior species. As Toulmin has indicated in his close criticism of Thomas Kuhn, it is not necessary to invoke hyper-dramatic terms like "revolution" and "paradigm shift" to understand alterations such as this; the processes are much more complex, less dramatic, more gradual.[11] But it is also not necessary to invoke some false belief about science as an activity that is free from historical, social, and cultural relations. Concepts and explanations develop within communities; modern science cannot be explained without taking these historical and social factors, these factors of human experience, into account.

The development of theology is similar in some respects to the development of modern science. The disposition toward change, however, is different in the dominant strands of each community. Theology is reluctant to change for reasons that cannot be lightly dismissed; science is open to change in concepts and explanations, though resistance occurs there as well. The methods and procedures for testing are radically different in each; whatever God is, he is not subject to the same kinds of investigations that lead to the disclosure of the double helix structure of DNA. The evidences adduced for a theological concept or idea simply cannot pass the same kinds of tests used in the hard sciences. The rate of change in theology is slower, not only because of the disposition to accept what is given, and not only because theologians do not get the munificent grants from the National Science Foundation and the National Institutes of Health, but also because the subject matter is radically different.

Nonetheless, the similarities to the development of natural science are worthy of attention as a way into descriptive and explanatory studies of theology. One need not say first that theology *ought* to develop like modern science develops. One can first establish that theology *has* developed in ways that have some similarity to the processes by which scientific thought develops. To establish this would require historical study in depth and detail for which I am not fully competent; nonetheless on the basis of general knowledge of theology I believe some processes comparable to those that have been indicated in scientific developments can be stated.

In both science and theology a particular phase of development begins with the wide acceptance within an interested and knowledgeable

11. Toulmin, *Human Understanding,* pp. 98–117.

community of a set of concepts and principles of explanation by which to construe the objects of investigation. Theology, as Julian N. Hartt has succinctly stated, is a way of construing the world.[12] Its concepts and principles function to interpret "the world" in the light of that reality it also construes, the Deity. There is a sense in which each of the modern sciences is also a way of construing that part of "the world" under investigation. What Kuhn calls "normal science" (a notion which Toulmin sharply criticizes) involves a widespread acceptance of certain principles and concepts as adequate for the fundamental understanding of what is under investigation. For example, while the genetic mechanisms of evolution are not fully explained, evolution as a general principle of explanation is accepted as a proper way to construe relevant aspects of the natural world. While there were philosophical and theological debates among late medieval theologians, as there were and are among biologists, a general way of construing the Deity, the world, and the relations between them was widely accepted in the Christian community of theologians.

In both areas of investigation there is a presumption in favor of what has been received: as long as what has been received passes certain tests of adequacy it remains unchallenged. Indeed, habit is strong among scientists and theologians in the history of our culture, and members of both groups find it hard to emancipate themselves from deeply ingrained dominant views within their areas of concern. But the difference between theology and the sciences to which I have already alluded must be noted here. Theologians tend to hold the tradition and what is received with a greater degree of reverence and respect than do scientific investigators. To be sure, in the history of theology there have been radical changes confined to short periods of time. The Reformation of the sixteenth century, while the result of developments in intellectual life, such as nominalism in philosophy and Renaissance humanism in textual studies, and of protest against ecclesiastical corruption from at least the time of the Lollards forward, altered Christian theology dramatically and swiftly. Luther, and subsequently others, were willing to challenge radically the received tradition. In our century Protestant theology went through a less dramatic but very significant change with the critique of the received liberal theology by Karl Barth and his contemporaries in Europe. In both of these movements, as well as in many other reforming movements, there was a return to the Bible as a source for the intellectual enterprise of theology. There was a retrieval of the past, and the texts of the past, which had been given normative authority in the early church. Developments in science are clearly different. While historians of science can find the earlier seeds of ideas which come to full development later, the

12. Hartt, "Encounter and Inference," p. 52.

practitioners of science do not return to those sources either for substantive information or for authorization of their concepts and principles.

It is important to note that in theology this retrieval of a past begins a process which is executed differently in the different historical periods. The "neoorthodox" and "neo-Reformation" theologians of our century had to work out their biblical theologies in the light of intellectual developments that occurred between the sixteenth century and ours. A long history of historical and literary criticism of the Bible had altered in significant ways the kind of authority that could be claimed for it. Even if Luther and Calvin were not fundamentalists in the twentieth-century sense of that term, they did not have to take into account the legacy of critical scholarship that recent theologians did. There has been retrieval, but what is retrieved is developed differently.

Retrieval is selective in theology. Because of the rich variety of materials in the Bible it is impossible to retrieve it totally and yet present its meaning in a systematic and coherent fashion. The Anabaptists of the sixteenth century accepted the renewed authority of the biblical materials, but were much more guided than were the major reformers by themes drawn from a more literal understanding of some of the teachings of Jesus, and by the centrality of the theme of following Jesus as faithful disciples even unto death. These themes were not absent from major reformers, but a selective process clearly made them more central to the Radical Reformation. Theologians who can be identified as the heirs of a particular stream of theological tradition, such as the Calvinist, select points of reference in the "father" of the movement, and develop different ways of interpreting the significance of the selected lines of continuity in their own religious and intellectual milieus. Brian A. Gerrish has shown brilliantly how five different theologians each maintained an authentic line of continuity with Calvin but developed their own theologies around particular interests and in ways that were significantly different.[13]

All retrievals are selective in theology, and necessarily so. Even the harshest proclamations of fundamentalism focus attention on certain aspects of the Bible, find ways to ignore other aspects, and construe the significance of what is retrieved in different ways. To be sure, theological justifications are given for the selection, and on the part of intensely biblical theologians these justifications are made on the basis of the centrality of the integrating theme or themes to the Bible itself. But the formulation of integrating theological themes from the Bible necessarily involves judgments in light of particular interests and convictions. Even

13. Brian A. Gerrish, *Tradition and the Modern World: Reformed Theology in the Nineteenth Century* (Chicago: University of Chicago Press, 1978).

theology that begins with biblical exegesis selects those passages which support a theological interest.

Theological development occurs as selected themes, often retrieved from the Bible, are reformulated in some way. One of the processes is recombination of concepts, themes, and principles. If a theologian seeks to be dominantly biblical and selects a biblical theme like eschatology as the proper central one, he or she must recombine the other themes of the Bible in relation to eschatology. In this process of new juxtapositions of traditional themes a measure of insight and imagination is required. The theologian does not simply recombine texts drawn from different parts of the Bible; he or she construes the meaning of texts and themes in ways that modify the work of others. A different central theme creates the possibility of different combinations of other themes, and the innovative aspects of a particular construction issue as a result. Almost necessarily some aspects of the sources used are abandoned. Certainly many aspects of the theological tradition are abandoned. Where the discarding is critical to the innovative recombination, a thorough theologian gives reasons for it. Often it is only in retrospect that a critical reader of theology sees just what and how much has been discarded. Abandoning and discarding are part of theological development. Even Luther was willing to consider discarding the Epistle of James, a canonical biblical book, because it was dissonant with what he believed to be the central theme of the New Testament. The Reformers of the sixteenth century were quite ready to discard a great deal of the philosophical apparatus of the tradition they inherited, an apparatus that was used both to provide an apology for the Christian faith and to interpret its significance for religious and moral life in terms of another aspect of the cultural tradition. The recovery of a more sympathetic understanding of myth in our time has lead to a general discarding of the creation narrative of Genesis as a causal explanation of how the world came to be without discarding its religious meaning and significance. The recognition that the ecumenical creeds of the early church were shaped in their concepts and principles by the metaphysics that was prevalent in the Greco-Roman culture of that time has led to a discarding of these creeds by some groups and to a reinterpretation of their meaning and significance by others.

These processes go on not only within the use of the Bible and of materials from the theological tradition of Christianity. They go on with reference to knowledge, concepts, and principles of explanation, and thus to communities, that coexist with the church in any given time. And they develop in these relations because Christians, and particularly theologians, are themselves participants in more inclusive communities of scholarly investigation or of the communities that absorb the significance of the results of these investigations. Selection of what is to be retrieved or sustained is relative to knowledge and understanding present in the culture that pertains to matters of concern to theology. Certainly the interpretation of the Genesis creation account in terms of its mythical significance was caused in part by the acceptance of the evidences and theories of historical geology, evolutionary biology, and physical anthropology. To be sure, theologians can assure us that the account was never meant to be taken as a scientific explanation, and that great theologians in the past really did not understand it in those terms. But both scientists and theologians in the nineteenth and early twentieth centuries (and a few now) would have been surprised to find this claim to be the ecclesiastical one. The idea of accountability for moral action, with its accompanying concepts of sin and guilt, is retained theologically and in some places ecclesiastically in the Christian tradition. Yet in the light of newer understandings of the causes or conditions of human action most modern theologians have extended the range of acceptable excusing conditions. We hear little of suicide as a sin any more; this act, so long judged and condemned and one whose eternal consequence was a particular place in Hell in Dante's vivid interpretation, is now almost always explained by spiritual and psychological factors beyond the control of the individual, or as an act of martyrdom in cases such as self-immolation in protest against a war or other injustice. Homosexuality, long judged to be a mortal sin against nature, is now interpreted by some Roman Catholic moral theologians as an excusable act in those instances in which the agent cannot be held accountable for the conditions which dispose him or her to act in this way.

Selection is made in the light of other areas of knowledge. So also, then, the processes of recombination, reinterpretation, and innovation take these into account. And the debates among theologians are partially about what aspects of knowledge are of such authority that they require abandonment of certain aspects of the Christian tradition, or require subordination of certain themes that had formerly been crucial. Theologians who freely and willingly acknowledge the truth of those principles of explanation derived from historical geology and evolutionary biology are properly unhappy when these principles per se become the principles of theology, when the processes described and the explanations given for them become the sole evidence for an articulation of the meaning of the Deity. Theologians are often willing to take into account the processes by which religious activity is explained by psychologists, anthropologists, and sociologists but are not willing to accept them as fully adequate explanations. But the recombination that takes place in the light of such explanations does alter the work of theologians. The continuing issues are those of authority—not of ecclesiastical institutional authority and exercise of powers of censure, though such remain, but of what weight the evidences and theories of the sciences are to carry in the reformulation of theological ideas. At what point are there beliefs and concepts the cost of whose abandoment would be the loss of identity and integrity of Christian theology itself? What degree of reformulation runs the risk of tipping the balance from a presumption in favor of the Christian tradition to a presumption against it? That theologians do select, reformulate, recombine, abandon, and innovate in the light of knowledge drawn from non-biblical sources is simply a matter of fact. The criteria for making judgments about what is proper in this process are matters of ongoing debate.

The point to be stressed, however, is that theology develops in a tradition. It does not merely make explicit what was always implicit in the seeds of its origins. It develops in ways somewhat comparable to the development of science, though at no point can it provide the means of investigation and the tests of truth for its theories that are available to scientists. It develops, honesty ought to require all theologians and churchmen to admit, in part by abandoning aspects of what is received, including what is received in the charter document, the Bible. It has its fossils of species that have not survived imbedded in the layers and folds of its past. Some of them are curious and humorous in retrospect; the gradual abandonment of some caused anguish, pain, and even death to many persons. The certainty about the truth of theological doctrines warranted suppression of thought within the community, persecution of Jews and others who were not convinced, conversions by force of countless persons, and stagnation of theology itself. What is at least ironic, and has been in many instances a tragedy, is that generally the grounds for repressions were themselves the products of historical development, unrecognized or unaccepted as such, by parties and powers within ecclesiastical institutions. Toulmin raises the question this way with reference to other intellectual activities: must truth be historically invariant?[14] Do the claims of theology, or of ethics, have to be defended as timeless and eternal in order to be true? Does the acknowledgment of the development of theology as related to and relative to the factors described in this section necessarily mean that there are no tests of adequacy for its doctrines? Is theology exempt from the processes of intellectual development that even modern science must accept? The answer to each of these questions is negative. The practice of theology, I believe, has demonstrated that the answers are negative, though the detailed historical evidence for this cannot be adduced here. Yet there remains, if not a pious reverence for what is received, at least a respect for it. And there remains that feature

14. Toulmin, *Human Understanding,* p. 45.

which distinguishes the "book religions," Judaism, Christianity, and Islam: a past text is authoritative—in some sense.[15]

Historically, one of the ways in which the development of theological thought has been governed and tested is by the use of a distinction between the "revelation," or Scripture, and the tradition that follows from it. Tradition necessarily involves development; it is accepted to some degree as relative to the historic periods in which phases and aspects of it are formulated. It is permitted to have some plasticity. Development of tradition occurs in response not only to investigations of the revelation and the prior tradition such as historical and textual scholarship on the Bible and on documents like the ecumenical creeds. It also develops in relation to relevant ideas present in the culture at given periods, as I have already noted. It also develops in relation to historical events within and surrounding the churches. For example, in our century, although no historian to my knowledge has been able to indicate with great precision what the impact of World War I was on Continental theology's turn from bland and optimistic liberalism to the stringent and awesome neoorthodoxies, there is general agreement that the impact was decisive. But traditionally Scripture has been the norm for judging the authenticity of tradition.

Scripture, or revelation, and tradition are in this way distinguished, and the question of the relative authority of each is a matter that has divided Western Christian theology since the sixteenth century. It is interesting to note that Jaroslav Pelikan, in his monumental multivolume history of Christian theology, seems to assume this distinction for either theological or practical reasons; Pelikan does not deal with tradition in the Scriptures but begins his study of the Christian tradition with the closing of the canon.[16] David Tracy's support of a "revisionist model" for contemporary fundamental Christian theology assumes something like this as well. "[T]he revisionist model holds that a contemporary fundamental Christian theology can best be described as philosophical reflection upon the meanings present in common human experience and language, and upon the meanings present in the Christian fact."[17] The critical part of the quotation is "the meanings present in the Christian *fact*." One can read Tracy to be saying that there is something called the Christian fact on which all theologians can agree; tradition in theology, like current theology, has developed in its fundamental form as philosophical reflection

15. The philosopher John E. Smith once observed in my presence that when theologians say "in some sense" they usually cannot say in what sense.

16. "What the church of Jesus Christ believes, teaches, and confesses on the basis of the word of God: this is Christian doctrine." Jaroslav Pelikan, *The Christian Tradition,* 5 vols. (Chicago: University of Chicago Press, 1971–), vol. 1, *The Emergence of the Catholic Tradition (100–600),* p. 1. The development of doctrine begins from the Bible.

17. David Tracy, *Blessed Rage for Order* (New York: Seabury, 1975), p. 43.

on this fact. But what is the Christian fact? What is it that counts as the datum of revelation on which subsequent theology is a process of reflection? Are all those "meanings" really present in the fact?

If the fact is what is given in Scripture, or a selection of what is given there, and if the Scripture is itself the result of historical developmental processes like tradition, what warrant is there for the radical distinction between the fact and the reflections on the meanings present in the fact? Why at one point does something become the fact, when the processes out of which it has come are like others whose yield is not facts in the same authoritative sense? One can realize the practical importance of not beginning a multivolume history of the Christian tradition in theology with a volume on the Bible itself, and one can acknowledge that the decision of the community to close the canon provides historical and theological warrants for giving the Bible a separate status. It is, however, clear to critical lay readers and even clearer to biblical scholars that the charter document itself contains many lines or strands of tradition, and that it cannot in a simple way become the datum for theology. Its own historical developmental character is acknowledged by all modern theologians; what is at issue is the theological significance of that historically developmental character. One can argue, as I would, that what is given in the Bible is itself reflection on the meanings of common human experience in light of an experience of the presence of God. The concepts and symbols for the presence of God within the Bible become one reference for further reflection on what Tracy calls "common human experience." Subsequent theological development is a process of reflection on experience in the light of generalizations warranted by particular interpretations of that rich and varied body of literature called the Bible. One might choose to draw the line between the Bible and tradition sharply on the basis of the presence of the Holy Spirit in the deliberations of those who determined what was in the canon. But even in that decisive judgment we know that certain historical criteria were used, certain texts rejected.

What is the revelation? What is the content of the revelation? For Christian theology it pertains to Jesus Christ; even from a social perspective the identity of the community through time is dependent upon the persistence of the distinctive significance of Jesus Christ. But we know that there are distinguishable Christologies in the New Testament as well as in the subsequent theological tradition. We know that different features of the New Testament accounts of the life and teaching of Jesus and of his universal significance lead to different combinations of other things indicated about him; one aspect is selected which becomes the principle around which others are drawn into coherence. My earlier book, *Christ and the Moral Life,* makes clear, I believe, that the various Christological themes in the theological tradition that lead to distinguishable characteristics in ethical thought can each be authorized from within the New Testament.[18] "Revisionist" models of theology are present in the Bible itself.

In making this case I not only prepare the ground for subsequent developments in this book but point to a theological issue which concerns all theologians in the Christian tradition: what is the special significance of the Bible, and particularly of Jesus Christ?

Another distinction that is present in the theological tradition is that between revelation and reason, between revealed and natural theology. I believe its most commonly accepted importance rests on the idea that revelation refers to a historically particular event or set of events which a community accepts as the effect of a choice by God to make himself known. It also refers to the records in which these events are known, and which contain the early reflections on the human and cosmic significance of these events. "Reason" most commonly refers to those procedures by which persons come to some knowledge of the same deity without giving the historical particularities a special authority in the development of the argument. What is the outcome of reason should be acceptable to all rational persons, those with feelings of piety and those without, and those living in Hindu and Buddhist cultures. In monotheistically inclined cultures both reason and revelation have to refer to the same ultimate reality, though the arguments persist about the correct answer to the ancient question, "What has Athens to do with Jerusalem?" There are those in the Christian tradition who argue that God can be known only through revelation; there are those who affirm that what can be known through revelation cannot be inconsistent with reason; there are those in the culture who argue that God, if he can be known, must be known through reason, and that anything claimed to be revelation is to be tested by reason.

The dichotomy of reason and revelation has been historically important. For polemical purposes, adherents to each extreme have forced polarizations. Revelation seems to some to be unreasonable and absurd; reason for others cannot build a rational bridge to God because God is totally other and free and not to be bound by the limits of human rationality. Indeed, he can only be known by revelation. The polarization is wrong and unnecessary.

Whatever claims are made for revelation, one cannot deny that human experience is an indispensable aspect both of how it is known and what is known through it. Whatever claims are made for reason, theological arguments for the existence of God are based upon human expe-

18 James M. Gustafson, *Christ and the Moral Life* (New York: Harper and Row, 1968; reprint ed., University of Chicago Press, 1979).

riences of other persons, of nature, and of society. Both revelation and
reason are human reflections on human experiences.

Even the most extreme arguments for a revelational foundation for
theology cannot deny that what is claimed to be known is based upon
human relations to the natural world, on human experiences of being
sustained by others, on human experiences of external requirements for
conduct and the ordering of societies, on human experiences of guilt and
release, and so forth. Not even the most extreme views of a revelational
basis for theology can deny that what is known is known through the
events and cultures in which it known. And unless one has the most
magical view of the Deity guiding the hands of the scribes who first wrote
things down, the medium of human reflection, symbols, and language has
to be taken into account.

Theology emerges from human reflection on a variety of human
experiences in the light of other experiences, and in the light of the experience of an Other present in, through, and beyond particular experiences. Whether that reflection is judged to be "reasonable" or not depends
upon the criteria accepted for determining the reasonable. If one confines
those criteria to the strictest forms of formal logic, one can make the case
that the reflection is unreasonable. If, however, the criteria are relative
to the nature of the "others" to be accounted for, then the theological
enterprise is not unreasonable. The enterprise is not simply "faith seeking
understanding," as if the data of faith were "unreasonable" and understanding a rational explication of it. It is that understanding is and always
has been present in faith, that there are evidences which, given conditions
of religious affections, both sustain confidence in the object and indicate
some characteristics of the object in which persons have confidence. The
creation account in Genesis is not "unreasonable" in the sense that there
are no justificatory premises from experience for the beliefs rendered in
what we have learned to call a mythic form. To be sure, theological
argument, as I have indicated previously, cannot provide the same kinds
of evidential warrants, and the same kind of confirming theories, that
arguments in some other arenas can. But this does not make them absurd.
And insofar as the apologists for an extreme view of revelation choose
to rely upon extreme claims they are not only doing their positions a
disservice apologetically but are also denying the experiential and rational
processes which are present and thus must be taken into account theologically.

Certainly "natural theology," theology based on arguments that do
not accept special authority for a particular historical strand of events and
culture, is reflection on human experience. It reflects in some forms on
the possibilities of distinctively human experience itself. It reflects in other
forms on the human experience of the rational ordering of natural pro-

cesses, on "design" either in terms of the ordering of the stars and planets or in terms of more limited evidences of design in nature. It is always human reflection. It uses what are deemed to be acceptable rules of evidence and acceptable canons of logical inference in justifying its conclusions. It is fashionable to suggest that apart from some nascent or lively natural faith or piety there would be no motive for engaging in such a theological argument. This is an empirical question I cannot answer exactly, but it is likely that the motivation to develop natural theology indicates the presence of religious sensibility—an aspect of human experience. One may not wish to call the awakening of that sensibility a moment of "revelation," but the affections that motivate the natural theological enterprise are certainly similar to the receptivity of persons to the acknowledgment of the presence of God that one finds in historic religious communities.

Not only are natural theology and revealed theology both grounded in human experiences; both necessarily refer to human mediations of the meaning and significance of aspects of nature and human experience through experience itself. Both share in a developmental process. I have already indicated the processes by which theological thought changes and develops. Not only does a "revelational" strand develop; natural theology changes as well. An argument from design based upon the assumption that, for example, species were determined by virtually Platonic forms could no longer hold after the work of historical geologists and evolutionary biologists proved this to be in error. But arguments from design themselves do not cease because the evidences for them have to be changed; the new evidences and theories are adduced in support for a different sort of design—more dynamic, more temporally changing in character.

This softening of the polarity between revelation and reason does not eliminate contention about what counts for sufficient evidence in a theological argument. But in my view the distinctions come not at the big and global level but in particularities of arguments. The distinctions have to be faced at more modest and precise points in theological discussion than the forced choice between reason and revelation indicates.

I have said little about morality and ethical thought in this section. The basic lines I have drawn would apply, I believe, to morality and ethics as well as to religion and theology. Certain patterns for understanding the nature of morality develop as a result of reflection on human experience. The classic distinction between the teleological and the deontological types of ethics is based in part on different perceptions and conceptions of the principal characteristics of the moral aspects of human experience. In theological ethics, H. Richard Niebuhr's development of an ethics of response and responsibility clearly rests on what he conceived to be an alternative model for understanding the moral aspects of human experience: "All life has the character of responsiveness, I maintain."[19]

The literature of philosophical ethics in the West has developed in a way similar to theology. One example can be taken from our century: G. E. Moore's *Principia Ethica* can be seen, in retrospect, as a text which, while developed from powerful antecedents in British moral philosophy, shaped issues that occupied scores of philosophers subsequently. The impact of logical positivism in this development was great. As the textbooks indicate, various responses were made to the issue of the relation of "is" to "ought " in this stream of literature; students read A. J. Ayer or Charles Stevenson for texts on the emotivist response; they read R. M. Hare to see the prescriptivist response, and so forth.

In Christian ethics the issues of the relation of revelation to tradition, and to philosophical (natural) ethics have long histories, comparable to the historical developments in theology proper. The Bible itself is seen not to provide one Christian ethic; there are several strands in the New Testament which have warranted historical alternatives in the development of Christian ethical thought. Even writers in Christian ethics who seek to relate the historic particularity of the Christian tradition to "natural" ethics choose among the options available in philosophical ethics to make their cases: some turn to the classic natural-law tradition, others to contemporary phenomenological philosophy, and others to seeking cross-cultural universals which can be developed from the work of cultural anthropologists.

Brevity and suggestion are in order here because I am moving toward a theological more than an ethical point in this volume.

Concluding Reflections

The basic themes of this chapter have been the significance of human experience in religion and morality, and thus for the reflections on these aspects of experience that take form in theology and ethics, and the historical developmental character of theological and ethical literature and ideas. A central tension has been indicated explicitly at some points, and alluded to at others: the tension between the historically particular and its relations, its relativities, on the one hand, and the universal on the other hand. My judgment should be clear by now. There is no way to be liberated from social, cultural, and historical particularity in religion and theology, but a dichotomy between this pole and a nonhistorical, immutable universality is often overdrawn. The historical particularities refer to human experience and to rational criticism and development; those

19. H. Richard Niebuhr, *The Responsible Self*, p. 46.

who strive for an immutable universality do so from intellectual communities which have their own traditions, development, and assumptions.

To strive for the universal is not only intellectually valiant but also a necessary motivation in theological work. It is necessary for apologetic purposes; the intelligibility of the particular can be made clearer and to some more persuasive by demonstrating that its insights and truths refer to the experiences of many if not all persons and that its justifications can be made clear in nonesoteric language. It is also necessary for purposes of internal criticism of a historical tradition. Blindnesses can be indicated; places where assumptions that were made in a tradition about such things as the ordering of the natural world, the motivations of human behavior, and the reliability or historical accuracy of critical texts have been made clear. The shifting within a tradition occurs in part by exposing it to lights which come from relevant knowledge and to ideas from other movements of thought. Undue parochialism becomes clear. Where historic particularity is adduced as support for ideas which are no longer viable or are marginal to the importance of what the tradition stands for, it can be eliminated.

The move toward the pole of universality is not novel in our time, and it is necessary. But to attempt to formulate a pattern and content of religious thought that can escape totally the impact of historic tradition is to pursue an end that cannot finally be achieved. It appears to me to make one of two assumptions, both of which can be radically challenged. One is that reflection and reasoning can and do take place in religion without any foundations that are relative to a particular culture or intellectual tradition, and correlatively that there exists in all persons a uniform capacity for rationality to which appeals can be made to evangelize them into a fictive and illusory community of all rational persons. The other assumption which might be made is that we have developed a sufficiently deep world culture upon which to build a rational theology, or a theology which is historically related to a world culture and thus is universal. I argue, on the contrary, that theology develops in traditions, and that religious traditions are always in relation to other traditions in a given culture and across cultures. Theological ideas do not need to be invariant in order to be significant or even to be true. But they must be tested; a theology of the creation, of the natural order, cannot ignore the information and principles of explanation of nature that are reasonably sound and accepted in our time. But theologies of nature have changed and will change in significant respects as our understanding of nature itself develops.

To be satisfied with the preservation of a religious and theological tradition at any given period of its development, however, is as problematic as is the effort to escape historical boundedness. It is clear from this chapter that this holds for the Scriptures as well as for subsequent developments in theology. Vast scholarly support can be adduced to show the extent and depth of development within the Bible itself. Received traditions are reinterpreted in the light of the religious and theological needs of other historic periods in the life of the Jewish people, and even within the short historic span of the New Testament community. We are driven to accept the idea that the theology of the gospel of Matthew is different from that of Luke's and Mark's gospels and even more clearly the theology of the gospel of John differs from that of the other three. *Sola scriptura* as a basis for theology is harder to defend now than it was in the time of the Reformation. We are too alert to the varieties of theology in the Bible to be able to go back to it for an indisputable, coherent, single theological viewpoint. Those who attempt to do so have to argue on scientific grounds that the view they find is *the* theology of the Bible, and as in moral philosophy and other humanistic studies, any effort to claim truth for one's own view is quickly responded to in a critical fashion.

Particular strands in the Christian theological tradition have sought either formally or informally to secure the thought of a figure or of an era as the timeless test of theological truth. Pope Leo XIII, in the encyclical *Aeterni Patris,* 1879, indicated clearly that the thought of Thomas Aquinas was to be the test for the orthodoxy of Christian theology and for teaching in Catholic institutions.[20] Creeds and confessions have been written in critical polemical circumstances in the history of the Christian churches, and have become the presumed invariant truth by which all subsequent theology is to be tested for its orthodoxy. Marvelous are the ways in which theologians manage to justify their own subsequent developments of thought as implicit in such institutionally authorized statements, or as selective developments of aspects of them, while quietly ignoring those that are intellectually embarrassing. Churches, such as the United Presbyterian Church in the USA, enable plasticity in theological development by adopting not one statement, the Westminster Confession of Faith, but several, and developing a contemporary one in addition to them. Leo's judgment is surpassed by history, and accepted as itself a time- and culture-bound statement.

Theological traditions develop. They develop not only in relation to the charter document, the Bible, and not only in relation to past theological writings. They develop in relation to aspects of the wider culture, and to historical and natural events in which churches and Christians participate.

---

20. Leo XIII, *Aeterni Patris,* in *The Church Speaks to the Modern World: The Social Teachings of Leo XIII,* ed. Etienne Gilson (Garden City, N.Y.: Image Books, 1954), pp. 31–54.

Obviously I have not stated anything novel. What becomes critical is the relative "authority" to be given to various points of reference involved in theological development. What weight will contemporary scientific accounts of nature, including human nature, be given, and how will they affect theological proposals? What weight will be given to the test of confirmation by human experience? And what will be the experiences, and whose will be judged to be significant? What will be retained from which strand of the Christian tradition? What will be incorporated from other strands? What will be the points around which ideas will be brought into coherence? How will ideas be recombined?

I shall be as clear about the choices made as I can, and give as good reasons for them as can be developed in limited space. Any more or less systematic account necessarily, as we saw in the first chapter, takes a theme, or several themes which are coherent with each other. The selected theme, as we have seen in this chapter, becomes critical in the determination of what is selected from the richness of the Bible and the tradition. It is critical in the determination of the order of significance of other themes, and in the ways in which they are recombined or developed. A statement of the themes is the purpose of the next chapter.

In sum, it is possible to isolate three ideal-types of purpose for a theologian. The types are ideal; they are exaggerations to highlight certain features, and in themselves do not accurately describe any particular endeavor. The first two that I shall develop are, I believe, less susceptible to historical evidential support than the third.

First, a theologian can defend a particular tradition by isolating its distinctive features on one of two grounds. First, it can be defended as the revelation of God or as the authentic recovery of the revelation of God in a subsequent historic period. Second, one can, on the basis of a deep historical and cultural relativism, decide that it is one's fate to construe the world in this particular way, and thus accept a tradition, or a time within the tradition, as one's theological location without making strong claims for its inerrancy or invariability.

On the basis of the foregoing paragraphs we have seen that this is a difficult type to realize in a disciplined and detailed way. Even those theologians who believe they are embodying this type in their work have made critical choices not covered by the principle that defines the ideal-type.

Second, a theologian can develop and defend an apology for the tradition, seeking to justify its truth in relation to some more general intelligibilities, and defending it in that way. If the first type is strictly "confessional," this type is strictly "apologetical." The purpose is to make arguments in support of the tradition from sources outside of the tradition. An argument for the existence of God from the design of nature, for example, is support for and defense of the theology that is found in the Christian tradition.

Any theology that is sophisticated enough to be remembered has some apologetical aspects to it. Even theologies that are more radically confessional give justifying reasons for taking a radically confessional stance. But there are efforts in the history of theology which are clearly more illumined by this ideal-type than by the first.

Third, a theologian can accept accountability for developing aspects of a tradition, being quite explicit about what is discarded from it, how various theological doctrines and principles are recombined as a result of the selection of certain themes to be central, giving reasons for how one works with traditional materials and also reasons for the selection one makes from other ways of explaining and construing the significance of "the world."

If the basic line of development in the latter part of this chapter is correct, all theologians to one degree or another can be illumined by this type. What distinguishes the type is the clarity of intention. This third is an ideal-type with reference to the present work; it will not fully meet all the tests of conscious recognition and defense that the type suggests. It is also ideal in another sense with reference to this work; it indicates formally an aspiration that motivates the subsequent chapters.

4

A Preference for the
Reformed Tradition

In theology, as in ethics, no contemporary proposals can claim radical novelty. In both of these fields there has been reflection upon the essential questions, formulation of basic alternative views, recombination of elements from various strands, and different primary principles for hundreds of years. If any contemporary scholar has illusions about his or her creativity in these fields, a conversation with a learned intellectual historian will quickly dispel them. By now probably all the basic options have been considered relative to primary questions in both fields. Those who glibly classify a current proposal in a large historical category, however, tend not to take seriously the finer points of argumentation in a book or article. For example, a theologian who had read John Rawls's *A Theory of Justice* said with a bit of condescension in his voice, "Rawls is a Kantian of sorts." No doubt that is true; the interesting and important innovations in the book are how he uses Kant, how these elements are combined with other elements from other traditions, how all the sources he uses are recombined into a coherent theory, and how the theory takes account of current literature including materials coming from the study of economics and psychology. The innovation is genuine, and it is very important; dismissal as a "Kantian, of sorts" trivializes the significance of Rawls's argument and contributions to political philosophy.

By the end of the twentieth century every theology that has some coherence (i.e., is not simply and foolishly eclectic) can be classified as "something, of sorts." The purpose of this chapter is to indicate the theological "something" of which the present book is, "of sorts." It is a Reformed theology, of sorts. This does not mean that no theologian writing before Calvin has contributed to it; Calvin was an Augustinian "of sorts," a biblical theologian, an heir to the classic tradition, and so forth. Nor does it mean that persons both before and after Calvin who would not be lined up among his principal antecedents and principal followers have not been sources on which I have drawn and from whose thought I have deeply learned. Thomas Aquinas is a case in point. I simply intend to make clear that there is a strand in the tradition from which I take my bearings more than from others. Obviously I shall not be able to defend the choices made in this regard against all the objections; I cannot provide a full apology even for what I select from the Reformed tradition.

Before developing my preference for the Reformed tradition, however, I need to provide some further explanation of how I view the purpose of the theological enterprise.

Theology as a Way of Construing the World

Julian N. Hartt has, in my judgment, stated clearly, succinctly, and forcefully, the primary features of theology. It is a way of "construing the world." He indicates that, in a religious context, construing "is more than a linguistic-intellectual activity." He goes on to spell this out in the following way: "It means an intention to relate to all things in ways appropriate to their belonging to God."[1] Subsequently I shall develop an emendation of this sentence to describe the primary task of religious morality; it is an intention to relate to all things in a manner appropriate to their *relations* to God. However, I accept Hartt's basic statement. It implicitly includes affective religious elements and more cognitive or intellective elements. It brings religion and morality together in a unity. It permits the development of theology as a basically practical discipline without eliminating from it more objective tests and requirements for its adequacy and validity.

If theology were merely a practical discipline, one might be led to believe that whatever concepts, myths, and symbols provide a coherent construal of the world and have some traditional or "generic" religious elements would pass for adequate. I have already indicated the reasons for not accepting such a possibility. If theology were merely a speculative discipline, there would be only a limited set of epistemological and metaphysical principles on which it could base its claims to truth. The operations of the human mind would have to be so perfectly coordinated with the operations of the divine mind that one could draw inferences from the ordering of human life and of nature to knowledge of God in a formally logical way.

Theology primarily is an activity of the practical reason. This it shares with ethics. (A great deal of scientific inquiry is an activity of the practical reason, but it is not in order here to make such a case.) The impulses to reflect theologically arise, as I have indicated, from human experience. Theology is an effort to make sense out of a very broad range of human experiences, to find some meaning in them and for them that enables persons to live and to act in coherent ways. It reaches to the limit-questions of not only human experience, but also our knowledge of nature. That there are deeply "speculative" dimensions to theology cannot be gainsaid; its principles, concepts, and arguments are not susceptible to the standards of verification that test areas of the natural sciences. But the basically practical character of the enterprise is clear; theology is testable in part by its consequences for those whose lives are informed by it: by its adequacy in the light of a broad range of human experiences,

1. Hartt, "Encounter and Inference," p. 52.

by the kind of direction it gives to human action, by the degree of coherence it provides for understanding the meaning of human life in the presence of "ineffable mystery" or "being-itself" or the "God who acts in history" or what have you. Theology, as Hartt emphasizes, is "more than a linguistic-intellectual activity," though clearly it is that. It is grounded in some kind of natural piety; it is a religious intellectual enterprise, a practical one.

There are many ways of construing the world. E. O. Wilson's work construes the world from a sociobiological perspective. The range of data and experience that he brings into his explanatory accounts, and the inferences drawn from them for the meaning of human activity, are as inclusive as any that systematic theology has provided. Not all functional equivalents to theology are as comprehensive as Wilson's.[2] Different religions, different views of human life (such as orthodox psychoanalysis), different stories all lead to different construals of the world—the meaning of human experience in relation to other persons, to history, and to nature. And different aspects of the world can be construed on the basis of different perspectives by the same persons. Theologians, as I have indicated, might well not challenge a current astrophysical explanation of the creation of the universe but continue to construe history and man in terms of the creation myth in Genesis. There are the instances of Christian fundamentalists who are at the same time hardheaded scientific interpreters of nature and man. The world can be construed according to Heidegger or Whitehead or others who have provided grand metaphysical systems. It can be construed from the perspective of A. J. Ayer's logical positivism. Theology is one way of construing the world; other ways of construing it are secular functional equivalents to theology. None are without practical impulses or practical consequences.

There are different ways of construing the world within the Christian theological tradition. There are persons within and outside the Christian community who would like to believe otherwise, but the literary and historical evidence belies them. There are secular thinkers, particularly those of a general conservative bent, who want nothing to do with a religious tradition but nonetheless believe it is better to keep it intact (e.g., a "biblical" view) than to have it altered by contemporary theologians. One may think Irish whiskey is not fit to drink but believe that those who mix it with something else are more reprehensible than either those who drink it straight or those who prefer beer. There are secular thinkers to whom theology means the Baltimore Catechism, Luther's

2. Efforts similar in scope to Wilson's sociobiology are made by economists. See, for example, Gary Becker, *The Economic Approach*. All such single-minded accounts are susceptible to the charge of reductionism.

Catechism, the Westminster Confession, or what they learned in Sunday School in the fifth grade; the reasons for rejecting what they once were taught are deemed sufficient for rejecting the enterprise as a whole. There are those in ecclesiastical power who seek valiantly to restrain any innovations in theological construals of the world. But, as I have indicated, there are different crucial principles that make even Matthew's theology identifiably different from Mark's and Luke's (which raises its own problems); it is only ignorance, invincible or culpable, that blinds persons to the fact that theological construals of the world vary, always have, and will continue to do so.

Such is also the case in ethics, in the interpretation of historical events, in the understanding of human actions, and in many other areas of scholarly inquiry. Pluralism in theology is probably no greater than in some other areas. Theologians are not the only scholars who have deep differences with each other within the field of their work; nor are they the only ones whose ways of construing the world have profound consequences for understanding the meanings of life and for the conduct of life among adherents. One can choose a psychotherapist according to his or her way of construing human life just as one can choose a theologian. One can also choose from the variety of moral philosophies currently available. There are identifiable historical traditions in theology; each is distinguished by the persistent continuity of one or more central themes. The same is true in theological ethics. Any beginning student of theology, for example, knows that central to the Lutheran theological tradition is the concept of justification by faith. That is not a sufficient basis for identification of the Lutheran strand of theology, as both historical scholars and theologians make clear. It is tenable only on the basis of certain Christological principles, certain principles pertaining to the nature of man, and so forth. There also were historical developments of Luther's own theology from his early writings to his later; these must be taken into account as well as the developments of Lutheran theology from the sixteenth century to the present. Not all Lutheran theologians agree on all points, either in the interpretation of Luther or on matters of how Lutheran theology can best be articulated and defended in later periods of history. Yet it cannot be denied that Lutheran theology construes human life in the world, and in relation to God, in ways which distinguish it from the mainline of Roman Catholic theology, from Anabaptist theology, and from Reformed theology.

Certain themes have characterized Lutheran theological ethics. For those who are Christians of a Lutheran sort the moral life is living out one's justification by faith.[3] This is, of course, not sufficient. When the law and the gospel are rightly divided, one can see that moral life requires adherence to the law; it is a dike against the forces of human sin which could lead to chaos, and in the orders of creation it is the ground of those fundamental social orders like family and state in which moral duties are defined. The ethics of the Lutheran tradition can be distinguished from, for example, the historic stream of the ethics of "the vision of God" that is described and analyzed in the classic work of Bishop K. E. Kirk. There the *telos* of man is the vision of God; mysticism and morality are related positively in a distinctive way.[4] The religious motives for moral action are very different from what they are in the Lutheran tradition. And both are easily distinguishable from the religious ethics of the Radical Reformation, with its primacy of the motif of discipleship, of following after Christ.

It suffices to say that in different theological ways of construing the world, of relating all things (including human beings) in a manner appropriate to their relations to God, critical judgments have been made in different historic strands of Christianity about which theological tenets are most central to ethics. The selection of particular tenets, if there is coherence to the strand, determines the ordering of other tenets, both theological and ethical. On the basis of different theological construals different reasons for action are described and prescribed: one is to move toward the vision of God, one is to live out one's Christian freedom, one is to follow Jesus in obedient discipleship even to death, one is to obey the commands of God, or one is to follow the law of love. Different "wellsprings" of action are described and prescribed: the desire for eternal bliss or for contemplative union with God moves moral action, the power of God's love flowing in and through Christians moves them to act morally, the threat of eternal damnation moves the will, and so forth. Different ends of action are described and prescribed: God is to be glorified, the neighbor's deepest need is to be served, social stability is to be fostered in the face of threats to peace and harmony, social conflict is to be instigated in the face of injustices in society, the Kingdom of God is to be approximated, and so forth.

The dominance of certain theological tenets shapes the prescriptive ethics and deeply informs the analysis of the human predicament and the circumstances of human action. As a result, one cannot argue for or against a view of ethics without arguing for or against the importance of

3. On Luther's ethics: "Luther's ethics is determined in its entirety, in its starting point and all its main features, by the heart and center of his theology, namely, by the justification of the sinner through the grace that is shown in Jesus Christ and received through faith alone." Paul Althaus, *The Ethics of Martin Luther,* trans. Robert C. Schultz (Philadelphia: Fortress, 1972), p. 3.

4. K. E. Kirk, *The Vision of God* (London: Longmans, Green and Co., 1931).

the theological principles that provide the vindicating reasons for the ethics. The importance of certain themes that almost all Christian ethics take into account differs according to ways in which theological tenets or principles are developed. The Anabaptists are not the exclusive adherents to the moral theme of discipleship to Jesus; it is present in Luther, in Roman Catholic moral theology, and in Calvin. But in order of its moral importance, in the religious motivations adduced for it, in its significance within a scheme of human salvation, and in the interpretation of its rigors the theme is quite different in each of these strands.

For a strand of Christian tradition to be identifiable there has to be some "discrimen," some central theme, symbol, or image, that is the point around which other beliefs cohere.[5] Perhaps it is too simple to suggest that there is one central theme; it is more likely that there are several which are correlated with each other, as we shall see in my delineation of the Reformed tradition. In the ordering of theological and ethical ideas the presence of the discriminating elements to establish the identity of a strand is apparent. It is not so apparent that the religious and moral lives of those who are raised in a particular strand and who give their assent to its tenets are as clearly marked as is the theology. This is to admit an empirical question that does not need to be answered here. Superficial observation, however, suggests that it is plausible that not only the lives of individuals and of members of congregations but also cultural life have been marked to some degree by the dominance of a particular strand of theological principles and by the communities that nourish people in accordance with them. Certainly many social and historical factors other than the presence of a theology are involved in the shaping of individual, communal, and cultural life, but there are characteristic "ways of life" which are justified and nourished by particular strands of Christianity. (The impact of religious traditions is, of course, clearer when one contrasts Hindu cultures with Islamic cultures and with a culture deeply affected by Judaism and Christianity.) Whatever economic, social, and other factors are adduced to explain the development of New England in the seventeenth century, they are not sufficient; some account must be taken of the "New England mind" as that was shaped by Puritan theology and by Puritan piety.[6]

Among the strands of Christian theology, among the identifiable ways of construing the world theologically, is the Reformed tradition. The

5. For an elaboration of this point, see David Kelsey, *The Uses of Scripture in Recent Theology* (Philadelphia: Fortress, 1975), pp. 160 ff. He credits Robert Clyde Johnson for the term *discrimen*.

6. See Perry Miller, *The New England Mind: The Seventeenth Century* (Cambridge; Harvard University Press, 1939). For my purposes Miller's discussion of piety is especially important: see pp. 3–63.

present work is most closely identified with that tradition. That I am a Christian rather than a Jew is an accident of birth; that I am a Protestant rather than a Roman Catholic is both an accident of birth and a matter of conscious assent; that I choose to develop my work out of the Reformed tradition is a matter of religious and theological conviction. That my work takes such revisionist turns that many of the adherents of that tradition will find the work an inadequate representation, or even a dissembling, of the tradition, stems also from convictions, some of which have been developed in the previous chapter. One which has not been acknowledged, and which is important, is that I am a "Free Church" theologian despite the perils of fragmentation that such a conviction brings; I do not believe that a theologian ought to be limited by commitments to historic creedal formulations.

The Reformed Tradition

When the Reformed tradition in theology is mentioned there is but one decisive generating source for its identity, the work of John Calvin. Within the proportions required for the development of this book it is not possible to engage in all of the exposition that seems to be promised by my identification with this tradition. I shall not offer an interpretation of Calvin's theology, or of the theologies of the Synod of Dort, the Dutch Calvinists, the Puritans, Jonathan Edwards, Schleiermacher, Barth, H. Richard Niebuhr, or others I consider to be within the perimeters of that tradition. Nor is a historical account of that tradition in order here, not even a brief one that would indicate the prominent lines both of continuity and of change within it. I also have in mind authors from whose works Calvin learned deeply, principally Augustine, and various aspects of the biblical materials. As I noted in the introduction to this chapter, to indicate a preference for the Reformed tradition is not to suggest that it is the only historic tradition that informs the present work.

Of course there are great differences in theologians who would be placed under the heading of the Reformed tradition. Again, it is not my intention to assess which representatives are, in my judgment, more or less satisfactory, or even to isolate the issues that are under debate among them. Indeed, in the end readers who most consciously and loyally adhere to the Reformed tradition in theology might well take great umbrage at my claims to develop my thought in continuity with it.

There are three elements in this theological tradition which I believe to be properly stressed, and which I affirm not because they can be authorized by a particular historical strand of Christian thought but because I believe they can be justified on grounds that are being gradually exposed in this book. These are (1) a sense of a powerful Other, written about in the post-Calvin developments as the sovereignty of God. (2) The centrality of piety or the religious affections in religious and moral life. By piety I mean not Pietism as that developed in Protestantism in many forms, nor do I mean piousness, that pretentious display of religion which offends me as much as it does anyone. I mean an attitude of reverence, awe, and respect which implies a sense of devotion and of duties and responsibilities as well. (3) An understanding of human life in relation to the powerful Other which requires that all of human activity be ordered properly in relation to what can be discerned about the purposes of God. These three elements are reciprocally interrelated; it is the powerful God who evokes piety; it is the powerful God who is the ultimate condition of possibility for human action and the ordering of life: individual, interpersonal, social, historical, and in relation to nature. Without piety it is relatively meaningless to make a case for the existence or presence of God. Without piety it is relatively meaningless to bring into the centrality of moral life the "senses" that are the hinges on which religious belief and moral obligations and opportunities turn. Without a disciplined ordering of human activities piety can become those instrumental, self-regarding practices which I criticized above; without God as the ultimate object of loyalty and ordering, moral concerns readily become limited to the anthropocentric concerns also criticized above.

I will not develop a historical theological argument that the three are related to each other in a unique way in the Reformed tradition, though I believe such a case is plausible. Some indications, however, of the bases in the Reformed tradition for these elements is necessary for establishing their importance for the present work. I shall subsequently indicate a number of points on which I deviate, in some instances radically, from that tradition.

John T. McNeill, in his Introduction to Calvin's *Institutes*, accurately notes the pervasive presence of a sense of piety in that great work. He interprets Calvin to be a man who lived and wrote with a constant awareness of God, a deeply religious man (not a theologian by profession) "who possessed a genius for orderly thinking and obeyed the impulse to write out the implications of his faith. He calls his book not a *summa theologiae* but a *summa pietatis*." "The whole work is suffused with an awed sense of God's ineffable majesty, sovereign power, and immediate presence with us men."[7] That Calvin was quite conscious of the importance of piety in religious life and in the theological enterprise is clear from the beginning of the text. Piety, he wrote, is "that reverence joined with love of God which knowledge of his benefits induces. For until men recognize that they owe everything to God, . . . that he is the Author of their every

---

7. McNeill, Introduction to Calvin, *Institutes*; McNeill ed., l:li.

good, that they should seek nothing beyond him—they will never yield him willing service."[8] Indeed, this sentence brings the powerful God on whom all depends together with piety and with the discipline of service to God. It is the "sense of the powers of God" that evokes and teaches piety.[9] Piety is no self-generated feeling but a response to the powers of God. These powers of God are known through the natural world; there is a natural piety which, of course, for Calvin is not sufficient. But whether one is thinking about "natural knowledge" of God, or about God within the life of the Christian community, knowledge of God is not "cold speculation"; it "carries with it the honoring of him."[10] Faith, like natural piety, is "a matter of the heart."[11] The Christian religion is not authentic in individuals or in the community without a profound experiential dimension.

For Calvin, God was exceedingly powerful; indeed, his providence ruled not only the general course of events but all particular events as well. He has a strong sense of dependence of all of life upon God, of the determination of the order of nature and of historical and interpersonal events ultimately by God, and a strong sense that whatever God does is done intentionally and justly. God, he states, "claims omnipotence—not the empty, idle, and almost unconscious sort that the Sophists imagine, but a watchful, effective, active sort, engaged in ceaseless activity." This is directed not simply toward "general motions" but toward "individual and particular motions." He "so regulates all things that nothing takes place without his deliberation."[12] Providence "governs all things," it is "lodged in the act and not merely in foreknowledge."[13] Indeed, he sets out to prove that "God so attends to the regulation of individual events, and they all so proceed from his set plan, that nothing takes place by chance."[14]

This understanding of God arises out of an interpretation of a large range of natural events and human experiences, as well as from an interpretation of the Bible. It stems from the simple observation that infants "immediately on coming forth from the womb . . . find food prepared for them by [God's] heavenly care" in their mothers' breasts. He is also careful to observe that "some mothers have full and abundant breasts, but others' are almost dry," and adds that "God wills to feed one more liberally, but another more meagerly."[15] The orderliness of nature, de-

8. *Institutes*, I, 2, 1; McNeill ed., 1:41.
9. Ibid.
10. Ibid., I, 12, 1; 1:116-17.
11. Ibid., III, 2, 36; 1:583-84.
12. Ibid., I, 16, 3; 1:200.
13. Ibid., I, 16, 4; 1:202.
14. Ibid., I, 16, 4; 1:203.
15. Ibid., I, 16, 3; 1:200–201.

pendent upon providence, is an occasion for gratitude; for those with
reason to be less than grateful there has to be a theological explanation
that refers to persons. (This, as we shall see, is one of the points at which
I shall distinguish my own work from Calvin's and from similar views of
providence.) Famine is a curse of God; a branch breaking from a tree and
killing a traveler is not to be attributed to chance. While persons cannot
know for certain the purpose of each event, since the ultimate reasons
and causes are often hidden from us, for Calvin there is evidence from
human experience interpreted by certain theological tenets not only to
establish the ultimate dependence of all upon God but also the meaningfulness of all events in his purposes. Further citations from the Reformer
are not necessary to establish that his Deity is powerful, indeed!

With this deep sense of divine providence it is clear not only that
are all things related to God—dependent upon him, intentionally ordered
by him, determined in particulars by him—but also that all things ought
to be properly related to God's ordering. The perennial puzzle of how one
can have Calvin's type of divine providence on the one hand and human
accountability on the other is faced at this point. For our purposes we
need not tarry long. Calvin valiantly distinguishes his position from what
he judges to be Homeric and Roman senses of fate. He assures us "that
we are not at all hindered by God's eternal decrees either from looking
ahead for ourselves or from putting all our affairs in order, but always in
submission to his will. For he who has set the limits of our life has at the
same time entrusted to us its care."[16] If God has committed the care and
protection of life to us, it is our duty to care for it and protect it; when
he offers "helps," we are to use them. If we acknowledge that God is the
"principal cause" by which all happens, we do not deny that secondary
causes have their proper place.[17]

The ethics that derive from Calvin's position logically are theonomous. The proper actions are those that are governed by the divine law.
The divine law is present in the natural ordering of things, and thus action
is to be in accordance with the natural law. The moral law of the Bible
is not different from the law of nature. The inward law that is engraved
on our hearts (the conscience) "in a sense asserts the very same things
that are to be learned from the two Tables." Because our consciences can
err in perceiving the natural law, "the Lord has provided us with a written
law to give us a clearer witness of what was too obscure in the natural
law, shake off our listlessness, and strike more vigorously our mind and
memory."[18] This is no ethics of autonomy. Actions are to conform to

16. Ibid., I, 17, 3; 1:216.
17. Ibid., I, 17, 6; 1:218.
18. Ibid., II, 8, 1; 1:368.

God's will, and since God's providence is omnipotent, there are no spheres of human action that are outside the divine governance and purpose.

The motives for obedience to God's law stem in part from piety, both natural and Christian. We act in accordance with God's law in part out of the gratitude that we have for his sustaining providence. We act also out of knowledge of what is displeasing to God. God as our Creator has, "by right the place of Father and Lord; for this reason we owe to him glory, reverence, love, and fear." We are not to "follow the mind's caprice wherever it impels us," but in dependence on his will we are to do alone that which pleases him. Piety and morality are unified in this view; "the only lawful worship of him is the observance of righteousness, holiness, and purity."[19]

There is an affinity between the argument developing in this book and Calvin's theology. There is a similar sense of the powerful Other, of that on which all things ultimately depend, to which all are ultimately related, which both limits and sustains human activities. That Other evokes piety; a sense of awe and reverence, the senses of dependence, gratitude, obligation, repentance, possibilities for action, and direction. Piety is, in a sense, the hinge which joins the frame of the moral and natural ordering of life to the door of human duties and obligations. Morality and religion are, for those of religious consciousness, inextricably intertwined. Both are evoked by God, both are directed in their activity toward God.

To be sure, there is a great deal in Calvin's theology that is left out by the process with which I have selected these three elements. Indeed, in the eyes of some I have left out the heart of the matter, the redemptive work of Christ known in the Scriptures. Subsequently I shall make quite clear the matters on which I disagree with this tradition, and in the next chapter shall indicate how a recombination of elements takes into account some matters that are not discarded.

To establish that there are bases in other theologians I consider to be in the Reformed tradition for the same three elements is not to assert that there are no differences between them in the ways that they interpret the three, or that they are even referring to exactly the same things when there are similarities. Nonetheless it is important to establish at least the grounds for the preference I have indicated. I shall, then, briefly indicate some resources in the work of Augustine, Jonathan Edwards, and Schleiermacher that are at least in a general way similar to those I have isolated in Calvin's *Institutes*.

19. Ibid., II, 8, 2; 1:369.

John T. McNeill's comment on Calvin's *Institutes* is equally applicable to much of the work of Augustine, especially the assertion that it "is suffused with an awed sense of God's ineffable majesty, sovereign power, and immediate presence with us men." Like Calvin after him, Augustine articulated a strong belief in the divine providence. While he could write at great length (and apologize for the length) about the Trinity, he also acknowledged that many of God's ways are beyond human understanding.[20] While he was concerned in the theological polemics of his time (as Calvin was in his) with correct doctrine, piety was essential. And, like Calvin, he had a strong sense of an objective right ordering of things, internal in persons and external in community, to which human response must conform. The general themes with which I identify in the Reformed tradition are strongly present and richly developed by the great bishop of Hippo.

Very early in *The City of God,* as in many other places, the reader meets expressions of Augustine's consciousness of the presence of God. At that point it emerges out of a practical problem; at others it is part of a more speculative argument; at still others it is expressed in prayer. The practical problem is that Christians have been taunted to explain why Christ has not rescued them from the fury of their enemies. "Where is your God?"[21] "Our God is everywhere present, wholly everywhere; not confined to any place. He can be present unperceived, and be absent without moving; when He exposes us to adversities, it is either to prove or correct our perfections; and in return for our patient endurance of the sufferings of time, He reserves for us an everlasting reward."[22] Not only is God everywhere, but there is meaning in all events in relation to God's purposes, and not only his purposes for Christians, but for all persons. He works within the creation of all visible things; his power operates through the "outward actions" of persons in the birth of children and in the growing of grain.[23] The ultimate course of history is in his hands. Nothing occurs fortuitously, as if events had no causes or as if such causes as they have "do not proceed from some intelligible order"; nor does anything occur by fate, by the necessity of a certain order which operates independently of divine or human will.[24] With the popularity of astrology and the presence of Stoic philosophical writings in his culture, Augustine had to distinguish his interpretation of the limitations of human control

20. Augustine, *On The Trinity,* bk. 15, 20 (50), *The Nicene and Post Nicene Fathers,* first series, 3:226–27.
21. Psalm 42:10.
22. Augustine, *The City of God,* trans. Marcus Dods, bk. 1, 29 (New York: Random House, 1950), pp. 34–55.
23. Augustine, *Trinity,* bk. 3, 8 (13, 14); *Fathers* 3:61, cols. 1 and 2.
24. Augustine, *City,* bk. 5, 1; p. 142.

over human destiny from other similar ideas. Against fate, the argument highlights divine foreknowledge, and the notion that, while human wills are included in the causes "certain to God" and "embraced by His fore-knowledge," they "are also causes of human actions." He assures the reader that "He who foreknew all the causes of things would certainly among those causes not have been ignorant of our wills."[25] We need not tarry over Augustine's struggles with the question of free will; he had to sustain it for the sake of human accountability even in the face of the foreknowledge and foreordination of events by God. That his Deity is powerful cannot, however, be denied.

The immutable and eternal Deity has created all so that there is a harmony, a proper order of relationship between all things, whether one is considering the order of human capacities or the order of the natural world. Life is to be governed and directed by proper relations to proper objects. While Augustine is often remembered to have said, "Love God and do what you will," that was no license to impulse. If one properly loved God, one's will and desires would be properly ordered. He had a basically aesthetic vision of the "whole" and the relation of parts within it. The heavens provided one analogy.

> When you contemplate the difference between bodies and observe that some are brighter than others, it is wrong to ask that the dimmer ones should be done away or made equal to the brighter ones. All must be contemplated in the light of the perfection of the universe; and you will see that all differences in brightness contribute to the perfection of the whole. You will not be able to imagine a perfect universe unless it contains some greater things and some smaller in perfect relation one to another. Similarly you must consider the differences between souls.[26]

All "natures" have an internal harmony, a rank and a species of their own, and a place in the order of nature. There is a "general scheme of the government of the universe" which makes parts and the whole tend toward their proper ends in divine providence.[27] Evil is disorder in the scheme of things; it is improper love of proper objects of love; it is improper objects of love. It is breaking the proper relationship between God, the supreme good, and the various lesser goods which he has created. By rightly loving God as the supreme good, man properly loves himself and his neighbors; by being properly oriented toward the supreme good man properly orders the lesser goods, as Augustine makes clear in many passages. Even the perverted disorder of things is dependent upon a prior

25. Ibid., bk. 5, 9; pp. 154–55.
26. Augustine, *On Free Will*, in Burleigh, ed., *Earlier Writings*, p. 186.
27. Augustine, *City*, bk. 12, 5, p. 384.

harmony.[28] God, the powerful Other, has created the order by which all things are justly and harmoniously related to each other—the powers of the human agent, the relations of institutions in society, the aspects of nature. Proper morality is proper ordering of the agent, proper ordering of actions in relation to the proper ordering of ends. The ordering of ends is defined by God's will; ethics is theonomous.

It would be an error to suggest that Augustine's consciousness of the importance of piety in any way denigrated the significance of knowledge and of right belief. "But who loves what he does not know?" he asks.[29] It is not unfair, however, to claim that for him piety or faith illumines the object of knowledge and of belief. "The true wisdom of man is piety," he wrote in the second paragraph of *The Enchiridion*.[30] Piety and worship are aspects of human affectivity as well as being oriented toward objects that are known. Religion is the pursuit of the proper objects of faith, hope, and love.[31] Faith, working through love, attains purity of life which finally attains sight. It is purity of heart that enables persons to "know that unspeakable beauty, the full vision of which is supreme happiness."[32]

More significant for my purposes, however, is Augustine's understanding of all of human life as being ordered and directed by desires. There is a sense in which his view of human activity is one long commentary on the saying of Jesus, "For where your treasure is, there will your heart be also."[33] The center of a person's "weight," the preoccupations of one's desires and affections, determines actions and the sort of person one is or becomes.[34] Desires, loves, direct the will; indeed, love is desire. All of human activity is motivated by desires, and desires directed toward the wrong objects are sources of human evil and of human dissatisfaction.

> The right will is, therefore, well-directed love, and the wrong will is ill-directed love. Love, then, yearning to have what is loved, is desire; and having and enjoying it, is joy; feeling what is opposed to it, is fear; and feeling what is opposed to it, when it has befallen it, is sadness.[35]

There is a natural desire for happiness; indeed most of human striving is for this end. While one cannot love what one does not know, it is also the

28. Ibid., bk. 19, 12; p. 689 and many other places.
29. Augustine, *Trinity*, bk. 8, 4; p. 118, col. 1.
30. Augustine, *The Enchiridion*, sec. 2, trans. J. F. Shaw, in *Fathers* 3:237, col. 2.
31. Ibid., 4; p. 238, col. 1.
32. Ibid., 5; p. 238, col. 2.
33. Mt. 6: 21, R.S.V.
34. Augustine, *Confessions*, bk. 13, 9.
35. Augustine, *City*, bk. 14, 7; p. 449.

case that love directs persons toward objects which will satisfy the deepest desires of the human soul. This is the "eros motif" in Augustine that, according to Anders Nygren, deeply compromises *agapē* as the unmotivated, self-giving love of the New Testament.[36] There is deep in human life a natural desire for God in Augustine's theology; and it is only in finding him as the proper object of our most fundamental longing that our souls find their rest. Religion, we can say, is a matter of human affections and desires; there is a "natural piety" in human longing for the right object of love; the fulfillment of life comes in the joy and happiness that occur when one loves God as the true and final end of life, and thus orders the rest of life in accordance with the proper ordering of goods. Morality is a matter of "affections." Actions are evil if the ends of human desires are evil, or if desires are improperly ordered in relation to the true good; actions are good insofar as the love that motivates them is good, insofar as human desires are properly ordered in relation to the proper ordering of the ends or objects of love. Religion and morality are deeply intertwined; they are properly realized when human life is oriented toward the Deity as the ultimate object of desire and as the Creator who has ordered all things in proper relations to each other.

As in the brief discussion of Calvin's theology, so in this one of Augustine's there is much that is left out. I have, I believe, established some general basis for showing that there is a deep affinity between the three critical elements of the present work and this significant predecessor of the Reformed tradition in theology.

In eighteenth-century New England there appeared a man who, it is fair to say, was very much in an Augustinian and Reformed tradition in his theology, Jonathan Edwards. His historical circumstances clearly influenced both his practical work as a pastor and preacher and his theology, as did the circumstances of Augustine and Calvin. He was heir to a Puritan tradition of piety and theology that went back to Elizabethan England, and that flourished in both New England and the mother country in the seventeenth century. This tradition was marked by its concern for the "preparation of the heart," by its preoccupation with a right ordering of individual life and society, and by its awareness of a sovereign Deity.[37] He was schooled in the new British philosophy of his time, and was a

36. Anders Nygren, *Agape and Eros,* trans. Philip S. Watson (London: SPCK, 1953), pp. 449–558. For a more appreciative interpretation, see John Burnaby, *Amor Dei* (London: Hodder and Stoughton, 1938).

37. The literature on Puritanism is vast. Two recent studies pertain to this sentence. Norman Petit, *The Heart Prepared* (New Haven: Yale University Press, 1966) surveys literature pertinent to the title. J. Sears McGee, *The Godly Man in Stuart England* (New Haven: Yale University Press, 1976), compares Anglicans and Puritans on the use of the two tables of the Decalogue. While the Puritans tended to stress the first more than the Anglicans did, their concern for moral order was not lax!

participant in the polemics against Arminianism—that latter-day version
of Augustine's foe, Pelagianism. The revivals of religion which in part he
generated were not only a matter of practical concern to Edwards but
also led to his fine discriminations between true religious affections and
defective ones. His vision had deeply aesthetic elements which were
combined with its religious and moral elements. Few theologians have
been as consistent in their focus on God's glory as Edwards. Indeed,
"the great end of God's work" is "but ONE; and this one end is most
properly and comprehensively called, THE GLORY OF GOD."[38] To be sure,
he had a deep utilitarianism in his religion and preaching; the justice of
his God was retributive as well as compensatory. Nonetheless there are
deep strands in his work that inform my own.

Affections were always part of distinctively Puritan piety. Religion
was "experiential." For full membership in a congregation the candidate
had to testify not only to right religious beliefs and have a record of moral
rectitude; he or she had to have an experience of regenerating grace.
Revivals of religion had occurred in New England before Edwards's time
as pastor in Northampton, but during that period they swept the region
and beyond. Affections called "religious" were intense, and discrimination was required to sort out those that were true. It is not my purpose
to delineate the twelve signs of true religious affections that Edwards's
treatise on that subject examines but to establish their centrality to his
thought and to indicate some of their features.

"True religion," Edwards wrote, "in great part, consists in holy
affections."[39] In expounding I Peter 1:18 ("Whom having not seen, ye
love: in whom, though now ye see him not, yet believing, ye rejoice with
joy as unspeakable, and full of glory") he notes the emphasis on love and
joy as "true and Pure" religious affections . By "affections," Edwards
meant "the more vigorous and sensible exercises of the inclination and
will of the soul."[40] As John E. Smith points out in his Introduction to the
Yale edition, "they carry the self well beyond indifference"; or in Edwards's more dramatic language, "the motion of the blood and animal
spirits begins to be sensibly altered."[41]

Edwards strives to make significant distinctions in his discussion of
the affections without dividing the "soul" into faculties. The inclinations
are distinguished from the understanding, but inclinations involve the
mind as well as the will. Indeed, without involving the mind there would

38. Jonathan Edwards, *Dissertation Concerning the End for Which God Created the
World,* sec. 7, in *Works,* 1:119, col. 2.
39. Jonathan Edwards, *Religious Affections,* ed. John E. Smith (New Haven: Yale
University Press, 1959), p. 59.
40. Ibid., p. 96.
41. John E. Smith, Introduction to ibid., p. 12. Edwards quotation, p. 96.

be no way of making judgments about the adequacy of affections that are claimed to be religious. True religion is the exercise of the inclination and will "towards divine objects."[42] They are the "springs of action," indicating the essentially practical character of true religion. Among the affections found in the Bible are fear, hope, love, desire, joy, sorrow, gratitude, zeal, and compassion. The chief of them is love: "The Scriptures do represent true religion, as being summarily comprehended in *love*, the chief of the affections, and fountain of all other affections."[43] Its object is God. But love is not purely emotive; it can become a settled disposition; and in a true religious affection of love "there must be light in the understanding, as well as an affected fervent heart." "If the great things of religion are rightly understood, they will affect the heart."[44] While Edwards seems to require an intensity of the affections that is not quite so evident in Calvin's view of piety, or in Augustine's discourses on love for God, the three share a common emphasis on "experiental religion."

Edwards's sermonic rhetoric could be very effective in evoking one of the religious affections, the fear of God. His portrayal of the sovereignty of God was itself sufficient to evoke an awe that would move the animal spirits. When that was coupled with his view of God's justice in determining the eternal destinies of individuals, and with his view of the divine election of some to be saved and some to be eternally damned, the sensitive heart was more than well prepared to be affected. God's sovereignty is a theme in most of Edwards's major theological works. Obviously he had to come to grips with it when he developed his treatise on the freedom of the will; the implication that God was then the "author of sin" had to be delicately handled in the treatise on original sin. (God permits sin, but does not cause it, he argues.)[45] It is a strong note in his preaching as well. The idea that man must acknowledge absolute dependence upon God for redemption is the theme of his famous Boston sermon of 1731.[46] Sermons on justification by faith, on the justice of God, and specifically on the sovereignty of God all state, develop, and apply the theme.

42. Ibid., p. 100.
43. Ibid., p. 106.
44. Ibid., p. 120.
45. "But if by 'the author of sin,' is meant the permitter, or not a hinderer of sin; and at the same time, a disposer of the state of events, in such a manner, for wise, holy and most excellent ends and purposes, that sin, if it be permitted or not hindered, will most certainly and infallibly follow: I say, if this be all that is meant, by being the author of sin (though I dislike and reject the phrase, as that which by use and custom is apt to carry another sense), it is no reproach for the most High to be thus the author of sin." Jonathan Edwards, *Freedom of the Will*, ed. Paul Ramsey (New Haven: Yale University Press, 1957), p. 399. This issue is the center of attention on pp. 397–412. See also, Jonathan Edwards, *Original Sin*, ed. Clyde Holbrook (New Haven: Yale University Press, 1970), pp. 380–88.
46. "God Glorified," in Edwards, *Works*, 2:3–7.

For Edwards, God's sovereignty included his right to do what he pleases. This is strikingly clear in the sermon "The Justice of God in the Damnation of Sinners."

> When men are fallen, and become sinful, God by his sovereignty has a right to determine about their redemption as he pleases. He has a right to determine whether he will redeem any or not. He might, if he had pleased, have left all to perish, or might have redeemed all. Or, he may redeem some, and leave others; and if he doth so, he may take whom he pleases, and leave whom he pleases. . . . It is meet that God should order all these things according to his own pleasure. By reason of his greatness and glory, by which he is infinitely above all, he is worthy to be sovereign, and that his pleasure should in all things take place. He is worthy that he should make himself his end, and that he should make nothing but his own wisdom his rule in pursuing that end, without asking leave or counsel of any, and without giving account of any of his matters. . . . He is the Creator of all things; and all are absolutely and universally dependent on him; and therefore it is meet that he should act as the sovereign possessor of heaven and earth.[47]

Clearly Edwards's God is accountable only to himself. This does not keep the preacher-theologian from rendering an account of the divine actions, or interpreting their importance to those who are affected by them, as we have seen in the letter about the collapse of the meetinghouse. It does not keep Edwards from making a case for the justice of some being eternally damned, deserving of that, even while they are eternally decreed to suffer that fate. But finally, it is God's sovereign will that determines all things, and all things are done, in the end, for his glory. A powerful Deity—no mistake about that.

Edwards's writings on particular moral problems are meager both in quantity and in substance. As Clyde Holbrook has demonstrated, he was concerned primarily with those "sins" that very conventional Christian piety, indeed pietism, has been concerned about.[48] He was worried, for example, about young people "frolicking" in the evenings, about excessive tippling in the taverns, about cursing. That he was no radical social reformer is clear; he was not greatly concerned with the just ordering of the relations of persons in communities, though he was sensitive to the fact that advantage was being taken of the Indians in Stockbridge after his undertaking to serve that missionary outpost. His concern for the religious affections and for an inward moral purity led him to keep

47. "The Justice of God in the Damnation of Sinners," in Edwards, *Works*, 1:670, col. 2-671, col. 1.
48. Holbrook, *The Ethics*, pp. 78–96.

one of those Puritan spiritual diaries. Spiritual and moral temperatures were taken almost hourly, not only by Edwards, but by his esteemed David Brainerd and others.[49]

The moral theory, however, particularly as developed in "The Nature of True Virtue," is quite a different matter.[50] In its impregnation with aesthetic language, its primacy of love of benevolence, its sense of the proper proportions of things in relation to each other, its final consent to being, to an objective order and reality, it is a latter-day Augustinianism. It is concerned to make a case for "natural morality" while indicating what a religious transformation of this means. While it is unfortunate that we have no testing of this moral theory in the details of particular moral problems such as we have in Augustine's reflections on the state, on marriage, and on lying, nonetheless Edwards provides a scheme for a theocentric morality, unified with his beliefs about religious affections.

"True virtue," Edwards wrote, "most essentially consists in *benevolence to being in general.*" It is "that consent, propensity and union of heart to being in general, which is immediately exercised in a general good will."[51] Virtue is an affection; it is love. And true virtue consists chiefly "in *love to God*; the Being of beings, infinitely greatest and best."[52] It is at this point that some of the strongest similarities to Augustine's religious moral vision occur. By loving God, the greatest and highest being, one also rightly orders other objects of love; one's specific virtues take on the character of "true virtue." Like Augustine, Edwards saw that "private affections" directed toward lesser goods deflect us from loving God, and thus disorder our relationships to particular things and to things in general. Both human vision and moral life are skewed because the parts cannot be seen properly in relation to the whole. The notions of the harmony and beauty of the whole, those aesthetic notions we saw in Augustine, come to play in this treatise as well. The "true goodness of being a thing must be its agreeableness to its end, or its fitness to answer the design for which it was made."[53] Since God is the supreme, governing,

49. "His Diary," in Edwards, *Works,* 1:xxiii-xxxvi. For Brainerd, "Life and Diary of the Rev. David Brainerd," in Edwards, *Works,* 2:313-86. See for example, Brainerd's entry, Friday, April 9, 1742. "Most of my time in morning devotion was spent without sensible sweetness; yet I had one delightful prospect of arriving at the heavenly world. I am more amazed than ever at such thoughts; for I see myself infinitely vile and unworthy. I feel very heartless and dull; and though I long for the presence of God, and seem constantly to reach towards God in desires; yet I cannot feel that divine and heavenly sweetness that I used to enjoy.—No poor creature stands in need of divine grace more than I, and none abuse it more than I have done, and still do." Ibid., p. 322, cols. 1–2.

50. Edwards, *The Nature of True Virtue* (Ann Arbor: University of Michigan Press, 1960).

51. Ibid., p. 3.

52. Ibid., p. 14.

53. Ibid., pp. 24–25.

and ultimate end of all things, the "truly virtuous mind, being as it were under the sovereign dominion of love to God, above all things, seeks the glory of God."[54] God's own end, his glory, becomes the supreme, governing, and ultimate end of man and human activity. The end of morality goes beyond morality to the glorification of God. And God is glorified when life is ordered with particular goods in their proportionate relations to each other, and to him as the greatest good. There is nothing short of a transformation of our vision in being rightly oriented by love to God; there is a reordering of our particular objects of valuation and of our affections in being turned from self toward the objective reality of Being, or toward God. Piety is oriented toward God; morality is oriented toward God. For Edwards morality is corrected by piety, and piety would not be true apart from virtue and actions which, to return to a key phrase, relate to all things in a manner appropriate to their relations to God.

While there is much in Edwards's theology that I discard, and much that will be reordered in its significance, his work, like Calvin's and Augustine's, sustains the three cardinal points of this chapter.

Richard R. Niebuhr, himself the author of the neglected but important book, *Experiential Religion,*[55] develops explicitly the affinities between Augustine, Calvin, Edwards, and Schleiermacher in his study of Schleiermacher's theology.[56] On the themes of piety and the religious affections and the pervasive governance of God in the universe these lines are clear. My reading of Schleiermacher's ethics, however, suggests that he takes a different turn from the others. His Christian ethical thought is focused on the agent and the actions that are forthcoming from the Christian God-consciousness far more than on a conformation of action to the objective ordering of life in the world.

About Edwards and Schleiermacher, Niebuhr wrote:

> These two not only shared a common idea of human nature, which Edwards stated as the conviction that "affections [are] the springs that set men agoing, in all the affairs of life, and engage them in their pursuits . . . he that has doctrinal knowledge only, without affections, never is engaged in the business of religion"; but they also agreed that theological discourse can remain faithful to the stuff of human religion and still be coherent, that theology can unite the affectional and rational dimensions of human nature

54. Ibid., p. 25. Any student of Edwards's ethics benefits from Holbrook, *The Ethics,* and especially from Roland A. Delattre, *Beauty and Sensibility in the Thought of Jonathan Edwards* (New Haven: Yale University Press, 1968). See also William C. Spohn, S.J., "Religion and Morality in the Thought of Jonathan Edwards" (Ph.D. diss., The University of Chicago, 1978).

55. Richard R. Niebuhr, *Experiential Religion* (New York: Harper and Row, 1972).

56. Richard R. Niebuhr, *Schleiermacher on Christ and Religion* (New York: Scribner's, 1964).

and therefore need not subsist either upon mere semantic and logical conventions nor upon esoteric and incoherent attestations of mystery. . . . Both Edwards and Schleiermacher, therefore, embraced a specific kind of empiricism.[57]

Not only did these two share a general empiricism, but this led them to an appreciation of the unity of the affectional and rational elements in man. Both also had powerful notions of the divine governance of affairs, something they share with Augustine and Calvin as well.

About Calvin and Schleiermacher, Niebuhr notes that "like Calvin before him, Schleiermacher freely exploited the conception of man as a being in whom his creator has sown the seed of piety."[58] Religion, to Schleiermacher, "is fundamentally man's affective response to the relationships into which the whole of human nature is bound, as the choice of the phrase, 'feeling of absolute dependence,' in itself suggests."[59] Theology articulates this fundamental piety, and "Christian doctrines are accounts of the Christian religious affections set forth in speech."[60] Piety, or the religious affections, is prior to theological formulations; the purpose of doctrine is to describe, explain, and justify piety. This piety, this feeling of absolute dependence, occurs "only along with the feeling of implication in a nexus of relative dependencies."[61] Schleiermacher, in my judgment, has a fundamentally organic vision of the relations of things to each other, and of persons in their relations to nature, to other persons, and even to God. He expresses these interdependencies, and the religious affections that they generate, in this way: "It can never be necessary in the interests of religion so to interpret a fact that its dependence on God absolutely excludes its being conditioned by the system of Nature."[62] It is also this vision, which made him so conscious of the divine governance of all things, that has led some interpreters to accuse him of being solidly in Spinoza's camp, and all interpreters to acknowledge a deep immanentism of God in the world in his thought. It is this vision of the "reciprocity of determination and freedom" that makes it impossible for there to be "room in his ethics for a doctrine of absolute freedom."[63]

Further exposition of Schleiermacher is not needed to establish certain affinities with his work, and to show that his work is in the Reformed tradition. The affinities go beyond the three major points highlighted in

57. R. R. Niebuhr, *Schleiermacher*, pp. 142-43. The Edwards quotation is from *Religious Affections* (Yale ed.), p. 101.
58. Ibid., p. 174.
59. Ibid., p. 181. See Schleiermacher, *The Christian Faith*, pp. 12–18.
60. Schleiermacher, *The Christian Faith*, p. 76.
61. R. R. Niebuhr, *Schleiermacher*, p. 186.
62. Schleiermacher, *The Christian Faith*, p. 178.
63. R. R. Niebuhr, *Schleiermacher*, p. 112.

this section. The "empiricism" present in his work is not unlike the account given in Chapter 3, above, of how religious affections emerge. The relation of theology to religion, that is, the claim that religion is prior to that theology, and that theology is a reflection on what Schleiermacher calls the religious self-consciousness, is clearly similar. The powerful sense of the divine governance, not only through historical events, but also in and through the nexus of relationships in and with nature is congenial. That a place for human agency is retained without leading to exaggerated claims for freedom is important both to Schleiermacher and to me. While the sense of dependence is the first in my ordering, and is present in not only the Reformed tradition but also in a great deal of Christian theology that looks to the basic human experiences, it has a dominance in Schleiermacher which I would modify.

Reasons for my preference for this tradition have been given in the preceding discussion. Experience is a central concept; the sense of human limitations is strong; ethics on the whole requires some discernment of the objective ordering of events; the Deity is powerful . I do not adopt and adapt these things because they have the authority of a tradition; rather, I believe the tradition expresses important and appropriate experiences and perceptions of the human condition in relation to the Other. As I shall show below, there are ways in which these elements of the Reformed tradition cohere with some of the well-established principles of explanation of both human life and the rest of nature that come to us from relevant modern sciences. To these matters of my preference for the Reformed tradition I shall return after some indications of the significant and relevant points at which I disagree with it.

Problematics in the Reformed Tradition

There are several aspects of this Reformed tradition which are noticeably missing from my account, and there are grave theological issues even at points on which I have a great deal of affinity with it. Some of these matters have been pointed out previously, but a more careful and focused development of crucial points is necessary. Not all of my objections would hold with equal force for each of the four theologians.

The sense of the powerful Other, of the divine governance of things, is a point for which I have great appreciation. On the whole the tradition has carried this to very extreme but logical conclusions in its notions of divine providence or divine sovereignty. Not only is there divine determination of the general course of events, limitation of human control over the destiny of the world, and a requirement of consent to limitations in nature and those forced upon human beings by historic and social circumstances. There is also divine determination of all particular events, with divine foreknowledge of them. I have quoted passages from Calvin and Edwards to establish this point. God regulates all things so that nothing occurs without his foreknowledge; his regulation is not merely in the foreknowledge but is lodged in "the act."

These strong claims are based on an anthropomorphism that has characterized Christian theology, and probably all religious myths and doctrines in which the ultimate power is personified. Intelligence, will, and power to control events in accordance with purposes are attributed to God. God is an agent in ways similar to those of a human agent. These characteristics become enlarged when attributed to the Deity; perfection seems to require the presence of these features to the nth degree, to the point that the limitations we experience are overcome. Indeed, there is an act of imagination in theological reflection at this point. What would these human features be if they were not limited by finitude? On the basis of laws of cause and effect, persons have some foreknowledge of consequences of action, with at least some degree of probability, in natural occurrences. Perfect foreknowledge would simply overcome the conditions of human finitude. To some extent, we can control our capacities and external powers (such as money, energy, etc.) in accordance with our intentions and purposes. The perfection of this capacity would not share the limits we have as human beings. By extension to the nth degree of these human capacities, theologians can claim foreknowledge and determination of particular events by a Deity conceived basically in terms of human agency. Criteria from *human* life are the basis for attributes of Divinity.

Anthropomorphism is religiously attractive and, to some extent, intellectually inevitable in theological reflection. I cannot undertake a discussion of the problems of analogical thinking at this point, but I do note its procedural and substantive importance in theology. It appears that in these extreme views of divine governance the analogy works in the following way. We, as human beings, have certain capacities; God has the same capacities in an exaggerated degree. The analogy seems to warrant moving from human limitation to divine nonlimitation. This is particularly the case at the level of theological abstraction on which the most personalistic language of piety is dropped. Piety also speaks of God as "Father", but here there is no assumption that because human fatherhood occurs through the biological process of the fertilization of the ovum by male semen the language of God as Father implies sexuality on his part. To be sure, other aspects of fatherhood are exaggerated to the nth degree: an idealized understanding of fatherly perfection in terms of the love of children, of the disciplining of children for their own good, and so forth. Language of Father seems, however, to be more clearly limited to metaphor; language of intelligence, will, intention, and purpose seems to be more specifically correlated with the being of the Deity itself. Thus God could be interpreted to have determined the precise movements of the falling meetinghouse in Northampton and the precise location of persons in relation to the falling parts of the building, all finally for his purposes with that congregation and for his ultimate glory. Even "natural" events are divinely determined according to God's foreknowledge and purposes. If one mother's breasts are full of milk and another's not, God intends for one infant to be fed well and the other meagerly. One is inclined to say that, happily, infants deprived of milk have sometimes had access to "wet nurses" and that now we have developed formulas to sustain infants naturally deprived. Such observations, however, have no severe effect on such arguments because our interventions are also foreknown and, while we are secondary causes of them, the divine agency is primary.

For now it is sufficient to indicate that the constructive view I shall develop in the next chapter must take account of "divine governance" and human limitation without getting into the difficulties that Reformed theology in its extreme forms has.

Those difficulties are tighter because of a second feature that is deeply problematic, the claim that the divine determination of events occurs for the sake of human well-being, or on the basis of human deserts, or deserving. The difficulty is serious because the focus of the "purposes" of divine governance is ultimately on the human beings. Features of events over which there is no rational basis for claiming any human accountability are interpreted as rewards or chastisements of persons, or in terms of their ultimate or long-range benefits for human well-being. Parents with a Down's syndrome child certainly are not accountable for the chromosomal abnormality in their child, but in this theological view there must be some meaning or significance for them in this affliction. Have they done something to "deserve" this? Is there some purpose in the birth of this defective child for them particularly? To put their marriage to the test? To try their capacities as parents? To give them an opportunity to extend their virtues? What lies behind this is the long and deeply held conviction that man is the crown of the creation, and that all that occurs is to be explained finally in the light of its meaning and significance for human beings. It is not that there must be an explanation of untoward events only in relation to natural causes; they must be explained in terms of human accountability, if not for the particular event, for some previous events; they must be explained in terms of what God is saying and doing to human beings for their own ultimate well-being in these events. While in many cases the meaning and significance remain a mystery, it is claimed that the mystery enshrouds what is meaningful and significant, and thus a deep resignation or consent is the appropriate response. The purpose might be hidden; God's ways might be inscrutable; nonetheless there is a divine purpose in relation to human life in all events. Even tragedy must be explained away somehow in terms of its meaning for those who suffer or for others who might learn from it.

There is something to be retrieved from such a view. Events, even those most tragic, which cause the suffering and deaths of persons and over which they have no control, can be occasions for human *responses* that are beneficial to others. But to claim that their purpose, their final end, is to provide these opportunities for the possible benefits to others is difficult to sustain from my point of view. When their possible beneficial significance becomes their causal explanation, this is wrong.

There are two theological corollaries that need to be called to attention. One is that the sovereignty of God in some representatives of the Reformed tradition implies the freedom of God to be arbitrary, that is, to not have to render an account of his choices, deeds, and will to anyone. We have seen this in the quotation from Edwards's sermon on "The Justice of God in the Damnation of Sinners."[64] God's choices and acts are sovereign; from the human experience of sovereign political powers that did not need to render account to anyone but were the final locus of authority and power, theologians have conceived the Deity to be the same. Yet to my knowledge no theologian in the Christian tradition who has claimed this radical sovereignty (indeed, perhaps only this radical view deserves to be called sovereignty) has accepted the notion that the arbitrary decrees are not finally in service of human deserving or human well-being. We may have no good clues to the arbitrary or secret will of God in some matters, but we are to believe that it is governed by a divine purpose for man. While God is free to decide as he will, his decisions are always just or beneficial for human beings.

The second theological corollary has thus been introduced. It is that God wills what is just and/or what is good for man. It is that not only is God sovereign but that he is good and just *for man.* Thus everything that occurs either as a result of processes over which we have no human control or as a result of the exercise of human agency must be meaningful in relation to God's justice and goodness for our species if not explained by it—our species, so late in developing, living on this small planet within our solar system. It is precisely at this point that the argument of this book comes to its most critical problem with the Christian theological tradition. Barth says vividly and categorically: "God is for man."[65] I do not say God is against man. But the sense in which God is for man must be spelled out in a carefully qualified way. But for much of the tradition,

64. See above, p. 174.
65. Karl Barth, *Church Dogmatics,* III/2, (Edinburgh: T. and T. Clark, 1960), p. 609, for one of many places.

Reformed and otherwise, our species, and we as individuals, are objects of divine benevolence and beneficence, or of the natural or decreed justice of God, in such a way that all events must be explained somehow in these terms. We are reaping the consequences of our previous actions for which we are accountable, whether the consequences are beneficial or destructive. Or we are reaping the consequences of the sins of our fathers, and somehow deserve to do so. Or in the light of an extended future, what we now do not know fully about what constitutes the good for us individually or as a species will be made clear; what we deserve either by reward or by condemnation will be forthcoming.

Again, there is something to be retrieved from the Reformed tradition. Many of the benefits and pains we receive we have been causally accountable for; many of the blessings of our time and culture as well as the threats to our well-being are attributable, in part, to the actions of previous generations. God is for man, in the sense that the possibilities of any human flourishing are dependent upon what we have received and on forces that are not ultimately under our control. But, as has been indicated over and over in this book, when man becomes the measure of all things, and when the ultimate power is conceived of having a purpose which ultimately focuses on human well-being or on human deserving, deep difficulties arise. They arise not only in the light of many aspects of human experience but also in light of what we have come to know in greater detail about the natural world of which we are a part. The Stoics perceived these matters to be problematic and resolved them in one way. Hindus and Buddhists perceived and resolved them in another; Parsees in still another. But the issue remains: is the Christian conviction that the purposes of the ultimate power are always and ultimately beneficial or just for individuals, or for the human species, tenable?

The Christian tradition, Reformed and otherwise, has used a doctrine of eternal life, of life beyond our present bodily life, as a way of resolving the deep doubts that arise out of human experience about both the justice and the benevolence of God directed toward particular persons. Calvin's doctrine of eternal life is indispensable in his theology; its coherence crumbles without it. So also for Augustine's and Edwards's. None of these theologians was superficial in his observations of the misery, the suffering, or the bitterness of human experience. Calvin wrote:

> [W]e can perceive the force and the usefulness of Christ's kingship only when we recognize it to be spiritual. This is clear enough from the fact that, while we must fight throughout life under the cross, our condition is harsh and wretched. What, then, would it profit us to be gathered under the reign of the Heavenly King, unless beyond this earthly life we were certain of enjoying its benefits? For this reason we ought to know that the happiness

promised us in Christ does not consist in outward advantages—
such as leading a joyous and peaceful life, having rich posses-
sions, being safe from all harm, and abounding with delights such
as the flesh commonly longs after. No, our happiness belongs to
the heavenly life! . . . Thus it is that we may patiently pass
through this life with its misery, hunger, cold, contempt, reproaches, and other troubles—content with this one thing: that
our King will never leave us destitute, but will provide for our
needs until, our warfare ended, we are called to triumph.[66]

The function of eternal life is to provide retribution for those who
enjoy things beyond their deserving in this life, and compensation for
those who have suffered beyond their deserving in this life. The well-
being, the happiness of those who are saved is deferred, but guaranteed.
This view, it seems to me, is a logical necessity from the dominant view
of divine providence in the Reformed tradition. And it is not only the
Reformed tradition that sustains God's justice and benevolence, and necessarily must posit a heavenly life to make it work in the end.

If one is agnostic about eternal life, or indeed believes that there is
no evidence from our bodily natures to sustain it, this critical move in the
argument for God's justice and benevolence toward human beings is not
possible. Nor is the utilitarian, prudential carrot that the promise of heavenly life sets before persons as a motive or end of their morality possible.
C. S. Lewis astutely noted this possible use of the notion of eternal life
when he wrote:

[T]he truth seems to me to be that happiness or misery beyond
death, simply in themselves, are not even religious subjects at all.
A man who believes in them will of course be prudent to seek the
one and avoid the other. But that seems to have no more to do
with religion than looking after one's health or saving money for
one's old age. The only difference here is that the stakes are so
very much higher. . . . But they are not on that account more religious. They are hopes for oneself, anxieties for oneself. God is
not in the centre. He is still important only for the sake of something else.[67]

The ethics of the Reformed tradition do not make the eternal reward
the motive for moral activity. The heavenly reward is assured to those
who have faith or to those who are elected by divine decree. Piety and
faith are special motives for moral action; they grow out of those subjects
who have faith. This is particularly clear in Schleiermacher's work. But
God's rewards cannot be purchased by moral propriety. Like Luther, one

66. Calvin, *Institutes,* II, 15, 4; McNeill, ed., 1:498 and 499.
67. C. S. Lewis, *Reflections on the Psalms* (N.Y.: Harcourt Brace, 1958), pp. 39–40.

must let God be God; human destiny is for him to decide. The conditions for arriving in some heavenly state were set by God and not by human beings. Nonetheless, the pious must be assured that there are rewards, benefits, for their piety. They will profit. It is a small step, taken by much of Christianity, to the assertion that the assurance of a heavenly reward for virtue, including the "virtue" of faith, is a reason for being virtuous.

The formulation of theology and ethics in this project, then, must develop a position in which life after death is not necessary. It cannot be necessary as a reward for those virtuous persons who have passed through life in misery, hunger, cold, contempt, and reproaches, providing them with an ultimate compensatory justice. It cannot be necessary for the condemnation of those who have enjoyed a rich and peaceful life beyond their moral deserving, providing them with an ultimate retributive justice. The key to this position lies within the Reformed tradition itself; the chief end of man is to glorify God, to relate to all things in a manner appropriate to their relations to God, in recognition of the dependence of all things upon him, and in gratitude for all things.

Reformed theology, for all of its awesome sense of the divine majesty and power, sustained a deep strand of utilitarian religion. All of Christian theology has; all of Christian piety has. One aspect of this is the centrality that human guilt has had in the Christian religion. Accountability for actions, and some accompanying guilt, is clearly present in other religions and, indeed in the lives of nonreligious persons as well. Human cultures are replete with devices to relieve guilt: gods are placated by sacrifices, penitential disciplines are required, psychotherapists are visited, encounter groups are formed, and liquor is consumed. The sense of guilt is deep, abiding, and I suspect quite natural. To be forgiven, to be reconciled with those from whom we have become estranged, is a significant desire in most persons.[68]

I indicated above that when a particular theological tenet assumes a place of particular importance, it affects the ordering of other tenets in a coherent theological account. That the doctrine of sin had great importance for Augustine, Calvin, and Edwards, is unmistakable. These theologians could not carry their views of divine sovereignty to a possible extreme partly in order to remain able to hold persons accountable for their immoral acts; to have the providential Deity be the author of sinful acts was an embarrassment both religiously and theologically. As we have briefly noted, each of these theologians worked out a position in which the divine sovereign causes the human conditions (capacity for agency)

---

68. On his deathbed my father recited in Swedish the words of I John 1:9, "If we confess our sins, he is faithful and just, and will forgive our sins and cleanse us from all unrighteousness." Without ecclesiastical authorization I was deeply moved to respond, also in Swedish, "Father, your sins are forgiven."

which make sin possible. He is the author of sin in this limited way; he permits it, but it occurs through secondary causes. These three theologians all had views of the human fault that were deep and broad; each in his own time conducted polemics against theologians and traditions that he felt were somewhat superficial in their conceptions of that problem, and thus superficial in their understanding of the importance of the atonement gained by the death of Christ. The divine sense of justice required the costly sacrifice of God's son to atone for the sins of the world; it is only through faith in God's mercy and benevolence, which are known only through the cross, that human beings can be rightly related to God.

The salvation of man becomes a preoccupation because the problem of sin is so critical. Edwards, in the famous Enfield Sermon, "Sinners in the Hands of an Angry God," could powerfully catalogue the circumstances in human life and the actions which manifested the depravity of the heart.[69] There was "profit," as Calvin said, in repenting, and in faith. This concern for sin and redemption is rooted in the Bible; it has continued throughout orthodox Christian theology. The human problems and their resolutions to which this concern points have nourished much of Christian piety and shaped much of Christian theology.

The perception of the depth and persistence of the human fault is something from this tradition that I shall retrieve and sustain. What is problematic is its placement within other tenets, and the significance that it has in the ordering of the relations of themes to each other. The question to be faced is whether one can take the human fault with deep seriousness, establish some sense of the possibilities of human alteration, and claim some benefits of the divine benevolence, without becoming trapped in utilitarian Christianity's preoccupation with human guilt.

Augustine, Calvin, Edwards, and Schleiermacher each made arguments from experience as well as arguments from Scripture. The first three had a confidence in the sufficiency of Scripture for theology that for various reasons is difficult to sustain in our time. A very typical pattern in major discourses of Edwards, for example, is a section in which evidences from experience are adduced with arguments from reason for his theological points, followed by evidences from the Bible. For example, the first part of his treatise on original sin adduces evidences for it from "facts and events, as found by observation and experience," together with some biblical and polemical arguments. The second part concerns "observations on particular parts of holy Scripture, which prove the doctrine of original sin."[70] The first contains not only evidences from experience but philosophical arguments about the problem of causality, the

69. Edwards, "Sinners in the Hands of an Angry God," in *Works,* 2:7-12.
70. Edwards, *Original Sin* (Yale ed.), p. vii and p. ix.

notion of free will. The second is basically exegesis of key biblical passages, with arguments against those who interpret the passages differently. Scripture proves the experience; experience does not prove Scripture. He proceeds from "reason, and the nature of things" to the "Holy Scriptures, the revelation that God has given of his mind and will," in the discourse on "Justification by Faith" and many others.[71] Reason and Scripture reinforce each other since both pertain to the same reality, but the biblical revelation is always the surer basis for authorizing the points that are made. Calvin works in a similar way, though the divisions are not made in the same way in the structure of his arguments. But for Calvin as well, the biblical revelation is the more secure; its authorization provides a basis for developing theology properly.

I have indicated that the biblical materials are themselves human expressions of and reflections upon human experience of a divine reality. This requires a qualification of the authority of Scripture as that was assured to the three earlier theologians in the Reformed tradition. I shall not undertake a lengthy discussion of biblical authority in theology in this work but simply state that my view of the subject is quite different from those of Augustine, Calvin, and Edwards.

I appreciate the strength of the views of the divine governance in the Reformed tradition; in my judgment this tradition has sustained a proper view of the limitations of human capacities to determine human destiny, and the destiny of the worlds. It has understood well how desires are fundamental in limiting the range of possible courses of action in persons. Augustine's interpretation of love as desire, and Edwards's affirmation that "it must be true, in some sense, that the will is as the greatest apparent good is," express important truths about human agency.[72] All of the theologians I have cited in this tradition stand in sharp contrast to views of the person that sustain a radical freedom, a "transcendental freedom"; all of them perceive accurately how past experiences condition, if not determine, future choices, how the range of possible actions is limited not only by the past experiences of agents but also by the external conditions in which particular choices are made. Each of them, as I noted, continues to hold persons accountable for their actions, and thus each finds a way to articulate a limited range of agency within a larger framework of deeply conditioned, if not utterly determined, choices. Their explanations of the freedom of the will become very intricate, and border on paradox.

The rigors of their views depend upon the interpretations they give of the nature of causality. An exploration of their views on this question

71. Edwards, "Justification by Faith," in *Works*, 1:630, col. 1.
72. Edwards, *Freedom of the Will* (Yale ed.), p. 142.

is not in order here, more than to indicate that all were heirs of a general understanding of causality contributed to Western thought by Aristotle and others in the Greek tradition. It can be argued that in the case of Edwards one finds some intimations of views that resemble those of Hume as well. With deep appreciation for the basic weight of their arguments about human actions, I shall attempt to qualify the stringency of their "determinisms" with an interpretation of human agency that rests on an interactional view rather than a stringent cause-effect view of human action. I shall argue that the possibilities of human action are severely limited both by the kinds of persons we have become as a result of natural capacities and experience and by the particular circumstances within which choices are made. But as agents within these structures we have capacities to respond to events and to others in such a way that we can in limited ways sustain or alter a course of events. The agents and the "fields" of interaction are both limiting; they both, however, provide necessary conditions for the possibility of action. Human beings and the events in which which they participate are not providentially determined in the highly specific ways that some of the Reformed theologians believed. They are limited by the governance which finally is divine; they are sustained by that governance; that governance provides the conditions for the possibility to intervene in events but does not determine the particular interventions. Like the strong determinists of the Reformed tradition, I shall argue that there are occasions on which we can only consent to what is occurring, but consent is a voluntary activity. I shall argue that much is to be appropriated from some modern understandings of the limitations of accountability for certain actions and for the consequences of actions. Most basically, I shall seek to replace what I believe to be a dominant cause-effect model in the tradition with one of interaction.

Perhaps in the eyes of some readers this discussion of problematics that I find in the Reformed tradition has effectively removed my claim to be an heir to it. The alterations that I have suggested may be sufficient for some to judge that my claim is false. I reiterate: the appropriation of some of its basic themes is based not upon the fact that they can be found in the tradition but upon my judgment that this tradition has perceived some of the fundamental aspects of life in the world in relation to the ultimate power and orderer of life. Imperious as it may seem, I appropriate those elements of the tradition which seem to me to be defensible.

Conclusions

The purpose of this chapter has been to indicate the particular strand of the Christian tradition that I prefer, to establish sufficient grounds from theologians in that tradition to warrant the claim to affinity with it, to indicate those aspects of the tradition which I find problematic that are closely related to the reasons I prefer it, and to show the main elements that I retrieve from it.

The final three chapters are my proposals for a theology which responds to the criticisms I have made of the Reformed tradition and of other theological options, and states the case for my own: my proposals for an adequate understanding of human life in relation to God and for human agency, and my general proposal for the shape that ethics takes in this developed theological context. Before turning to this task, however, I shall indicate how a number of strands or themes introduced in the first four chapters are being drawn on and already, to some extent, woven together.

The interpretation of the relevant religious and cultural circumstances developed in Chapter 1 pointed clearly toward the importance of retrieving a theocentricity that has eroded. Culturally, such a view can be articulated in terms of a clear acknowledgment of the ultimate dependence of life on realities or powers beyond human control, and in terms of the importance of reassessing the place of our species in the universe, and of individuals in society and in nature. Chapter 2 went ahead of the story, so to speak, to begin to see the implications of the direction that was suggested. Some of the revisions I make of the Christian theological tradition were introduced there, and continue to be developed. The principal one is that we cannot be as certain as the tradition has been that man is so centrally, so exclusively, the object of divine beneficence or divine providence. In an effort to explain why this is the case, evidences and explanations for the development of our universe, of life, of the human species, and of the likely terminus of our universe were introduced. The theologians introduced in this chapter all have developed strong doctrines of the divine governance of all things; they are strongly theocentric, and thus a preference for them was indicated. They also have strong doctrines of divine providence and justice focused on man, and thus create a major problem.

The critique of contemporary religion in Chapter 1 raised the issue of the self-serving, utilitarian, instrumental character of both religious activities and of religious ideas. The validity of this interpretation rests on observations that religious practices are developed and sustained not because they honor God but because they offer comfort and happiness to human beings, that religious ideas become supporting props and ideological principles for meeting a variety of human needs. Not only is this the case for individual and interpersonal life; it is true also for the developing morality and ethical thought of the churches. Persons adopt moral and social causes, whether from the extremes of right and left, or in the middle, and develop from the theological tradition those principles which provide religious authorization for their moral preferences. The ideas developed about the Deity can easily be manipulated to support human needs and moral causes without sufficient tests of the adequacy of the theology that informs them. We strive valiantly to put God in the service of man; we avoid facing the question of how man is to be put in the service of God. Even theologians in the Reformed tradition wanted to secure "profit" for human beings in religious life and faith. Yet the Reformed tradition, with its stress on divine sovereignty or governance, can be developed in the direction that this book is taking. The chief end of man is, after all, to glorify God.

The problem of the knowledge of God—how he is known and what can be known about him—is, of course, vast. The interpretation of several theological options given above exposed some of the perils of too quickly resorting to the language of mystery and to language that provides excessive certainty in detail about these matters. One needs to note that even our Reformed theologians, who on the basis of their confidence in the biblical revelation as well as in reasoning from human experience seemed to be able to say a lot with great certainty, acknowledged the limits of human accessibility to the workings and will of the Deity. The most suitable way to seek God, Calvin wrote, "is not for us to attempt with bold curiosity to penetrate to the investigation of his essence," but to contemplate him in his works through which he in some manner communicates himself.[73] In a brief section on the function and limits of the arts he warns, "let not God's majesty, which is far above the perception of the eyes, be debased through unseemly representations."[74] There always remains an element of the divine majesty that escapes our verbal representations, there is always an element of inscrutability to the will of God which in certain circumstances properly qualifies our claims to knowledge. Similar acknowledgments can be found in other theologians in the Reformed tradition. Prudence, or judiciousness, is always in order when one attempts to delineate with some specificity just what God's ordering of life requires; as Rahner vividly points out, silence before unspeakable mystery is often in order. Yet if the turn is taken toward theocentric ethics, readiness to risk more, rather than less, is required. The basic principle of divine governance at least warrants careful reflection for purposes of ethics and openness to indicators of what is required from many sources. One cannot propose that human actions are to relate to all things in a manner appropriate to their relations to God without claiming some knowledge of what those relations to God are, and what is required of us.

73. Calvin, *Institutes*, I, 5, 9; McNeill ed., 1:62.
74. Ibid., I, 11, 12; 1:112.

The move toward more "objective" ethics than has often recently been defended in Protestant ethics is possible on the theological bases I have been developing. The Christian tradition has in one way or another generally sustained more objective ethics; the commands of God are given in Scripture or natural law; there is a pattern to relations which are appropriate to our approximations of the Kingdom of God; we are to obey and apply the law of love. But as I have indicated, the penchant in both Christian ethics and in much of Western philosophical ethics is to make man the measure of all things. Theologians find ways of developing a happy coincidence between the divine law and what fulfills human life. If, however, a theology develops views of the divine majesty and governance in which this happy coincidence is not always and in all cases true, the ethics have to be altered as well. One moves closer to some aspects of the Stoic tradition than most of Christian theology and ethics has. One entertains the possibility that the "law of God" does not guarantee benefits to oneself, to the perceived interests and goods of one's community, or even to the human species as a whole.

I have developed the primacy or centrality of human experience as the matrix in which the presence of the divine reality is sensed. The Reformed theologians, as we have seen, characteristically rely on various dimensions of human experience and on their reasoning about those dimensions to establish the plausibility of central tenets of their thought. The "senses" which I delineated are aspects of piety; they are imbedded in the religious affections. Theology as a practical enterprise has regularly tested doctrines by experience, showed how symbols, myths, and concepts illumine profound aspects of human life. The range of experiences used by theologians varies from case to case. The extent to which experience does not confirm religious beliefs is a persistent question in the history of religious consciousness and activity. I have noted that our experience of the natural world, interpreted and explained by relevant theories from the sciences, is not denied by theologians, but its significance can be avoided in what they write. I noted that we have a Ptolemaic religion in a Copernican universe; religion and theology have to do with God in relation to man and history, not so much in relation to the natural world. Theologians find ways to assure the believer that if his or her experience does not confirm religious beliefs in the present vale of tears, those beliefs will be confirmed in the long run in eternal life, or there are hidden reasons that keep the beliefs from being confirmed in experience. Piety—the religious affections—however, is no guarantee of self-fulfillment. Piety evoked by a powerful Deity is not always comforting to human beings. Yet the theological enterprise has significance largely to those whose affections are evoked by certain dimensions of human experience, and whose reflections are moved and in part governed by these experiences.

The theme of affections will be developed further for other reasons indicated in this chapter. I noted how Jonathan Edwards sought to develop a view of knowing and acting that did not separate affections from mind and that did not separate desire from critical analysis about the objects of desire. Augustine's development of love has strong similarities with this. I have indicated my own judgments about the interpenetration of affectivity, intellect, and will in making judgments and choices. These themes will be further developed when I make a case for viewing human beings as "valuing beings." As valuing beings they are not irrational; they can be critical about what they value and why. The centrality of valuing helps to hold together rationality and volition; both are integral to the way in which I shall develop this idea. Religion and morality are both valuing activities; the religious and moral "affections" can be seen to be positively related. And when the ultimate object of religious affections is God, the power and orderer of the worlds, morality becomes central to religion; one cannot have piety that does not issue in morality. Both religious and moral activity are directed toward an end beyond themselves: the honoring, or glorifying, of God.

Inferences that can be drawn from this view of God about the limits as well as the possibilities of human life are not dissonant with inferences that can be drawn from scientific interpretations of astrophysical, geological, and biological sorts. Ethical themes suggested earlier can be brought together with themes drawn from the Reformed tradition in Christian theology. The rhetoric of the "grandeur" and "misery" of man is too simple; it can mask the need for a careful assessment of the place of our species in the whole of nature and the place of one individual life in the context of its communities. Both theologically and ethically we need to take into account not only the dependence of man on other features of the ordering of nature but also the significance of culture and the human capacities for agency. Proper restraints of human culture and activity, as well as proper interventions, need to be delineated within the vision of the human species as related to a divine governance. This cannot be done in our period of culture and history without taking into account those indicators from the sciences which can give some clues as to what human activities will relate all things in a manner appropriate to their relations to God under present conditions.

The biblical religions have been very alert to the indicators of a human fault. Augustine, Calvin, and Edwards were more extreme than some in portraying its depths and its pervasiveness; Luther and others have been their equals in this regard. One does not need to appropriate the traditional explanatory theories of the origin and continuation of sin to profit from many of the astute perceptions of the human condition that are forthcoming from traditional Christian theology. One does not need to cast some of these conditions for which humans are accountable in traditional religious terms; but to do so gives some clues to the continuing importance of the tradition. There is idolatry; from early biblical writings forward the term persists. It refers to absolute confidence in objects, realities, and persons that do not merit that confidence. It refers to the surrender of accountability for oneself by in effect enslaving oneself to some person or cause. It refers to too much confidence in appropriate "objects", that do not bear the excessive trust we have in them. There is pride; we know about it not only from the biblical religions but also from the Greek literary and moral traditions. It is that overweening trust in the rectitude of our judgments, the superiority of our perspectives, that keeps us from due self-criticism and from hearing the criticisms of others. There is infidelity. It refers to the breaking of bonds in which duties and obligations are formed, to our capacities for betrayal of persons and deception of them, to our resort to expedience to justify our failures to act when our moral obligations clearly demand our defense of those human values to which we profess loyalty. There is sloth. It is not only laziness per se, but also complacency, diffuseness, irresponsibility, and lack of effort to discipline ourselves. These and other themes of the human fault, which draw on the Christian tradition, Reformed and otherwise, will be developed later. These roots of improper actions are, in a theological account, seen to be grounded in part in being improperly related to God, and to other things in relation to God.

Finally, a number of matters introduced in previous chapters point toward the importance of the way in which we construe the world for the ways in which we act in it. Julian Hartt's warning that a religious construal of the world is more than merely a linguistic phenomenon is correct. Indeed, a religious "vision" of the world affects our very perceptions of others, of the events in which we participate, and of nature. In the Reformed tradition, and particularly in the thought of Augustine and Edwards, as in their modern heir, H. Richard Niebuhr, there is a strong doctrine of "conversion," of significant alteration if not transformation of the perspectives of those who are oriented finally toward God. In Augustine, as we have seen, this doctrine is developed in terms of having the proper ultimate object of love or desire, God. With this, he was convinced, one would rightly order all other desires, rightly relate to other things in a manner appropriate to their relations to God's purposes. Edwards's *Nature of True Virtue,* as I have noted, develops a very similar theme. It is no accident that Niebuhr expounds Augustine and Calvin as examples of the type of Christian ethics he calls "Christ The Transformer of Culture," the type with which his own work is most closely identified.[75] In *Radical Monotheism and Western Culture,* Niebuhr's diagnosis of the disorders of modern life are made possible and deeply informed by his construal of the world in a radically monotheistic way.[76] An alteration of the world, meager as its effects might be, occurs in part through the alteration of our visions of the world; that is, by perceiving, construing, interpreting, and understanding life in a theocentric focus. In Niebuhr's favorite terms, with God as the object of our ultimate confidence and ultimate fidelity, our other "trusts" and other "loyalties" are reordered.[77] This theme of "conversion" of perspective, drawing deeply on the Reformed tradition, will be central to the practical claims I make for theological ethics.

I have drawn on a number of strands introduced in the previous chapters and in this one to indicate again, and in a way developed somewhat differently, the program of the subsequent three chapters. The task now is to formulate the crucial concerns of this volume: an adequate understanding of God, an interpretation of man in relation to God thus understood, and the pattern of ethics that follows from these.

75. H. Richard Niebuhr, *Christ and Culture* (New York: Harper, 1951), pp. 190–229.
76. H. Richard Niebuhr, *Radical Monotheism*, pp. 49–89.
77. Ibid., pp. 11–23.

5

God in Relation to
Man and the World

In Chapter 4 I indicated three principal features of the Reformed tradition which form the basic theme of this work: (1) piety, which is evoked by (2) the powers of God, (3) in relation to whom we are to relate ourselves and all things. Theology, I indicated, is a way of construing the world, a way of perceiving, interpreting, and articulating life in the world as it is related to the power that brings it into being and in whose "hands" is its ultimate destiny. As a way of construing the world, theology is a practical discipline; what makes this practical discipline theology, however, is that the world is construed theocentrically. This does not mean that a human being can construe the world as God might, but that in a theological construal of the world God is the ultimate reality to be taken into account. In Chapter 3 I indicated that the "truth claims" that a theologian can make are "soft" in comparison to those that natural scientists can make according to their procedures of confirmation. Yet some evidences for the reality of God need to be adduced if only to avoid the charge that God is purely a projection of the human imagination. Calvin, Schleiermacher, and others have argued persuasively that we cannot know God in himself but only through his works, or only in relation to the world and to man. In keeping with this point of view, I shall develop a theology in the restricted sense of the term; that is, a view of the Diety. I will, however, make no claims to know God in what has classically been called his aseity. I have previously indicated that theology is persuasive only in the context of religious affections, and that these affections are grounded in certain "senses."

This chapter develops the following general line of discussion and argument. First, religion is, in an important way, a matter of affectivity. This is not to argue that religion is a matter of passing feelings, or that because religion is affective it is not also a way of knowing the world. The first section of the chapter develops various concepts and terms that are used to deal with human affectivity, and establishes the principal terms and distinctions that I find to be appropriate. I use the term "affectivity" as a general term to include "senses," piety, and affection. I intend "senses" to mean those terms I introduced in Chapter 3; I shall develop the idea of piety in terms of basic attitude and disposition; and I shall refer "affections" to particular "emotions."

With the terms and distinctions delineated, I argue that affectivity is evoked by responses to a wide range of events and "objects" that we experience. It is not the presence of affectivity that makes particular attitudes religious, but the object of the affectivity. The affectivity that "becomes" religious, however, is a response to very particular events and objects; in the religious consciousness these objects and events are perceived to be ultimately related to the powers that sustain us and bear down upon us, to the Ultimate Power on which all of life depends. The rise of the affections that become religious within basic piety and within a theological construing of the world is illustrated not only to clarify the argument but also to evoke empathy for what I believe is involved in religious life.

Since I am not convinced that one can argue from a wide range of particular experiences to a logically necessary conclusion that a powerful Other—a monotheistic God—exists, the discussion does not take this turn. Rather it shows descriptively how, given affectivity and the ways in which it is engendered not only by common experience but also by participation in a religious tradition, the religious tradition provides warrants and symbols for moving from particular experiences to the experience of responding to an ultimate power. But, as I made clear in Chapter 3, a contemporary theological construing of the world works selectively from a tradition.

Following this I argue that some classic terms that the Christian tradition has used to refer to the presence, power, and activity of the Deity in the world continue to be meaningful in our own cultural circumstances. There is a development of the themes of God as Creator, as Sustainer and Governor, as Judge, and as Redeemer. What can be said in these traditional theological terms can also be expressed in more abstract language, and one can find warrants for it in nonreligious construals and explanations of the world of which we are a part. This is followed by a brief discussion of the relation of my argument to some themes in the Christian tradition.

I: Religion

Religion is described and defined in many different ways. I shall not argue for the particular usage I have chosen.[1] The brief descriptive accounts given by two contemporary theologians indicate what is central to my view. Richard R. Niebuhr wrote:

> To exist as a religious being is to be awakened from seeing and hearing, from working and thinking, from fearing and despairing to the consciousness that all these actions are affections aroused in us by the presence of power. Human religion is the sense of being aimed at—by strengths coercive and persuasive, which affect men as intellectual beings, as moral beings, as aesthetic beings, as sentient, and as biological beings. . . . Religion arises as human reaction and answer to the state of being affected totally.[2]

1. See James M. Gustafson, *The Contributions of Theology to Medical Ethics* (Milwaukee: Marquette University Press, 1978), n. 2, pp. 96–97, for my critique of some views of religion.
2. Richard R. Niebuhr, *Experiential Religion,* p. 34.

In Julian N. Hartt's terms, "We ought to say that [a man] is not really religious unless he feels that some power is bearing down on him, unless, that is, he believes he must do something about divine powers who have done something about him."[3] In both of these descriptions affectivity is central to a religious response to the world. In both, the affectivity is evoked by a power or powers that limit and sustain life in the world.

The Use of Terms

A wide range of human affections is evoked by a sense of being limited and sustained by powers beyond the self. There is no canonical list of the emotions or senses that can have religious significance. And those that can have religious significance are not per se different from those without religious significance. In Chapter 3 I introduced six "sense" terms that have deep affective dimensions: dependence, gratitude, obligation, remorse or repentance, possibility, and direction. Jonathan Edwards lists the biblical religious affections as fear, hope, love, hatred, desire, joy, sorrow, gratitude, compassion, and zeal.[4] In his classic discussion of the emotions Thomas Aquinas delineates five contrasting pairs: love and hate, desire and aversion, pleasure and sadness, hope and despair, fear and courage; to these he adds anger.[5] St. Paul lists the fruits of the Spirit as "love, peace, patience, kindness, goodness, faithfulness, gentleness, self-control." These are contrasted with the "works of the flesh": "immorality, impurity, licentiousness, idolatry, sorcery, enmity, strife, jealousy, anger, selfishness, dissension, party spirit, carousing, and the like."[6] Edwards and others have sought to designate the affections which are truly religious; a normative concern is coupled with the descriptive. St. Thomas deals with the "gifts of the Spirit" as a separate topic from the emotions, and in accord with tradition he expounds them according to Isaiah 11:2-3.

> And the Spirit of the Lord shall rest upon him with the spirit of wisdom and understanding, the spirit of counsel and might, the spirit of knowledge and the fear of the Lord. And his delight shall be in the fear of the Lord. (R.S.V.)

A sorting out of these affections and the claims that are made for them, the relations of the gifts of the Spirit to the virtues, and so on, is

---

3. Julian N. Hartt, *A Christian Critique of American Culture* (New York: Harper and Row), p. 52.
4. Edwards, *Religious Affections*, p. 102.
5. For the complete discussion, see Thomas Aquinas, *Summa Theologiae*, 1a, 2ae, Qq. 22–54.
6. Gal. 5:19–23.

not immediately germane to this discussion.[7] I shall describe a broad range
of affective responses that can be understood as human responses to the
powers that bear down on us.

In addition to the question of what affective responses should be
included, there is the problem of how to order them. The discussion of
affections, passions, emotions, feelings, desires, attitudes, sensibilities,
dispositions, and related terms is extensive in the literature of "philosophical psychology." In this discussion I have chosen to use the term
"affectivity" to include "senses," attitudes, dispositions, and more particular affections or emotions.

Earlier I introduced a series of "senses of. . . ." They are a sense
of dependence, of gratitude, of obligation, of remorse and repentance, of
possibilities, and of direction. A term that helps elucidate what I mean
by a "sense" is "consciousness"; we are conscious of our dependence,
conscious of possibilities, and so forth. But consciousness, if it is interpreted exclusively in cognitive terms, limits the range of meaning of
"sense." "Sense" in my usage covers both affectivity and awareness.

The second and third aspects of affectivity are a set: attitude and
disposition. When I develop the meaning of piety I shall use these terms.
By attitude I mean a basic "posture" of the self toward the world that
has persistence but is not an immutable state of the person. Attitudes are
"settled" but subject to change. The old idea of "filial piety" indicates
a persisting attitude of children toward parents, one of respect. Attitudes
and dispositions are related to each other in an intimate way. By "disposition" I refer to a readiness to act in certain ways. Particular actions
are not determined by a disposition, but dispositions predispose us to act
in particular ways, and to act with some degree of consistency. Piety as
disposition is a precondition for courses of action that will express our
respect for others and the world and our awe and respect for God.

7. I have eliminated a lengthy discussion in which literature that informs my conclusions was analyzed. The following was included: Aristotle on the emotions, in "Rhetoric,"
bk. 2, 1–11, in *The Basic Works of Aristotle,* ed. Richard McKeon (New York: Random
House, 1941), pp. 1379–1403; Augustine, *City of God,* bk. 9, 4–6, pp. 282–86; Thomas
Aquinas, *Summa Theologiae* 1a, 2ae, Qq. 22–54, and Q. 68; Eric D'Arcy, Introduction to
St. Thomas Aquinas, *Summa Theologiae,* Blackfriars edition (New York: McGraw-Hill,
1967–), vol. 19 and vol. 20; works by Shaftesbury, Hutcheson, and Adam Smith in L. A.
Selby-Bigge, *British Moralists,* 2 vols. (Oxford: Clarendon Press, 1897), vol. 1; Rousseau,
Emile; Edwards, *Religious Affections*; Max Scheler, *The Nature of Sympathy,* trans. Peter
Heath (New Haven: Yale University Press, 1954); Scheler, "Ordo Amoris," in *Selected
Philosophical Essays,* trans. David L. Lachteman (Evanston: Northwestern University
Press, 1973), pp. 98–135; Richard R. Niebuhr, *Experiential Religion*; and Don E. Saliers,
The Soul in Paraphrase: Prayer and the Religious Affections (New York: Seabury Press,
1980), especially pp. 1–20. For my earlier discussion of related issues, see *Can Ethics Be
Christian?* pp. 25–47; for bibliography, see Chapter 2, n. 2, pp. 180–81.

The fourth term is "affection." As I use the term it refers to emotion. If emotion is understood to be purely nonrational, however, a distortion is involved. Affections are evoked by particular events, others, and occasions; they do not have the same settledness that attitudes and dispositions have. Yet to some degree they are governed by our senses, our attitudes, and our dispositions.

All four are object-related. Our "senses" are senses *of*; what they are senses of stems from our relations to others, to the world around us, and, in the religious context, to God. Our dispositions are dispositions *to act* in particular ways. In the religious context they are dispositions to act in ways that respect the world as given by God, that honor God, that relate all things in a manner appropriate to their relations to God. Our attitudes are attitudes *toward*; they are our stances or postures toward persons, things, and events. In a religious context, piety is an attitude toward the power that sustains and governs the world. Affections are evoked *by*; while we may well be disposed to respond affectively in certain ways as a result of settled beliefs and the fruits of experience (for example, some persons are "prone to anger"), particular affections are aroused by very particular circumstances, events, persons, and so forth. Religious affections are evoked by particular occasions in which persons of religious consciousness perceive the presence of the powers of God. Sometimes it is fear of God; sometimes it is joy in response to a perceived goodness of God.

Our senses, our attitudes and dispositions, and our affections qualify our perceptions of events and persons, as well as the ways in which we think about them and act in relation to them. Such qualifications are not confined to religious persons. They are part of the life of the scientist, the dedicated hedonist, the hard-driving corporate executive, and every person. What makes them religious is their ultimate object, not the qualities or particular descriptions of each. We all have times of fear; what makes fear a religious affection is that it is evoked by the powers of God.

There is nothing sacred about these distinctions. Some aspects of experience, such as love, cannot be confined to affections; love refers to attitude and disposition as much as to affection. In the end the distinctions and concepts have heuristic value; I use them to illuminate and elucidate religious aspects or dimensions of human experience.

It is important to remember that affectivity as it is used here is not set over against intellect or reason. The Reformed tradition in theology never set affections against cognition. Affectivity and intellect are interrelated. To separate them radically leads to misleading interpretations not only of religion but also of morality.[8]

The radical separation in morality leads to ethical theories that take little or no account of motives for actions other than "reasons," of failures of "will" to do what reason requires, of the importance of desires and dispositions toward values in moral activity, and of the importance of affective responses such as indignation in the presence of gross injustice, for raising moral questions to consciousness. But morality is not simply a matter of feelings and emotions either. Morality is more than a feeling for values, more than simply pro or con attitudes toward actions, persons, and events. Purely emotive theories of morality are as much in error as rationalistic ones.

There have been, and continue to be, rationalistic theories of religion and arguments for the existence of God which rely on "reason" alone. And there are always temptations to view religious life as purely a matter of feelings and emotions. For the most part, however, religious affectivity and knowledge of God have been held together. Augustine's theology, as we noted, is based on a deep and natural desire or love for the Good. But one cannot love what one does not know, so loving involves knowing. Also, as we have seen, Jonathan Edwards was careful in his discussion of the religious affections to include understanding and willing as well as feeling.

Intricate interrelations between what can be distinguished conceptually as emotion and reason occur not only in religious and moral experience but in many other areas as well. Experience occurs in relation and response to realities objective to persons, and not to mere figments of human imagination, projections of human feelings, or self-generated moments of significance. There are cognitive aspects of our relationships and responses; there are "reasons" for our particular emotions, and for our attitudes, dispositions, and senses. Our affectivity is evoked by our perception and understanding of others, of things objective to ourselves, as well as by subjective conditions.

Take the example of riding in a small automobile during high winds and very heavy rains. There are reasons for fear; the control of the car by the driver is far less than under normal weather and road conditions. Previous experience and knowledge, as well as the current perception of conditions, all make anxiety "rational." Certain knowledge conditions can alter the passengers' perceptions of reality, and in turn revise the degree of anxiety. If, for example, the driver knows the road, has had a great deal of experience driving in such conditions, and "knows" the car

8. For contemporary examples, see Gewirth, *Reason and Morality,* and Ronald M. Green, *Religious Reason.*

well, the anxiety diminishes. Perceived confidence in the driver and the car qualifies the immediate response of fear.

Intellectual activity and knowledge-conditions that are object-related inform our affectivities. What persons accept as good explanations of the realities that evoke affective responses makes a difference. A person, for example, who believes that his or her destiny from day to day is determined by the positions of the stars and the planets will respond differently to the "starry heavens above" than will a person informed by contemporary astronomy, astrophysics, and psychology. Astronomical explanations for some persons might eliminate a response of awe and wonder by providing natural explanations for all that can be seen. For others the same explanations might even enhance a religious response to the course of the planets and the stars. Beliefs, explanations, perceptions, and affections are intricately related in a great deal of human experience.

This is not to say that "reason" and "emotion" cannot and ought not to be distinguished. Dispassionate, disinterested pursuits are intellectually appropriate in many circumstances. The proverbial search for truth by the natural scientist is a case in point, though even there the endeavor is related to a deep (and thus "affective") interest on the part of the investigator. The clear, refined arguments of a moral philosopher, at each point developed in relation to the arguments of other moral philosophers, is another case in point. Religious affections can be altered, indeed "corrected," by testing the adequacy of the beliefs that inform and express them in the light of biblical research, human experience, and scientific accounts of the world. The principal contention, however, remains: affectivity and cognition are intimately related in experience.

Piety, a basic disposition and attitude, has primacy in religious affectivities. Piety is a more accurate term than faith, the most traditional one used in Christian discourse. Because of the importance of this shift to language of piety rather than faith some justification is needed.

Piety is not a transient emotion, though consciousness of piety ebbs and flows with circumstances. It does not refer to piousness—the kind of sanctimoniousness that lends itself to caricature in novels, films, and drama; or to intensity of religious emotion. It is a settled disposition, a persistent attitude toward the world and ultimately toward God. It takes particular colorings or tones in particular circumstances, but awe and respect are the fundamental and persisting characteristics of piety.

I choose piety rather than faith as the primary characteristic of a religious disposition and attitude for important reasons. Faith is often contrasted with reason. Most modern religious thinkers do not hold that faith begins at the point where reason ends, that faith is an absurd leap beyond a sure and certain rational knowledge to knowledge that comes by virtue of the authority of the Bible or the authority of an ecclesiastical institution. Faith does mean this, however, to many Christian believers and secular people. In this distinction the contrast is drawn between two different sources of authority: reason and faith. Either things are known on the authority of faith that cannot be known by reason and experience, or faith authorizes beliefs that are not subject to critical investigation. The contrast is between two different sources of knowledge and in some cases between different things that are known. Reason and experience are one source; the Bible and tradition are the other. Or, one knows certain things about man, the world, and nature by reason, but one knows about God by faith. I have indicated that this dichotomy is wrong in part because of the experiential basis of all our knowledge, including our knowledge of God.

Faith, in the sense of trust or confidence, is often contrasted with unfaith, lack of confidence. This was the central meaning of faith in Luther's reformation of religious life. Sin was the absence of trust in God; faith was a sure and certain confidence in God. Trust in God was not resignation to fate, not consent to the limits of finitude, but confidence in God's love and mercy for man. Calvin also makes this plain.

> Now we shall possess a right definition of faith if we call it a firm and certain knowledge of God's benevolence toward us, founded upon the truth of the freely given promise in Christ, both revealed to our minds and sealed upon our hearts through the Holy Spirit.[9]

It is the true and certain knowledge of divine benevolence toward us that makes trust possible.

In my judgment there is a rightly measured confidence in the divine benevolence toward man, a benevolence adduced from a whole range of human experience, including that which is distinctively Christian. But the benevolence that we know and experience does not warrant the confidence that God's purposes are the fulfillment of my own best interests as I conceive them. Imaginatively, a scenario can be developed in which the divine benevolence will lead to the extinction of our species when conditions for its sustenance no longer exist on this planet; this, however, is not the sense in which the certainty of divine benevolence has been fostered in the mainstream of the Christian tradition. Both Christian piety and Christian theology have had excessive confidence in the divine goodness toward individuals and communities, and toward our species. The gift of life is from the divine goodness; the means of its sustenance and the measure of fulfillment it has are dependent upon that goodness: true. For these and other things one can have confidence in God, one can trust God, and one can affirm the benevolence of God. But I reject the notion

9. Calvin, *Institutes,* III, 2, 7; McNeill ed. 1:551.

of trust as ultimate confidence that God intends my individual good as the usually inflated and exaggerated terms portray that good.

Faith is often contrasted with unfaithfulness, with infidelity, with disloyalty. While faith in contrast with lack of trust is included in piety to a measured degree, faith in terms of fidelity is wholeheartedly affirmed. Richard R. Niebuhr comes close to my meaning in this regard. He has the faithful man ask, "How may I play my part in this field of powers? How may I be freed so that I may be aimed in the direction in which all true power and virtue move?"

> [M]an as a faithful being is not one thing only but is a being-in-process or a becoming, exhibiting and exercising a many-sided strength that is an elemental force of his nature, enlarging, enlivening, and intensifying his daily world and his own actions in that world. . . . [H]uman faithfulness presents itself as the great personal act or course of actions in which a man, or some family of men, commits and aligns himself to the one coercive and persuasive power in the world that is the recapitulating expression of the meaning of the whole. So wherever and whenever we see men giving themselves for that which is greater than themselves and greater than all the particular forces impinging on them, there we meet faithful human beings.[10]

Faith, in Niebuhr's sense of faithfulness, is central to piety. It is an aspect of respecting God; it is the honoring of God. It cannot in any respect be self-referential in terms of rewards or assurances to individual self-realization.

The term "piety," then, is more inclusive than the term "faith." Piety cannot be contrasted with reason. Faith as a measured confidence in God is part of piety, but faith in the benevolence of God to fulfill human purposes as we desire them to be fulfilled in all respects is not part of piety. Faith as fidelity is central to piety. It is an alignment of persons and communities with the "coercive and persuasive powers" that order life. It is, as Niebuhr makes clear, not simple resignation to fate, but a participation in the ordering and enriching of life. Faith, as excessive trust, puts God primarily in the service of humans. Faithfulness puts human beings in the service of God. Faithfulness, like measured trust, is part of the basic disposition toward the world and toward God that I call piety.

There are other reasons for choosing the word "piety." Faith as sure trust seems to exclude the propriety of that aspect of awe that is expressed in fear, not to mention anger, toward the Deity.

If piety is understood primarily in terms of awe and respect, there is a place in the religious affections for both an attraction toward the

10. Richard R. Niebuhr, *Experiential Religion,* p. 40, p. 38, and p. 39.

powers of God and an aversion from them; both a love of God, the giver of the possibilities for value and meaning in life, and fear and anger in the face of conditions which frustrate human aspirations and threaten or deny human life. Edwards believed that the affections that are religious in the Scriptures include a broad range: fear, hope, love, hatred, desire, joy, sorrow, gratitude, compassion, and zeal.[11] Piety does not foreclose anger, fear, and even hatred from being honest religious affections. The emotions as distinguished and listed by Thomas Aquinas can each, on occasion, be authentic expressions of piety: love and hatred; desire for God and aversion from God; pleasure in the signs of his benevolence and sadness when they are withdrawn; hope on those occasions when conditions provide possibilities for action and improvement of life, and despair when God appears to fate us or others; fear in the face of inexorable bad consequences of our actions as a result of the divine governance, and courage to act within the limited possibilities that the same governance provides; and anger against God, an authentic expression of piety vividly portrayed in the story of Job, in the life of Jeremiah, and in countless others throughout human history.[12]

My distinctions have only heuristic value. All are affectivities, and each is important in religious life. The term "affectivity" includes inclinations and understanding as well. To make it an inclusive concept is not to deny that under certain circumstances it is appropriate to make sharper distinctions between cognition and intellect on the one hand and emotions on the other.

The point has been made that religious affections are not unique; indeed, as affections per se they cannot be distinguished. I will therefore inquire how the variety of human affectivites is evoked in human experience, and how some of them can be described, construed, and understood in their significance to be religious. If the affectivities are evoked in human experience by a broad range of "objects" which in themselves are not religious, how is it that the religious consciousness understands both the affectivities and their ultimate object to have religious and theological significance?

"Nonreligious" Experiences, and Their Religious Significance

Putatively nonreligious experiences of persons and communities, as we have seen, can have religious meaning and significance. This theme is here elaborated in more detail. The issues are as follows. Affectivities that can be construed religiously can be evoked by many different objects,

11. Edwards, *Affections*, p. 102.
12. For Thomas's delineation of the emotions, see *Summa Theologiae*, 1a, 2ae, Qq. 22–30.

events, and persons. We do not have, except perhaps in the case of the true mystic, experiences of God as a distinct and isolated object. Our immediate experiences are of trees and germs, of strikes and wars, of life-support systems and television shows, of fathers and income-tax laws, of our bodies and our habits. Affectivities are evoked by things such as these rather than by a Deity experienced apart from such things. Thus, the objects that evoke our affectivities are not uniquely religious, and the affectivities themselves are not uniquely religious. How, then, can we describe and explain how objects of ordinary human experience which evoke ordinary human affectivities can have religious significance? That is, how do we perceive and construe them to be manifestations of powers bearing down on us, sustaining and limiting us? How can ordinary human affectivities evoked by ordinary human events be at the same time religious affectivities?

Much that I have said is similar to the basic claims of William James. A theological interpretation, however, takes a sharply different turn from a psychological one. I agree with James's observation that it is the object that makes affections religious.

> [T]he moment we are willing to treat the term "religious senti-
> ment" as a collective name for the many sentiments which reli-
> gious objects may arouse in alternation, we see that it probably
> contains nothing whatever of a psychologically specific nature.
> There is religious fear, religious love, religious awe, religious joy,
> and so forth. But religious love is only man's natural emotion of
> love directed to a religious object; . . . religious awe is the same
> organic thrill which we feel in a forest at twilight, or in a moun-
> tain gorge; only this time it comes over us at the thought of our
> supernatural relations. . . . [T]here is no ground for assuming a
> simple abstract "religious emotion" to exist as a distinct elemen-
> tary mental affection by itself, present in every religious experi-
> ence without exception.[13]

James points out that various thinkers have sought to specify more particularly what the religious affectivity is. "One man allies it to the feeling of dependence; one makes it a derivative from fear; others connect it with the sexual life; others still identify it with the feeling of the infinite: and so on."[14] If one remains close to experiences of many sorts, as James did and as I shall do, it is difficult to establish that the varieties of affectivity can be reduced to a single theme, or be adequately interpreted on the basis of a single response to a single object. Even if the "sense of de-

13. William James, *The Varieties of Religious Experience* (New York: Random House, n.d.), pp. 28–29.
14. Ibid., p. 28.

pendence" is primary, it is not sufficient to account for the varieties of affections that can become religious.

James's conclusion from his general account of this variety nicely poses the issue that must be confronted. "As there thus seems to be no one elementary religious emotion, but only a common storehouse of emotions upon which religious objects may draw, so there might conceivably also prove to be no one specific and essential kind of religious object, and no one specific and essential kind of religious act."[15] If one takes into account the many religions of the world, both historic and primitive ones, this guarded generalization is accurate. If there are many religious emotions (to use one of James's terms), and these are evoked by many different objects and experiences, one will not be surprised by the existence of polytheism. If agriculture and human reproduction evoke a sense of dependence upon fertile powers, it is understandable to have a goddess of fertility. If the same community finds itself at war from time to time, it develops a god of war.

Even monotheistic Christian theology makes significant distinctions to account for similar varieties of experience and of affectivity. Both theology and the language of prayer and worship indicate that God is experienced and conceived as the Creator on whom all things depend, and the Judge before whom all persons and communities are morally accountable. His wrath is experienced, as well as his tender mercy. Rather ordinary experiences of normal people in the Christian community can be adduced to sustain this view; one need not concentrate on the extreme and marginal types of experience that James examines. The classic types of prayers in the liturgies of Christian churches point to this: prayers of adoration which express awe in the presence of God's ineffable majesty; prayers of thanksgiving for the "goodness" of nature, institutions, and culture; confession of sin, in which remorse is articulated for moral faults; prayers of supplication for aid to be and do a variety of things; prayers of intercession in which persons open themselves to the divine governance and intentions for other persons, institutions, and events. Various religious affectivities, evoked by many experiences, are taken into account in the primary language of Christian piety.

Monotheism finally concludes that there is "one specific and essential kind of religious object"; but that conclusion does not preclude variety in religious affectivity and many different kinds of religious acts. Different concepts are used by theologians to account for this variety. For example, God's creative activity is distinguished from his redeeming activity; God has his moments of wrath and his moments of mercy. In monotheism, of course, what is distinguished must finally be brought again into a unity.

15. Ibid., p. 29.

This gets us ahead of our story, but suggests some factors that have to be taken into account in the argument. For now, other questions require attention. What objects and occasions evoke awe and respect, a sense of obligation and of possibility, fear and hope, joy and sadness? What ordinary experiences evoke these affectivities, which in piety and in a religious construal of the world, become religious? What moves the mind and heart to perceive and create these affectivities as religious? Why and how do persons and communities perceive the presence of God in and through these common experiences? My initial task here is descriptive.

Many arenas of putatively nonreligious experience have profound religious dimensions. They provide warrants within the religious consciousness for affirming the reality of an ultimate power that orders and sustains the world. I have chosen to distinguish five such arenas: experiences of nature, history, culture, society, and self. The division of these arenas is a matter of practical convenience; in experience they are usually interrelated. Our experiences of nature are culturally affected; culture has affected the development of the natural world; we are distanced from nature by many aspects of culture; culture provides explanations of nature. Historical events are conditioned by natural events and by human dependence on the natural world; they are also conditioned by the cultures of those who shape and respond to them. Social organization and social processes arise in part out of human relations to nature and of the nature of human beings; the particular forms of these organizations and processes are conditioned by cultures; they both shape and are shaped by historical events. Selves are bodies but are deeply conditioned by culture, historical events in which persons participate or to which they respond, and the social institutions in which they are nourished and through which they act.

Theologians have tended to write about each of these arenas in the abstract. We have treatises both ancient and modern, for example, on the relation of grace to nature, or on the natural orders of creation. But persons never experience nature in general, in the abstract. We experience aspects of and events in the natural world as they affect our interests and identities. There are many different responses to nature; some are passing, others are deep and perduring. Theologians usually write about history in the abstract. We have treatises dealing with faith and history, with the meaning of history, with the relationship of salvation history to universal history, and with Christ as the center of history. But we experience particular historical events, not history in general. Ordinarily, we do not worry about "the meaning of history," but we do attempt to judge the wider significance of particular historical events in past time and in our own time. Ordinarily, history in general does not evoke hope or despair; particular events evoke hope if they open possibilities for alterations of

conditions deemed detrimental to particular human interests, or despair
if they seem to foreclose possibilities of fulfilling particular human aspirations.

There are theological works on the relation of Christ to culture,
various theologies of culture, and works that deal with the relations of
religion and culture. Culture in such works is an abstraction; we never
experience culture in general. Recently more attention has been given by
some theologians to particular aspects of culture: literature, art, and technology. Technology is sometimes dealt with at a high level of generalization; increasingly, particular aspects are theologically interpreted, and
subjected to religious moral evaluation. But, technology in general is not
experienced; word-processing equipment, respirators, and jet airplanes
are. Some theologians respond to the "ethos" of modern culture; our
affective responses are more likely to be evoked, however, by alterations
in certain values that we deeply cherish, such as self-reliance or "the
work ethic." Religion and science are often discussed in general terms;
science becomes an abstraction in such discourse. We know sciences,
and respond to nuclear physics and its applications, or to human genetics
and its applications. We do not respond to art but to particular musical
compositions, paintings, sculptures, novels, dramas, films, and poems.

Society has usually been dealt with on a highly generalized level by
theologians. The Protestant tradition discusses the "orders of creation,"
such as family, state, and "economy." There are discussions of the theology of law and of the uses of law. To be sure, some topics such as usury
have been treated in detail. But we respond to a particular family, a
particular government, particular corporations, and particular laws.

Many treatises deal with "man" in the abstract. Theologians write
about human nature and human destiny; theological "anthropology" has
been a focus of concern for centuries. Our experience of ourselves, however, is always more specific. We respond to the pains and the pleasures
of our bodies, to memories of past deeds and experiences and to aspirations for future ones.

These arenas of human experience have, initially, a different function
in my argument than they have had in most theological ethics. They
provide the particular occasions for our affective responses. I am describing an order of experience. The order of experience, if I am correct,
is not a sense of the powers of God ordering nature, but experiences of
the natural world that evoke affectivities that can be religiously significant.
The intellectual construal of the theological significance of the objects that
evoke the affectivities and of the affectivities themselves is a further step
in the discussion. Generalization and abstraction become necessary, but
it is generalization about human experiences, and abstractions from them.
The ultimate power that sustains us and bears down upon us is experienced

through the particular objects, events, and powers that sustain us, threaten our interests, create conditions for human action, or evoke awe and respect. Both the description and the explanation of religion is excessively foreshortened by too hasty abstraction and generalization. This is important for theological ethics and religious morality as well; those things that are to be related appropriately to their relations to God are not nature, history, culture, society, and selves in general or in the abstract, but in the very specific circumstances in which human relationships and actions occur.   *goes back to experience*

Nature

One arena is our experience of the world of nature. Some of the richest experiences of beauty are evoked by aspects of the natural world. It may be the beauty of a cell viewed through an electron microscope, or the beauty of a landscape or seascape rich and subtle in its variations of color, movement, and form. It may be the beauty of the deeply lined, leathery face of an aged seaman, or that of an infant's smile. The experience may be evoked by something as small as a patch of lichen, with its hues of green, blue-green, and gray, on a granite boulder in a forest, or something as large as the range of the Canadian Rocky Mountains viewed from a distance. We respond to the beauties of nature with delight, with awe and wonder, with joy and with respect. Indeed, it is difficult not to be deeply grateful for these gifts that are not created by man.

We experience aspects of the natural world as sources of the sustenance of human well-being and flourishing. Without sun and rain, soil and plants, our species could not survive. Without the powers and processes of human reproduction we could not propagate our own kind. We use materials from the natural world to protect us from heat and cold, to build our homes and make our clothing. We harness natural powers to provide energy that eases the burdens of human work and living. We often rely on the natural healthy processes of our bodies to overcome illnesses and infections. Even when technology comes between us and nature, we continue to rely on it. We are deeply and inexorably dependent upon aspects of the natural world for human survival and flourishing. For these we are grateful, since we did not bring them into being. They deserve our respect, for without them we could not be. We recognize a duty to care for them.

But aspects of the natural world also threaten human interests. Carcinogenic cells, germs, viruses, and other causes of diseases and death are natural. Earthquakes, typhoons, droughts, and floods are natural. Tropical mountain streams are naturally "polluted" and their waters unsafe to drink. Even when human activities put us at greater risks, many of the risks are mediated by nature. The air we breathe, the waters we drink, the food we eat can all be contaminated by human interventions;

it is nonetheless pollutions of nature that threaten us. The threats of nature are both raw and mediated through human activity. We properly fear certain features of the natural world; it is not always a "friend" which serves our best interests. Its threats provoke awe and respect; its destructive as well as sustaining powers bear down on us. We are a part of the natural world; it brings us into life and sustains life; it also creates suffering and pain and death.

The natural world provides the materials and occasions for human creativity; it provides the conditions of possibility for developing our most distinctive human capacities. Much of humanly created beauty, if not an imitation of nature, relies on nature for its inspiration: English landscape paintings, Michelangelo's portrayal of God in the act of the creation of man on the Sistine Chapel ceiling, or Georgia O'Keeffe's painting of a cow's skull. Science investigates the powers and processes of nature: nature challenges human beings to search out its secrets, whether enshrouded in orderly movements of the planets, the layers of rock on earth, or the DNA molecule. Natural phenomena are there: they inspire, tease our curiosity, stimulate the development of human culture, provide the occasions for human achievements. Again, from nature come the senses of dependence, of gratitude, of possibility for human development and achievement; the occasions for delight and pleasure, for hope and courage, for zeal and joy.

Human achievement is not demeaned by recalling that many man-made objects have come from human assembly of aspects of nature, often cooperating with it more than fighting against it. One thinks of musical instruments; for example, the gourds that resonate sounds in Indian stringed instruments. One thinks of human interventions that remove or control impediments to natural processes: the surgical removal of diseased organs so that healthy ones can function; drugs that lower blood pressure so that strokes, heart attacks, and kidney disease can be avoided; artificial insemination and *in vitro* fertilization. One thinks of interventions that improve the operations of nature: fertilization and irrigation of soils, and the development of hybrid seeds. Human creativity in many forms relies on possibilities nature provides; to acknowledge dependence on nature does not demean the value of culture. We can be grateful for the malleability of the natural world, for the possibilities of human activity and meaning that it provides. Our participation in it evokes a sense of accountability for it; our misuse of it engenders remorse; our capacities to use it for the sake of human well-being evoke hope and joy.

The total array of affectivities that religious thinkers have enumerated are evoked by our experiences of aspects of the natural world. We respond with awe and respect; nature elicits piety. Our sense of dependence on powers that bring us and all things into being, powers we did not create, and some which we cannot yet control, becomes very strong when we reflect on our experiences of nature. For what is given that we did not create or earn, thankfulness is fitting. Human capacities make possible our interventions into the natural processes; for the consequences of these we are blameworthy or praiseworthy, for them we are accountable. Pleasure, fear, joy, sadness—these and other affections come into being. For persons of piety the powers of nature manifest the power of the ultimate reality, enabling and requiring us to respond to God. Worship, praise, moral activity, and other responses are appropriate.

History

History is another arena of experience to which we respond affectively. My distinction between nature and history is this: historical events occur as a result of the choices and exercise of powers by human agents. Natural events, such as earthquakes and hurricanes, are neither caused by human initiatives nor can they be avoided by human actions. Revolutions, changes in governments, and similar events are the consequences of the capacities of humans to establish aims or ends, and to exercise powers to achieve them. The control of consequences in historical events, however, is limited; other persons and institutions respond in the light of their own aims and ends, and with their powers. Nature and history are related in important ways, and the distinction I have drawn does not rule out similarities in some particular instances.

Just as particular aspects of nature evoke our affectivities, so particular historical events do. Our affective responses are to particular events with their particular contingencies and the particular aims of those who instigate them—such as a strike, an election, or the assassination of a president. Persons do not fear history, but they do fear the outcomes of particular sequences of historical events. We do not vacillate between hope and despair about history; we often do, however, about the outcome of a political revolution.

Wars are one class of historical events to which we have passionate responses. We can respond to a war, such as World War II, as a total event that has been given configuration by historians. If we participated in it, or in any other war, however, the configuration seems to miss the particularities of the sequence that can be viewed as a whole. War stories told by veterans, like war novels, do not depict in a general way the justifications, aims, successes, and failures of a war. They tell of very specific enemies, of particular battles, of very concrete times and places. The reader of a war novel, like the narrator of war experiences, in a sense lives through or relives the event in a way that a historical interpretation cannot capture.

Wars are experienced and responded to differently by various persons and communities. A war may be perceived to be the means to fulfill
lofty purposes and ideals such as saving the world for democracy; it may
be perceived as a grim necessity, a last resort by which evil intentions
and powers can be restrained and subdued. Wars are the occasions for
deep human misery and for exuberant feelings of glory. They are the
deaths of the innocent by obliteration bombing, the devastating destruction of cities with their replaceable modern artifacts and their irreplaceable
historical and cultural treasures, the defoliation of forests; they are
wounds, gory deaths, terror in the face of battle. Resources are destroyed
that could have been allotted for other purposes. Wars are also exuberant
parades after victory, and the occasions for individual and group heroism;
they reward victors with spoils. Wars bring cultural intrusions: modern
technology into relatively primitive cultures, Stalinism into Roman Catholic countries, and Islam into Christian and Hindu countries. They generate rapid development of technology; they require self-sacrifice and
strenuous effort that can be exhilarating or repressive. They leave their
aftermath in countless ways: tyrants defeated or victorious; economies
exhausted, destroyed, or "taking off"; families bereaved or joyous; new
alliances or different enemies; and many more. Wars bring changes more
rapidly and of more kinds than do most historical events to large numbers
of persons and communities.

Wars are historical and not natural events; human choices and actions bring them into being, conduct them, and deal with their consequences. The "inevitability" of a particular war can only refer to the
direction that a course of events seems to take inexorably; the direction,
however, is the result of cumulative choices and actions by persons and
nation-states.

Because events occur in war which are unusually critical for individuals and groups, and because persons and states can be praised or
blamed for war, it elicits particularly strong responses. (WAR)

War evokes hatred; one hates the enemy in a way that one does not
hate a drought or a flood. Persons respond with a sense of fatedness;
individuals are powerless in the face of choices and actions of others that
deeply affect their personal and collective destinies, whether the "other"
is an enemy infantryman or the leader of the enemy country. Hopes are
engendered: for the elimination of a particular power deemed evil, for a
new order of peace, for the spoils and the glory of success. Fear and
courage often alternate in combatants and in the noncombatants who
support them. The outcomes of wars are decisive for the destiny of a
people; defeat leads to deep despair. Feelings of remorse as well as of
pleasure are experienced by individuals and by groups: remorse for the
destruction of lives and communities; pleasure from having successfully

fulfilled individual or collective aims. The sense of accountability is deepened because of the decisiveness of the consequences of human choices and actions.

Particular historical events seem both to "happen" and to occur as a result of collective and individual initiatives. It is the task of historians and other scholars to explain how particular events occur. But persons respond to particular events with a sense of both their inevitability and their possibilities. The civil rights movement in the United States is a good example. Groups had actively engaged in the pursuit of this cause for decades prior to the flourishing of the movement, yet their successes were minimal. A concatenation of events, each of which had some effects, led to the historical possibilities of a given time for various persons and groups to achieve more than had been achieved before. Some initiatives were decisive, such as the suit against the Board of Education in Topeka and the 1954 ruling of the Supreme Court. Some events were not so deliberately planned, such as the refusal by Rosa Parks to sit in the section of a Montgomery bus reserved for blacks. There were responses by gifted individuals such as Martin Luther King, Jr., but the success of their leadership depended on many conditions that made their actions possible. The movement could not have developed as it did without the results both of complex multicausal factors and leaders who perceived the possibilities of interventions and shaped the power to achieve what did occur.

Depending upon how their interests are affected, persons and groups respond to historical conditions as providing hope and possibilities or as leading to consequences they feel obliged to resist or to which they finally acquiesce. An aspiration for individual and group fulfillment is nourished, or a pleasant way of life is threatened. Persons respond to events with a sense of the significance of their potential consequences, with a sense that the consequences are dependent upon interventions made in the light of particular interests and aims. Both aspirations and fears are intensified; desires and aversions become passionate; fear and courage are engendered; anger results on all sides. Gratitude is sometimes a natural response: gratitude for conditions which, however they have come into being, provide for the possibility of release from oppression, and for persons who emerge with the talents, courage, wisdom, and ideals to give direction to a course of events. In retrospect history may appear "providential" to those whose aims have some success, but fateful to those whose aims are defeated.

A concatenation of events can evoke a powerful sense of dependence on forces beyond the control of individuals and groups, a sense of being at the mercy of choices and actions over which we have little or no control. Such is the response of much of the industrialized world to the "oil crisis." The OPEC nations became a decisive force in history during the 1970s.

Their power was the result of "accidents" of nature. They happened to have political and economic control of resources that were the effects of millions of years of geological processes in earth history. But those resources gave them power only because societies and cultures had become dependent on them as a result of technological developments only a few decades old. The historical significance of these nations would be minimal at this time in history apart from the confluence of their "accidental" control of oil resources at the time when technology became dependent upon them. To be sure, these nations are responding politically and economically (i.e., historically) to the unplanned historical circumstances; they are intervening in history in a decisive way as a result of what nature has provided them. The possibilities, however, are the result of contingencies and not of long-range aims and aspirations of these countries.

Peoples respond with anxiety, fear, and even anger to their dependence upon events beyond their control. They might respond in resignation to accidents of nature, but the effects of human agency through political and economic power deepen their emotions. Persons and governments over which they have limited influence are causally accountable for alterations in their ways of life.

Affective responses to historical events cover the range of possibilities. Human accountability for them, limited as it often is, can evoke a different tone than is the case with nature. To a greater extent things could be, and can be, other than they are. In religious consciousness this recognition can move in several ways. If the outcomes are beneficial, there is gratitude, and even gratitude for a providential care; if deleterious, the events may be construed as the retribution of God. The sense of being limited by and dependent upon past historical events is coupled with the sense of accountability for future ones, at least for persons with the power to affect events. Moral accountability, not merely to immediate others but to the divine governance, is evoked. It is no surprise that theologians, particularly Protestant theologians, have viewed history as a distinctive sphere subject to peculiarly theological construal.

Culture

Culture elicits affectivities that can be construed religiously. As a concept, culture is not used in a uniform way; in this respect it is similar to the concepts of nature and history. As has been noted, it has been brought into theological discussion frequently as an abstraction. I am more concerned with particular aspects of culture, and human responses to them, though generalizations are necessary.

"Culture," as I use the term, refers to three areas of human experience which are related to each other but can be distinguished. It refers to artifacts, and preeminently in our time to systems of artifacts called technology. It refers to meanings and values, to world views, and to what is included in that suggestive term "ethos." Myths, symbols, theories, and other forms express these meanings and values; religion is part of this aspect of culture. It refers to the sciences and the arts: to those realms of human initiative and creativity that manifest the most distinctively innovative and creative fruits of intellectual and spiritual life.

Culture, like history, is an arena of the distinctively human; it is the realm in which causality, if it exists, is so complex that it is not well understood. To be sure, there are accounts of the particular natural and historical conditions which are necessary for various manifestations of culture to develop; indeed, there are cultural conditions necessary for further cultural developments. But the conditions cannot be specified as sufficient causes for what flourishes.

Culture becomes a "second nature" to human life. It is the milieu in which we relate to natural events: we distance ourselves from the immediate and raw effects of nature through culture. We are not wild plants, immediately susceptible to changes in natural environmental conditions. Cultural developments have deep consequences for nature itself; they even affect biological evolution. And cultures are historical; they have their own developments through time, altering and recombining what has been received, innovating and reassembling. There is no "creation out of nothing" in culture, though there are periods of rapid cultural change, and highly creative persons whose work decisively alters various aspects of culture.

Culture in general does not evoke our affective responses; particular aspects of culture do. Technology is a case in point. Although technology can be reified and dealt with as a power in its own right in such a way that it becomes the object of hopes and fears, our responses are more normally to particular technologies; our affective responses vary accordingly, and are themselves culturally conditioned. We rely upon future technologies to repair some of the costs of previous technologies.

We respond with gratitude and pleasure to those technologies that eliminate human drudgery: fork-lift trucks, ditch-diggers, grain combines, and many more. These become problematic only where they cause further unemployment in areas that already have large surplus labor markets, as for example in India. There the response might well be one of pity, despair, and even anger. Human drudgery evokes compassion; the elimination of drudgery at the cost of jobs among those who are already poverty-stricken also evokes compassion. Technologies that restore health and eliminate human suffering with no bad secondary effects are received with approval. Persons derive hope and new possibilities of realizing their aspirations.

To other technologies we respond with more ambivalent emotions. In medical care the lives of radically defective infants can be sustained, but often with severe impairments of their capacities and with continuing needs for intensive and extensive medical care. Families that are grateful for the preservation of a cherished human life frequently bear economic and personal strains as well as satisfactions. The development of peaceful uses of nuclear energy after its destructive forces were first visited upon cities generated waves of hope: ships would move by its powers; cities would be lighted; heartbeats would be regulated by pacemakers that used it. Safety was always a concern; hope was tempered by anxiety, if not fear. With nuclear accidents fears and anger have intensified, and deep emotions are stirred. Evidences are marshalled to relieve fear, if not to increase hope; others are marshalled to intensify anxieties.

Most technological developments are justified by their proponents on the basis of benefits they are expected to bring to human beings. While some persons fear that life is being "dehumanized" by technology, more have, in retrospect, many things to be grateful for as a result of it. Unanticipated consequences that are deemed bad and long-range consequences that cannot be foreknown temper gratitude and hope. Technology is a creation of human beings; it is developed and guided by finite creatures; it has its costs and its benefits. Human responses are mixed.

Ethos is a more elusive aspect of culture than technology. In modern pluralistic societies there are competing beliefs, valuations, world views, and life orientations. It may be the case, as some analysts claim, that "technical rationality" is a dominant feature of the ethos of our time and that our basic orientations toward life and our valuations are deeply conditioned by the methods and aims of technology, but other currents are also strong. Ethos is expressed and transmitted in a society by many means: traditional myths and symbols, but novel ones as well; explanatory theories about the world; religious and secular cultic and liturgical activities; advertising and other aspects of the media; and so forth.

Persons become deeply emotional about aspects of the ethos, no matter how elusive these aspects may be. About some, persons have deep and consciously developed convictions: what America means, what their religion means, or the moral ideology of the free market economy. We simply share in others without much self-awareness of their significance for the ways we live, the choices we make, the desires and aversions we have, and the aspirations we have for our lives.

Emotions become particularly charged when passionately held beliefs and values are threatened. In national life this occurs frequently: the freedoms of American life seemed to be threatened by communism or socialism, and McCarthyism flourished. Christian religious beliefs seem to be at risk when the breezes of modernity blow through the churches, and Protestant fundamentalism or Catholic traditionalism gains strength. The "work ethic" appears to be eroding and anxieties are intensified about the general state of the self-discipline, individual responsibility, and the achievement orientation that made Western industrial economies successful. The loyalty to the traditional family is perceived to be diminishing, and anger, fear, and despair result. Anxiety is enhanced because ethos is so nebulous; it is difficult to locate who or what is responsible for the changes. Scapegoats are fashioned as the object of blame.

Sometimes the prevailing ethos is perceived to be hostile to persons' interests and aspirations. Certain beliefs and values are judged to repress aspirations for individual self-fulfillment. Signs of change become signs of possibilities and hope. Male domination of many rewarding features of modern life is attacked by the feminist movement, and every indication of success is seen as a sign of liberation from cultural and social repression. What are deemed to be archaic beliefs and authoritarian practices in a religious community undergo rapid change; there is a new spirit of freedom and vitality on the part of those who favor change. "Reforming mentalities" become as passionate as "conservative mentalities."

Ambivalent responses are frequent. The ideology of the free-market economy supported and, in turn, was supported by the tradition of civil liberties. The ideology of the paternalistic state compensates for many of the individual and social costs that resulted from the free-market economy; it has also reined and qualified the pursuit of individual liberties in the pursuit of distributive justice. Many persons and groups are deeply ambivalent about these ideologies, and recognize some merits in each. Perhaps it is the American "liberal" ideology that takes shape in an effort to combine aspects of both, and thus finds its own group of adherents.

The responses to aspects of an ethos might be all the more affective because, unlike in responses to technologies, there is no "object," no thing, that causes human emotions. Blame and praise are hard to fix, and yet persons sense the importance of beliefs, values, and ideals. Changes in them are not easily perceived and explained. Moral judgments flourish in response to ethos: both defenders and reformers are quick to justify their positions in moral terms. For all its elusiveness, persons and groups rely on it, feel obliged to sustain or to change it, respond to it in hope or despair, and even in deep anger.

The third aspect of culture is the arts and sciences. In both technology and the arts and sciences there is a great deal of human creativity and ingenuity. The ends, however, are different; ideally the arts and sciences are "ends in themselves." We recognize those high degrees of human intelligence, those creative powers of the human spirit, that probe into the world and explain it, that create powerful and beautiful paintings and literature, sculpture and music, movies and dramas. Both the sciences and the arts redescribe the realities that we immediately experience, and interpret them in ways that alter their significance for our believing, our self-understanding, and our doing. These perceptions and interpretations evoke deep affective responses.

We respond to the natural world with gratitude, awe, and respect. The sciences that explore this world and give more accurate understandings of it elicit the same responses. A better understanding of how our planet came to be, how life emerged from combinations of chemicals, how human beings evolved, how the organs of the body function, how human actions are conditioned, evokes gratitude to the sciences and their investigators; awe and respect are proper. The capacities of human intelligence to create plausible hypotheses, to develop appropriate means of investigation, and to confirm or disconfirm received explanatory theories, provoke admiration and appreciation. The possibilities for human life are enhanced as a result of the achievements of various sciences. Since human effort and commitment are required for these achievements, this dedication is honored; it is no less ascetic than that which is honored in religious saints or military heroes. Awareness of the ambiguities in the uses of scientific knowledge does not diminish gratitude and respect for its achievements.

The arts, because they appeal more immediately to affectivity, for some persons are even more powerful. Color and design, texture and form, may evoke delight and pleasure or a haunting sense of doom. A Henry Moore sculpture can suggest both vast power and a sense of control over it at the same time. Some works bring spontaneous smiles: the fantasies of Chagall, for example, whether in glass, mosaics, or paint, are simply delightful. Others bring a sense of tranquillity, for example, some of the best of Constable's and Turner's landscapes. There is no mystery to why Picasso's *Guernica* affected Paul Tillich and others very deeply; its depiction of the results of human evil are overwhelming, even more profound than photographs of My Lai and other human brutalities.

Drama can be painful or delightful. Its painfulness comes in part from its powers to make us live through the depressing and tragic experiences of others; one thinks not only of classic Greek tragedies but also of Pinter's *Betrayal*. One feels the power of human evil in forms of betrayal or of perverse domination of one person over another; one feels the strangeness of being fated and accountable at one and the same time. One relives, and not just remembers, similar experiences in one's own life, or the temptations present in one's own relationships. Delight comes in the exaggerated highlights of the human comedy; one laughs with Prince Hal at Falstaff. Our responses to music, poetry, and novels are similar.

We affectively respond to what the artist creates and to the capacities of artists so to move us. Art not only redescribes human experiences; it enlarges them, it brings new ones. Emotions and intellect are both evoked, and surely both are present in the creative artist. Not only emotions but

new and deeper understandings of realities come to us through art. It is
the realm of human creativity par excellence, for it is not bound to verification of its "truths" in ways that sciences are. If sometimes it cor-
responds to deep aspects of reality, at others it creates new realities. The
range of human possibilities is expanded in a dramatic way; the limits are
fewer than in other forms of human activity.

Our experiences in and of culture affect us in many ways, and with
many different degrees of intensity. We respond to culture with a sense
of dependence on this very human realm for many aspects of human
experience. We respond with gratitude for its sustaining powers and for
the human flourishing that it expresses. We acknowledge a sense of obligation to be its bearers from one generation to the next, to restrain its
developments that threaten human flourishing, and to enhance those that
provide richer experience. We are the cultivators of culture; we, in diffuse
ways, are responsible for it in ways in which we are not accountable for
natural events. Pleasure and sadness, love and hate, desire and aversion,
hope and despair, fear and courage—all the rich and deep emotions of
human experiences are evoked by our participation in culture. Not only
our affectivities but also our reflections are provoked, and not only in
relation to culture in the abstract but to aspects of culture that immediately
affect our interests. In religious consciousness there is a reconstrual of
culture and our responses to it. Its "objects" evoke affections that become
religious.

Society

The fourth arena that evokes powerful affectivities is ordered social
life. Some social institutions and social processes have received attention
from theologians throughout the history of the Christian tradition; family,
state, and "economy" or work. Sometimes these discussions have been
general, and institutions have been dealt with in the abstract; sometimes
the moral assessments of particular patterns and processes have been
detailed and specific. Just as we do not respond to nature in general, so
our immediate experiences of society are quite particular; we participate
in particular families, react to the governance of particular states and
laws, feel victimized or flourish in relation to particular economic institutions.

Institutions and their functioning are not natural in the same sense
that, for example, the processes of human reproduction are. Major institutions, of course, meet fundamentally natural human needs; the shapes
that they take and the ways in which their purposes are executed, however, are the result of historical and cultural developments and the actions
of many individuals. They are shaped by human choices and human activities. Social necessity requires a division of labor; how labor is divided

varies according to historical and cultural conditions. Sexual life needs to be ordered; how it is ordered varies. Aims, purposes, ends, and intentions enter into the shaping of social life just as they do in historical events and culture.

Family life of some form is deeply natural. It meets survival needs of both old and young; it is a major socializing institution that prepares children for the relative autonomy of adulthood. How persons respond to family life depends on many factors, and in modern Western societies the responses are frequently ambivalent. Family can be the nexus of sustaining affection, of prudent restraints, and of nourishing social and personal development. It can provide the earliest and most immediate experiences of repression, of neglect and estrangement, and of fear and hate. The intensity and intimacy of marriage and family life evoke deeper dissatisfactions and deeper gratitude than other institutions evoke. In family a sense of dependence becomes strong; both the liberating and repressing effects of dependence can result. Families are a network of natural duties that flow from the interdependence of the family members; we learn moral accountability to others and to a common good. Our earliest and perhaps deepest feelings of both remorse and satisfaction come in family life. From it we derive our earliest experiences of proper and improper aspirations; some of our deepest desires and aversions are shaped by it. Love and hatred, joy and sorrow, fear and courage: these and other affectivities are deeply elicited not by family as an order of creation but by our particular families, our relations with particular persons. And the most tortured ambivalence that humans experience occurs in family life. It is not surprising that parental and familial metaphors have played such powerful roles in the perceptions and conceptions of man's relations to God.

We do not react to economic institutions in general, but we do feel the powers of particular ones sustaining or repressing us. If the effects of a particular industrial corporation have been to meet our interests in a favorable way, if it has provided our job security, our affluence, and our sense of professional achievement, we not only acknowledge dependence on it but respond to it with thankfulness. If it has exploited us, put our job security at the mercy of the vicissitudes of the market system, or sold us inferior and defective products, we respond with aversion, anger, and hate. Our sense of justice or injustice is elicited by the ways in which we have been treated by industrial corporations. If the power of corporations is perceived to be feeding their own narrow interests at the cost of the proper interests of others and of the common good, their activities are signs of disorder in human life. To this persons might resign themselves, or they might zealously exercise powers of restraint by means of

law or countervailing economic powers. Often our feelings toward economic institutions on which we necessarily depend are deeply ambivalent.

Government evokes ambivalent responses. Its powers impinge upon
us in many ways. For the provisions of public safety, the works it does
for public health and cleanliness, and the powers it exercises to restrain
excessive pollution of our natural environment, we are grateful. It sustains
our individual and corporate well-being. Its institutions and activities that
compensate for the costs persons cannot bear for themselves are praiseworthy: welfare and medical assistance programs, social security and
compensations for injuries and unemployment. Opportunities for personal
development are sustained: public education and support of the arts and
sciences enlarge the realm of human flourishing. Government also becomes the object of our anger and our hate. When its agencies determine
from paternalistic motives what is in our individual or collective interest
without consulting us, we feel trodden upon. Its powers to make choices
and to act without participation by those who are affected is deemed an
undue intrusion into the private sphere. Its proper concern for the collective interests of a city or a nation often necessarily infringes upon our
individual interests to our deep dislike. Yet when individual and group
interests and rights are neglected or violated, it is to the powers of government that persons turn for protection and compensation. Its powers
provide the possibilities for the alteration of conditions we deem harmful
to ourselves, our social group, or the common good.

It is not surprising to find political metaphors used to express and
construe the relations of God to the human community. The powers that
bear down on us through government, restraining and sustaining us, evoke
those affectivities that human beings feel in relation to God.

The ordering of social life evokes the full gamut of human affectivity
that can be construed religiously; it is not accidental that society has been
the object of religious and theological interpretation and understanding.
Ordinary human daily life relies upon social institutions: functions are
performed by such institutions which make human activity possible. Individuals often look to their families, for example, as a source of spiritual,
emotional, and other sustenance. Insofar as institutions function benefi-
cially for our interests and for the common good, the response of gratitude
is appropriate. Institutions are the realms of our moral duties and obligations; we learn morality in the context of both natural institutions (like
family) and contractual ones. We have a sense of moral accountability for
them; through them we influence the course of events. They are realms
of possibility and of restraint. We love and hate them; we fear them and
we participate in them with courage. Like our response to the natural
world, so also our response to the world of institutions is a major area
of human experience that is construed religiously. To the religious con-

sciousness the divine governance of life occurs in and through orders in human society.

The Self

Human beings respond affectively to themselves. We experience ourselves as an "other" to a limited degree. We do treat ourselves as objects, but not like material in a tissue culture in a laboratory, or a political process under social scientific investigation. Probably the notion of a mind-body dualism arose from views that the body could be responded to as an object by the mind. Self seemed to be mind or spirit, in distinction from body. With self, as in other arenas, there is some tendency to generalize and to develop an abstraction. The self is thought of as a thing: one begins to assume that in some generalized way we can relate to our own "selves" as entities. But we probably do not respond even to our bodies as wholes, except in a very philosophical mood. We respond to pain in the shoulder, we assess the strengths and limits of muscular capacity if we plan to climb a high hill, we correct a deficiency in our vision. In a similar way, what it is about our "selves" that evokes affective responses can be sorted out.

We become "observers" of ourselves largely through the function of memory. Our observation is seldom, if ever, disinterested; memories of particular occasions evoke affective responses. Memory, whether faulty or accurate, provides the "data" to which we make responses. The events which we remember most vividly are those which affected us most deeply while they were occurring. Our past deeds evoke affectivity. We can recall what we did; we can often sort out what our motives were for doing it, what ends we chose, and what the consequences were. If, for example, our motives for an action were vindictive and successful we might take delight in our success or be ashamed for our intentions, or both. If our intentions were good, but the consequences of our actions were damaging, we examine our errors. Were we not adequately informed? Did we misjudge our capacities to bring the desired ends into being? Did we deceive ourselves about our intentions? Remorse is evoked by memories of such experiences. We might excuse ourselves because we were not culpable, or we might feel guilty if we were. We recall events in which our good intentions led to the intended good consequences, and respond with a feeling of satisfaction, if not of pride. Our remembered actions evoke affective responses to our "selves." The gamut of affectivity covers a wide range of human emotions: love and hate, remorse and delight, anger and pride, respect and loathing.

Most persons have some sense of identity; they have a sense of the "sort of person" they have become if they are reflective about their aspirations and their actions. Persisting characteristics are accounted for in classical ethical literature under the concept of *habitus,* a lasting disposition. When we respond to our "selves," we respond in part to our settled dispositions. We may resign ourselves to them as if no change were possible. We may consent to them, affirming them as reliable. We may accept accountability for them. There is a love of self, respect for self, not merely as an abstraction (as a rational autonomous agent), but as it is given in what G. H. Mead calls the "Me" aspect of the person (in contrast with the agent, or "I," aspect), the self as it is present in our habits and dispositions.[16] Self-loathing, or self-hatred, is an affective response to felt and believed perceptions of the sort of persons we have become. We may fear ourselves; we fear what we might do under certain circumstances, because we "know" our dispositions. Despair occurs when the self is perceived to be fated, locked in, incapable of any improvement of its adverse circumstances. To the extent that we acknowledge accountability for what we have become, we feel satisfied or guilty not only about particular actions but about ourselves. We have informed feelings about ourselves.

The "senses" that I have described can each be evoked by our relations to ourselves. We have a sense of dependence on our bodies, with their capacities and limitations, and on our settled dispositions. There is a sense of gratitude for what we have become; for the conditions that have made possible what is pleasing and satisfying. We feel duties to ourselves; we feel obliged to maintain our moral integrity, or to seek to realize our moral ideals. Remorse and repentance are directly evoked by our sense of accountability. We have a sense of possibilities; while there are limits to our capacities to become other than what we are, we can alter some of our external conditions, and shape our inner lives and identities. Our ideals and habits provide a sense of direction to our actions and to the course of our lives.

Responses to self are construed religiously, as one can see in prayers of confession and supplication, and in the language of theology.

This account of how various "objects" or realms of experience evoke affective responses lends credence to William James's view that religious affectivities contain "nothing whatever of a psychologically specific nature." It is the object that makes affections religious. There is no doubt that James is correct when he indicates that the delineation of an object that is religious is a human activity. Theologies are human constructs; they are the works of human intellects. Theology is not "revealed." I have indicated some of the ways in which persons and communities move from experiences to religious interpretations of their

16. George Herbert Mead, *Mind, Self, and Society* (Chicago: University of Chicago Press, 1934), pp. 192–222.

ultimate object. This is done by asking "religious questions" about experiences.

In all these arenas of experience persons find themselves asking four general questions of great religious significance. First, in whom or in what can we have confidence? This, in traditional Christian language, is the question of faith, or trust. What or who are the proper objects of our reliance, our confidence? Which are trustworthy, or reliable? On what improper objects do we rely? The question is not only one of the objects. Do we rely, for example, on certain institutions more than they can bear, or more than they merit? Ought we to be relying on certain things more than we do? In the context of these questions, as we shall see in the next chapter, one form of sin, or the human fault, arises. It is sin understood as idolatry, of the wrong objects of ultimate confidence, and of the wrong degree of confidence in proper objects. In the religious consciousness these questions become generalized. Is there an ultimate power that is trustworthy, in whom we can have confidence? And as I have noted, there is a further question even at this point: *for what* is it proper to have confidence in God, and for what is it improper to rely upon God?

The second question is, as H. Richard Niebuhr has so clearly indicated, the question of loyalty, or fidelity.[17] To whom, or to what, do we owe loyalty? To whom and to what ought we to be faithful? Part of living is a matter of finding the appropriate answers to these questions. We do live by loyalties, explicitly and implicitly; there are persons and institutions to which we are faithful or unfaithful. It is not only a question of the proper objects of loyalties but of the extent of loyalty that is proper to these objects. Excessive loyalty to improper objects leads to many personal and social difficulties. Again, the idea of sin as idolatry arises: idolatry is fidelity to improper objects, or excessive or deficient fidelity to proper objects. Is there an ultimate power that commands our ultimate loyalty? This is the question that the religious consciousness asks.

The third question is, For what can we, and ought we, to hope? What aspirations are appropriate to human life? Which are inappropriate? What objects or grounds of hope are viable? Do we have an excessive hope, improperly grounded? The obverse side of the question of hope is the question of dread or fear. What are the appropriate objects of our dread? In religious consciousness the question becomes, Can we and ought we to hope in God? The matter of trust is trust *in*; the matter of fidelity is fidelity *to*; the matter of hope is hope *for* or *in*.[18] If we can and ought to hope in God, for what is it fitting to hope? One form of the human fault is inappropriate objects of human aspiration.

17. H. Richard Niebuhr, *Radical Monotheism,* pp. 11–23.
18. Ibid.

The fourth question is, What are the appropriate objects of human
loves and desires? What are the proper objects of aversion? Like the rest
of the animate world we are moved by needs and desires; our activity is
implicitly or explicitly purposive. We have the capacity to choose our
ends, to form intentions, to expand almost without limit the things that
we desire. There are misplaced loves, misplaced objects of human desires.
There are excessive and deficient desires for proper objects. Therein lies
another way of coming to the problem of the human fault; this is the
problem of sin as stated in basically Augustinian terms. In religious consciousness we ask if it is proper to love God, to have our orientation
toward the world governed by our love of God.

These questions intimately unite religious and moral life and unite
the affective and the cognitive aspects of human experience within religious and moral life. Our answers to them delineate our "religion." The
functional religious questions are: In what do we ultimately have confidence? To what are we loyal? For what do we hope? What do we love?
For many persons the answers do not lead to an affirmation of the presence
of an ultimate power sustaining and bearing down upon life. There are
functional surrogates to religion as I understand it. It is also the case that
those who profess God to be the ultimate object of confidence, fidelity,
hope, and love live religiously and morally in ways that belie their confession.

The Religious Construal of the Affections and Their Object

I am engaged in a process of giving reasons for the kind of piety and
theology I advocated in Chapter 4. Two kinds of reasons are involved:
explanations of how a monotheistic piety and theology comes about, and
justifications that commend it. William James was cognizant of this distinction. His explanation was given in terms of the best psychology of his
time, and as psychologist he sought to provide a sufficient explanation of
the varieties of religious experience without recourse to a deity. Yet he
was clear that the value of religious experiences could not be assessed
simply on the basis of their explanations. For him the criteria of value
were pragmatic. Thus, for example, a chapter in which he explains saintliness is followed by a chapter on "The Value of Saintliness."[19] Interestingly, the value judgments are based on Edwards's principal criterion,
"By their fruits ye shall know them." Edwards's explanation, of course,

19. James, *Varieties,* lectures 11–13 on "Saintliness" and lectures 14–15 on its value.
See a similar contemporary caveat: "This is not a book on religion. It is a clinical study of
the possible origins of the individual's private representation of God and its subsequent
elaborations." Ana-Maria Rizzuto, M.D., *The Birth of the Living God: A Psychoanalytic
Study* (Chicago: University of Chicago Press, 1979), p. 3.

was radically different from James's;[20] for the theologian-preacher the explanation was the presence of a new principle in the agent as a result of the work of God's spirit through conversion.

Obviously, I am not averse to taking seriously "naturalistic" explanations of the emergence of religious affectivity and of the varieties of actions that express it. I am not explaining or defending religion on the basis of "supernaturalistic" interventions of a deity which bypass natural causal factors.[21] The problem I have shaped is how to account for the experience of God in and through the particular affective experiences; how to explain and justify a response to the divine governance and powers in and through our other responses. The way in which I have shaped this problem has important features. The empiricism of the approach leaves, accurately, the impression of pluralism, indeed, perhaps of something like James's "pluralistic universe." How can we move from this pluralism to a single powerful Other? The empiricism also leaves the accurate impression that what is received in a tradition is to be tested in part by human experiences, both ordinary and critical. It is also to be tested by modern accounts and explanations of nature and other objects to which we are related. This precludes the radical "leap of faith" of existentialist theologies inspired by Kierkegaard; it precludes Pascal's famous wager; and it precludes orthodox confessionalisms. To Job's famous words, "Yea, though he slay me, yet will I trust him,"[22] it responds with the query of what kind of trust is warranted, and for what do we trust. The problem is a very old one in religion and in theology.

If a whole range of ordinary affections can be religious affections, then how do they come to be religious? If affections become religious by reference to their object, and if, as we have seen, there are many "ob-

20. James: "What I then propose to do is, briefly stated, to test saintliness by common sense, to use human standards to help us decide how far the religious life commends itself as an ideal kind of human activity." James, *Varieties,* p. 324. The asceticism of saintliness, while it takes perverse and destructive forms, can be partially commended because it sustains something James valued: the "strenuous life." Edwards, the twelfth sign: "Gracious and holy affections have their exercise and fruit in Christian practice. I mean, they have that influence and power upon him who is subject of 'em, that they cause that a practice, which is universally conformed to, and directed by Christian rules, should be the practice and business of life." *Religious Affections,* p. 383.

21. One reason that I have always appreciated Schleiermacher's theology is that he is quite clear about which side of a polarity of "magical" and "empirical" explanations of the work of redemption and other things he chooses. The "magical" way, he says, "admits, of course, that the activity of Christ is redemptive, but denies that the communication of His perfection is dependent on the founding of a community; it results, they maintain, from His immediate influence on the individual." The contrasting "empirical view" also admits redemptive activity on the part of Christ but sees it as taking place through participation in a community with its particular activities and forms of life. Schleiermacher, *The Christian Faith,* pp. 429–30. See also pp. 434–35.

22. Job 13:15. K.J.V. Cf. R.S.V., "Behold, he will slay me; I have no hope." For a discussion of the textual problems, see Marvin Pope, trans., *Job,* pp. xliv–xlv.

jects'' that evoke affections, in what ways do these objects meaningfully refer to God? What is involved in construing human affections religiously? What is involved in construing their objects theologically?

No one asks or answers these questions de novo. They have different answers in different religious traditions; they are dismissed as meaningless by secular tradition; or they are not experientially significant for many persons. I developed earlier the theme that theology and religion develop in a tradition. I turn to the human experience of a historic religious tradition and the institutions and activities that bear it across time and space to give some explanation (if not full justification) of answers.

The explanation can distort the character of the experience. The way in which I have progressed lends itself to this distortion. One might think there is a process with several stages by which an affection becomes religious. It could be something like this. One responds affectively to the beauty of a landscape. The sight evokes awe, pleasure, and gratitude. From the particular objects that make up the landscape, one is convinced that there must be a creative and ordering power to bring them into being. Now one responds to this power, and not to the particular objects that are arranged in a pleasing order. The response to the object then converts the affections evoked by the objects into religious affections evoked by God.

While these stages might, with some huge gaps, suggest a rational plausibility for religious affections, they are hardly an accurate description of the experience of religious affectivity. No more accurate would be a description of an experience of the presence of the Deity in itself, apart from the particularities of the occasions of the affections. Recall the statement by Julian N. Hartt that is central to this project. He states accurately that theology (and religion), as a way of construing the world (including, for our purposes, human affections), ''is more than a linguistic-intellectual activity.'' It ''means an intention to relate to all things in ways appropriate to their belonging to God.''[23] This suggests that the particular objects that evoke affectivity from time to time (i.e., not on every occasion) are perceived in piety as related to God. The same objects might also be perceived differently. One can have a scientific perception and explanation of the same phenomenon that can be perceived and construed aesthetically and religiously. A scientist can be as moved by beauty as a religious person. But a scientific view does not preclude both the objects and the response from being construed religiously. For some persons the more that is known about how natural events come to be, the deeper is the awe in their presence. It is not necessary to be able to give a theological explanation of the natural occurrences to which one responds in order to have a

23. Hartt, ''Encounters and Influence,'' p. 52.

religious response. One does not need to have an Aristotelian-Thomistic philosophical theology of a prime mover, or a process theology. To be sure, the religious affectivity can provoke reflection on how the ultimate power is disclosed in and through such an event, on what relationships can be rationally delineated between the Other and the particularities, and on why one's awe can be denominated religious as well as aesthetic. But the perception is prior to explanations; a religious construal is not merely a "linguistic-intellectual activity."

The religious perception implies a different description of the meaning of the objects. For example, if one knows something about Nordic folk religion, it is not difficult to imagine why in earlier times Scandinavians believed in trolls in response to their natural environment. Perception, description of what was perceived, and their meanings for persons all interpenetrated in their experience. The roots of this were, in part at least, the sense of dependence upon natural forces beyond their control, a sense of the contingency of events that determined their fate, and a personification of the powers bearing down on them to which they were subject. We do not see trolls, nor do we believe that the contingent powers bearing down upon us are manipulated by them. Our perception is affected by observations and explanations that rule out the existence of trolls.

For some persons these observations and explanations rule out any religious dimension to their affective responses. For some a naive religious response occurs. For others the response is qualified by experiences and beliefs that come from a religious tradition. The religious language and symbols of one's tradition penetrate one's perception both of the meaning of what is seen and one's affective responses. What one sees may be an expression of the power and the glory of God; one's responses might be a quiet expression of praise of God; one's joy and delight may be in the beauty and the goodness of God.

I have argued that the Christian religious tradition is multifaceted; its charter document, the Bible, provides the possibilities of different religious developments. Subsequent development has taken various religious and theological forms. One can imagine that Jonathan Edwards, with his doctrine of specific providence, might construe a lovely landscape accordingly. God, in his foreknowledge and in his ultimate control of secondary causes, determined both the landscape and the observers . All would be caused by God, the objects and the responses; and while the observers are agents to the extent that they consented to the causes, God even foresaw their consent. And all would be caused for the purpose of its human benefits. Some would respond in natural piety; those with the new principle of the spirit in them would have a new sight and see the glory of God.

Such a view is not one of a bare divine transcendence. God is not an ineffable mystery through and through. It insists that there is a religious meaning to particular events, indeed, to all particular events. And the events are for the sake of human beings. The divine determination is, in the strong words of Calvin, "in the act ," and not merely in foreknowledge.

The views of this book, as indicated above, move away from this rigorous deterministic view of the activity of God developed in the Reformed tradition. But they do not depart from the claim that the particular experiences we have of nature, history, culture, society, and self can be religiously significant. Through them we feel powers sustaining and bearing down on us.

The religious affections are human *responses.* They are not acts, in the sense that I choose to respond with delight to a landscape or with remorse to suffering I have caused. Nor, as has been indicated, are the affectivities uniquely religious. But their character as religious affections is a consequence of other experiences to which one gives consent, and to beliefs that have become meaningful (and, one hopes, critically tested). *Persons* construe the meaning of the affectivities, just as they construe the religious significance of the objects that evoke them. Often affectivities are responses to particular events, but they can become general dispositions to respond to many events.

The language of affectivity, we must again recall, does not imply that emotions are contrary to intellect. There is a knowing that comes through loving, through fearing, through pleasure. The intellectual construal of the religious meaning of the affections and their objects is continuous with the primary experiences. But while theology is not merely a linguistic-intellectual activity, it is a constructive intellectual activity using imagination and imagery as well as concepts. Its primary language is first-order religious language of metaphors, analogies, similes, myths, and symbols. Even its more abstract forms are constructive; arguments are made that do not follow the strictest rules of formal logic but which commend themselves as reasonable ways to deal with the realities of religious life. External observers with sufficient empathy might comprehend the arguments but not be persuaded by them. Their persuasiveness is relative to piety. Theology is a response to and expression of experiences of religious affectivity, evoked immediately by many objects. It is a knowing activity, though the tests of its validity are not those of solid-state physics.

Two "subjective" factors must be acknowledged in theological work. One, which I note without further comment, is the individuality of any effort. Ernst Troeltsch understood and dealt with this accurately. The formulation of religious ideas "is an individual, creative act which arises out of the possession and appropriation of previous acts, but which con-

scientiously shapes the development of what is possessed in such a way
that in the new formulation . . . the acquisition of the past coincides with
personal conviction."[24]

The second "subjective" factor is the reliance upon a particular
historical tradition, at least initially. This is the problem of historical
relativism on which I have already commented. The point here is to admit
that a religious and theological interpretation of life in the world is deeply
informed by the religious tradition and community of its author. Two
familiar questions come to mind. How do aspects of the tradition function
in a constructive account? This is the explanatory question. What reasons
does one give for such reliance as one has on the aspects of tradition
drawn upon? This is the justificatory question.

Religious affectivity and reflection depend upon not only responses
to the putatively nonreligious aspects of experience but also upon experiences in a religious community. This project depends upon experience
of and in the historic Christian community—its institutions, its activities,
and its traditions. One's own religious affectivity is informed by the constituting events, the significant persons, the history of the community,
and the stories that are borne through time by the Christian tradition and
by the churches. This is unquestionably the case.

From one perspective this appears to be a severe limitation, for it
may dispose one blindly to accept the accounts given, and to live and
think only within the margins of the tradition, and in some cases the
margins of the tradition that have been judged by ecclesiastical authorities
to be orthodox. This is a limitation. For all my empathic capacities, I
cannot enter fully into the Hindu religious construal of life in the world.
For all my efforts to grasp the significance of its various myths, doctrines,
forms of cult, and its personal and social moralities, I never understand
Hinduism as well as I understand Christianity. The limitation does not
close one to insight and understanding from other traditions, or to exploration of one's own tradition in the light of one's knowledge of them. But
what is explored, stretched, expanded, revised, or reordered remains
basically the heritage of the biblical faiths, particularly the heritage of
Christianity.

From another perspective the limitation presents a concrete possibility. From the recorded experience of a particular religious community

24. Ernst Troeltsch, "What Does the Essence of Christianity Mean?" in Robert
Morgan and Michael Pye, *Troeltsch: Writings,* p. 166. With almost agonizing honesty
Troeltsch deals with the problems that this subjectivism creates. He believes that penetrating
individual constructions of religious ideas can express "a perception which will prove itself
to others" (p. 167). He also is conscious of the possibility that a constructive formulation
might "lead unnoticed away from Christianity and issue in a new religion only loosely
related to Christianity" (p. 169). Such are the risks.

come particular insights into the meaning of a religious response to the world and to the powers and ultimate power that bear down upon human beings. The community's own theological affirmations arose out of its members' responses to nature, history, culture, society, and selfhood as they were shaped by the community and its history. If it is granted that religious interpretations, like others, develop in traditions, and if it is granted that particular traditions carry perceptions of the meaning of human experience that are at least partially valid, then it can also be granted, I believe, that one's own historic tradition (to which one necessarily gives some consent) is bound to affect one's construal, and can affect it in a positive way.

I argued years ago that a process of "socialization" not only carries a recognizable tradition through time and across cultures and societies but also provides for the "internalization" of its meanings by those who participate in it.[25] In many respects one becomes a Christian in the same way that one becomes identifiable by any other social distinction—nationality, class and so on. The stories, symbols, cultic life, preaching, and other aspects of institutional religious life provide the participant with a perspective from which to respond affectively and intentionally to nature, historical events, culture, society, and themselves. Persons may drift away from these symbols and their meanings as those of other communities provide a more satisfying way to form the persons' aspirations, interpret the events in which they participate, and judge their own worthiness. Persons may consciously reject them in the light of what they perceive to be illusions, repressiveness, intellectual weakness, or defective morality. Or they may rigidly and dogmatically hold certain symbols and meanings to be orthodox, adhere to them as the exclusive ways to interpret the meanings of events and experiences, and close themselves off from anything that would threaten the security that the tradition offers. But the tradition, expressed in various forms, does inform those who participate in it. The current interest in the significance of narrative, metaphor, biography, and other literary genres for establishing religious and moral identity is only, in the end, an exploration of processes that have always taken place. It is part of a process of "traditioning." The tradition is not just remembered; it is not just a curio of the past available for scholarly investigation; it is often relived.[26]

25. Gustafson, *Treasure in Earthen Vessels*.
26. See ibid., for an explication of this in the light of the arguments of Wilhelm Dilthey, George Herbert Mead, and others who have attended philosophically to these matters. Social and behavioral scientists have, perhaps, more detailed and conceptually refined ways to do the same, confirmed by procedures of experimentation and investigation that Dilthey, Mead, and others did not have.

The tradition's symbols become personally meaningful as ways of construing the world when participants consent to them. "Consent," Samuel Johnson tells us in his *Dictionary*, has three meanings: "To be of the same mind, to agree," "To cooperate to the same end," and "To yield, . . . to allow, to admit." The third meaning overlaps with some of his definitions of "resign": "to yield up," "to submit without resistance or murmur." The distinction between consenting and resigning is important. By indicating that the tradition's symbols become meaningful by our consent to them, I do not mean to indicate resignation: submitting to them because of their institutional, or traditional authority. To consent does not mean to submit to their authority "without resistance or murmur." Dr. Johnson's first two meanings of consent come close to my use of the term. We come to be of the "same mind," to share in the meanings and disclosing powers of the symbols of the tradition, by agreeing with those meanings. To agree, however, is not to yield up, not to resign one's capacities to make judgments about the adequacy or inadequacy of the symbols. To agree is to be persuaded that there is value in the symbols and in what they yield as a way of construing the world. To agree is not to submit to authority; it is to find what is proposed to be reasonable and meaningful. To consent, to refer to Dr. Johnson's second definition, is to cooperate to the same end. With reference to traditional symbols, this suggests an openness to the capacity of the symbols to yield meaningful accounts of human experience. If "complacence" had not come to mean "self-satisfaction" as it currently does, it would be an appropriate word; I believe its classic meaning of "receptivity to" (in this case) the symbols and their meanings is central to consent. But cooperation implies that agency continues. Not only do persons or communities use the symbols to construe events; they can test, revise, judge, and choose among them. To cooperate is not to resign oneself to coercive authority but inwardly to participate in the community and its symbols, to be receptive to the interpretations that the symbols elicit, and to assess their adequacy.

The tradition and its symbols are prior to our consent to them. They are not the creation of a new generation; rather, they are the manifestations of many generations of continuity and development. There are instances of genuine "conversion" from one set of symbols or one tradition to another, of consent to one tradition that involves a rejection of another, but the conditions of historical existence bring persons into particular communities and traditions, religious or otherwise. There may or may not be a dramatic moment in which one consents to or cooperates with what is given. Confirmation in the classic Christian tradition is a specific rite of passage whose high purpose is to indicate that the confirmand gives consent and pledges cooperation with the community and the tradition. To acknowledge the possibility of consent is to indicate the possibility of dissent; to include a voluntary aspect based upon some persuasion is to indicate that disagreement is also a possibility; to suggest that consenting implies a cooperation to a common end with the tradition indicates that one can be noncooperative and, indeed, reject the community and tradition.

To interpret the affections and their objects in a particular religious tradition, then, is to recognize a "social-psychological" or a historical process. My being a Christian rather than a Jew is an accident of birth; my being a Protestant rather than Eastern Orthodox or Roman Catholic is largely an accident of birth. The range of choice of religious symbols for construing the world is limited initially by events beyond individual control. In this sense one is "fated" to be a Protestant Christian, or whatever one's religious identity early in life is. To say this, however, is not to imply that the Deity so governed all the events that led to my being what I am with a particular intention in mind for me. Nor does it mean that I must "resign" myself to this "fate." To give consent to the direction in which accidents of birth and history have turned one is to be persuaded of the adequacy of that direction, if not its eternal validity. What is true for the individual is true for the religious community as well. In some complex ways it consents to its history and its tradition. But the processes of selection from the tradition, of judging aspects of it in the light of contemporary knowledge and experience, of reordering, revising, and rejecting, go on. If a community can consent to its tradition, it can dissent from it; it can select aspects to which it consents and from which it dissents. The tests for the community or for individuals are many: lived experiences of many sorts, coherence or incoherence with other ways of construing the world, and the like.

The experience of a lovely landscape, or of remorse for causing suffering, does not evoke religious affectivity because somewhere in the Bible it says the heavens declare the glory of God or that one is guilty when one causes harm to others. Rather, a moment of deeply appreciated aesthetic response is, in the consciousness of the beholder who has consented to certain fundamental aspects and outlooks from the biblical tradition, also a moment of "natural piety." But it would not be religious piety without participation in a tradition that affects the perception of the phenomenon as one that is ultimately dependent upon powers that make possible such beauty, that sustain the natural world. My religious construal of both the objects and the affectivity is different from, for example, that of the Nordic people of old, for whom Teutonic religious mythology and popular beliefs in trolls no doubt penetrated their construal of similar natural events. My perception of the event and its significance as a moment which declares the glory of God is permeated by the religious symbols and consciousness that characterize the biblical religious traditions. *There is no avoiding acknowledgment of a circularity in this;* the experience confirms that which I am predisposed to have it confirm. But confirmation is subject to assessment by me and by the community. (It no doubt disconfirms what a militant atheist is predisposed to have it disconfirm as well.) A reliance on the religious tradition is inevitable; but consent to it is not. The larger meaning of the event is experientially confirmed.

Why does one give consent, even selectively, to the symbols of a tradition? The orthodox answer is that God has chosen to reveal himself in the events recorded in that tradition. The authority of the symbols stems from their authorization by the Deity. I have already indicated that I reject such a view. I return briefly to a theme I have just developed, and again use the term "consent." What the tradition records is the consent of a people to the powers that bear down upon them, that sustain them, and in the light of which they evaluate themselves. The people consent to their dependence upon the powers of nature to bring them into life, to sustain their being, to provide opportunities for human development. It is in their cooperation with these powers, and their agreeing to the conditions of these powers, their receptivity to them, that they come to interpret the meaning of life in relation to them. They come to construe the world theocentrically rather than anthropocentrically out of their consent to these powers. But consent, once again, is not resignation. It is a voluntary agreement with the powers, a cooperation with them to the ends that they are perceived to have. It implies the possibility of dissent, of rebellion against these powers, of denial of their reality and of human dependence upon them. These experiences gave rise to myths, symbols, interpretations of the significance of historical events, and cultic procedures. We share piety and experiences of "the world" with our ancient forebears. The religious heritage to which we consent arose out of the construal of the world in dispositions and attitudes of awe and respect, out of experiences of the natural world, historical events, and so on, in a religiously affective way. A knowing came through religious affectivity, a knowing that was confirmed or disconfirmed, sustained or revised, of the presence of God in and through human experiences. The tradition is not an ancient bag of irrational nonsense; it carries a way of relating to all things in a manner appropriate to their relations to God that has been forged by human experiences both similar and dissimilar to our own. It is not a series of inferences developed from the "facts" of human experience to a conclusion that the powerful Other exists. Rather it is penetration in piety of meanings of various experiences and their expression in various symbols and cultic rites.

No current generation of a religious community construes the world theologically de novo any more than a current generation of scientists cuts itself off from the preceding generation. There is at least a presumption that the theological perceptions and construals of the world that are given in the tradition have a significant degree of adequacy. If they did not they would not have survived; their inadequacy for interpreting the religious responses to the world would have rendered them totally obsolete. As I have noted, aspects of the tradition have been abandoned; others have been reinterpreted, altered, extended, and recombined in the light of the tests of various aspects of human experience and various forms of knowledge. Those who have drifted away from a traditional theology they once affirmed or at least were exposed to have found other ways of interpreting the purposes of life in the world to be more to their liking, more adequate to their experiences. Those who have consciously rejected traditional theology have deliberately dissented from it because it does not meet certain tests. Some of the tests are experiential: the story of Job is read by many to be, in its "happy ending" version, a too simple resolution in the face of his afflictions. Some test theological interpretations by other ways of interpreting the meaning of the same events and experiences. The belief in a powerful Other, for example, is deemed not necessary to explain the existence of the world in which we live; it is a hypothesis that is disproved, or at least is unprovable, and therefore it is abandoned. Or, the sense of accountability, and its accompanying senses of guilt or self-approval, is explainable by various theories of the person; no Other to whom we are accountable is necessary to explain this aspect of human experience. Those who continue to give a measured consent to aspects of the tradition find that a heritage from the past provides a worthy way of understanding certain meanings of present human life and experience. Theology is an enterprise that extrapolates from piety, and other affective responses to the world, to say some things about God. Consent to a particular theological retrieval from the past, however, is not given merely because it is "subjectively satisfying." There are multiple tests of the adequacy of what can be said about God, and since God is not an object alongside other objects, and therefore not subject to the same investigations as other objects, there are limitations to what can be said and "verified."

II: God

In Chapter 1 I briefly, but critically, surveyed several current options in theological literature for articulating the meaning of God. Some observations I made about those options are worthy of recall. All that I chose have the merit of attempting to say some things about God and his relations to the world; none of them intentionally reduces theology to anthropology, into a way of understanding only man and the human situation. In some cases recourse to the language of mystery was taken too soon and too often; the degree of abstraction of the language used removed God from a more experiential context; on the whole they did not pay sufficient attention to nature, and when some of them did, the purpose of nature was the fulfillment of human beings as individuals. All, at least, agreed that some things could be said about God, and although I did not develop the points fully, all gave some reasons why and how these things can be said. Limitations of claims for knowledge of God have been in the Christian tradition for centuries; this reflects not only proper intellectual modesty but also the ineffability of the object of theological knowledge. No contemporary theologians within the range of our discussion want to make God an object like other objects. It is not only the limits of humanity that make all discussions of the Deity circumspect; the Deity is not knowable as other things are knowable. Yet, unless religious and theological language is to be left vacuous, some things have to be said about their ultimate "object."

In this section I shall first articulate in traditional religious and theological language some of the themes about God and his relations to the world that have been meaningfully sustained in the Western religious consciousness for many centuries. I shall develop certain classic symbols: God as Creator, as Sustainer and Governor, as Judge, and as Redeemer, and show in what ways these continue to be viable ways of speaking about God in relation to man and the world. The traditional language of God's love is not independently treated because, in my judgment, it is often used in an excessively vague way, and many of the terms I shall employ could be developed as more precise specifications of it. This will be followed by a section in which I draw upon some evidences from other branches of investigation to indicate the meaningfulness of interpreting or construing the world theologically.

God as Creator

Claus Westermann, in an exegetical study of the first eleven chapters of Genesis, argues that creation accounts arise in response to man's surroundings, not out of a philosophical or scientific investigation of human origins.[27] Westermann stresses that man was threatened by his surroundings; this is no doubt the case. The imagery also indicates (as Westermann subsequently develops) that the surroundings sustain the life of the human community, and that part of the problem of human living is to be appropriately related to our surroundings. Westermann perceptively calls attention to the breadth of human experiences that are explored or alluded to in the early chapters of Genesis. There are the experiences of time in

27. Claus Westermann, *Creation*, trans. John J. Sullivan, S.J. (Philadelphia: Fortress, 1974), p. 11.

the differentiation between night and day; of space in the differentiation of land and waters and sky; of teeming animal and plant life; of the distinctiveness of human life with its capacities for "dominion" over other forms of life; of human possibilities to work and to cultivate what is given in the charge that Adam was to till and to keep the garden; of "marriage" and family; and of moral accountability and guilt. The capacities to develop culture are presented in the naming of the animals, the establishment of cities (4:17), the development of nomadic life (4:20), music (4:21), and the development of technology (4:22). In all of these experiences, human beings are depicted in interrelationship with nature and with other persons, responding to possibilities given in the world. There is a strong sense of dependence on what has been given prior to human intervention into the world, of interdependence of aspects of the world, of the capacities to develop what is given, of appropriate relations of things to each other, as well as of man's accountability for being properly related to what is given and for relating things properly to each other. The world is there to be tilled and kept by human activity, but what is given is also deemed good in its own right—without specific claim that all things are good for man.

In my terms, these narratives express human consent to the powers that have brought life into being; that order the range of "objects" and experiences; that create the conditions for possibilities of human development biologically (genealogies), historically, socially, culturally. The traditional myths and symbols express the awe and respect that the senses of dependence, gratitude, possibility, and the rest nourish as a result of participation in the powers of life in the world. Religious affectivity is evoked by objects of experience, and in the religious consciousness of the Western religious traditions this evokes piety toward manifold powers and toward the powerful Other that is perceived to be present in and through the world.

My argument is not an exegetical or historical one; it is not a claim that one finds only a monotheistic religious consciousness in the biblical materials, or that there was a consistent historical development from the perceptions recorded in the beginning of the Bible to our own generation. It is that the "objects" experienced by persons early in the tradition were responded to in religiously affective ways and led to a theological construing of the world that symbolized the power and the powers in the name of God as the Creator. There are similarities between our experiences of our surroundings and those described in these narratives: our surroundings evoke similar senses, attitudes and dispositions, and affections. The world is not "in human hands"; we also depend upon and respond to many things that are given both as limits and as possibilities for our species. No Eden is given to us, but we receive the natural world, culture, and society of our own times. We also have the capacities and the responsibility to "till and to keep" what is given. Like those whose experience is depicted in these myths, we need to discover the limits and the boundaries which we overstep only to our peril and the peril of the world around us. We also need to live in the world with a sense of the Divine Reality on whom all things depend, who was before our species evolved, and will be long after it has disappeared from this planet. Respect and awe evoked by nature, history, culture, society, and by our capacities as persons, lead to acknowledgment of the creative powers on which all things depend. God as Creator remains, in piety, a vivid religious symbol.

God as Sustainer and Governor

The theological tradition has often used the symbols of Sustainer or Governor to refer to God's presence and activity in the world. Often the term "divine order" has been used to designate the characteristics of a fixed, eternal, immutable order of nature and society. Thus we have traditions of the "natural order" and of the "orders of creation." All such notions begin with the perceptions and interpretations of nature and society and go on to speak about God as Governor or Sustainer. They have been influenced by speculative thought about nature. If nature was described as timeless and immutable, the religious response was affected by this. Certainly in the piety of Augustine this is the case; beyond the realms of change was the reality of the Diety who was changeless and therefore perfect. Birth and degeneration, history and human catastrophes, were all perceived to be in the realm of the imperfect precisely because of their temporality and mutability. The perfect had to be the changeless, immutable, timeless, eternal. It is consistent with this view for moral responses to the Deity to require a conformity of institutions, historical events, and cultural achievements with this changeless, timeless divine order.

The history and the debates about such notions need not be attended to here. One of the contributions of periodic returns to the biblical accounts as the exclusive source for theology has been to demonstrate that in the biblical tradition itself there is a distinctive strand of expressions and symbols: the idea of God acting in history. While this idea did not reduce the significance of the Deity to random appearances in a contingent series of events, it did at least suggest that there was a dynamism to the presence of God in the world. God was not an eternal, immutable, abstract order, but an actor in the world. Certainly the process theologians have contributed to the shifting of metaphysical thought about God from the more "classical" view to the more "historical" or dynamic view, for example, in Whitehead's distinction between the "consequent" and the "primordial" natures of God. Lutheran theologians, saddled by the tradition of a far too static and conservative understanding of the "orders of creation" used to justify particular social institutions, have shifted from the idea of order to the idea of God's creative activity. Gustaf Wingren's systematic account, *Creation and Law*, is a case in point.[28] For Wingren, even the notion of law becomes transposed into activity; God's law is God's ordering activity in the world. The classical arguments for the existence of God from the design of the universe, which reached a particular peak in the eighteenth century in the clockmaker metaphor, were shaken by developments in geology and biology that indicated the presence of costly and chaotic developments in nature, but were again attempted in the light of a more developmental view of the design and thus of the designer.[29]

The perception either of an order or of an ordering process in a whole range of life in the world continues to be a warrant for an attitude of piety on the part of many persons and communities. And the significance for our species of what is perceived as the ordering continues to be a subject of serious reflection. A divine governance in the ordering of nature, historical events, and culture cannot be a justification for those human aspirations and ends that exceed what is fitting to our place in the universe. There are warrants for the symbol of God as Sustainer and Governor in our human experiences of the world. For Sustainer there is not only the sense of dependence that warrants the symbol of Creator but also the continuation of the ordering of the universe, of life on this planet, and of human relationships. Human dependence is not only on the creation but also on the sustenance of life within the natural and more distinctively human world. We continue to rely upon processes and relationships that are not of our creation, we are continually sustained by natural, social, cultural, and historical processes to which we give tacit consent. The symbol of God as Sustainer brings this to consciousness.

Life is sustained through ordering as well as through creative powers and capacities. A governance of the world is perceived in many ways. If the sun's temperature were higher or lower by a relatively insignificant degree, the conditions necessary for life on this planet would not exist. Continuities in the genetic code make possible the replication, generation after generation, of creatures with the capacities we call human. A natural "food chain" sustains not only human life but all other forms of life on this planet. There are orderings of human relationships, varied in their particular forms, but nonetheless operative, that must be complied with

28. Gustaf Wingren, *Creation and Law,* trans. Ross MacKenzie (Philadelphia: Muhlenberg, 1961), pp. 46–47. Wingren stresses the creative activity of God rather than orders of creation.

29. See Neal C. Gillespie, *Charles Darwin and the Problem of Creation* (Chicago: University of Chicago Press, 1979), pp. 82–108.

for the biological, educational, and social nourishing of human young. There are many prerequisites for the world of nature and for human societies to survive and to flourish. Meeting these prerequisites does not guarantee my well-being as I might perceive it, nor that of a particular community. The divine governance not only creates the possibilities but also the limitations of human flourishing.

To indicate that the prerequisites must be acknowledged, respected, and tended, is not to claim sufficient warrants for a clear and unambiguous delineation of a *telos* in the mind and power of God, and most certainly not a *telos* that guarantees that the prerequisites exist for the sake of our species or any one of us as individuals. To remember the natural contingencies which made life possible on this planet, and which made possible the development and survival of mammalian life, is to recall that, had a few natural events been only slightly different, we would not be. To argue that these contingencies are indicators that the divine governance intentionally worked through them to bring our species into being as the crown of creation is its own leap of faith. To ponder the meaning of the forecasts of the demise of our species should be sufficient to deter us from such a faith. The visions of Teilhard de Chardin of the steady development to the Omega of spirituality's dominance over biology cannot be defended.[30]

To remain agnostic about an ultimate *telos*, however, is not necessarily to deny the indicators of the divine sustenance and governance discernible in the necessary conditions, the prerequisites for life. To claim that such prerequisites exist is not to argue that the particular forms and requirements of them do not change over the course of human evolution, and of historical, social, cultural, and personal development. In the realm of nature, or those aspects of life that can be investigated by the "hard" sciences, much more can be said about these necessary conditions with greater confidence than in the realms of society and culture. An infant with a particular chromosomal defect will not have the capacities for human development that a genetically normal infant has. The biological prerequisite for normal development is not there. But when we seek to discern and articulate the necessary conditions, for example, for the flourishing of a human society, our observations are less precise, more generalized (and perhaps even quite formal). These conditions change over the course of human development. Some ordering of sexual relationships seems to be required; precisely what that will be is subject to many biological, historical, cultural, and social factors. (No doubt the near equality between male and female human births provides the biological prerequisite for monogamy as a normative form of marriage. If the ratio

---

30. Teilhard de Chardin, *The Phenomenon of Man*, trans. Bernard Wall (New York: Harper and Row, 1959).

of male to female births in our species were 1:4 we can be sure that polygamy would be both statistically normal and morally normative.) Some ordering of labor is necessary even in relatively simple societies. What the ordering is depends upon a multitude of conditions, including cultural traditions. Some articulation of the processes by which disputes are settled between competing interests in a given society is required, whether by the establishment of legal or moral codes, processes of negotiation and adjudication, or physical strife. These prerequisites must be acknowledged. Life is sustained by acknowledging them and meeting their conditions.

We return to the notion of ordering, rather than order, as the more fitting designation of the meaning of the symbols of God the Sustainer and Governor. What can be discerned about how the world is being ordered changes with knowledge-conditions, as is clearly the case in our understanding of the natural ordering. Whether the focus of attention is on human genetics, psychology, or nutrition, the sciences inform us regarding the ordering conditions and laws. While we can, in modern cultures, intervene in these processes to alter them, we still consent to them in a significant measure, cooperating with them as they are given. If a chromosomal defect cannot be corrected, we can consent to it (not merely resign ourselves to it) and participate in the development of a limited natural capacity. If we understand the chemical components that make for high yields of food grains, we consent to that and augment the yields by, in a sense, cooperating with the necessary conditions. The conditions both limit possibilities and make possible our cooperation with them for some developments. This is relative to our knowledge.

In the ordering of social and cultural life, we might state in a highly generalized manner what the prerequisites are for individual and social flourishing. Our perceptions of these, however, are altered by our knowledge. Numerically larger societies cannot be ordered in the same way that small ones can. Industrialized societies require a different ordering from preindustrialized societies. Societies in which there is the dominance of a single religion are ordered somewhat differently from societies in which there are several religions. Yet there are some persistent prerequisites. While the material principles of justice might differ in different societies and cultures, there seems to be a fundamental need to determine what is due to each person, and which equals shall be treated equally. In the West we have had centuries of discussion about the preferability of monarchy, aristocracy, or democracy, and under certain historical conditions each seems to have fulfilled a corporate need; but the need for some allocation of power and authority, and for some legitimation of it, persists. The persistent prerequisites are, in the religious consciousness, signs of an ordering process of social life, ultimately under the divine governance.

Morality in this perspective is the task of discerning what the divine ordering requires under particular conditions in a particular time and place. It is not a task of knowing what the immutable divine moral order of the universe is, and then developing institutions and human relations to conform to it. Because the sustaining and the governing of life is itself both continuous and changing, the human cultural venture of moral and political ordering must be open to extension, development, and abandonment of some features of what is received. The religious community responds to the signs of ordering of nature and society as marks of the divine sustenance and governance. It perceives its moral and social task to be to relate to that sustenance and governance in a fitting way, to relate to all things in a manner appropriate to their relations to it. Not only is dependence on the divine ordering acknowledged but also accountability to it. God as Sustainer and Governor remains a powerful religious symbol. The vocation of the human community is to consent to the divine governance, to cooperate with it (not merely be resigned to it) toward those aims that can be discerned. It is to participate in it, while acknowledging dependence upon it, and acknowledging the limits and possibilities of human activity that are consonant with it.

God as Judge

The traditional religious symbols of God as Judge, and of the wrath of God, currently do not receive much attention. In part they have been displaced by the cheap grace of contemporary Christianity. In part they have been modified by the powerful theological trends that argue that the grace of God is prior to the judgment and wrath of God. In part they are ignored because a historic emphasis on them is believed to be accountable for an excessive sense of guilt, and even for severe mental disturbances. Reference to them has become jocular in recent American culture; one remembers the frequent quip on a popular television comedy show in which, after each occasion when something was done that was offensive to her, the principal actress says, "God will get you for that." Some claims made about the wrath and the judgment of God have been fairly arbitrary. Sometimes the terms have been used in the context of a highly personal understanding of God penetrating each human experience so that every pain or affliction was the sign of the wrath of God for some known or unknown deed or thought that was sinful. When the penal-judicial symbols have achieved a paramount position in the interpretation of Christianity, this symbol has come to have an excessive impact upon Christian morality. Whether in Jansenist Roman Catholicism, or in evangelical Protestantism, the need of human beings for salvation from sin has been correlated with the stress on the wrath and the judgment of God.

The fact that a symbol has been used excessively, or misused, in religious life is not a sufficient reason for eliminating it. If one's perception of human life is deeply social in character, and stresses the interdependence of persons with other persons and with society, culture, and nature, the symbol of God as Judge can be retrieved and used in a meaningful way. This can begin with the biblical materials themselves. I believe Westermann is correct when he argues that, in the Genesis accounts, "Man is not only set before God; he appears from the very beginning as a social being who must work and bear the problems consequent on this state."[31] Sin, then, is not properly understood in the narrow, individualistic ways that have usually dominated the Christian tradition. "It is viewed in a broader perspective. It is seen as that other limit, that inadequacy or overstepping of limits which determines the whole of human existence."[32] Thus it affects many aspects of human life. It is a disordering of proper relationships between persons. The disorder is not only the result of transgression of proper limits but also of deficient participation in the care of other persons, society, culture, and nature. It is not only a matter of pride but also a matter of sloth.

In some aspects of human experience the limits are clear; the narrative of the murder of Abel by Cain reflects the basis on which the commandment against murder was established. Adultery is morally wrong because it involves a betrayal both of trust and of explicit commitments that establish proper relationships between the sexes. Theft is wrong because it violates morally justifiable rights of control over various goods. In other aspects of human experience the proper relationships are not so clear. While the eating of the forbidden fruit suggests that there are limits that cannot be transgressed without untoward consequences for the transgressors, the narrative does not establish what sorts of knowledge and intervention would count as transgressions for all social and cultural conditions.

The lines that can be drawn to indicate deficiencies in relationships and mutual participation are less clear than the lines that can be drawn around excessive transgression. To ask, "Am I my brother's keeper?" is to raise, in a very particular human relationship, the question of our obligations not only to limit our interventions in the lives of others but also to be positively responsible for their care and sustenance. It is to raise the question not only of what it is proper to refrain from doing but also what we are obliged to do to sustain and develop the lives of other

31. Westermann, *Creation*, p. 18.
32. Ibid., p. 19.

persons, the common good of human communities, and even the natural world and culture.

We are not privileged to know with clarity and certainty just what our proper relationships and activities are in the ordering of life in the world in many areas of experience.[33] An understanding of the proper relationships, and consequently of those actions which are fitting, is relative to knowledge-conditions, to capacities that have developed to control the consequences of interventions, and to other aspects of society and culture. And each extension of what had been deemed to be proper limits involved risks. This is not a matter simply of theological ethical speculation; it is a matter of quite particular import in the history of society and culture, and in contemporary life as well. There have been, and still are, those who in great anxiety decide that certain investigations are morally wrong because they intrude into a forbidden knowledge of nature. Often this is a retrospective judgment: in the light of the development and use of nuclear weapons, for example, ought physicists not to have developed nuclear physics? In the light of the potential for control of human behavior that increases with more accurate knowledge of the human brain, ought there to be restraints on this kind of investigation? In the light of the unforeseen consequences of rapid growth in population, was it wrong to use the public health measures that have extended the life expectancies of millions of persons in various parts of the world? My point is that as human experience and culture develop, the understanding of the proper relationships between not only man and nature but also society and culture and nature, require continual reassessment in light of new knowledge-conditions, and in the light both of the possibilities and the limits of controlling consequences of interventions. This is to affirm positively the necessity to take risks; but it is also to affirm the necessity to assess the limits that come to our awareness. Similar examples could be drawn from social experimentation and other realms of contemporary life.

How, in the light of these considerations, are the symbols of God as Judge and of the wrath of God meaningful? Certainly in the biblical materials these symbols represented the historical and personal consequences of disobedience to the commands of God. The prophetic moral indictments of the prophets Amos, Hosea, and Micah were based upon the assumption that the people knew what was cultically and morally

33. For generations the biblical tradition was assailed by scientists because it seemed to deter aggressive experimentation; its ethic was an ethic of restraint. In the past decade the opposite accusation has been made against it; the passage on "dominion" has been accused of being the source of Western culture's excessive aggression into nature for the sake of human well-being. I suppose that if one is against religion one will find one reason or another to express the antipathy.

right, and that they were accountable for their disobedience to those requirements. Events were judged to be marks of the divine judgment for this disobedience. In a similar way in the Deuteronomic materials the future well-being of the people was assured if they lived in conformity with the Torah.

There are clearly difficulties in this view. Theologically it assumes the divine determination of all particular events according to the principle of just deserts to their agents. And, given the model of moral and social life as properly conducted through obedience to commands, both persons and communities were accorded a very high degree of moral accountability for what occurred. Whenever there were untoward consequences, the impulse was to seek out persons or groups which might be held morally or cultically accountable for them. Moral blame had to be located, and not only repentance but also retribution was required.

The position I am developing has affinities with this description of what is assumed in this aspect of the biblical tradition. A notion of divine judgment and wrath requires a view that "discerns" the presence and the purposes of God in and through a whole range of events and processes. An utterly transcendent conception of God provides no way to construe the particular participations in the ordering of life in the world as occasions not only in which fidelity to the divine governance occurs but also as occasions in which the judgment and wrath of God are perceived. Human accountability to God occurs through the actions and relationships which are consonant or dissonant with what can be perceived as the indications of the divine ordering. One of the ways in which we sense that actions and relations are not properly ordered is by their adverse consequences. But since we are not given a blueprint of an eternal divine order, and are not given precise commands that are to be obeyed in all circumstances, the divine ordering is discovered in the processes of human experience.

Three aspects of a biblical model of moral accountability that sustain the Deuteronomic and prophetic views are thereby qualified. First, the commands, at least within the scope of activity covered by them, provided certainty about what conduct was required. This is somewhat of an exaggeration, for clearly the Torah itself developed, and there were procedures for interpreting its implications for events not precisely covered by given commands. But if one knows the commands, one is culpable to a high degree for one's disobedience to them. My qualification of this aspect is not so extreme as to sustain a view that the divine governance is necessarily discovered or rediscovered only in particular events and occasions, but it does imply a lesser degree of certainty about what our proper relations to "all things" are.

Second, there is a qualification of the extent to which persons and communities can be held morally culpable for the consequences of their actions. The limitations of knowledge and the limitations of capacities to control consequences are part of human finitude. While both expand in many areas as culture itself develops, limits nonetheless remain. The scope of accountability increases with expanding knowledge and capacities to control our interventions in nature, society, and human life. But human beings are not the only "causal agents" in sequences of events, and thus consequences cannot be ascribed to their moral blameworthiness or praiseworthiness to the extent that some of the biblical interpretations appear to do.

The third aspect is that this biblical model, like models of particular providence that have followed from it in subsequent Christian theological tradition, assumes that the divine intention directs all particular events, and that consequences thus can be attributed not only to the moral responsibility of agents but also to the specific intentions of the Deity to punish and to reward particular persons and communities. Thus all adverse conditions have their final "cause" in God's intentions to punish, and not only Job but many others are forced to examine their pasts to find out if they deserve what they have received.

I believe that the symbols of the judgment and wrath of God are meaningful even with these qualifications. The religious consciousness confronts the judgment and wrath of God on those occasions when the consequences of our commissions and omissions signal a serious disordering of relationships between persons, in society, in relation to nature. When we perceive that human activity has "overstepped" limits and has created adverse consequences, we meet not only the divine ordering but the divine judgment as well. When we perceive that a deficiency of our activity is responsible for adverse consequences we also meet the divine judgment. The circumstances in which this occurs are very different. In a more primary order of biological life, the "natural reaction" is sometimes immediate and fully explainable; the ingestion of a poison violates the proper ordering of bodily processes, and the consequences are immediate. But even in such a case technology and "culture" can intervene to ward off the natural consequences; an antidote can be taken. In areas of greater scope, the "natural reaction" is delayed, cushioned, or altered by myriad processes of society and culture. Population growth is a case in point. Widespread malnutrition and starvation due to excessive population growth would have occurred much sooner in our century had it not been for a large number of technological, cultural, political, economic, and other activities that have warded off catastrophe. Culture provides ways in which human beings can participate in various processes of life to sustain a larger number of persons. Yet one need not be apocalyptic in outlook to perceive the signs of the judgment of the divine governance; without many forms of actions, including actions to restrain the growth that culture has now made possible, there will be more suffering and more deaths related to malnutrition.

One does not need to use the symbols of God the Judge and of the wrath of God to explain adverse reactions to the disordering of relationships between persons, man and nature, and within societies. Explanation is not the point of such religious symbols. Their meaningfulness is within the context of a religiously affective response to events and of a theological construal of them. While for many persons the presence of the signals I refer to as signs of the divine judgment are hardly warrants sufficient to affirm a power which orders and limits, as well as provides possibilities for life, to the religious consciousness they are. As I stated more homiletically above, God will not be denied; human activity must find proper ways to consent to the indications of a divine ordering; without such ways human life and other aspects of the world are put in peril. Such is the judgment and the wrath of God.

God as Redeemer

The biblical materials, both Old and New Testaments, are replete with themes of the redemptive work of God. Indeed, through the centuries Christian piety has placed a central importance on this; it is affirmed as well in Jewish religious and liturgical life. God is good not merely in the sense that there is a power that brings life into being, sustains, and orders it. God is good also in the sense that human beings are liberated from bondage, transformed from their old creaturehood into signs of a new being or new life. And, as we saw above, there has been the persistent belief that God's goodness will be made clear in eternal life to those who have undeservedly suffered in this life in spite of their faith and their morality. Or, as we saw in the discussion of Moltmann's theology, redemptive possibilities are seen to be deep and radical: they provide the ground of hope for a new "creation," largely in terms of a new and better ordering of society.

Redemption has to be "from" something; salvation and liberation are "from" something. Traditional distinctions have been made in theology between the goodness of God's grace in creation—the provision of the natural possibilities of human life—and God's special grace given through Jesus Christ which redeems persons from sin. Indeed, redemption from sin is the persistent historic theme. Sin itself, as shall be indicated more fully in the next chapter, has had a number of different references in the Western religious tradition. It is disobedience to the laws of God, and thus takes on a deeply moral component. It is disorientation of life, life striving for the wrong ultimate object, love of that which is less than God with a love that is appropriate only to God, as we have noted in Augustine. It is failure to have the proper object of trust, and thus is basically spiritual and moral idolatry, as Luther held. It is now attributed to "structures" of society that repress legitimate aspirations for justice and self-fulfillment. It is, in some instances, even wrong beliefs about God. While there are discussions of the relations between creation and redemption, the primary focus has been on sin and redemption. The deep affirmation of hope in the Christian tradition is grounded in a confidence that God is the Redeemer, that in the end sin itself has been overcome, and that not only the results of the human fault but also the limitations of human finitude will be overcome in individual eternal life or in the coming of the new blessed community, the Kingdom of God.

I have, particularly in the discussion of the "sense of possibility," indicated that within the religious consciousness the ultimate power provides the conditions for human (and other) possibilities. While there are the limitations within which the human community and individuals must live, and while particular ranges of choice and action are limited as a result of antecedent events and individual experiences and capacities, fatalism is incorrect. We are "fated" (deeply conditioned) in many ways; we have to consent to particular conditions over which we have no control, recognize limitations in personal capacities that are natural or a result of social and cultural nurture, and confront institutions and events that we cannot radically alter. Yet there are capacities for change present in ourselves, in our institutional and other external conditions, and in the course of events. Hope, as William Lynch, S.J., has so carefully shown, is the consciousness of possibilities.[34] Its contrast is despair, which is evoked and sustained by the absence of significant possibilities for oneself or one's community. To speak of God as the "provider" of conditions of possibilities, or of the goodness of the creation and ordering of life, does not capture the meaning of redemption. These things are forms of grace but not what the tradition calls "redeeming" grace.

It is proper, I believe, to speak of redeeming grace in two ways: as redemption from conditions of fatedness, and as redemption from sin.

Those limits and burdens to which we are "fated" as particular persons and communities are beyond our immediate control. For example, many black persons and families in the United States have been deprived of opportunities as a result of historical and social conditions neither they nor their ancestors brought into being in a voluntary way. Many persons suffer from diseases that are genetically transmitted. Some societies are located in areas of few natural resources. It is proper to speak of redemption from these conditions when the capacities to alter them for the better can be exercised by the victims and by others. The "times" can

34. William F. Lynch, S.J., *Images of Hope* (Baltimore: Helicon, 1965), p. 32. "[H]ope is, in its most general terms a sense of the possible."

be redeemed by the alteration of the fated conditions through the exercise of powers and capacities in the human community. Legislative and judicial powers are used to alter the conditions that have fated members of some minority groups in American society. Medical interventions can manage the symptoms if not cure the causes of some inherited diseases. Persons and communities that suffer deprivation because of droughts and other natural conditions can be attended to by the actions of other persons and communities. Where human agency can rectify the effects of fatedness, can bring some good out of natural evils, can create possibilities in society and culture for those who are in despair, and can alter institutional arrangements to restrain threats to human well-being and create possibilities for human flourishing, a form of redemption is occurring. We can be redeeemed even from the particular fatedness of nature in some circumstances; interventions into nature can sometimes release persons and communities from the scourges that bring suffering. Within religious affectivity it is meaningful to construe such occasions as signs of the presence of God the Redeemer: the power or powers that make possible rectification, renewal, and recombination of the elements of life that contribute to proper human well-being, and to the well-being of the ordering of life with which we are interdependent. These powers do not absolutely overcome limitations but create and extend the conditions of possibility.

It is proper to use the term "sin" only for actions (including failure to act) and states of life for which persons can be held causally accountable, and therefore religiously or morally accountable. Guilt cannot be fairly attributed to persons for states of affairs or behaviors beyond their control. Experientially, a sense of guilt is a reality of human life. It is distorted or even false when fated conditions provoke it. Unfortunately there are still persons who feel guilt for the birth of a defective child, or who feel guilty for their poverty when it is due to forces beyond their control. In my judgment, release from distorted or false senses of guilt occurs when the real causes are understood. Release from proper guilt, however, comes only by forgiveness.

The biblical materials and the Christian tradition are replete with evidences that the experience of guilt is a central aspect of construing life theocentrically. The biblical moral codes stipulate the offenses for which persons are held accountable. Infractions of them render persons guilty with reference to persons they have offended, to the community, and to God. They are, in a sense, failures to consent to the divine governance as that is understood and articulated. Like most religions, the biblical ones describe cultic rites by which God or the gods can be placated; disciplines of penance in Christian ecclesiastical life are modifications of the same purpose. But equally strong is the motif of divine forgiveness: the ultimate power is experienced and perceived in part to be one of

steadfast love, of mercy, and of reconciliation between persons and between God and persons. The evidences that warrant this are varied, and
in orthodox Christianity the supreme evidence is Christ, as the meaning
of his life, death, and resurrection are construed in the light of the experience of sin and guilt. The biblical religions are salvation religions in
a strong sense; God is not only Creator, Governor, and Judge but is also
Redeemer.

From the perspective of the present work, this attribution of mercy,
redeeming power, and renewing power to the Deity arises out of the
human experiences of loving forgiveness. Forgiveness is never deserved,
never something earned. It is proffered, tendered. It can be sought: the
occasions of one's guilt can be deeply acknowledged; contrition can be
expressed in word and in attitude. But forgiveness is always an expression
or an act of an other. Only metaphorically can we say that we forgive
ourselves. Forgiveness can be withheld, for it is the capacity of an other
to give it. Life can be quite unbearable without forgiveness. Indeed, a
readiness to be contrite and a readiness to forgive are necessary conditions
for intimate human relationships. Family life is one such relationship. In
it there are occasions of sins of omission: those times and places when
we ought to have done what we did not do. There are sins of commission:
those times and places when we have done that which we ought not to
have done. There are breaches of mutual trust, failures to fulfill natural
and contractual duties, and insensitivities to the deep needs of others. It
is love in the form of proffered forgiveness that heals the breaches, moves
us to fulfill our duties, and reconciles us to others. In piety one aspect of
the ultimate power is construed to be mercy, forgiving love. The gratitude
for and joy of being forgiven, for being tendered possibilities in the most
undeserving circumstances, rests finally on the divine governance. Consent to and cooperation with the direction of the powers that order life
involve both consent to being *forgiven,* reconciled, and renewed, and
consent to being *forgiving,* reconciling, and renewing. The historic tradition provides symbols of the merciful and reconciling love of God that
are experienced in human occasions of forgiveness and reconciliation.
But, to paraphrase H. Richard Niebuhr, to say that God is merciful is not
to say that mercy is God.[35]

The traditional symbols of God as Creator, Sustainer and Governor,
and Redeemer express aspects of the human experience of powers that
sustain and bear down upon us, and powers that create possibilities,
including that of human renewal. They express religious affectivities in
response to many aspects of nature, history, culture, society, and self.

35. "Though God is love, love is not God for [Jesus]," H. Richard Niebuhr, *Christ and Culture* (New York: Harper, 1951), p. 17.

They articulate a theological construal of life. One finds them, or terms similar to them, in prayers and hymns, in sermons and in liturgies. They are terms of piety as well as, in more precise formulations, concepts. They are not used simply because they are biblical terms, or terms that express significant biblical ideas; even in the Bible these sorts of terms express meanings of human experience in various surroundings, in response to natural and historical events, in social relationships. It must be acknowledged that apart from piety the symbols are not confirmed.

The objects of our experiences are interpreted, construed in non-religious language as well. As modern culture develops, there are more competing symbols and theories to explain and express the meaning of what is expressed religiously and theologically. While I believe it is not possible to construct, for example, a purely "natural theology" of nature and experience, in the sense that the existence of the power and powers of God is proven apart from religious affectivity, scientific descriptions and explanations can correct and alter some traditional religious claims, and the realities to which they refer can be indicators of matters which inform and make plausible certain theological affirmations.

The Use of Scientific Explanations in the Retrieval and Reconstruction of Theology

John Calvin wrote, "I confess, of course, that it can be said reverently, provided that it proceeds from a reverent mind, that nature is God. . . ." His qualification of this bold statement warns that it might lead to a confusion between God and "the inferior course of his works."[36] McNeill notes, in a footnote to this passage, that this reflects statements by Lactantius, who was in turn influenced by Seneca.[37] Whether or not it is ultimately the historical influence of Stoicism that leads some theologians to take nature and its laws seriously, it is clear that for Calvin God was not simply the "God of history." The orderly operations of nature were for him, as for the psalmists, Augustine, Edwards, the Deists, Schleiermacher, and many others, signs of the power and presence of God.

"The idea of God is admittedly not directly accessible in any other way than by religious belief," wrote Troeltsch. "Yet it asserts a substantial content which must stand in harmony with the other forms of scientific knowledge and also be in some way indicated by these."[38] I believe that Troeltsch is essentially correct. The substantial content of theology, if it is not in perfect harmony with scientific knowledge, cannot be in sharp

36. Calvin, *Institutes,* I, 5, 5; McNeill ed. 1:58.
37. Ibid., n. 22.
38. Ernst Troeltsch, "Religion and the Science of Religion," in Morgan and Pye, eds. *Troeltsch,* p. 117.

incongruity with it, and what we say about God must be congruent in some way with what we know about human experience and its objects through the sciences. This is not to say that scientific knowledge does not develop, nor is it to say that one draws theological inferences directly and immediately from what we know from sociobiology or physics. To affirm that there cannot be deep incongruity between theology and scientific knowledge, and that such knowledge can also be theologically construed, is to continue in a very old strand of the Christian tradition. But new knowledge of nature and society requires that God be spoken of in ways different from those which relied on a Stoic view of nature.

The ways in which evidences from various sciences are used in theology can be indicated by a brief ideal-typology. One type uses theological propositions as if they were scientific. The currently renewed pressures on the part of fundamentalist Christians to require that the "creationist" account of Genesis be included in science textbooks for public schools represents this type. To be sure, the arguments in favor of this are a bit more subtle than those used in the 1920s when fundamentalists were certain that the Genesis account was true and Darwinian evolutionary accounts were false. Now the assertion is that scientific accounts have not been finally proved to be true, and thus the Genesis account is an alternative hypothesis deserving equal time. But the qualifications are not serious; there are still impulses to believe that one can deduce scientific explanations from biblical theological statements. If there is incongruity between theological explanations and scientific ones, the theological are correct.

Similar arguments are not fundamentalist in form. For example, the biblical faiths are interpreted to show that the relationship between a human person and God is an I-Thou relationship. A second premise is that an I-Thou relationship with God must be an eternal relationship. If these premises are correct, then on theological grounds particular human beings must be immortal. Any submission of counterevidences from biology, for example, that with the demise of the brain the center of personal identity is gone, are not persuasive to persons who argue in this way. One might say that their own "biological" conclusion is deduced from theological premises: if God is a Thou to whom individuals are related eternally, there must be some "scientific" basis to assure the immortality of individual persons. Paul's argument in I Corinthians 15 is sometimes adduced: "It is sown a physical body, it is raised a spiritual body. If there is a physical body, there is also a spiritual body."[39] Either a theological explanation is a scientific explanation, as in fundamentalist views of cre-

39. 1 Cor. 15:44. R.S.V. The whole chapter is relevant.

ation, or a theological principle requires a sufficient "scientific" explanation to render the theological one true.

At the other extreme is the approach that draws theological deductions from scientific explanations of the world. I say deductions rather than inferences; loose inferences have been drawn from perceptions of the natural order to a Creator and Orderer throughout the history of religions, including the biblical ones. The psalmists, Augustine, Edwards and many others perceived a divine ordering in nature. Their accounts, however, were persuasive only in the light of a religious attitude toward nature, in the light of piety. In contrast with those who carry on this looser kind of inferential process, there have been those who would make purely rational arguments not only for the existence of God but for particular characteristics of God on the basis of the sciences of their times. No more could be said about God than what was warranted by the scientific data and theories available. The Stoics and the Deists represented this type of theologizing. Among contemporary theologians the most striking example of this type is the work of Ralph W. Burhoe. Burhoe, who is more widely known and respected by religiously interested scientists, particularly biologists, than he is by academic Christian theologians, has two purposes. One is to reform religion so that it is based solidly on scientific data and theory and not on blind faith or vague appeals to mystery; the other is to show that science is itself a very religious enterprise.[40] God is equated with the laws of nature in this work. Religion is explainable by brain functions; the laws of genetics and other areas of science tell us

40. Burhoe was the founder and long-time editor of *Zygon: Journal of Religion and Science*. In the Statement of Purpose of the journal the following indicates its intentions: "The aim of this journal is to present . . . scientifically based revisions or innovations of belief and practice for religion." *Zygon* 1 (1966):8. The "salvation" interest is clear: "One might say that because of its radical mutation the cultural 'gamete' from father science has not yet found any corresponding 'gamete' from mother religion with which it can unite to form a workable new culture for civilization." *Zygon* hopes "to unite, in full integrity, the sciences with what men hold to be their sacred values, their religion" (p. 2). In 1975 *Zygon* published Burhoe's most extensive systematic account of his thought, "The Human Prospect and the 'Lord of History,'" *Zygon* 10 (1975): 299–375. The following quotations generally substantiate my generalizations about his work: "Religion has biological roots in ancient, genotypically programmed patterns of the central nervous system, traceable back more than a hundred million years" (pp. 304–5). It is brain functions that "allow us to account for religious experience" (p. 307). "To the extent that there could be shown to be an equivalence between what is denoted by the theological term 'God' and this scientific term 'nature,' to that extent we could say that scientists are engaged in the attempt to talk about God and hence are doing theology" (p. 330). "In general, I would say that the new scientific pictures of man's creation by natural selection again allow for the restoration of the validity of a god concept as a reality which maintains perpetually a concern for what is going on in the cosmos, even a complete control of the process" (p. 335; after this sentence Burhoe quotes Jonathan Edwards with approval). "If we understand the 'nature' described by the sciences as the system of laws, according to which events in the history or evolution of the underlying reality system proceed in time, which, together with the given or 'initial conditions' and the

what can be said about God. It is both interesting and important to note that the great sociobiologist E. O. Wilson, in his synthetic secular equivalent to a systematic theology, *On Human Nature*, relies on the work of Burhoe to establish his own interpretation of religion.[41] The critical criterion in such a way of working is this: if a statement is not scientifically demonstrable, it cannot be theologically meaningful, not to mention true.

A type somewhere between these two extremes is that which is constructed on the foundations of classical realistic epistemology and metaphysics. The most recent significant statement of this type is found in Stanley L. Jaki's Gifford Lectures, *The Road of Science and the Ways to God*. Jaki takes his readers through an erudite critical examination of the history of science, laden with frequent evaluations based on this classical realistic view. His basic belief is that apart from this view neither good science nor good theology are possible. The alternatives of idealistic metaphysics, positivism, and what he calls "naive realism" are fundamental errors with disastrous results both for science and theology. There is an "urge" which moves human beings toward a rational argument for traditional Christian beliefs about God. Some of his summary statements will suffice for our purposes.

> Just as this very same science cannot be understood without recognizing the existence of a mind able to hold within its reach the wholeness of nature and be thereby superior to it, the understanding which science gives of nature will fully satisfy the urge to understand only when that urge is allowed to carry one to the recognition of that Existence which is not limited by any singularity. . . . With an inexorable urge that limited mind reaches out for the unlimited in existence which, precisely because it is genuinely unlimited, cannot happen but can only be and is therefore most aptly called He Who Is.[42]

Jaki is as critical of "mystery-mongering" as he is of rationalistic metaphysics and positivism. "Moderate realism" is the proper alternative.

> The singularity of the universe is a gigantic springboard which can propel upward anyone ready to exploit its metaphysical resilience

'hidden relations' or 'preferred configurations' of the reality system, explain (as far as man can explain) the varied history or evolution of the universe and the living systems (including human minds and societies) in it, then we do have a concept akin to the ultimate reality or God of the high religions. It possesses the aseity (absolute self-sufficiency), omnipotence, and the other attributes of God that make it natural to speak of a 'Lord of history'" (p. 361). "[T]he religious reformation now, already begun but not yet widely known, will be a theological adaptation of traditional religious beliefs and rituals to modern science." "Modern science is the new revelation about human nature and the world that is universally credible and compelling for most men today" (p. 328).

41. Wilson, *On Human Nature*, p. 171.
42. Jaki, *The Road*, p. 277.

and catch thereby a glimpse of the Ultimate and the Absolute in the form of a unique inference. Catching that glimpse, or sensing the truth of that inference, is always transitory, nay momentary. Our need of and hunger for the sensory quickly pulls us back to things tangible which, when properly touched, will again propel our minds toward the Absolute as the explanation of what is singular and contingent. The alternative to this continual surging upward is to envelop existence in a never-to-be-resolved mystery.[43]

There is an urge to draw this inference to the Absolute from what can be scientifically known and explained. Jaki develops a parallel argument, which I shall not discuss here, with reference to the presence of a purpose in creation. The inference leads to the final explanation of all that is explained scientifically; theology is in the business of explanation; its claims are made inferentially from science. Yet the truth of the inference is sensed only momentarily. Perhaps it is piety that enables this to be done. But, I believe, for Jaki to introduce piety too forcefully is a threat to his theological enterprise. The inference is theological and not scientific; "it is not for science to answer the question about the reason for the existence of a unique or singular universe." Natural theology will not benefit science qua science in the strict sense, but it

> will greatly strengthen the scientist's trust in the existence of an objectively existing, rationally ordered universe which can be investigated by the human mind, a pursuit which is man's privilege and responsibility.[44]

But the religious import of the natural theological inferences requires something more to be fully apprehended. The natural theology is, in the end, only "a skeleton of the flesh-and- blood reality" of man's relation to God. "A theism without prayer and worship is mere reasoning, which can at most show its rationality and the inconsistency of its critics, who most of the time are unwilling anyway to carry their assumptions to their logical end."[45] Piety puts flesh and blood on the skeleton of a natural theology inferred from science, but the theology is based on the sciences.

A fourth type is the ancient view of several independent truths; the truth of religion and theology, for example, standing alongside the truths of science. Since they have different basic references, they do not get into each other's way. This view has been articulated in Judaism, Islam, and Christianity by very philosophically sophisticated persons. Sometimes two sources of truth are noted: revelation and science. Sometimes human consciousness is differentiated into its aesthetic, moral, religious, and

43. Ibid., p. 278.
44. Ibid., p. 326.
45. Ibid., p. 330.

scientific aspects, and to each of these are attributed appropriate languages and meanings. In a very subtle way the work of the theologian and philosopher Paul Holmer represents this type.

Holmer is a keen polemicist whose purpose is to get important matters of theology and religion properly sorted out, and in the process to make a case for his view of religious language. His polemics create such a strong impression that he is an enemy of learning and the intellectual life that he has to assure his readers over and over that this is really not the case. His enemy is confusion in the theological enterprise, confusion created by the modern assumption that scientific language *about* religion (or other things) is necessary in order properly to use the language *of* religion. One can interpret Holmer's work to be a philosophically sophisticated project that justifies an intellectually simple act of faith and gives assurance to the simple believer. The means for accomplishing these purposes is a sharp differentiation between kinds of explanation. His article "Scientific Language and the Language of Religion," first published in 1961, remains, in my judgment, the clearest statement of the issues as he discerns them.

> [T]he logic of the discourse of science is not the same as the logic of religion. . . . [T]here are many kinds of explanations. Each kind has its context, its occasion, its own province, and its own function, relative to a specific need. We are gradually learning that kinds of explanations are not necessarily incompatible. They are in fact incommensurable with each other, and hence there is no logical incompatibility of a radical sort. A scientific explanation is a particularly apt ingress to the difference between scientific language and religious language. For a scientific explanation discloses the constituent circumstances of an event or phenomenon and then the universal relations or laws by which these circumstances come to be as they are. . . . A religious explanation is a direct use of pathos and does not resolve a dispassionate query of interest. Here a person seeks to know oneself and to explain everything relative to faith and to his or her God. So one can well say that a religious explanation is a kind of achievement and hence a heightened instance of the religious life.[46]

For Holmer, then, the language of science and the language of religion are incommensurable, but each is meaningful within its proper sphere. The purpose of theological language "is to intensify and to purify religious passion."[47] Its primary role is a practical one, "to root believers firmly in the Christian life."[48] In view of this sharp separation between

46. Paul Holmer, *The Grammar of Faith* (New York: Harper and Row, 1978), p. 69.
47. Ibid. , p. 67.
48. Ibid., p. 50.

the purposes of religious and scientific language, religious language is exempt from criticism by scientific language; indeed, historically, theology has always mishandled religious language when it has borrowed and used scientific, moral, and metaphysical terms to explain the object of its attention or to justify religious beliefs.

From Holmer's standpoint, all three previous types have erred. The error of the first is to use religious language as a scientific explanation of, for example, the creation of the world. The error of the second is to assume that scientific language can function theologically and religiously. The error of the third is to establish epistemological and metaphysical foundations which permit a unification of the tasks of science and natural theology at least to the point where the believer makes the final inference to God. And surely Troeltsch's assertion that the idea of God must be in harmony with scientific knowledge, and indicated by it, is another example of the confusion Holmer intends to clear up. Holmer, of course, has his own view of what religion is about; it is about faith (in quite Lutheran and Kierkegaardian terms) and practice. With the aid of Wittgenstein and Kierkegaard, faith and religion have autonomy; not only does a violation of this lead to intellectual confusion, it pollutes and harms religion.

From the previous developments of this book it follows that Troeltsch's statement of the case is closest to my own.[49] I would amend it in the following ways. First, piety (rather than "belief") is a necessary condition for ideas of God to be subjectively meaningful and intellectually persuasive. I do not intend by this to assert that arguments for the existence of God cannot be intellectually interesting to persons without religious affectivities, but the worthwhileness of the theological enterprise is apparent within the context of personal and communal piety. Second, the "substantial content" of ideas of God cannot be incongruous (rather than must be "in harmony") with well-established data and explanatory principles established by relevant sciences, and must "be in some way indicated by these."

This delineates a fifth type of relation of theology to science. Relative to the first type, it is clear that one cannot draw scientific conclusions or hypotheses from theological statements. Theology cannot explain the world scientifically. Relative to the second type, it is clear that one cannot draw theological conclusions deductively from scientific data and theories; there is a measure of autonomy in religion; it makes sense only with the acknowledgment of piety. What are for Ralph Burhoe data and theories for theology are for this type tests of the plausibility of certain things that are said about God. Since science is itself a developing intellectual venture, theology cannot rest its case so exclusively on the established results

49. See above, p. 251.

of science in a particular era. Yet theology cannot make claims about
God's relations with the world that are incongruous with well-established
scientific data and theories. Burhoe's excessive confidence and enthusi-
asm for identifying the two activities at least force the general point on
more traditional theologians.

Unlike the third type, for which Stanley Jaki's work is used as an
example, my position does not share the confidence in realistic epistemology and metaphysics that are essential to Jaki and others. That confidence is cast into doubt by the evidence for social and cultural relativism
in perceptions of the nature of ultimate reality. One result of development
within the physical sciences themselves, and in the historical and philosophical analysis of theoretical change within the natural sciences, is a
radical qualification of the correspondence theory of truth which the metaphysical enterprise seems to me necessarily to presuppose. Also, in his
case, the moment of piety, so to speak, comes near the end of the argument. It permits the theological inference beyond what science establishes. Piety is, so to speak, at the beginning of the religious and theological
enterprise in my position.

In distinction from the fourth type (Holmer's) this type takes a larger
view of the meaning of religion which requires that evidences from the
operations of nature be taken into account in theology. If piety is an
attitude and disposition toward the world, then what is known about the
world affects piety and must be taken into account in theology. Holmer
is correct to indicate that confusions occur when explanations become
mixed. No doubt from his standpoint my position still has explanations
too mixed and thus confused. But I believe it is proper and necessary to
test what is said theologically in the light of relevant sciences, and to use
indicators from the sciences in what one says substantively about God.
This is particularly the case if one asserts with Calvin that "it can be said
reverently . . . that nature is God," provided one does not confuse God
with the "inferior course of his works."

What indications from the various sciences are relevant to what is
said about the characteristics of the powers that bear down upon us and
sustain us? What data and theories from the sciences are appropriate tests
of the intelligibility and plausibility of theological affirmations? Which are
proper tests of a theological construing of the world? With which theories
must theological statements be congruous? Answers to these questions
cannot be fully developed here, but a general response to them and some
illustrations of particular answers are necessary to further the argument
of this book.

It must be noted that the questions are asked in terms of sciences,
in the plural, rather than science in the singular. There are different ranges
of theory in the sciences, relevant to the scope of the problem delineated

for investigation. Thus, some theories are subject to more substantial confirmation than are others. Cosmological theories have been generally alluded to previously in this book as important for theology. It has been argued that theologians cannot make theological claims about the creation or about the end (finis) of the world that would be contradicted by sound cosmological theories. Yet cosmologies are in dispute; this is in part because the cosmological question is so "global," and the evidences for particular theories so complex and partial at one and the same time, that inferences from the data can be quite different. They fit different "ideals of natural order."[50] Geological theories of earth history use a far more limited range of data, and theories can be relatively well confirmed by the corroboration of evidences not only from strata and types of rocks but also from fossil data interpreted by evolutionary theory. Yet new hypotheses about various aspects of earth history emerge. When I studied earth history in 1947 the hypothesis of continental drifts, plate tectonics, was dismissed as the product of fanciful imaginations; today it is one at the forefront of geological investigations. Evolutionary theory in biology enjoys a general confirmation and acceptance. The history of its intellectual development still excites the scholars, in part because of the "evolution" of the theory of evolution itself.[51] Lamarckian explanations of observed phenomena have no serious defenders in our time; the mechanisms of both continuity and change were better specified only after the work of Mendel was retrieved from obscurity and the science of genetics developed, and so forth. Much remains to be explained, but investigations now focus on more detailed phenomena and one cannot foresee that the general lines of the theory will ever be doubted again.

One must refer to "sciences" rather than "science" because the primary objects of investigation differ, and the scope of theories and hypotheses differ. The detection of chromosomal defects and their effects in human beings makes possible a degree of confirmation of theory that is not the case in cosmology. Different ranges or scopes of theories have different degrees of confirmation. Any reference to these matters by theologians has to take these factors into account.

The social sciences are distinguishable from the natural sciences, and vary among themselves in terms of the ranges of hypotheses and theories and the possibilities of confirming them. Demographers using aggregated data can make forecasts of the proportion of future populations in each age cohort, and even of how much the life span will be increased if a particular disease is "conquered." In other areas of social scientific research the same sort of long-range forecasting is not possible because

50. See Stephen Toulmin, *Foresight and Understanding*, pp. 44–82.
51. See ibid., on "The Evolution of Scientific Ideas," pp. 99–115.

the "variables" are too numerous, and the course of events more subject to unpredictable choices and action by persons and institutions. Thus one cannot write, as some persons are prone to do, that because "social science" indicates certain things to be true these things have to be taken into account in theology and ethics. Such appeals to general authority do not take into account the plurality of the ranges of hypothesis, degrees of adequacy of data, and the impact of the perspectives of the investigators that are involved in different human studies. Changes in life outlooks, moral beliefs, and other human valuations are even more difficult to explain in a way that will satisfy various investigators. The relevant data of changes in ethos are in themselves difficult to isolate and delineate, and are subject to so many different explanations that arguments about what theories are "true" are indecisive. Thus one must think not about "science" but about "sciences."

The Reformed tradition in theology, as that was amended in the previous chapter, is the central theme of this project. Thus our Troeltschian concerns must be specified a bit more. What data and theories from the sciences indicate the presence of powers bearing down on us and sustaining us? What indications from various sciences sustain, for example, the view developed of a radical dependence on powers beyond full human control? Do any of the sciences warrant the conviction that there is an ordering of life by these powers, to which some measure of conformation is required in human action? Do any indicate that these powers create conditions of possibility for human action? Do any indicate some fundamental directions by which human activity can be oriented? Some illustrative affirmative answers to these questions will be given before turning to the second Troeltschian inquiry: whether some traditional theological affirmations are so incongruous with certain sciences that they must be discarded or amended.

> The religious sense of dependence upon powers beyond ourselves is supported by many of the data and theories of many sciences. In nonreligious terms, this simply indicates that human life is a part of nature, and dependent upon the processes of nature. This is true with reference to individual human life and its potentialities for development that are determined in part by genetic endowments. It is also true with reference to the development of life over the long sweeps of time: for examples, the chemical and other conditions that existed on this planet to make possible development of life, and the evolutionary process by which our species came to be. The religious recognition of human dependence on the order of nature, of course, did not have to await the explanations of modern science; it is present in primitive religions, in non-Western religions, and in the history of Western religions prior to the modern age. The forms and processes of this dependence, however, are known in more

precise ways, and the range and scope of the dependence can be elaborated with greater refinement.

Theologians who have been metaphysical determinists, totally or with few qualifications, have always perceived the depth of this dependence. Their generalizations were based both on evidences from experience and on what they believed to be the proper rational extrapolations from this to an all-powerful God. In the process of drawing inferences, they did not have the same understanding of the complexities that are available to us now. Nor did they have to take into account the intricate ways in which the extension of human intervention into natural processes has developed as a result of modern technology. When he wrote that nature is God, Calvin referred to a radical dependence on nature; a contemporary theologian must take into account a substantial dependence upon culture as well. And culture is the result of human activity within many forms of dependency upon nature. The developments of culture do not follow laws in the way that nature does. Culture shows that we can do something about these powers that bear down upon us and sustain us, while still being dependent upon them and being limited by them.

It is not only to the natural sciences that one can turn for warrants for the religious sense of dependence. In the social and behavioral sciences the connections between social and interpersonal environments and what persons become are looser and more disjointed than they are in our understanding of how chromosomal defects limit certain capacities. Nonetheless, evidences of the effects of "social conditioning," cultural conditioning, and the impact of interpersonal relations (for example, in infancy) are strong enough to warrant the claim that what we become individually and collectively depends heavily on circumstances (powers) beyond our full control. These circumstances shape both some of the particular limits we cannot easily break through and some of the particular possibilities of communities and persons for flourishing and achieving. Retrospectively, if not prospectively, it is possible to understand many circumstantial factors for which individuals and communities are not causally accountable that have decisively conditioned what they have become. Moral theologians have generally been aware of these factors; for example, discussions of whether one is culpable for particular ignorance that leads to an immoral act recognize the limitations of accountability. The scope of that limitation has been extended as a result of studies in the social and behavioral sciences. The point here is a more general one. Evidences from these sciences warrant a religious sense of dependence upon powers that bear down upon us, sustain us, and create the conditions of possibility for human achievement. There are always "powers" and circumstances that are necessary conditions for human activity.

Evidences from the sciences not only indicate that there are powers on which we are radically dependent; they also indicate that there is an order and ordering of natural processes and developments. I use the word "ordering" as well as "order" for two reasons. First, it qualifies the more static sense of an immutable natural order that informed the theological appropriations of nature until the developments of the sciences that began in the seventeenth century. Even in the eighteenth century, for example, the Swedish botanist Linnaeus assumed an immutable order of the species he distinguished; this was coherent with a more general view of nature, and one which had been appropriated by theology in its views of creation. More recent science has demonstrated the error of such an assumption; more recent theology that takes nature as an indicator of what can be said about the powers of God must be altered accordingly. The process theologians have moved in the right direction. The second reason is that moral inferences from the discernment of an ordering, rather than an immutable order, can take into account the differences between societies and cultures, and the differences in various "stages" of social development, while still accounting for requisites for the well-being of human life and the world of which it is part.

A rudimentary understanding of the natural sciences is sufficient to indicate that ordering exists in nature. Science, of course, would be impossible without it. Whether it is in the movement of the planets or the double helix structure of the DNA molecule, order and ordering is perceived. The presence of order and ordering does not warrant the confirmation of a final purposiveness in nature. Any inference to a teleological construal of nature as a whole requires other convictions than the confirmed theories of particular sciences. Nor can one say that the remarkable ordering, and the even more remarkable capacity of the human mind to discern and understand it in greater and greater detail and accuracy, is sufficient in itself to warrant belief in a Designer. At most one might say that a "governance" is occurring. Its presence, however, evokes awe and respect, natural piety, toward nature. And it warrants the affirmation within piety that the powers and the ultimate power are ordering; they are not purely contingent or chaotic.

In the realms of history, culture, and society, no such precise understanding of an order and ordering is confirmable. Yet certain fundamental requisites for the survival of human life, even in relation to nature, can be inferred from the presence of ordering in these realms. For example, some division of labor is required in society for individuals and the social unit to meet their survival needs and the requirements for a richer human flourishing. While a precise formulation of the right ordering of affective relationships between parents and an infant cannot be given, studies of human development indicate that certain conditions must be met if the infant is going to develop with the "ego-strengths" that make both for individual and social well-being. Cultures are elastic: they develop not only on the basis of human creativity and initiatives but also as a way of making satisfactory and fulfilling adjustments to the natural and social worlds. While laws of cultural development cannot be delineated with precision, aspects of culture are ordered responses to many ordering conditions in nature and in persons.

Piety can respond to such discernment of ordering as is found in society, history, culture, and even in self, as the presence of an ordering power. The power or powers create the conditions of possibility for initiative and creativity, for the development of institutions, for the achievements of the arts and sciences, and for personal development. They also are recurred to in order to discern those requisites for the sustenance of life in the world which can be ignored only at the peril of human fulfillment, human survival (individually and collectively), and human development. This can lead even to the discernment of the requisites for a moral ordering of life. The absence of respect for persons is the root of much moral evil, whether it takes the form of murder or less violent forms. Unjust social arrangements and relationships in which persons are not given their due, or in which equals are treated unequally, lead to stresses and strains within and between human communities. The particular forms of respect and just-ordering vary under social conditions, and normative reflection on the fundamental ordering of human respect and justice provides principles for criticizing various arrangements. There is, however, a perception of a proper ordering even in the moral sphere: certain fundamental requisites must be met in some way for human life to flourish properly. In piety this is construed to be discernment of the moral governance of the ultimate power.

Various sciences contribute to the substance of theology. They can be construed to inform the religious thinker even of certain directions that the empowerment and ordering of life takes, and with which human beings must cooperate. I say cooperate, rather than resign themselves to, though some of the processes, like those of dying, are in the end overpowering. Human cooperation with and consent to these directions are necessary not only for biological survival but also for that measure of individual and collective flourishing that is proper to human beings. This is not to assert that the direction of the ordering powers ensures that all other things exist for the sake of human beings, that the divine benevolence and beneficence has our species in mind as the supreme recipient of value. Nor is it to say that there are not inevitable limitations of human flourishing. However, flourishing occurs within the possibilities given by the divine ordering powers, and within limits that they set. But it is not only for the sake of human flourishing that we must pay attention to the "direction" of the ordering of nature, culture, history, and persons. It is for the sake of the natural world itself. The moral dimensions of human interventions into nature are located at those junctures where interventions that go "contrary to nature" or seek to redirect the course of nature are under consideration.

I believe enough has been said about what can be said of God from various sciences to sustain the general point: "God" refers to the power that bears down upon us, sustains us, sets an ordering of relationships, provides conditions of possibilities for human activity and even a sense of direction. The evidences from various sciences suggest the plausibility of viewing God in these terms. These terms, and any warrants for them from the sciences, however, find their full religious significance only within piety, religious affectivity.

The second Troeltschian query is a test of plausibility: are some traditional affirmations about God incongruous with well-established data and explanations of the sciences? I have in earlier chapters indicated that I think some are. Even liberal theologians, however, find ways to avoid this subject. In at least one stage of his theological development Gordon Kaufman was a case in point. Like all mainline Christian theologians, in spite of his aura of critical hardheadedness, Kaufman preserves the idea of a moral God—a God whose purposes sustain the anthropocentrism and geocentrism that I bring under radical question. Kaufman distinguishes between two models of transcendence. One is teleological, and leads to a theology of being (his example is the classical analogy of being). The other is personalistic, and draws its analogies from interpersonal relations. In it God is conceived "as an autonomous agent capable of genuinely free acts (not merely activity)."[52] This distinction is often drawn in terms of a more speculative philosophical theology that draws inferences from nature and the more anthropomorphic biblical theology that draws inferences from personal relations and human actions. Like all critical contemporary theologians, Kaufman is careful to make limited claims for the truth of theology. The theologian "has as the principal object of his inquiry this imaginative construct, God."[53]

His chapter "God as Symbol" is couched in hypothetical terms, offering a disinterested account of what theology is; nevertheless it seems to disclose his own views. In his proposal for the imaginative construct, God, he acknowledges (as I and other contemporary theologians acknowledge) that there is no escaping the "subjectivist trap." Scripture provides

52. Gordon D. Kaufman, *God The Problem*, p. 78.
53. Ibid., p. 87.

a methodological principle, "we walk by faith, not by sight,"[54] for the transition to what can properly be constructed.

The question under discussion is this: if the subjective element cannot be avoided (Troeltsch's "belief," my "piety" and "religious affectivities"), what are the tests of what can be plausibly stated from within it? Kaufman, it seems to me, rules out any tests that might come from science or even metaphysical speculation.

> [T]he question of a man's fundamental orientation in life—his deepest commitments and ultimate values—is not decided by rational assessment of the (metaphysical) structure of the world and a judgment about the form of life appropriate to that structure. It is determined on other grounds.[55]

This, I take it, is an empirical generalization that is subject to its own tests of validity. If this is the case, then

> the only relevant question of truth that can be directly considered here concerns the ordering of life and the world which faith imposes: is such an ordering appropriate to the world as we experience it and to the nature of our human existence, or does it involve misapprehensions of our situation and result in a stunting of human life and its ultimate breakdown?[56]

The test of a theological construction becomes its moral effects, and its moral effects appear to me not to take into account man's continuity and interdependence with nature.

54. 2 Cor. 5:7.
55. Kaufman, *God The Problem*, pp. 98–99.
56. Ibid., p. 99. For Kaufman's critique of recent theologies of nature, see his "A Problem for Theology: The Concept of Nature," *Harvard Theological Review* 65 (1972): 337–66. His criticism reasonably follows from his earlier work. "[The concept of nature] proposes a conception of the overall context for human life which does not have built into it the dimensions of purpose, value, and meaning, all of which are drawn from man's linguistic and cultural institutions and activity. The notion of God, on the other hand, as agent characterized by freedom and purposiveness and love, is based on the model of human freedom and agency as experienced within society and culture" (pp. 345–46). "[T]he metaphysical tendencies implicit in [the concept of nature] are not obviously congruent with those of Christian faith" (p. 348). "A concept of God (or of gods) is a means by which man gives ultimate metaphysical significance to the moral and personal side of his being, for it involves doctrines which interpret ultimate reality as moral and personal in character" (p. 351). "The natural world, thus, is of an ontologically different order from man. Though man is a part of nature and has been made from natural materials, he is lifted far above the rest of nature by his moral and personal character: he is, indeed, the very image of nature's Creator and absolute Lord" (p. 353). Kaufman is correct to indicate that there are far-reaching consequences for Christian faith in the implications of the nature-oriented view; see p. 355. His modest concession to such a view is not developed: "Thus man cannot be understood as a merely natural being, i.e., in terms of merely natural powers and processes; if he is to be understood at all, it will be as a historico-natural being" (p. 363).

Even on Kaufman's own terms, I believe that to test an ordering appropriate to the world as we experience it, and to human nature, requires that what is said about God be assessed in light of many aspects of human experience and by material from the sciences. Kaufman, again without fully committing himself, takes recourse to the "the Western conception of God." "God is conceived as the absolutely *moral* being, invested with perfect righteousness and love, and demanding the same of his devotees." He adduces rough historical evidence for the moral benefits of this view: "it has contributed substantially to the transformation of man into a fully moral—and in the modern sense, personal and human—being."[57] "God serves as the supreme symbol for a life-policy of humanizing and personalizing the world. From a practical point of view, one does not ask first whether it is true that God exists (a speculative question), but rather whether this is an appropriate life-policy for men to adopt."[58] A moral test becomes the exclusive test of a theological affirmation.

The hard question that I believe Kaufman and others avoid is this: what if a rational assessment of the structure of the world requires that we consider the form of life that is appropriate to *it*? What if there is a deep incongruity between what we know about nature and the continuities of man with nature on the one hand, and on the other hand a life-policy of humanizing and personalizing the world? What if there are good reasons to believe that some stunting of human aspirations is required by "the structure of the world"? The terms "humanization" and "personalization," shibboleths in a great deal of recent Christian theology, of course can be construed in such a way that some of the more unreasonable human aspirations are ruled out. But on what grounds can one rule them out if one does not take into account what can rationally be known about "the structure of the world"? If it is correct, on the whole, that our deepest commitments and ultimate values are not derived from our views of the "structure of the world," it is still possible, and I would add morally required, to assess them in the light of what is known about "the structure of the world." If the analogy of personal agency is appropriate to use to construct imaginatively a view of God, it does not necessarily follow that the intention of that agent is so exclusively toward "humanization and personalization." It does not mean, either, that such purposes as can be discerned are contrary to human interests and aspiration, but that the human species must be set in a wider context before one is able to discern what is proper.

57. Kaufman, *God The Problem,* p. 106.
58. Ibid., p. 107.

I have chosen Kaufman as an example; the same problems arise in other theologians' work. It is my conviction that a number of things attributed to God in the Christian tradition that sustain this anthropocentric view and the morality that is derived from it must be called into question in the light of some of what we learn from various sciences. Since these things have been introduced in previous chapters, I can briefly indicate them here. Certainly there is no firm consensus among astrophysicists and cosmologists on the most adequate explanatory theory to account for the universe of which we are a part. But there is consensus that the biblical accounts are not scientific. That does not bother most theologians, who have long recognized that these accounts are mythical, just as the accounts of the early history of the biblical people are legends rather than scholarly histories. The difficulty with the Christian tradition is not that it is bound to Genesis as science but that it has sustained some of the questionable meanings of the mythical accounts in the face of other explanations of the origins of the universe. The critical one is the anthropocentric centering of value, enforced by the view that the divine intention is finally focused on our species. The issue is how the span of time and space within which the emergence of human life is scientifically explained is taken into account theologically. Do the accounts of the billions of years of development of the universe, the emergence of the chemical necessities for life on this planet, and the presence of conditions that made evolution to our species possible, alter in any way the claims that have traditionally been made for the place of the human species in the intention of God? The issue is how the evidence is to be construed theologically. For some scientists of a religious disposition, such as John Eccles, it is to be interpreted as a matter of design, the created *telos* of which is our species.[59] Events which can be interpreted as contingencies, such as the survival of the mammalian strain, are seen as marks of divine intention. An argument against this cannot be decisive; the position involves a weighing of scientific theories and judgments and a drawing of a theological inference from them that is not a necessary deduction. Thus an argument that the *telos* of the whole is not man cannot be decisively defended either. In my judgment, however, both the time- and the space-spans indicate that of all the possible things that could develop many did, and many did not; that if there was divine "foreknowledge" of human life, there was no particular merit in bringing it into being through such an inefficient and lengthy process. Further, our biological dependence on past developments and on present relations of aspects of our planet to each other, and the deleterious as well as useful intrusions into nature that our species can make, suggest that our capacities and their uses must

59. John Eccles, *The Human Mystery.*

be seen in this wider context. Such further inferences as could be drawn need not undercut the response of piety to nature, or the response of gratitude for the conditions it provides. But it does undercut a self- and species-interested conviction that the whole has come into being for our sake.

I previously indicated that Christian eschatology, a theme used in our time to create conditions of hope for oppressed persons in the world as well as for those who aspire to immortality, must be questioned. "As the beginning was without us, so will the end also be without us." Again, there is not complete consensus on how the demise of our planet will occur; the last hundred years has seen some theories, such as the cooling of the sun, flourish only to be discarded. Also, since the forecasted demise is so long in the future that it has no significant bearing on present conduct, some wonder whether the humane values and aspirations that traditional eschatologies sustain need be questioned at this time and in the light of current scientific speculations. With Woody Allen in the movie *Annie Hall*, most persons feel that it is silly to wonder and worry about the end of the universe. But that is not the point. The point is whether some things that are affirmed about the Deity need to be tested by what is forecast on the basis of established data and theories. We may not be able to say what the end will be, but, as Troeltsch stated, it will not be the Apocalypse of traditional Christian thought. To be sure, if God is free to act, and is not merely engaged in activity (Kaufman's distinction), then anything is possible. Laws of nature could be amended or abolished. But if our perceptions of the Deity are in and through nature and human experience, and what is imaged is a divine governance of the world, then the biblical eschatological symbols or the contemporary Christian developments of them are not sustainable. Again, the impact of this is to set the human species in a larger time-span, and to reduce the traditional assurance that everything is for our sake.

Christian theology has always been divided on the issue of the depth and breadth of human freedom. The struggle between Augustine and the Pelagians was one historical instance, that between the Calvinists and the Arminians another. At issue is not so much a doctrine of God, at least not in the first instance, as a proper understanding of man. Is human life to be interpreted more in terms of continuities with nature or in terms of distinctiveness from nature? Are individual actions to be interpreted more as the directing of natural impulses, desires, and capacities or as the fruits of "free" acts? This traditional question is discussed with great philosophical refinement in contemporary action theory and in literature on the mind-brain problem. These issues cannot be fully developed or adjudicated here. It is my judgment, however, that some of the traditional and contemporary claims for radical freedom, such as those espoused in theologies influenced by existentialism, cannot be sustained in the light of what we are learning not only about the biological nature of human life but about other aspects of life as well. The powers that bear down on human beings and sustain them through their bodies, through the "accidents" of birth into particular families, through their nurture and conditioning in particular societies and cultures, and in other ways, shape the "natures" of the particular individuals—their capacities, their desires and aspirations, and their ways of interpreting life. These particularities are both limiting and the conditions of possibility. They are not merely the conditions of action, they also shape dispositions to act in particular ways. It is my conviction that the radical transcendental freedom claimed for human beings in existentialist theologies does not pass the tests of well-established scientific views of "human nature."

The theological issue that comes to the fore in this discussion is that of the analogy or metaphor most appropriate for imaging God. The two that Kaufman suggests in his chapter on types of transcendence are the personalistic one of agency, modeled after interpersonal relations, and the metaphysical one of being, modeled more on the perceptions of the causal laws involved in nature. The debate is an old one, and has sometimes been sorted out on the basis of the degree to which the biblical notions, deemed more personalistic, are to be controlling.[60] The model of personal agency carries with it the notion that the ultimate power has intelligence similar to our own, and can exert its will in ways comparable to ours. This means that God has "intentions": God can "think about" the ends of his activity and control the forces available to bring these ends to fulfillment. Thus far the agency model does not necessarily require that the divine intentions are directed to human beings as the supreme object of creative and redeeming activity. Some other warrants must be brought into the discussion to argue that, because the divine agent has intentions, those intentions are directed most centrally to the well-being of human beings. Biblically, there is a resource for this; the Genesis assertion that man is made in the image and likeness of God can be interpreted in such a way that man is therefore the special object of divine favor. But every doctrine of the *imago Dei* is very circular. What one says about man determines what one says about God, and what one says about God in turn reinforces what one says about man. Thus, if man is conceived primarily in terms of the capacities for agency, and these capacities are expounded in terms of a doctrine of radical human freedom, God is similarly construed. And this construal of God reinforces the understanding of man as agent. If, however, man is conceived more in terms of the

60. See, for example, Paul Tillich, *Biblical Religion and the Search for Ultimate Reality* (Chicago: University of Chicago Press, 1955).

continuities of action and agency with "nature," and man is conceived more in terms of the continuities with other animals, both the scope of human agency and, by analogy, of divine agency are more limited. Since, as I have argued previously, all of our construals of the Deity emerge out of our interpretations of human experience of the world, it is not possible to think about God as God might be in his aseity. "Our concepts are at best metaphors and symbols of his being, not literally applicable."[61] The question is the choice of analogies, metaphors, or symbols.

The choices raise ancient issues of pantheism versus theism, and of the relation of the immanence of God to his transcendence. "High" doctrines of divine transcendence are sometimes defended on spiritual and moral grounds. One stands silent before the ineffable mystery of God who is transcendent; this is an experience of great power and significance to those who have it. God who is the "One Beyond the Many" provides the ultimate principle for the moral criticism of all false objects of confidence and all improper objects of moral and human valuation. A powerful prophetic religion and morality can be grounded in a high doctrine of the transcendence of God. A high doctrine of transcendence has also been claimed to sustain a favorable view of secularization with its great benefits for science and culture. One can have a truly secular, that is, worldly and not divinized, view of nature and culture on the basis of the transcendence of God. The kind of animism that might restrain investigations of nature because it is sacred and the kind of reverence for nature that predisposes human beings to refrain from intervening into its processes, are both ruled out by a high view of the transcendence of God. Such opinions are deemed not to be theological accommodations to radical secularization, but to be a theologically appropriate view of things. Indeed, there was a period within the past two decades when "theology of secularization" was in vogue; the argument was that the biblical construal of God and his relations to the world necessitate a desacralization of nature and the world, and is beneficial and correct.

It is my conviction that if we choose to use the analogy of agency for construing the Deity, it must be developed with great circumspection. Insofar as the analogy leads us to assert that God has intelligence, like but superior to our own, and that God has a will, a capacity to control events comparable to the more radical claims made for human beings, the claims are excessive.

A distinction has frequently been made between purpose and intention. Animals have purposes but, so far as we can determine, they do not have intentions; they cannot think about their ends and the means of fulfilling them in the way that human beings can. I believe that we can

61. Kaufman, *God The Problem*, p. 95.

discern through experience (not simply in terms of sensationism or phenomenalism) and through our knowledge of life in the world what some of the divine purposes are for the creation. Some of these have already been introduced: ordering, creating conditions for possibilities, and so forth. I do not find sufficient reasons to move from our perceptions of the purposes of the divine governance to the assertion that these imply an intelligence similar to our own, or a capacity of radical agency similar to certain claims made for human beings. Even in piety, in religious affectivity, such a move is not in my judgment warranted. This is to some persons surely an impoverishment of religion; in my assessment it is not. One can acknowledge dependence on ordering powers that sustain life and bear down upon it without conceiving these powers as gifted with intelligence and arbitrary will. One can be grateful for the divine governance, for all that it sustains and makes possible, without conceptually personalizing the Governor. The language of piety may well use personalized symbols; they have some warrants from our perception and construal of the divine purposes and from their expressive appropriateness for religious affectivity. But they do not warrant the theological construction of an anthropomorphic divine agency. In this way I agree with Tillich that we can be personally related to the divine governance without conceiving of God as a person.

My argument radically qualifies the traditional Christian claim that the ultimate power seeks the human good as its central focus of activity. "Goodness" or "value" are not terms that refer to some entity or entities in and of themselves. It is always appropriate to ask, Good for whom? Even the terms "right" and "wrong" are ultimately relational in usage. This does not make them utterly relativistic, as if because an act or a relationship seems right for someone or for members of a particular community, there are no better reasons for the claim. Murder is always wrong. For now, we need not discuss the problem of what acts of killing are to be called murder. But murder is wrong because it violates a proper relationship between persons, one that acknowledges the respect for the life of the other that is needed for human flourishing. The terms "goodness" or "value," however, are more germane to the immediate discussion.

The purposes of the ultimate power can be deemed generally good without necessarily claiming that they have to be good for human beings. This is not to claim that we can fully know for whom or for what they are good in their comprehensiveness and completeness, or even that they are. But even the Genesis account can be interpreted to indicate that the Creator viewed the whole creation as good, not merely as good for our species. To claim that the purposes of the divine governance can be good for the whole creation, and not exclusively for human beings, is not to deny that God is "the source of human good."[62] It is, however, to say that the human good must be seen within limits of what is possible for finite natural creatures, creatures gifted with capacities no others known to us have.

This view is not as contrary to the Christian tradition as it might initially appear. At least in recent times, theologians and members of churches have accepted certain evils as "natural," evils for which neither human intentions and powers nor the divine intention are held to be accountable. Modern theology, though not all contemporary piety, has ceased to discern a divine intention in the fact that a tornado hit Topeka but left Lawrence, Kansas, unscathed. It has ceased to discern a divine intention in the fact that a brilliant and gifted leader is struck down by cancer at the peak of his powers. It does not seek an intention of divine justice in any such events, or claim that there are benefits intended by God for others through them. It would not deny that such events can provide conditions for possibilities of human response that are beneficial. If there is a geological fault through a California city, this might be a consideration to be taken into account in subsequent urban development and in the choices of individuals about where they will live. But these are not ascribed to a divine intentionality.

Nor am I prepared to argue that tornadoes and cancer are good for anything. They are realities that emerge from natural processes; the divine governance through nature is not necessarily beneficent. It is limiting; it indicates the relative powerlessness of human beings in such drastic events. But it is not necessarily good for anything or for anyone. Indeed, we ascribe evil to natural events in relation to our perceptions of the human good. We judge such natural events evil according to our human desires and aspirations. We properly attempt to avoid them, but in the end we may simply have to consent or resign ourselves to them. Piety stands in awe of the powers that bear down on us and sustain us; it does not trust them to fulfill all our perceptions of the human good. Piety in the presence of such powers can be expressed in fear as well as gratitude.

Perhaps Jonathan Edwards was closer to the truth when he described the end for which God created the world as God's glorification of himself.[63] To say that God intends to glorify himself through the creation requires an assurance that he has this capacity for intention and volition that I believe cannot be sustained. What might be right about the direction of Edwards's argument, however, is that the purposes of the divine governance are, insofar as human beings can discern them, not exhausted by

62. Henry Nelson Wieman, *The Source of Human Good* (Chicago: University of Chicago Press, 1946).
63. Edwards, "The End for Which God Created the World."

its benefits for us. Whatever they may be directed toward, they are not all directed toward us. This perception is the appropriate basis for acknowledging the transcendence of God, the ineffable mystery before which we stand in silence.

The personalistic metaphor or analogy for God has the practical benefit of viewing human beings (in the image of God) in terms of agency. And this view sustains a deep moral conscientiousness and sense of accountability. Theologians who use more impersonal language, or who use the personal language to make the point that God intends each effect of each cause by the presence of his immediate agency in all events (Calvin and Edwards), have all sustained within various limitations the notion of human agency and accountability. None has been so single-mindedly deterministic as to reduce human capacities to links in a necessary causal chain. Scholars who attend to human action, whether brain physiologists attempting to solve the relation of the operations of the organism called the brain to our thought and actions, or philosophers concerned with the mind-body problem, have not yet resolved the issues involved. No "hard" determinist has successfully accounted for human action, though the aspiration to do so motivates some investigators and theoreticians. Luther says somewhere in the *Table Talk* that man is more acted upon than acting. This, I take it, is an observation of experience, not a pure theological opinion, and is correct.

To speak of God as a powerful Other, and to discern processes of the divine governance in the world, does not reduce human actions to effects of describable and knowable sufficient causes. It does acknowledge the existence of conditions which both limit and sustain the possibilities of human action. To stress the continuities of the human beings with the rest of nature does not deny the import of our capacities for agency. An interactive, or response, model of human action is more fitting to human experience, to what we now know about the nature of human life, and to the theology here developed, than is a rigid determinism. Readers of theology will recognize this as similar to H. Richard Niebuhr's view in *The Responsible Self*. As scholars of his work know, he was informed by the work of both George Herbert Mead, a social behaviorist, and by Martin Buber's development of the I-Thou relationship.[64] The views espoused here differ from Niebuhr's principally on a theological point. For Niebuhr, God is "acting" in all actions upon us. He had more confidence in the agency model of God than I have. In distinction from that view, I believe we can appropriately say only that we have capacities to respond

64. G. H. Mead, *Mind, Self, and Society*; Martin Buber, *I and Thou*, trans. Ronald Gregor Smith (Edinburgh: T. and T. Clark, 1937). For a discussion of these writers, see Paul Pfuetze, *The Social Self* (New York: Bookman Associates, 1954).

to persons and events in an interactive way, and that through those actions we respond to the divine governance, to the powers that bear down on us and sustain us. We have capacities to discern in particular events and relations something of what the divine governance requires, what our appropriate actions and relations are to nature, to other persons, and so forth. God is the ultimate source of the conditions for the possibilities of all our actions; we not only respond to these possibilities but, in some instances at least, they respond to us and interact with our action. Even natural processes respond (react) to our interventions; the normal course of nature is affected by our actions. In the personal and cultural spheres the responsiveness, or responsive actions, of others to our actions is clearer and more dramatic. A heightened sense of dependence on these powers does not eliminate capacities of human agency, though it is likely to lead to an acknowledgment of more limitations than many persons find desirable. Limitations and possibilities are both within and external to ourselves. Our responses to divine governance are always in particular occasions, times, and places.

Has this view left behind so many tenets of the Christian theological tradition that it is beyond the pale? Troeltsch thought that a modern theological construction pursuing its lines of inquiry might lead to the point where it would espouse some other religion than that from which it came. Why do we ask such a question? Why is this a legitimate worry for a theologian? For many sorts of reasons. One may have a sense of the importance of preserving the vitality of a historic tradition as one among many that provides values and outlooks in culture. One may be concerned about commitments one has made, such as vows taken at ordination. One may be concerned about a potential rift in one's own "inner life," on the one hand deeply identified with the symbols and rites of a particular tradition, and on the other identified with the task of assessing the adequacy of these in the light of other sources of understanding. One may be concerned about a possible imposition of ecclesiastical sanctions against dissenting opinions. Or, one might worry that there is more misconstruing than plausible and meaningful construing of God and of life in relation to God in the Christian tradition.

I earlier laid the groundwork of being selective within the tradition. The lines of divergence have been stressed more than the lines of continuity. It would be dishonest to claim that the views I have developed are what certain traditional symbols of Christianity have really meant, or that what I have written is the development (especially the only possible development) of the seeds of the Christian gospel. Nor do I desire to alter radically the traditional meanings of many Christian symbols and doctrines while appearing to preserve them. Yet the views espoused have been in part the fruits not only of the Christian religious tradition but also of a particular historic Christian piety.

Christology is the most critical doctrinal issue for any Christian theology. The definition of an orthodox Christology, it must be remembered, took several centuries, and was motivated by many conditions that were nondoctrinal in character. And scholars of the New Testament have demonstrated that within those texts there are several views of the nature and the significance of Jesus. He is given many "titles," not all of which are readily merged into one. His works and their significance are plural. Even within Christian churches governed by creedal orthodoxies there are retrievals of different emphases in different historical and social conditions. For example, without calling into doubt a creedal elaboration of the "high" Christology of the Epistles to the Colossians and the Ephesians and of the Prologue to the Gospel of John, much of contemporary Roman Catholic political theology accents an interpretation of Jesus' identification with the poor and the oppressed based on the accounts of the synoptic gospels. The Pauline interpretations of Jesus as Savior are construed as warrants for political and social revolution; he liberates human beings from sin, but a new form of sin, sinful social structures, is accented. In some recent Protestant social ethics there was an effort to ground the social witness of the churches on the Christological themes of Colossians and Ephesians; the gnostic-like principalities and powers that the Lordship of Christ has overcome are interpreted to refer to historical and social "principalities and powers" such as technology and money. Every effort to formulate a coherent Christology is selective of the biblical materials, and is determined in part by the issues that theologians and the churches face in particular times and places. Debates about Christology are never exclusively debates about what the New Testament really says about Jesus.

The Christian piety that moves and sustains the views developed here is derived more from the narratives and teachings found in the synoptic gospels than it is by the Book of Revelation, the Epistle to the Hebrews, and many themes within the Pauline corpus.[65] This is not to deny that there are continuities between it and what can be found in these and other New Testament books. Nor is it to claim that it does not select themes from within the gospel accounts.

65. This preference for a Christology derived primarily from the narratives of the synoptic gospels arises from three sources: (1) a strong sense of the priority of narrative over more abstract language in evoking and sustaining piety, (2) my rejection of biblicistic views of revelation, and (3) epistemological suspicion of the meaningfulness (in other than highly theoretical or symbolic terms) of claims about the nature and activities of the "preexistent Christ," of Colossians and Ephesians, etc.

Jesus incarnates theocentric piety and fidelity. Through the gospel accounts of his life and ministry we can see and know something of the powers that bear down upon us and sustain us, and of the piety and the manner of life that are appropriate to them. This in no way denies continuity between Jesus and the Jewish history and tradition of which he was a part; indeed what is known through him is so dependent upon that history and tradition that its distinctiveness could not have occurred in other cultures.

The gospel accounts, with their depictions of the life, teachings, and ministry of Jesus, bear down on the receptive human spirit with their own compelling power. Their spiritual and moral authority is not finally dependent upon the intricate scholarship that seeks to determine which data about him stand as hard evidence and which words and phrases are truly his own. Nor is it vitiated by an awareness that each gospel has its own theological purpose which colors its selection of accounts and its interpretation of their meaning. Nor does the spiritual and moral authority of the gospels depend upon the votes of ecclesiastical councils which have claimed one or another interpretation of Jesus' person and work to be exclusively true.

The gospels clearly testify to the compelling power of Jesus' unique life and ministry, of his devotion to God whom he called Father, of his sensitivity to the discord between conditions of oppression and poverty, and a vision of what perfect fidelity to God's governance requires. They powerfully show what human life, in fidelity to God and in openness to his empowering, can and ought to be—a life of courage and love grounded in an object of piety and fidelity that transcends the immediate objects of experience. They make clear the costs of such piety and fidelity, as well as their beneficial consequences for others. Without the compelling power of Jesus bearing down upon and sustaining his vacillating followers we would not have the gospels, the other books of the New Testament, and the tradition from which the Christian community continues to gain its sustenance and by which it is constantly informed and tested. His teachings, ministry, and life are a historical embodiment of what we are to be and to do—indeed, of what God is enabling and requiring us to be and to do.

The primitive church consented to the powers of Jesus, and thus saw him to be the Christ. The Christian community through history—falteringly and without purity of heart—has consented to the power of the gospel, that is, has been called to align itself with the purposes of the divine governance as that is informed by the gospel. This community's empowering and ordering of life, with all the blindnesses of the community's finitude and all the faults of its unfaithfulness, have taken place through its confidence in the gospel. Its being and doing have been sustained, informed, and judged by the historically particular source of its fundamental perceptions of why and how God is to be honored, obeyed, and celebrated. Its perceptions of how persons and communities are to be related to God—indeed, how all things are to be related in a manner appropriate to their relations to God—is indelibly colored by its consent to the piety and fidelity of Jesus. The only good reason for claiming to be Christian is that we continue to be empowered, sustained, renewed, informed, and judged by Jesus' incarnation of theocentric piety and fidelity.

In developing religious affectivity earlier in this chapter I deliberately did not recur to the gospels, but rather indicated that these are part of our common human experience. In a sense I followed an implied injunction of Richard R. Niebuhr's.

> All of the dogmatic labors a theologian may devote to the definition of Christ, all of the research that a historian may expend in the search for the historical Jesus . . . will fail to create clarity in the figure of Jesus—until we understand what it is in our world/ age that endows our own experience with resonance to the world of Jesus and that enables us to recognize his conduct and his method of taking hold of the known and paying deference to the unknown as authoritative, augmenting, and attractive to us in our enigmatic world.[66]

Our experience of our enigmatic world resonates to the gospel accounts of Jesus' world; indeed, some features of widely common human experience resonate to his experience of his world. The similarities of fundamental human experiences of our surroundings to those described in the gospels is one basis for our capacities to find in the Christian story of an earlier time insight into the correctness of a theocentric vision. The world of experience described there not only resonates with the conditions of our human experience; the piety and faithfulness there described appeal deeply to our own natural pieties and fidelities, and guide and direct them within the Christian community.

I shall illustrate this briefly by recurring to some of the aspects of religious affectivity developed earlier. Among other things, I delineated six "senses" that have deep religious dimensions. Acquaintance with the gospels should make clear to the reader that each of these senses is expressed in and through the teachings and the accounts of the life and events of Jesus. The "natural piety" that I described is similar to the attitudes and dispositions, the sensibilities of Jesus. There is in the gospels the record of a person who had a deep and powerful sense of dependence

66. Richard R. Niebuhr, *Experiential Religion*, pp. 82–83.

upon the powers that bear down upon us and sustain us. This dependence, ultimately on God, is known through very common human experiences like the provision of what is needed for our basic physical sustenance. Gratitude to God is expressed over and over. There are both teachings and examples that indicate the scope and the character of our obligations to others which fulfill our obligations to God. There is no less a sense of remorse and repentance for human failures to act faithfully toward others and toward God. But the message is not only one of obligation and remorse; in the symbols of the times it points to possibilities for human renewal in the interior life of individuals and in the external conditions of the world. Also in the apocalyptic symbols of the times there is a sense of the directionality that life ought to take.

In the events that the Christian community remembers and relives in Holy Week, we perceive most deeply the meaning of fidelity to the divine purposes and powers. There is no general disclosure of the precise requirements of that faithfulness that covers every event from the entry into Jerusalem to the trial and crucifixion. The power of the narratives rests in large part in their dramatic form: there is adulation and honor, fear and despair, betrayal and faithfulness, courage and sadness. The cacophony of events and of the responses of participants to them show in poignant detail how Jesus and his disciples struggled to discern what God was enabling and requiring them to be and to do. What does fidelity to the divine governance and purpose require in this particular set of historical and social events? For Jesus this is found only through struggle and suffering, through doubt, and through confrontation with religious and civil powers beyond his control. Consent, not resignation to the inevitable, is finally given. In that consenting we gain insight into the purposes of God. One such insight is that fidelity does not lead to what we ordinarily and immediately perceive to be a human good, but that what is of human value must be sacrificed for the sake of the purposes of God.

Theology is the noun, Christian is the modifier. The sketch of a Christology I have given, even if elaborated in more detail and more systematically, does not meet the claims of many creeds and many churches. To many Christians it may reduce the significance of the tradition to a social-psychological function, to a way of sustaining and vivifying a memory and way of life that has more significance for the subjective side of piety than the objective knowledge of God. But religious affectivities, nourished, informed, and vivified by the record of a historically particular set of events, "in-form" (form in us) our perceptions of the ultimate power and our articulations of its meaning. They motivate as well as express piety; they move us toward the faithful consenting to the powers of God that is required for moral life. To acknowledge that the particularity of the Christian story is more important for our individual and communal "subjectivity" than it is for what we are finally able to say about the powers in whose hands are the destinies of the worlds does not render it meaningless. With their liturgies and preaching, religious communities function to awaken and nourish our religious affectivities, to provide the symbols by which we consciously acknowledge God, and through which we praise God. Their symbols always appropriately point to the reality of the divine powers, but never exhaust them. They help us to discern both the presence of the divine governance in and through particular experiences and events and its ineffable mystery before which we stand in silence.

I have sought, in this chapter, to make a case for religious affectivities, and for their evocation by the powers that bear down upon us and sustain us. The effort, to be sure, is unsatisfactory to many adherents of Christian faith and theology. It lacks the philosophical-theological refinement of those more adept than I in speculative matters. It does, however, form the basis of a theological ethics which I believe bears continuities with the Christian tradition and can be warranted by many human experiences and by data and explanations from some well-established sciences. It has not been developed as an ad hoc rationale to sustain a prior view of morality or a prior view of the Christian faith and religion. Its goal has been to find what can be most truly claimed about God rather than to defend traditional Christianity.

6

Man in Relation to God and the World

The focus of attention now turns to man—man in relation to God and the world. Calvin began *The Institutes* with this statement:

> Nearly all the wisdom we possess, that is to say, true and sound wisdom, consists of two parts: the knowledge of God and of ourselves. But, while joined by many bonds, which one precedes and brings forth the other is not easy to discern.[1]

The basic line of argument of this book begins principally with knowledge "of ourselves"; that is, it begins with aspects of human experience, and knowledge of our natural world. The theological construal of our experience and knowledge, however, invokes the powerful Other. Now it is time to return to a more coherent interpretation of human life in the light of "the knowledge of God." What features of our humanity are salient in the light of that knowledge? In an order that resembles that of traditional theological treatments, the answer falls into three sections: nature, the human fault, and the correction that I believe a theocentric vision makes possible—in more traditional language, nature, the fall, and redemption. Following these sections I shall use more traditional religious language and concepts to indicate the lines of continuity of this work with Christian themes.

"Natural Man"

The perspective from which persons view human life, as with anything else they view, affects what they see, and how they describe it. Certain features take on greater salience; other features are reduced in significance. The anthropocentric or homocentric interpretations of the world I have earlier criticized stress those features that distinguish human beings from the rest of the animals. Those features of human life that are judged to be unique become the starting points for reflections on the "nature of man." Interpreters of the biblical tradition have for centuries turned to the symbol of man made in the image and likeness of God as the starting point for their theological anthropologies. Modern Anglo-American moral philosophy has attended to man as agent, and to the criteria to be used when this autonomous agent decides to act. Appropriately, recent philosophical and theological literature has attended to the concepts that distinguish our species from the other animals. The "margin" of human freedom defended has varied from the extreme claims of existentialism to highly deterministic views based on psychoanalysis, the social sciences, or brain physiology. My preference for the Reformed tradition has indicated that the balance in this work is tipped toward the

1. Calvin, *Institutes*. I, 1, 1; McNeill ed., 1:35.

side that stresses a more deterministic view of human action and greater similarity between the human and other animals. What perspective an observer takes on this matter makes a great deal of difference to his or her interpretation of many features of human life such as individual acts and the nature of social relationships.

Mary Midgley, in her *Beast and Man: The Roots of Human Nature,* develops a viewpoint on biological and philosophical grounds that is in many respects similar to mine. "What finally (you may ask)," she writes, "does distinguish man from the animals?" The question needs rephrasing, she says: "Unless we take man to be a machine or an angel, it should read 'distinguishes man *among* the animals. . . .' "[2] In apt turns of phrase and with intellectual poignancy she over and over shows how interpretation of man in continuity with nature enables us to take into account the contributions of sociobiology, behaviorism, and other views that many humanists, including theologians, often find distasteful. "Why should not our excellence involve our whole nature?"[3] "Our dignity arises *within* nature, not against it."[4] To acknowledge our kinship with other species is not to say we are identical with them.[5]

It follows, I believe, from the theological interpretation of the world that I have been developing that human life is to be construed in continuity with "nature" as much as in distinction from it. This does not mean endorsing the mechanistic view of cause and effect that sometimes creeps into Jonathan Edwards's efforts to develop his interpretation of the nature of human life. Nor does it mean that God's causal agency has an immediate presence in the sequence of events, as some passages of Calvin and Edwards suggest.

Since some of the features of a theocentric construal of human life have been developed previously they can be treated briefly here.

First, I have stressed the sense of radical *dependence* of human life on the rest of the natural world: not merely contemporary dependence, but also the historical and biological dependence upon the processes that brought our species into being. A theology that highlights radical dependence is coherent with a biological interpretation of radical dependence. I have indicated that we are also dependent upon history, society, culture, and on our own individual bodies and histories. This dependence is species-wide in fundamental respects; it takes particular communal and individual forms in particular circumstances. Dependence does not imply enslavement; it requires acknowledgment of limitations and of the possibilities for human initiative and development.

---

2. Midgley, *Beast and Man* (Ithaca: Cornell University Press, 1978), p. 203.
3. Ibid., p. 204.
4. Ibid., p. 196.
5. Ibid., p. 198.

We are radically *interdependent* as well as dependent. The notion of dependence alone is susceptible to implications of human passivity; it might suggest a greater measure of determinism than is warranted by human experience and by various studies of human life. Interdependence reflects more the interactive relationship between human life and activity and the rest of the world that I introduced in the previous chapter. In most circumstances we are "more acted upon than acting." Prior events and occasions have established both the limitations and the possibilities for our intentional interventions, whether into nature, culture, historical events, society, or even in giving direction to ourselves.

The ordering that scientific investigation discovers, analyzes, describes, and explains exists prior to the investigations of it. Yet at least metaphorically, that ordering "responds" to the investigator; it is disclosed, can be further examined, and in many instances altered by subsequent investigations and by technology based on them. Culture, while more malleable than nature, is inherited by each generation; its particular forms are received by any person who has special interests. There are no creations ex nihilo in culture, but human interventions of many sorts can alter what is received—whether a literary or artistic tradition, technology, or values. In responding to historical events and in giving direction to them, persons must anticipate as best they can how their own interventions will be responded to by those on whom they act, and with whom they interact. In interpersonal relations the process is similarly one of interaction, and even well-established social institutions are affected and changed as a result of the exercise of human powers according to specific purposes. Metaphorically, at least, we even interact with our "selves." Our actions are dependent upon our capacities—upon what we have become as a result of our natures and our experiences—but our "selves" are affected and changed by our choices, our new experiences, and our aspirations.

Dependence and interdependence point to the limits of human capacities to affect courses of events in accordance with intentions. These limits, of course, vary greatly in different areas of experience and under different specific conditions. Not only does "ought" imply "can"; "should" and "will" imply "can," unless one desires to maximize life's frustrations. In the sphere of nature, our interactions frequently require greater conformity to the ordering that is present than they permit a new ordering or even a mastery of the ordering that exists. Other spheres of life are more malleable, more subject to control by human initiatives. The extent of human foreknowledge of the consequences of interactions varies in different spheres of activity, as does the extent of capacities to control subsequent interactions. To recognize limitations inherent in our interdependence is not to recommend passivity in the face of all that is received or given; it is not to recommend that nature, history, or culture be permitted to take their "natural courses." But it is to acknowledge finitude, and strongly to affirm the necessity of taking risks in human activities. In extreme instances it is to face honestly the possibility of inexorably tragic outcomes.

No human activity would be possible without what is received or given, and all human activity is interaction in specific contexts. The possibilities of action depend upon the combination of elements that are present on particular occasions and in particular contexts. Current investigations in cellular biology, for example, are possible on the basis of prior developments in the disciplines of biology, chemistry, and even physics. They are dependent upon the natural and trained capacities of the investigators who undertake them, and upon the technological developments that make modern means of investigation possible. Creative genius, whether found in a scientist or an artist, is not demeaned by a recognition that its fruits are part of a network of interdependence between past and present as well as between elements that are present.

Interdependence is communal as well as individual. Christian theologians who propose radical social revolutions are interacting with the social orders established in the past, and with those groups in particular societies that have been awakened to the injustice of their circumstances. Revolutions do not occur without "prerevolutionary" circumstances being ripe for them. This is not to assert that social changes and revolutions occur as the natural course of events in a given society; the impact of leadership that construes circumstances to be repressive and unjust, that persuades persons of the validity of their interpretations, and that inspires the risks of action, is always present. But the efficacy of the leadership is interdependent with many economic, social, and political factors.

A construing of man as a radically interdependent creature is coherent with the theological views that were developed in the previous chapter. As we shall see, this basic conviction makes a difference in the interpretation of the ethical enterprise.

Man is a *valuing* animal; as such, man shares a great deal with other animals. As Midgley so nicely points out, "We did not, personally and unassisted, invent every aspect of humanity. Much of it is drawn from a common source, and overlaps with dolphinity, beaverishness, and wolfhood."[6] A contrasting perception has been dominant in the Western humanistic tradition, both in its religious and its secular strands. This is quite understandable; we define any particular thing, whether a fork or a species, according to those features that distinguish it from other similar

6. Ibid., p. 160.

things. Forks are unlike spoons in ways that can be articulated; human beings must be unlike other animals in ways that can be articulated. One way in which we describe the distinctiveness of a given thing is by its particular purpose or function. Spoons and forks share a common function; within that common function forks are useful because the tines permit one to "spear" food, and spoons are useful because they permit one to carry liquids to the mouth. Human beings have been distinguished not only by certain features such as rationality, capacities to develop intentions, and the like, but also by the different purpose they have been asserted to have. On the basis of distinctive capacities has come the humanly-interested distinction of value, the assertion that we are not only different but "higher." The metaphor of "up and down," as Midgley indicates, has had a decisive impact on our evaluations as well as our descriptions.[7] And from the assurance of greater value has come the assurance of a special purpose for humanity; the assurance that all other things were created for our sake.

Midgley is quite correct in her critical observation that recent moral philosophy has posited the assumption that our capacities to reason are somehow discontinuous with the capacities we share with other animals. I agree with her criticism of the decades-long debate over the relation of facts and values. We "can indeed only understand our values if we first grasp the given facts of our wants."[8] And our wants are to a great extent shared with other animals. "[W]hat is good does not have to be unique to a species."[9] Moral choices involve the sorting out of our plural and often conflicting motives, and these motives are not just our "reasons" for acting but are grounded in our biological and social natures. Our rationality is expressed in our sorting out our motives and our desires, and in directing our actions in a fitting way.

This insight, of course, did not have to await the modern scientific investigations of the biological and social bases of human behavior. Jonathan Edwards, in *The Freedom of the Will,* made a similar point.

> By "motive" I mean the whole of that which moves, excites or invites the mind to volition, whether that be one thing singly, or many things conjunctly. Many particular things may concur and unite their strength to induce the mind; and when it is so, all together are as it were one complex motive. And when I speak of the "strongest motive," I have respect to the strength of the whole that operates to induce to a particular act of volition, whether that be the strength of one thing alone, or of many to-

7. Ibid., pp. 145–64.
8. Ibid., p. 178.
9. Ibid., p. 205.

gether. . . . [T]hat which appears most inviting and has, by what appears concerning it to the understanding or apprehension, the greatest degree of previous tendency to excite and induce the choice, is what I call the "strongest motive." . . . [W]hatever is perceived or apprehended by an intelligent and voluntary agent, which has the nature and influence of a motive to volition or choice, is considered or viewed *as good*. . . . And therefore it must be true, in some sense, that the will always is as the greatest apparent good is.[10]

Man is a valuing animal. Other animals are also valuing; they direct their activities to the meeting of their needs and desires. They have purposes; in this sense it is not purposiveness that distinguishes between man and other animals as wanting, desiring, valuing creatures. But human choices and intentions are "built" on desires and wants; the continuities between the biological, social, and cultural aspects of what we are, and the intentions we form and choices we make, must be taken into account more than they often have been in moral philosophy and in theology. What can be construed biologically, psychologically, or sociologically are data not only for a description of moral and religious life but also for more "normative" constructions of the ethical and religious aspects of human experience.

To stress that our purposes express our wants and desires is not to deny that from among our multiple "motives" we can choose ends and think rationally about what motives, ends, and means we ought to follow. Perhaps even this capacity to find the appropriate means to fulfill our desires is not unique to our species. Animals are "cunning"; we describe them as such when we observe their clever behavior in catching their prey, for example. Some animals have the capacities to find complex means for achieving their purposes. And animals can have conflicting motives, it appears. We are distinguished, however, by our capacities to examine critically various objects of our desires, ends of our motives, and objects of our valuations. We have capacities to recognize conflicting desires and valuations, and to consider in the light of many other things, including our moral and religious beliefs, which values we ought properly to pursue. But values, like "the good," do not exist independently of needs, wants, and desires, or of what we perceive to be needed, wanted, desired, or necessary for persons, society, culture, and even nature. To be rational is not simply to reason logically from certain abstract or general principles, or from some moral ideals and values, to their application to the particular "facts" at hand. Our rationality is exercised in determining what things are good for, for whom they are good; how to order and

10. Edwards, *Freedom of the Will*, pp. 141–42.

govern our subjective and often conflicting motives; and how to relate things to each other in the "external world."

I have argued that Edwards was correct in his belief that religion is largely a matter of affectivity. To affirm valuing as the central descriptive term for man, rather than "reasoning" or "intending," is to claim that affectivity is a principal feature of all of human activity. As was argued in the discussion of religion, the radical distinction between "reason" and "emotion" creates a false dichotomy. Midgley makes the same point: "Reason, though not always equated with mere intellect, has usually been sharply opposed to Feeling or Desire."[11] Jonathan Edwards would have been pleased with her argument. Emotion or affectivity is not antirational; rationality means more than intelligence or following the rules of formal logic, "[i]t includes a definite structure of preferences, a priority system based on feeling."[12] Even this kind of structure, Midgley argues, is also found in higher animals. The term "valuing" can take account of the primacy of desire and affectivity, but valuing, at least in human beings, involves a consciousness of conflicting motives and of alternative objects of desire. It involves careful reflection about choices, and the principles, duties, obligations, and ends that are proper. Valuing does not denigrate the rational component of moral life, any more than it does the work of the scientist. Valuing requires a critical examination of the objects of valuation, of whether some things are valued too little and others too much; it requires the formation of clear intentions in many circumstances of human action. It is easier and more correct to interpret the significance of rationality and intentionality in intimate relation to affectivity than it is to adopt mere rationality as the distinguishing feature of humanity and then find some relation of it to desire and emotion. As Midgley says, "'Reason' is not the name of a character in a drama. It is a name for organizing oneself. . . . It is the process of choosing which that is rightly called reasoning."[13] To reify reason and emotion, and to think about their relations as if they were separate characters in a drama of deep conflict, is to falsify the nature of man.

Man is an *agent*. Our species, in continuity with other animals, has the capacity to exercise powers in accordance with purposes and intentions so as to affect the course of events. How one describes human agency depends upon the standpoint from which human life is viewed. The proper account of what is called "freedom" is always at stake; more particularly, the question is one of how freedom is related to its contrasting term. Dialectical theologians are likely to contrast freedom with destiny,

11. Midgley, *Beast and Man*, p. 256.
12. Ibid.
13. Ibid., p. 258.

and to see a dialectical relationship between them. This polarity is central to Paul Tillich's theology. Sartre's *Being and Nothingness* makes an even starker contrast between the references of the term "freedom" and that which is not freedom.[14] Kant's distinction between the noumenal and phenomenal aspects of the self often gets reified into two selves: the phenomenal that is subject to causal analysis and the noumenal that is radically free.[15] In addition to these discussions the recent literature on action theory has various precise arguments about whether action is caused and, if not caused, how it is to be explained. Are reasons for actions causes of actions? Are what some deterministic theorists view as causes of action to be interpreted as conditions of action?

One wonders why this discussion is so extensive, and what the underlying motives for pursuing it are. Surely there are many, and the issues are not trivial. There is a genuine philosophical problem. One can observe the human behavior of an arm rising. It is readily susceptible to two very different types of explanation.[16] A neurologist could account for it in terms of the physical processes that took place to move the arm from a lower to a higher position. If the agent was gesturing to make a point in a lecture, he or she would account for it in terms of the intention of the act. No one has yet satisfactorily explained how the intention itself can be accounted for neurologically. A behavioristic psychologist might explain the act as learned behavior, but one who is partial to the language of intention would only query whether the behaviorist could account in rigorous causal terms for the choice of this learned behavior under these circumstances. Other human actions that are much more complex than the raising of an arm present greater difficulties. One chooses to be married, for example. While there are many explanations of the choice, and even of the choice of the particular person, none is sufficient to account for the act. Enter intention and choice. The philosophical problem is genuine.

Another motivation for the discussion is moral. Moralists through the centuries have acknowledged that there is some behavior that cannot be fully controlled by "reason" and the "will." And certain persons, because of their states of "mind," are excused from accountability for their immoral acts. But a broad and rapid extension of the range of behavior that is accounted for as natural, that is, as caused, carried with it a restriction of the range of behavior for which persons can be held

14. Jean Paul Sartre, *Being and Nothingness,* trans. Hazel E. Barnes (New York: Philosophical Library, 1956), pp. 433–556.
15. I. Kant, *Critique of Practical Reason,* trans. Lewis White Beck (Chicago: University of Chicago Press, 1949), pp. 118–28. I do not read Kant to reify the distinction, but some subsequent literature does.
16. A. I. Melden, *Free Action* (New York: Humanities Press, 1961), pp. 26–42.

accountable. Crime rates, for example, have been significantly correlated with the presence of certain social and economic conditions. The correlation does not prove causality, but the plausible suggestion is that these conditions are significant in predisposing persons to crime. If a criminal is not excused on the basis of such circumstances, he or she is often judged with a measure of leniency. A deeply moral society seems to require that human activity be construed with a maximum stress on human freedom, on the accountability that persons have for their behavior. What is believed to be the satisfactory explanation of human behavior affects the extent of persons' moral accountability. There is an important practical consequence for society in the arguments.

A further practical consequence, I believe, is in the thoughts of some persons. There is something dehumanizing about efforts to account for human behavior in terms of causal processes that can be sufficiently explained by various sciences of man. Humans become construed as automata, as flotsam and jetsam directed only by the motion of currents over which they have no control. The explanatory principles can become the basis for the extension of technical reason: those who have power to determine the currents have power to manipulate human life, and manipulation is a violation of respect for the autonomy of persons. Holes appear in the dikes against the "thingification" of man, and in the barriers that hold back tyranny. Mechanistic or biological analogies take over as the basis for interpreting human life, to the peril of the distinctively human experience.

The practical reasons for adhering to particular views of agency are not sufficient. At their worst they could become useful fictions, rationalizations for the sake of morality and a certain view of humanization. Philosophical or moral beliefs that are defended solely for their utility value deserve no more credence than religious beliefs so defended. The philosophical issues of action theory are the real issues. And one way in which they are distinguished is by looking at action from the agent's perspective on the one hand and the observer's on the other. Intentions as causes are always more persuasive from the agent's perspective. The reduction of intentions and volitions to the end stages of a particular causal sequence is more or less plausible from an observer's perspective; in retrospect, many intentions and actions are susceptible to more refined causal analysis than the agent is conscious of in the moment of choice.

As Midgley says, "Central factors in us *must* be accepted, and the right line of human conduct must lie somewhere within the range they allow."[17] This certainly would have to be admitted by even the most radical libertarians (not political libertarians but theorists of the "will").

17. Midgley, *Beast and Man*, p. 81.

Our intentions and choices, whether moral or otherwise, draw upon and give focus to our biological natures. Other factors must be accepted; at least they are not subject to radical revision and alteration in most persons under most circumstances. Cultural and social conditioning, while unpredictable to a degree in their effects, certainly predetermine the range of choices and actions under most circumstances. What we have become as a result of habituations and conscious commitments is a preselective reality that particularizes the limits and possibilities of action at a particular time. Similarly, the specific external location of our activity in both time and space limits and particularizes our human possibilities.

This is not to deny several important things. We can care for and develop our natural capacities so that more possibilities exist for us. This is a matter of choice and discipline. We need not be the prisoners of a given culture or society in the modern pluralistic and mobile world. The relativization of our "natural" cultures and societies occurs not only as a result of unintended exposures to different ones but also by deliberate effort to make contact with alternatives. We appear to have quite natural revulsions against repressive ways of life that have formed us; I take it that much of modern psychotherapy offers explanations of such resentments and individual rebellions. We need not resign ourselves to the limitations and possibilities of action that are prima facie apparent. We can act to alter those conditions so that the range of possibilities is amplified; we can choose to relate ourselves to other circumstances than those that immediately confront us.

In all of these possibilities, however, our agency is exercised to marshall and to direct realities that exist prior to our choices and actions. The scope of our "freedom" is not as vast as it is claimed to be from some points of view. Edwards, in his own eighteenth-century terms, makes a similar point. "[T]he will always follows the last dictate of understanding. But then the understanding must be taken in a large sense, as including the whole faculty of perception or apprehension, and not merely what is called reason or judgment."[18] Our freedom is the exercise of various capacities that are involved in human agency, capacities that earlier were called "faculties." Understanding, motives, desires, will, reason, and judgment are all involved. This view, it seems to me, does not denigrate humanity, and has the merit of more accurately portraying human agency. As Midgley so poignantly asks, "Why should not our excellence involve our whole nature?"[19]

Human accountability is not abolished from this point of view. To be sure, we can rightly indicate that persons have been held accountable

18. Edwards, *Free Will*, p. 148.
19. Midgley, *Beast and Man*, p. 204.

in the past for more than they actually should have been. A great deal of misplaced guilt has been evoked by beliefs about the range of human freedom that are not defensible. Persons have been held morally accountable for events and effects for which they were only partially causally accountable. But one might argue that what we are held accountable for can be more complex and more particularized than can be included in a dialectic of freedom and nature, or freedom and destiny, when those are understood as specific and independent roles in the drama of life. We are accountable for the ways in which we bring our "natural" capacities to a focus of choice and action, for the assessment of our interrelations with other persons and other things in determining how we will exercise our powers, and for the understanding of the circumstances of our action. We are accountable for the ordering of our motives, drives, and desires, as well as for the consequences of our actions that are within our powers to control. We are accountable to ourselves, to the communities of which we are a part, and to those who are affected by our actions.

In contemporary moral philosophy it is almost axiomatic to say that we are to respect the rational autonomy of other agents; that we are to respect their freedom.[20] Certainly it is correct to respect their capacities for agency. But persons are more than their capacities for agency. We must also respect their bodily natures, and we have responsibilities to see that they are not deprived of necessities. We are to respect persons not merely as individuals but as "members one of another" in their communities. What any moralist means when he or she insists on respect for persons depends upon the image or view held of persons. A view can be more or less comprehensive, more or less complex. If persons are viewed as biological entities with an unique capacity for agency, what is respected is amplified beyond "rational autonomy." Indeed, when one sees how restricted is the range in which autonomy is exercised, and when one sees how the exercise of agency is dependent upon and limited by biological, social, cultural, and other conditions, respect only for autonomy can be viewed as denigrating.

It is my conviction that a reader can learn more about human agency from great novels than he or she can from philosophical treatises or scientific accounts of the subject. Novelists such as Jane Austen, George Eliot, and Tolstoy show with poignancy and detail how human agency and particular acts bring to focus many drives, many motives, and require assessments of complex circumstances. In novels that are perspicacious in their development of character and action, we see how choices are made in continuity with what persons had become as a result of their whole natures.

20. See, for example, Alan Donagan, *The Theory of Morality*, pp. 33–74.

Man is an agent. But agency draws upon all that persons are; it is the capacity to exercise our powers in accordance with purposes and intentions to affect, either by overt action or by restraint, the subsequent course of events.

Our views of the nature of human beings are affected by the selection of a dominant metaphor or analogy for understanding social relations. Social theory in Western culture tends to be divided, in this respect, between an organic analogy and a contractual view of human interrelations. Of course there are combinations of these; the family emerges as a result both of a "contract" of marriage and the natural bonding between the couple and children. As a more or less natural (organic) unit, the family shapes our natural duties; parents do not make contracts with their children that define their obligations to them. In professional life and business transactions the contractual relationship is dominant; we consciously undertake obligations that are specified, and are bound to meet them.

Each of these, when driven to extremes or when used too exclusively, falsifies human experience and misconstrues human nature. The organic metaphor excessively highlights the processes of continuous mutual determination between persons, between groups, and in some instances, as in the extreme sociobiological views, between human beings and the rest of nature. It overcomes the dichotomy between body and "soul" by construing the activities of the intellect and other forms of human agency as necessary and determined outcomes of other processes. Only their ignorance, it would appear, keeps investigators from giving sufficient explanations of human activity, and that is being overcome. The individual is seen primarily as the outcome of the processes of life as a whole, and his or her "autonomy" is underestimated. In morality it is easy to claim, from this perspective, that the good of the whole body is of greater importance than the good of its individual parts. "Surgery," the denial of life and liberty to an individual "organ," is more readily justified.

The contractual model rests strongly on the primacy of individuals. Their being is implicitly if not explicitly judged to be of prior significance to the "whole." The agency of individuals has a more central role; society is seen to be more the result of the actions and choices of individuals, or of contractually bound groups, than as the outcome of "natural" processes. The distinctiveness of man among the animals is stressed more than the similarities and continuities. The autonomy of individuals is highly respected, and with this comes a moral stress on the respect for the autonomy and rights of individuals. In situations of conflict between the rights of individuals and benefits for a social group, the presumption is always in favor of the former. It is more difficult to make a case for restraints and denials of liberty and life for the sake of the well-being of a whole.

An interactional model of society takes into account what is valid in each of the other two models. It can account for the priority of society in the sense that we are the "products" of it to a large extent, and our initiatives are always in response to what exists and to the actions of others upon us. It recognizes that individuals and even most groups do not have the power to create or to recreate their larger societies. Novelty takes place within the developments in social life that are beyond the control of individual and corporate actions. Yet it recognizes the individual and corporate capacities for action. The processes of social change are not mechanically or organically construed; the exercise of powers does alter social orders and the course of historical events; it affects the development of culture. An interactional view provides no simple way of deciding in hard cases whether the individual's autonomy should be curbed for the sake of a larger good any more than it simply sustains the "good of the whole" over against the claims of individuals. Whether the moral weight rests primarily on the individual or particular groups over against the well-being of a larger community—a nation-state or the species—depends on valuations that are not determined by the model itself. Such critical choices, in any case, could not be universally predetermined in the abstract, or in very general terms. They are determined in relation to a particular set of circumstances and events. Societies are developing; their development is governed by a whole complex of processes of which particular events initiated by particular persons and groups are only a part. Multicausality, including human agency, must be taken into account in understanding individual, social, historical, and cultural developments.

An interactional view of society is coherent with the interpretation of the salient features of human nature and with the theology that I have delineated.

The "Human Fault"

Theological discussions of the origin, transmission and extent of the human fault, and of the capacities affected by it, are very extensive. Certainly consciousness of such a fault arises out of human experience, primarily the experience of obligation and remorse. It is not my intention to rehearse theories of original sin at this point, or to analyze critically how it is "transmitted." It is enough to say that the human experience of accountability for moral wrongs is present in all persons who accept the fact that they are agents and that they are responsible to some extent for their choices and their actions. Different religious myths and different interpretations of what causes such wrongs are available from many sources. The extent of accountability for moral wrongs attributed to agents varies with the interpretations of their cause. The ancient theological argument of whether God is the "author" of sin was particularly raised in relation to the Reformed tradition. That is not an argument that is germane here, for it presumes a different view of the "moral character" of the powers that bear down upon us and sustain us than I hold. Nor do I find it necessary to presuppose a time when there was no human fault, when moral innocence reigned, if only briefly and in a very tiny community. The capacity for fault is part of our human nature. The faults that we perpetrate are of various sorts, and for some we can be held more accountable than for others. Some are errors due to the inevitable partiality of our perspectives and our times and places in history, society, and culture that limit our capacities to view the world differently. We do not blame persons who lived prior to Newton for not understanding and interpreting those laws of nature that he articulated, any more than we blame Hindus who practiced the immolation of widows prior to the introduction of a different view of the value of persons in Indian culture. Subsequent to such innovations, however, we do. And as cultures develop and are in contact with each other, we find fewer good reasons for gross partialities and narrow-mindedness.

There are four facets of the "human fault" that are experienced, I dare to affirm, by all human beings. The Christian tradition has had insight into all four: the experience of misplaced trust or confidence (the traditional problem of "idolatry"), the experience of misplaced valuations of objects of desire (the traditional problem of wrongly ordered love), the experience of erroneous perceptions of the relations of things to each other and of our understanding of things (the traditional problem of "corrupt" rationality), and the experience of unfulfilled obligations and duties (the traditional problem of disobedience). The doctrines of sin in the theological tradition arise out of these experiences; what makes them "sin" is that persons have a measure of accountability to God in each. Each involves a disordering of proper human relationships to other persons and to the world around us and each involves a somewhat disordered relation to the powers that sustain life and bear down upon it. The four are frequently interrelated with each other both in the sorts of agents we are (thus references to "sinful human nature") and the sorts of actions we engage in (thus references to "sinful acts"). All four are "inevitable."

The problem of idolatry for most modern human beings in Western culture is hardly that we bow and make sacrifices before the altar of Baal or Kali, or manipulate Kachina dolls. The traditional language of "false gods" however, does meaningfully refer to common human experience. Luther was particularly astute in seeing the significance of this. In his exposition of the First Commandment he noted the point very clearly:

A god is that to which we look for all good and in which we find refuge in every time of need. To have a god is nothing else than to trust and believe him with our whole heart. As I have often said, the trust and faith of the heart alone make both God and an idol. . . . That to which your heart clings and entrusts itself is, I say, really your God. [21]

Idolatry refers to objects of ultimate trust or confidence that do not and cannot bear the weight of reliance that we place upon them for providing sustenance and meaning. In this functional sense, any person whose life has coherence around an ultimate object of trust and loyalty, or around an "ultimate concern" that distorts human life by wrongly centering it, has an idol. The range of objects of confidence that can be idols is very great indeed. Identity with a particular race can be idolatrous when a person's sense of worth and significance is tied to a biological contingency. The twentieth century has seen the horrors that can be perpetrated on humanity when both race and nation function as the objects of ultimate trust for vast numbers of people. If one's professional success is the sole or central source of one's sense of achievement and worth, so that professional failure devastates a person totally, the profession has become one's idol. For the sexual hedonist, I presume that prowess in sexual relationships is what provides the sense of worth, and sex functions as the idol. Technology, money, ideology, nature, one's home and garden, health, or any other object can become so much the focus of human confidence that it bears more meaning and weight in life than it merits.

The issue is not only one of misplaced objects of ultimate concern. It is also that of misplaced degrees of confidence in proper objects. No one has ever relied solely on a single object of trust; for his day-to-day continuity and decent functioning everyone trusts in many persons as well as "things." We rely upon drivers to keep in proper lanes, and we rely upon technology of many sorts to function as it was designed and programmed to function. There are many objects of human confidence that are proper; not even the most pious person trusts in God alone. But it is also part of human experience to have trusted excessively in certain persons, institutions, or things, and to have had insufficient trust in others. Also, we have confidence in persons or things to do particular things. We rely upon a lawyer to protect our interests in a particular legal situation, but on a doctor to diagnose our illness. Even self-confidence, a characteristic that is properly prized, requires some discrimination. Overweening confidence in oneself in matters in which the reliance is not warranted is hardly a virtue; it can lead to an excessive sense of self-sufficiency that

21. T. G. Tappert, trans. and ed., "The Large Catechism" in *The Book of Concord* (Philadelphia: Muhlenberg, 1959), p. 365.

is deleterious both to one's self and to others. Persons can have proper respect for themselves without the perils of inordinate self-esteem. Knowledge of one's capacities and competencies is necessary for discriminating self-confidence. Overweening and indiscriminate self-confidence can lead to arrogance and pride; an insufficient sense of worthiness or confidence can lead to sloth.

The assessment of proper objects of trust, and of the proper degrees of trust and distrust in various objects, comes through human experiences of many sorts far more than it does through general and abstract knowledge. Both wariness and trustfulness are formed in the course of human relationships and human actions, and involve affective dimensions as well as rational assessments. They involve assessments of the trustworthiness of other persons, institutions, and things. Naive, "childlike" confidence that indiscriminately trusts is no more to be honored than is a deep cynicism that harbors radical doubt about the reliability of others. Each extreme is likely to carry its costs as well as its rewards for the agents involved. Innocent trust is vulnerable to events that can cause great pain to oneself; cynicism can inhibit much of the spontaneity of human relationships that brings deep satisfaction. This is the case as much in the relations of groups to each other as of relations between individuals. Servants, slaves, and industrial workers who trusted their employers or owners to protect their best interests have always been vulnerable to exploitation. When the balance is shifted to the other side, conflictual and adversarial perceptions of groups in society dominate, and antagonism and strife occur with both costs and benefits to all parties involved.

In what sense can we say that "idolatry" is a fault? Since any object of reliance, including religious belief and practice, can become an idol in the functional sense I have described, in what sense can one be held accountable for the improper degrees of trust in the right objects? Is idolatry, to use a distinction drawn by Reinhold Niebuhr, universal, but not necessary?[22] Can God become an idol? Can persons rely upon God excessively, expecting those things to be done and those meanings and values to be supported that are not in God's power? I shall treat these questions more fully after the other three aspects of the human fault are described. For now, it is sufficient to indicate that the inevitability of idolatry stems in part from human finitude. We are not capable of fully foreknowing what objects are worthy of what degrees of trust. In this sense idolatries are necessary as well as inevitable. But our capacities as human agents are the basis for making discriminating assessments of the objects of reliance, and for managing to some degree our attitudes. The

22. Reinhold Niebuhr, *Nature and Destiny of Man*, 2 vols. (New York: Scribner's, 1941, 1945), 1:242.

proper responses to the complexities of human experience in this regard are not resolved by highly generalized beliefs about which persons still fruitlessly argue, such as whether humankind is too corrupt to be trusted. Such general beliefs certainly affect our attitudes and actions; the believer in "original sin" is likely to be more wary of others than those who believe in human perfectibility. But it is an error to live from day to day as if such beliefs were universally true.

Wrongly ordered objects of desire constitute the second classic form of sin. The difference between this form and the first is largely a matter of the basic paradigm of human relationships to God. The second views human beings as primarily creatures of desires, of *eros*, as motivated by their loves. The first views human beings primarily in terms of relationships of trust and distrust. The second is dominant in the theology of Augustine, and continued through the classic Catholic tradition. It is not important for this project to judge which of the two is most accurate; we experience both and they are closely related to each other. We tend to trust what we love, and we tend to love what we trust. The basic view of human life in the second aspect of the human fault is teleological. Human beings are viewed as desiring ends and objects. The fault is that of desiring the wrong ends and objects; that of being wrongly directed. In one classic passage, Augustine wrote:

> The right will is, therefore, well-directed love, and the wrong will is ill-directed love. Love, then, yearning to have what is loved, is desire; and having and enjoying it, is joy; fleeing what is opposed to it, is fear; and feeling what is opposed to it, when it has befallen it, is sadness. Now these motions are evil if the love is evil, good if the love is good.[23]

ojects of desire, of "goods." For Augustine, of
good; God is the ultimate object of our desires.
whether individual or collective, is pursuit of that
ith the strength of desire that is appropriate only
of the fault is rightly ordered loves: the love of
and then the proper love of other things as they

Augustine is noting is the problem of misplaced
ion and of the wrong intensity of valuation of
onal terms, we often love the wrong things; and
love, as the medieval writers put it, with either
ects can be many: one's own self; other persons;
n become chosen ends such as health, comfort,

od, bk. 14, 7; p. 449.

and satiation of appetites; power; money; a variety of material things; and so forth. It is probably the case that a highly integrated person has an implicit, if not consciously affirmed, order of loves. Some objects have primacy; perhaps a single object or end is primary. Other loves are ordered in relation to the primary object, and human activities are shaped and graded in importance by the ordering of loves; the ordering of valuations.

The problem of idolatry, when it gets refracted so that we see multiple objects of trust and their relations to each other, is a problem of properly proportioning those things on which human life, and indeed, the life of the world must rely. The problem of ordering our loves, our valuations, is also a problem of proper proportions between our many desires and chosen ends. The proper proportions cannot be worked out in a timeless fashion, a priori; different proportions are proper in different stages of the life cycle, and in different natural, social, and historical circumstances. The sense of proper proportions, such as might be achieved, results from the experimental character of human life. Persons do not learn an abstract and general *ordo amoris,* and then govern their behavior according to it. Yet there is a reflective process, a process of intellectual assessment of our desires and their objects and of our chosen ends, that comes from experiences of human satisfaction and human bitterness and disappointment. We can and do consider what the proper objects of our valuations are, and what the proper intensity of valuation of proper objects is.

Because of its prominence in Jewish and Christian scriptures and its centrality to human experience, a great deal of literature exists about one set of proportions: love of self, of neighbor, and of God. While there have been those stringent views, such as Pascal's, that we are to hate self only and to love God only, a more moderate view has been dominant.[24] Jonathan Edwards, for example, states that "[i]t is not a thing contrary to Christianity that a man should love himself, or, which is the same thing, should love his own happiness." To make such a stringent claim as Pascal's would "tend to destroy the very spirit of humanity." That a person should value himself is necessary "to his nature."[25] The problem, as Edwards and many in the theological tradition phrase it, is inordinate self-love, the love of self that is "too great in degree." One of his discussions of proper proportions is rather typical of much literature in the tradition.

> If we compare a man's love of himself with his love for others, it may be said that he loves himself too much—that is, in proportion too much. And though this may be owing to a defect of love to

24. Pascal, *Pensées,* no. 476, p. 156.
25. Edwards, *Charity and Its Fruits* (Edinburgh: Banner of Truth Trust, 1969), p. 159.

others, rather than to an excess of love to himself, yet self-love, by this excess in its proportion, itself becomes inordinate in this respect, viz. that it becomes inordinate in its influence and government of the man. For though the principle of self-love, in itself considered, is not at all greater than if there is a due proportion of love to God ånd to fellow-creatures with it, yet, the proportion being greater, its influence and government of the man become greater; and so its influence becomes inordinate by reason of the weakness or absence of other love that should restrain or regulate that influence.[26]

Of course there is a "quantification" process in this kind of discourse that never accurately portrays the dynamics of valuations of and desires for ends and objects. But the observation is apt: those things which one values most highly and intensely influence and govern one's activities to a greater degree.

With less precision, this pattern of the human fault discloses aspects of societies, cultures, and even periods of history as well. Currently, for example, it is common to read about America's "love of the automobile." The valuation of this particular piece of technology and the purpose it serves for human convenience and satisfactions has considerable effect upon how many aspects of life are "governed" or conducted: economic, ecological, political, and others. This "love" determines to a considerable extent what other desires and ends can be "sacrificed" for the pursuit of the satisfactions of the automobile. One can even play upon the theme of "the expulsive power of a great affection" as a heuristic device for understanding the decline of alternate modes of transportation. Patriotism, the high valuation placed upon one's nation, while it appears to wax and wane in intensity historically, becomes under certain social and historical circumstances a collective love that reorders other valuations, including the valuation of one's life. A collective great affection can become disastrous in its consequences when it is not properly proportioned to other ends and valuations.

Human valuations, individual and collective, grow out of our natures; there are "natural" and cultural bases for the desires we have and the ends that we choose. This does not imply that conformity to nature in a simplistic sense determines the proper objects of love or the proper intensities of valuations. Augustine makes this point in the following way: there "are gradations according to the order of nature; but according to the utility each man finds in a thing, there are various standards of value."[27] The critical matter for human accountability of valuations is the choice

26. Ibid., pp. 162-63. See also Joseph Butler, sermon 12, sec. 11, in *Fifteen Sermons* (London: G. Bell and Sons, 1948), p. 191, and elsewhere.
27. Augustine, *City,* bk. 11, 16; p. 360.

of the standards of value. While loves are grounded in nature, ends are chosen. And since human life involves many desires, many valuations, and many ends, our agency is involved in ordering our desires and valuations. This is not to claim that we can choose a "rational life plan" that is imposed upon our collective and individual desires—affectivity is primary. But, as I have insisted over and over, affectivity is not mindless, and natural valuations are not always to be suspected. Yet agency involves choosing, ordering, and governing our valuations; it involves a determination of the proper proportions of our loves. For this we are accountable. One aspect of the human fault is wrongly ordered loves, or valuations. Such wrong orderings are inevitable; "sin" is universal. Yet we can learn a more fitting order of valuations. For Augustine, the oft-quoted aphorism, "Love God, and do what you please," was not an invitation to a divided life or to license; he believed that if one had the proper ultimate object of the most intense and proper ultimate desire, human activity would be properly ordered. Other things would be loved in proper proportion to their place in God's ordering of all things. Edwards's view, in *The Nature of True Virtue,* is similar.

A third traditional aspect of the human fault is corrupt rationality. The literature on this topic displays intricate argumentation about whether human reason has been corrupted by the fall, and about the extent to which it is corrupt. The limitations of fruitfulness of this discussion rest primarily in the assumption that reason is virtually some "thing" that can be corrupted, partially corrupted, or even "saved." To be sure, what theologians have believed about this matter has had deep effects on other things that they wrote, and has had cultural effects in communities that their thought penetrated. One has a far more "pessimistic" view of human possibilities if one believes that not only the "will" but also "reason" is totally corrupt. If, however, rationality is considered as an activity, not a faculty, the traditional issue can be reformulated. If rational activity is faulted, it is not necessarily always faulted, and the fault has different consequences for different kinds of rational activity. The rational activity of the investigator of the functions of the nervous system is quite different from the rational activity of the policy maker who is trying to determine what is best for a given nation-state under particular historical circumstances. The rational activity of a metaphysician qua metaphysician is different from his or her rational activity in ordering natural desires or determining proper relationships to other persons.

The fault of rationality is not so much a matter of errors in logic as it is in misconstruing that realm of reality that engages us; it is a matter of the wrong depiction and interpretation of the particular "world" that attracts our attention and that evokes our activity. In accord with much that has previously been written in this book, it is clear that one's place in history, society, culture, and even nature affects what is seen, and how what is seen is construed. There is no possibility of human emancipation from the particularities of a perspective. The bias that naturally occurs, however, has different consequences depending on what it is that one is construing. The results of the descriptions and understandings of a cell studied through an electron microscope are from a perspective, to be sure, but the tests of validity are far different from those that can be applied to descriptions and understandings of a social revolution or the nutritional crisis in many parts of the world. We cannot be held accountable for our finitude, which is part of our nature. Our rationality, however, is flawed by our refusals to "see" certain aspects of the world to which we are attentive, our refusals to take into account relevant information and explanations, our refusals to be corrected in the light of substantial evidences and persuasive arguments. It is corrupted by sloth, the self-satisfaction that makes us content with the level of development of our intellectual capacities we have achieved, and with the sufficiency of our partial perspectives and interpretations so that we do not submit them to criticism and correction by others. Closed-mindedness can be rooted in either pride or sloth.

Of course, as I have noted, persons cannot be held fully accountable for the partialities and corruptions of their rational activities. This has been long recognized, for example, in moral theology's discussions about invincible and culpable ignorance: is a person held accountable for that which he or she could know but did not make an effort to know? We do not hold a Bengali villager accountable to modern scientific standards of explanation for events in personal and historical life if he has access only to astrological and mythical ways of construing them. Nor, at the other extreme, do we hold out the possibility that one way of rationally construing the world will ever be sufficient in itself or universally available to persons in all societies and cultures.

As some philosophers and historians have long noted, our rational activity is grounded in our interests. That grounding is not to be understood as solely negative. Without the passionate interest in expanding a scientific understanding of a given phenomenon, the pursuit of knowledge would lag. Without a passionate interest in finding the powerful similes and phrases that express a poetic perception of various aspects of the world and our experience, we might be insensitive to some of the deeper meanings of human experience. Certainly much of social scientific research, Marxist and other, is motivated by interests in practical social reform. But our interests also constrict our rational activities. A social science that is deemed to be valid, finally, because the research sustains the moral interests of a particular group in society is hardly adequate; a passionate religious interest that zealously excludes consideration of information and explanations from other perceptions is hardly honorable; a political interest that leads to the denial of the importance of certain data in development of a policy or course of action is properly suspect. Rational activity is always related to interests, even if only the interest in being disinterested; without such relation there would be no passion, no motivation to engage in it. Thus one measure of the corruption of rationality is the propriety and the breadth or narrowness of the interests that motivate it. This points to one root of the corruption: human affectivity, human valuations. But this rooting is, as we have seen, ambiguous; without it there would be no rational activity at all.

As in matters of trust and love, so in matters of rationality, there is a graded relevance to any charges of corruption or culpability. It is simply wrong to say that reason is corrupt or, worse, totally corrupt. Any accusations about faulty rationality are relative not only to the knower and the community of which he is part but also to the object of knowledge. There are some things that human beings cannot fully know; there are some issues that have so many variables, so many contingencies, that we must be content with far less than perfection. There are some aspects of the reality of human experience that transcend our capacities to explain fully according to a single method of investigation, or from a single perspective. Judgments of adequacy are not thereby ruled out, but the standards used must be graded with reference to the object under investigation and the present cultural and procedural resources for investigating. Human beings live and act according to probabilities; "corruption" of rationality is grounded in human finitude. The actual corruption lies in the resistance to being corrected, the resistance of closed-mindedness. And this resistance in excess is fairly universal; mighty are the efforts and capacities of even intellectual giants in the defense of their rational activities, and in the extension of their self-assurance to matters far beyond their demonstrated competence.

The fourth traditional aspect of the human fault is more narrowly moral; in traditional terms, it is disobedience. A legal pattern of thought dominates; Thomas Aquinas quotes Augustine, "Sin is a word, deed or desire against the eternal law."[28] There are ample grounds for this idea of sin in the biblical materials; Torah was to be obeyed. And in the Christian tradition, both before Augustine and long after him, this moral and legal interpretation of sin is very strong. For much of the tradition the focus was on disobedient acts, and this assumed some things about the flawed nature of persons, but in many forms of both Catholic and Protestant ethics emphasis was on behavioral conformity to what were judged to be correct rules of moral action. Augustine, it is to be noted, also

28. Thomas Aquinas, *Summa Theologiae,* 1a, 2ae, Q. 71.

included desires, and surely this is grounded in the biblical material and is continually present in theology and piety.

Whatever the traditional claims might be for knowing the eternal law, or the law of God, the formulation of the moral rules developed out of human experiences. Not only is there a cultural history behind the biblical moral laws that is traced by scholars of the ancient world; there is a "natural" history to them as well. It is not implausible to argue that, for example, the moral rules of the "second table" of the Decalogue were formulated in light of the consequences of those actions that violated those principles. In keeping with the approach of this book, it is conceivable that these and other rules were deemed to have divine authorization because they provided the requisites for human beings to get along with each other in a community. While obedience to them was authorized because they were deemed to be the commands of God, there were other reasons for requiring it. Given the anthropocentric focus of attention, there were moral reasons for the laws; God commanded them because they were right. Disobedience became a basic form of sin and, given human propensities and desires, it was inevitable that the moral rules would be disobeyed. As they became extended and refined, and as desires and attitudes were included as subject to God's laws, the possibilities of a life free from disobedience became less and less.

The primacy of the notion of disobedience points most clearly to the idea of moral fault. Insofar as disobedience implies clear rules, it is too restrictive an idea for the complexity of human experience. To illustrate this, recall the discussion of trust. One human fault is trust in the wrong objects, or trust in excess or deficiency in proper objects. But the objects of trust, in personal and social relations, have the capacities to be untrustworthy. Most dramatically, persons or institutions in whom we have confidence can betray our trust. The experience of betrayal of trust is, perhaps, one of the most bitter in human life. To be sure, many of the moral rules attempt to ensure the keeping of trust: committing of adultery or stealing are more fundamentally violations of trust. But the problem of untrustworthiness is grounded in the characters of agents, not merely in the violation of rules of conduct. Something about human relations that cannot be fully encompassed in a rule is violated in broken trust—whether promise-keeping, expectations that the other will tell one the truth, reliance on institutions to meet their commitments and fulfill their functions, or reliance of nation-states on each other to fulfill their explicit or implied obligations. Betrayal and deception are the sins against trust, and elaborate indeed are the cultural and social devices that have been developed to guard against them: vows, contracts, promises, surveillance procedures, laws, and regulations.

Disobedience in its restricted and expanded modes is a universal fault. Again, the moral theological literature is replete with definitions of conditions which excuse persons from obligations. Physical and other forms of disability excuse: "ought" implies "can." Coercion and duress, from physical torture to mental and spiritual manipulation, excuse. And the judgments made about whether conditions were sufficient to excuse vary both circumstantially and historically. But accountability for adherence to moral rules and principles and to natural duties and implied commitments of trust is sustained. As Jonathan Edwards and other theologians have long pointed out, there is evidence for sin from the history of mankind that needs no bibilical terminology or authorization to be perceived. Modern moral philosophers have, on the whole, shied away from the deeper sources of the human fault: the restriction of interests to the self, the difficulty of the "will" in fulfilling what moral reason dictates, and the taming and directing of natural desires. But the theological tradition carries more wisdom; it construes the moral fault to be not only the failure of action to conform to rationally defensible rules but also the desires (to use Augustine's term) and propensities of our full human natures. It is the perception of the propensities of agents to act immorally that has led to the theological notion of corrupt persons as well as corrupt acts. It is the recognition that actions are governed by the desires persons have and the sorts of persons they have become that has led the religious tradition to look for a correction of the moral fault in places that rationalistic views eschew.

No single metaphor is sufficient to account for all aspects of the human fault. In their discussions of the "fall," however, both Augustine and Jonathan Edwards use the powerful one of the "contraction" of the human spirit. Augustine wrote, "But man did not fall away as to become absolutely nothing; but being turned towards himself, his being became more contracted than it was when he clave to Him who supremely is."[29] Edwards, in a very Augustinian spirit, wrote:

> Immediately upon the fall, the mind of man shrank from its primitive greatness and expandedness, to an exceeding smallness and contractedness. . . . Before, his soul was under the government of that noble principle of divine love, whereby it was enlarged to the comprehension of all his fellow-creatures and their welfare. And not only so, but it was not confined within such narrow limits as

29. Augustine, *City,* bk. 14, 13; p. 460. See also, "Upon this account it seems worthwhile to inquire whether private interest is likely to be promoted in proportion to the degree in which self-love engrosses us, and prevails over all other principles; *or whether the contracted affection may not possibly be so prevalent as to disappoint itself, and even contradict its own end, private good.*" Joseph Butler, sermon 11, sec. 1, in *Fifteen Sermons,* p. 166.

the bounds of creation, but went forth in the exercise of holy love to the Creator, and abroad upon the infinite ocean of good, and was, as it were swallowed up by it, and became one with it. [With the fall] all this excellent enlargedness of man's soul was gone, and thenceforth he himself shrank, as it were, into a little space, circumscribed and closely shut up within itself, to the exclusion of all things else. Sin, like some powerful astringent, contracted his soul to the very small dimensions of selfishness; and God was forsaken, and fellow-creatures forsaken, and man retired within himself, and became totally governed by narrow and selfish principles and feelings.[30]

I obviously am not interested in arguing that a historical event occurred that more traditional theologians name the "fall" of man. We know too much about how our species developed biologically and culturally even to dream of sustaining the notion that there was once the purity of the vision of God, the enlargement of the human soul, from which we have fallen. But the perceptions of Augustine and Edwards are accurate with reference to a very salient aspect of the human condition—an aspect that is perennial through history and universal across the species. The metaphor of contraction can refer not only to individual persons but to particular human communities, from the intimacy of the family to the breadth of the nation-state; it can refer even to the species as a whole. Each of the four aspects of the human fault can be explicated in large part by the metaphor of contraction.

Idolatry is a contraction of human trust and loyalty. It is a foreclosure of confidence in persons and institutions that are worthy of it. It is a fixation of trust and fidelity on persons, institutions, values, and ideas that distorts proper relationships among these things. Contracted trust and loyalty can lead to demonic fanaticism; one's nation, one's creed, one's moral code, one's political ideology—each can be deemed so absolutely worthy of confidence and loyalty that they are falsely imposed on others, and defended with a degree of fervor that belies their partiality. Appropriate "distribution" of our confidences and our loyalties is warped by our tendencies to idolatry, by contraction of our loyalties.

The quotations from Augustine and Edwards illustrate the significance of the contraction of our desires and our loves. The "selfish principle," as Edwards calls this contraction, reigns in excess. We become insensitive to the needs of other persons, other groups, other nations, and even of nature by a contraction of our desires, by an undue focus on the individual self, on one's family or nation, or on one's profession or institution as the object of love.

30. Edwards, *Charity*, pp. 157–58.

The corruption of rationality is largely a matter of the contraction of human vision. Excessive confidence in the propriety of particular interests blinds us from seeing aspects of the world that are relevant to our knowing and our doing. Defensiveness about our perspectives and methods makes it difficult to acknowledge their limits and to be open to correction from others. We readily assume that our ways of knowing, our concepts, our procedures for making judgments, and our reasons for choices are applicable beyond proper bounds. Imagination becomes stultified by this contraction; we are unwilling to imagine other ways of ordering experience, other ways of relating aspects of knowledge to each other, other contexts in which what we know can be interpreted.

Disobedience is a contraction of our moral interests. It is a fixation on what is deemed beneficial for the self or for a particular community that leads to inconsideration of the rights and the needs of others. Deeper than the issues involved in failing to act according to a particular moral rule or principle are those involved in selective preferences for self-interest or the interests of particular groups that tempt us to such disobedience. Betrayal and deception of others, for example, is rooted in expedient preference for what one judges to be his or her immediate self-interest or group interest.

The human fault, then, is our tendency to be turned inward toward ourselves as individuals, or toward our communal interests. It is, in the words of Augustine, becoming more contracted in our being than we ought to be. It is, in Edwards's words, "like some powerful astringent" that narrows our compehension of all our fellow creatures and their welfare. It is a shrinking of self and community "into a little space, circumscribed and closely shut up within itself." It is retiring within the self or the group, either out of the pride that takes the form of excessive confidence in the partialities of our particular ways of life, or out of the sloth that sustains a self-satisfaction in what has already been achieved. The human fault is not only moral, in the restricted sense of that term; it is a deeper misplacement of ourselves and our communities in relation to other persons and communities, and in relation to nature. Recall my general principle: we are to relate ourselves and all things in a manner appropriate to our, and their, relations to God. The human fault keeps us from a proper understanding of our proper relations by contracting our trusts and loyalties, our loves and desires, our rational construing of the world, and our moral interests. The distortions that are forthcoming penetrate many areas of human experience and human action and they become pervasive. This is what the theological tradition has understood to be the corruption of man and of human life. The fault is universal.

The Correction

If the human fault can be indicated by the metaphor of the contraction of soul and of interests, and its consequences as improper relations of ourselves and all things to God, the correction can be indicated by an "enlargement" of soul and of interests, and by a more appropriate alignment of ourselves and all things in relation to each other and to the ultimate power and orderer of life. This is the correction that a theocentric view can evoke and sustain.

Of course, the enlargement is not sufficient in itself to resolve the practical issues of how things are to be appropriately related to each other and to God. The kind of conversion or transformation that is entailed in a theocentric view is no more sufficient to resolve particular moral choices or to establish the particulars of a more adequate human self-understanding than is any other religious conversion, or any of the secular surrogates for religious conversion that contemporary culture provides. If it is not sufficient, enlargement of soul and interests is at least necessary.

Also, I am not so naive as to believe that large numbers of persons or various interest groups in the human community are going to be converted to a new perspective. Indeed, such correctives are more likely to occur as a result of events which provoke reconsideration of the human contractions and of the actual relations of things to each other. Such changes as occur will stem from an enlightenment of narrow self-interest, a perception that even our proper self-love cannot be realized without attention to love of other persons and objects. Edwards makes this point.

> Self-love may not only influence men, so as to cause them to be affected with God's kindness to them as parts of a community: as a natural principle of self-love, without any other principle, may be sufficient to make a man concerned for the interest of the nation to which he belongs: . . . self-love may make natural men rejoice at the success of our nation, . . . they being members of the body. So the same natural principles may extend further, and even to the world of mankind, and might be affected with the benefits the inhabitants of the earth have, beyond those of inhabitants of other planets; if we knew that such there were, and knew how it was with them.[31]

Or the changes will occur in a more coercive way. Undue turning in on self or community will be corrected by economic restraints, by political activities within and between nations, by legislation and regulation, and by the alterations of the natural resources that are available for our use. In the language of the Reformation fathers, there is a civic

31. Edwards, *Religious Affections*, pp. 246–47.

or political use of the law; it, together with whatever powers enforce it, properly restrains the effects of the human fault. It is, in Luther's powerful metaphor, a "dike against sin." Indeed, the divine governance affects human activities by forcing consciousness of the relationships that are necessary and proper for the measure of human self-fulfillment that is appropriate. In language that others are more prone to use than I, "necessity" will require that the human community do certain things that conversion to a theocentric view might induce it to do voluntarily.

Nonetheless, if the fault and its consequences are at root a religious problem, the resolution of the problem can be delineated in religious dimensions. It is not my purpose here to use traditional or first-order religious language to describe the correction that a theocentric view evokes and sustains. In the next section of this chapter I shall make a case for the importance of such language, and of a community that uses it and is informed by it. For now the correction can be described in three parts: an alteration and enlargement of vision, which is in part a correction of the flaw of our rational activities; an alteration and enlargement of the "order of the heart," which is in part a correction of the flaws of idolatry and of disordered loves and desires; and different standards for determining proper human being and action as a result of the other corrections, which is in part a correction of the flaw of "disobedience."

Theology, to repeat Julian Hartt once more, is a way of construing the world. Construing involves a perception of the world. The theocentrism I have developed provides a perspective from which the human species is perceived and interpreted in relation to the rest of the universe. The primary turn is one that has been reiterated several places in this book; it is from self to other, from anthropocentrism to God as the primary object of attention. I have properly denied that this enables human beings to see things from "God's point of view." But it does force persons to perceive and interpret man in relation to the ultimate power and orderer of all of the creation. Man is perceived and interpreted in relation to the purposes of the divine governance that can be grasped by humans, and the divine governance is of the whole of the creation. This is not to claim that Mary Midgley and many others cannot adequately perceive the place of man in relation to nature without a theology or an avowed theocentric interpretation of life. The enlargement of vision that a theocentric perspective enables certainly can be achieved, at least in considerable measure, from nontheological perspectives. But the theocentric view does enlarge the context within which humanity is perceived and interpreted.

No doubt in the eyes of many persons, including theologians, the effect of the perspective on man that is developed here is "dehumanizing." A great deal of contemporary theology is intentionally anthropocentric; I noted some examples of this above. The political and liberation theologies of both Protestants and Catholics provide examples. Among Catholic theologians such theology is espoused in reaction to what they perceive to be the impersonality of traditional theology of Being, and a denigration of the interests of man that results from placing humans in the context of an impersonal ordering of life. They react against the observed moral consequences of this theology: particular social orders are virtually sacralized and the poor and relatively powerless are exhorted to fit into a repressive scheme of things. The passion for social justice, for alteration of the conditions of the wretched and deprived peoples of the world, is evoked and sustained by giving primary attention to the needs and interests of the poor, and to "history" rather than nature as the arena of God's action. The question, to be faced more specifically in the second volume of this work, is whether the construal of man in relation to the rest of the universe that I am defending *necessarily* leads to complacency with present unjustifiable distributions of power and resources in human society.

My response is that it does not. The context is enlarged in which the human historical venture of creating institutions, economic and political orders, and international relations is set. The social, historical, and cultural ventures of the human race are here perceived not only within the context of the ordering of nature (of which man is a part) but also within the ultimate ordering of God, insofar as this can be grasped and stated. To construe *all* things in relation to God, to relate to *all* things in a manner appropriate to their relations to God is to construe human relations in this context. The problem of injustice is quite properly perceived in its particular historical, social, economic, and political dimensions. But the problem of particular constellations of injustice is deeper and more pervasive; it is the failure to perceive the requisites for the measure of human flourishing for individuals and groups that are expressions of the divine governance. The moral problem of the ordering of societies is the failure to establish institutions and relationships that are in agreement with the order and ordering of life that bring to each person and group its due. Injustice is a sign of disordering, and the disordering is in part due to a failure to construe human life in its relations to the purposes of the divine governance. But we do not properly perceive what is due to persons and groups by taking them out of the context of nature, with both the limitations and possibilities that it provides. We do not properly perceive a just ordering from a theological perspective that limits the significance of the Deity to the process of history or to an eschatological Kingdom which will finally bring human life to its consummation. Human life is related to the divine governance as much in nature as it is in history.

Another charge against this enlargement of vision is that human life becomes absurd and meaningless. The biblical witness, and particularly the Christian witness, provides an assurance of the ultimate meaningfulness of human life, and of its final consummation and fulfillment. It is the case that the view espoused here sets the quest for meaningfulness in a different context. It is also true that in construing human life in this wider context a long coveted aspiration for an exaggerated meaningfulness is rejected. What can be hoped for is set in a different context because the place of human life is set in a different context. A theocentric view that takes into account well-established explanations and data from various sciences, and that stresses the affinities of man with the other animals, cannot sustain any view of the meaningfulness of human life, now or in the future, that contradicts these sources of understanding.

This does not mean that apathy, or resignation, or slothfulness is warranted. Rather it requires that the quest for meaningfulness be guided and tempered by a more accurate and adequate view of the place of man in the universe. It does not deny that there are conditions for possibility, that is, hope, of development of human life, of better conditions for human living, of achievements that surpass our present ones. It does not, however, provide the prospect of a gradual and ultimate triumph of spirit over matter as the vision of de Chardin does. It negates the aspiration for the perfectibility of man, if only because man in nature, culture, history, and society is in a process of change, and thus it asserts that the eternal criteria of human perfection are impossible to establish. Much that is richly meaningful now is not threatened by seeing our species in a larger context: interpersonal love, a sense of worthiness, satisfaction in human achievements, the establishment of just institutions, the zest for competition, the appreciation of beauty, the satisfaction of physical desires—these and many more loci of meaning will continue.

One can properly ask why some larger, more dramatic, ultimate meaning and perfection is desired. Why do persons want a hope that is beyond the conditions of possibilities for them? What is so attractive about the assurance given in the New Testament that all things will be made new? From the religious standpoint of this book, part of the explanation is that we do not consent to our finitude properly, that we do not consent to the place of the human species in the universe. There is a corruption of our rational activity, a wrong perception of the place of man in the universe. The vitality of that wrong perception, to be sure, is grounded in our interests, but the error of it is also cognitive. It is a failure to take fully into account what is known from many different sources. To question the biblical claim that all things are or will be made new in Christ, to see such a claim as hyperbole, is not to deny that "newness" is possible, that what now exists for man can be surpassed, or that there are conditions for hoping. To construe man in this theocentric perspective does require that aspirations be tempered by what we know of our place in the universe. Religiously grounded and theologically defended aspirations for more dramatic meaningfulness, for greater hopes, and for newness might have great utility value to believers, but this does not make them true.

How we construe the place of man in the universe, and in the divine governance of all of creation, clearly has profound effects upon what can be reasonably meaningful, upon our aspirations and our hopes. Altered understanding brings with it other alterations. The expansion of vision that I have proposed entails reassessments of many other features of what has been religiously and culturally traditional.

The second correction is of the "order of the heart" and affects the traditional faults of idolatry and wrongly ordered desires. The ordering of the heart and the perception of the place of man in the universe are intrinsically interrelated; which prompts the other is not a matter of concern here. Indeed, on principles previously stated, it is not important to attempt to answer this question in general. Intellectual activity is affective, and our knowing is informed by our affectivity. This correction requires, in the terms of Nietzsche, a "transvaluation of values."[32] Such a transvaluation has always been implied in the theological tradition that has claimed that only God is worthy of ultimate trust, loyalty, and devotion; that (in Kierkegaard's language) we are to be absolutely related to the absolute and relatively related to the relative.[33] It is implied in the Augustinian tradition that has claimed that the human fault is having the wrong objects of love, or the wrong intensity of love for proper objects. The antidote to this poisoning of life is, in this tradition, the love of God as the supreme good, and the reordering of other loves in relation to God. The "heart" and the "will" must be reordered; the values that guide human activity must be transvalued.

A correction of the order of the heart is enabled by a theocentric piety and view. By this I mean a governing and reordering of our natural desires, loves, natural instincts, and aspirations. I am not suggesting that the natural order of the heart is replaced by a new order. Rather, I am building on what I wrote about natural man, and about the primacy of affectivity in human experience. There is a continuity between our natural loves and the ends that we choose, between our affectivity and our rational activity. The relationship is not, as Midgley so aptly phrases it, a

32. Nietzsche, "Beyond Good and Evil," trans. Helen Zimmerman, sec. 46, in *The Philosophy of Nietzsche* (New York: Random House, 1927), p. 433.

33. Søren Kierkegaard, *Concluding Unscientific Postscript,* trans. David F. Swenson (Princeton: Princeton University Press, 1944), p. 371: "But the maximum of attainment is simultaneously to sustain an absolute relationship to the absolute end, and a relative relationship to relative ends."

"colonial" one, "in which an imported governor, named Reason, imposes order on a chaotic alien tribe of Passions or Instincts."[34] Nor is the relationship a colonial one in which a "new principle" of grace or spirit expels the old principle and replaces it. Human nature does not have to be exterminated and replaced by a new and different nature.

Here we are in the middle of ancient theological debates that have many aspects, and have their own historic symbols and language. In effect, I am affirming that whatever disorders of our loves there are, they do not involve a "total corruption." Of course, even theologians who are popularly accused of adhering to "total corruption" of human nature qualify their positions with care. Or, with reference to another classic debate, I am affirming that "nature" is redirected or transformed by "grace." We are also in the middle of an ongoing philosophical debate about the relation of "reason" to the "passions." It is clear that I affirm rational activity to be an ordering of our natures, and in continuity with them, rather than an incessant warfare against them.

Every person who has some semblance of personal identity, some measure of integrity, and some identifiable character has a personal center of gravity. Some persons are more rigorously integrated than others, but no one lives without inner tensions, or serious conflicts—between various natural desires, various objects of their affections, duties and obligations that claim them, ends that they have chosen, aspirations such as professional success and that of being a good parent, groups to which they are loyal, and so forth. Such conditions are a necessary part of our finitude. The "purity of heart, which is to will one thing" (Kierkegaard) is never completely achieved in human experience.[35] Yet both our natures and our chosen ways of life resolve many of the tensions and conflicts, or at least give shape to some priorities. If we do not have a single and supreme purpose that orders and directs all our activities and impulses, most of us have "loves" that cohere sufficiently to keep us from being riven. Happily such coherence is sufficient to sustain us and our relationships to other persons and things in ordinary daily life. And happily, the social and natural worlds in which we live are generally ordered in such a way that there is rough coherence between our personal lives and our environments. To a considerable extent we are "at peace" with ourselves, and "at home" in our world. Or, in pluralistic societies, we can find those communities in which we feel at home.

The term "order of the heart," however, needs qualifying. There is *ordering* of the heart. A center of personal gravity can keep us from

34. Midgley, *Beast and Man*, p. 260.
35. Kierkegaard, *Purity of Heart Is to Will One Thing*, trans. Douglas V. Steere (New York: Harper and Bros., 1938).

falling, but it does not inhibit movement. Particular circumstances and events require a reordering of the heart; our rational activity induces particular expressions of passions and desires for particular purposes, and is provoked by particular events or persons . The "order of charity" that Thomas Aquinas designs so precisely is at fault in part because it does not provide the space for an ordering that is appropriate under particular circumstances, and his capacity to resolve possible conflicts on the basis of philosophical distinctions does not ring true to human experience. For example, he asks "whether a man ought, out of charity, to love his children more than his father." To Ambrose's claim that the order is God first, our parents second, our children third, and our household last, Thomas answers in the following way.

> [T]he degrees of love may be measured from two standpoints. First, from that of the object. In this respect the better a thing is, and the more like to God, the more is it to be loved: and in this way a man ought to love his father more than his children, because, to wit, he loves his father as his principle, in which respect he is a more exalted good and more like God.
>
> Secondly, the degrees of love may be measured from the standpoint of the lover, and in this respect a man loves more that which is more closely connected with him, in which way a man's children are more lovable to him than his father. . . .
>
> It is natural for a man as father to love his children more, if we consider them as closely connected with him: but if we consider which is the more exalted good, the son naturally loves his father more.[36]

Clearly for Thomas this order and the distinction on which it rests is not sufficient to resolve a conflict that might exist between love of father and of children. Also there is merit in reflecting on how our loves ought to be ordered; love is not pure spontaneity. And how our loves are ordered will be directed to some extent by our "natures." Yet, Thomas's effort to develop an "order of charity" implants on the dynamism of human nature a rigidity that violates it.

To have a center of personal gravity or, to change the metaphor, to be oriented in life by a basic intentionality that is grounded in a pattern of coherent loyalties or affections, does not imply that a fitting reordering of the heart ought not to occur in relation to particular circumstances: those interior to the person, those events in which a person acts, and those objects to which persons are attracted.

36. Thomas Aquinas, *Summa Theologiae*, 2a, 2ae, Q. 26, art. 9, in St. Thomas Aquinas, *Summa Theologiae*, trans. Fathers of the English Dominican Province, 3 vols. (New York: Benziger Brothers, 1947), 2:1301–2.

The center of gravity varies in different persons. As we saw in the discussion of the human fault, almost anything can function as one's god; almost any object can function as one's supreme good. Integrity in itself is hardly a moral virtue, or a sign of a religious life. The critical question is, What is the center of gravity? What is the basic direction of our orientation? The claim of a theocentric piety and view of life is that the center of gravity of affections and of our construing of the world is the Deity. In Augustine's terms, to love God as the supreme good is to reorder our other affections so that we can love others and all things in relation to God. To love other things as the supreme good is to have the wrong center of gravity; it is to be basically disoriented in the proper valuations of other things. What is claimed about God, of course, makes a great deal of difference to a life that is ordered by supreme loyalty and supreme love. It is my position that God in relation to man and the world is an appropriate center of gravity; orientation to God will govern and order the heart in a way nearer to what human life is meant to be.

With significant qualifications this pattern of thought is appropriate to human communities as well as to individual persons. Communities too can be idolatrous. Their collective affections and interests can be turned in on themselves; their interests can be constricted in such a way that members of other communities suffer for their sakes and injustices are done to persons and to other groups. The reordering of a "collective" heart is greatly more difficult than the significant difficulties involved in reordering an individual one. Shared values, common objects of love, and corporate aspirations are all parts of culture, and not so readily affected by transformations or conversions. To raise the question of the difficulty, however, is not to say that there are no beneficial natural interests and desires in communities to be sustained. While there are "corruptions" of social values, there are also social values that under many circumstances do work for a common good. The correction of social vision is much easier to prescribe than is the correction of those shared loves and values that deeply condition ways of life and choices of public policy. Perhaps all one can expect is the intellectual and affective recognition that there are limits within which corporate interests have to be kept for the sake of the well-being of one's own community and of others.

A reordering of the heart can be enabled not only by a theocentric vision, but also by theocentric love, loyalty, fidelity, and devotion. Correction, even in one individual, is never complete, not only because of perversity but because of the dynamic interrelations of human life. While the Eden experience is myth, it is suggestive, especially as Edwards describes it: it is an enlargement of soul that comprehends all our fellow creatures and their welfare. It is not even confined to "such narrow limits as the bounds of creation," but goes forth on "the infinite ocean of good."

Theocentric piety enables an enlargement of affections and loyalties, and an ordering of them under the divine governance.

A theocentric vision and piety can also enable a correction of the moral fault of disobedience—in the enlarged sense of that term described above. Correction of constricted vision and valuations, of course, bears upon the correction of the moral fault in a restricted sense. The moral life becomes one, in Edwards's metaphysical terms, of "benevolence to being in general."[37] It becomes one of living one's life, ordering one's activities and "all things," in such a way that they agree more with the ends and purposes of the divine ordering of life. The enlargement of vision is clearly necessary as a condition for this view of moral life. So also is a reordering of the heart. Human responsibilities and obligations are enlarged, and particular obligations are set in a wider context of life.

There is merit in the traditional Protestant concern about the constrictions of "legalism" in morality, though some of the reasons for it are not adequate. The concern of the Reformation fathers was religious: that of justifying oneself in the eyes of God by one's morally righteous life. This denied that salvation was a free gift of God's gracious mercy. But there are also moral concerns with legalism. The justification of a moral act tended to be located in the act of obedience itself; if one obeyed a moral rule, one was a good person and the act was good. This militated against any openness, out of love, to actions and attitudes that were creative or responded to needs that were not covered by the rules. The Pharisees have been much maligned and misinterpreted by Protestant theology and piety, but the charge that Jesus was believed to lay against them was to this point. There is a consenting to the divine purposes that can be restrained by the notion that human goodness rests in obedience to rules and that the rules given are sufficient to cover all occasions of choice and action.

Other aspects of the distaste for legalism also have some merit. The authorization of the rules to be obeyed is often properly questioned. Sometimes this authorization was by institutions claiming, if not inerrancy, excessive certainty about their wisdom and their power to determine for all persons what conduct is right. Sometimes this authorization came from dubious metaphysical and theological principles. A view of Being as eternal and immutable tended to authorize deductions from that Being of rules of conduct that also were prescribed as timeless and changeless. Sometimes this authorization was claimed on the basis of a literalistic view of the revelation of a morality in the Bible, though those who claimed such authorization always found ways to ignore many of the cultic and other laws that are given in the Bible.

37. Edwards, *True Virtue*, p. 3.

The theology proposed in this book does not eliminate moral rules and principles, but it does require a strong sense of the need for them to be general rules whose application must be addressed to changing historical conditions. This is the case for two principal reasons. One is that it is not given to people to know inerrantly what the divine governance requires under some special circumstances. Our understanding of what is morally required is not infallible, and it develops historically in relation to events and to other forms of knowledge, just as theology and the sciences do. The other is that the divine governance is an ordering and not an immutable eternal order; rules and principles have to be open to revision and extension in the light of alterations in natural, social, historical, cultural, and individual conditions.

Another charge against legalism is that it is excessively rationalistic. I would agree that some Protestant and Catholic moral theology, as well as moral philosophy, has been excessively rationalistic. Rules and principles have been justified rationalistically, without due attention to the desires, drives, impulses, and affections that need to be rationally ordered. Application procedures have been rationalistic and have been based upon that sharp distinction between reason and affectivity, reason and "nature," that I have argued is incorrect. An often hidden assumption is that, as Midgley so nicely puts it, reason and desires are separate roles in a drama, as if the old "faculty" divisions of the person could still be defended. Or, in another of her metaphors, this drama often takes a "colonial" view of reason, as if it were an outside power that is necessary to dominate the crudities and incivilities of human nature. The correction that theocentric vision and piety bring is not antinomian and antirational. Rather, as I have previously indicated, it understands rational activity to be an ordering of not only our individual motives and desires but also of the natural world and social world in the light of what can be perceived and interpreted about the proper relations of things to each other and finally to divine governance.

A theocentric construal and an alteration of affections and valuations open the moral task to greater readiness to extend, revise, and alter some of the traditional moral rules. This construal is grounded in an interpretation of the divine governance that cannot claim the complete certainty that seems to be subjectively and objectively desirable in morality, particularly as novel occasions and possibilities for human action arise. It does not relieve the anxiety of taking risks; it does not eliminate the need sometimes to act unjustly for the sake of a wider justice; it does not resolve the deep ambiguities of moral choices in certain particular conditions; and it does not eliminate the possibility of genuine tragedy as a feature of human moral experience. It does not provide a bland assurance that something good will issue from every circumstance of what is injurious to human welfare, that every "crucifixion" will issue in a glorious "resurrection," that all things work together for good for those who love God.[38]

Indeed, the correction occurs most centrally in the displacement of the constricted anthropocentric sources of the material considerations of morality, and thus in interpreting the moral life to be more complex than the Western tradition has often taken it to be. I recur to an Augustinian distinction: while he perceived an order of nature (in his case an eternal and immutable one), he saw that the order of utility for human beings was not coincident with it. The human reference of morality is always one of utility for us; this does not imply that "utilitarianism" as a philosophical movement is the only way in which that utility is to be thought about. What the tradition has on the whole sustained is a view that the purpose of nature, and of society and culture, is finally to benefit man exclusively. Theocentric piety and vision claim that utility for man is not the sole criterion of an enlarged view of morality. Consenting to the divine governance requires that other ends and values and other aspects of nature be taken into account in developing the general rules and principles of moral action. Consenting to the divine governance, or "obedience to God," turns the moral question into, "What serves the divine purposes?" And the construal of the divine purposes, as we have seen, brings into consideration much more than human interests and ends. Other relationships become more significant than they traditionally have been. The scope of the vision of the divine governance sets the scope of the material considerations for human morality. Human agency based on our distinctive capacities expands our causal accountability beyond the well-being of the human life to the well-being of various "wholes" of which we are parts.

The Christian Religious Context

One of the themes of this book is that visions, ways of life, and intellectual activities take place in particular historical and communal contexts. They grow out of aspects of cultural histories and societies, and can be sustained only in communities that have their distinctive symbols, languages, and rites. This is true not only of religious views and activities, but it is necessarily true of them. Communities are bound together by common interests, common loyalties, common standards, and common languages. If a community of autonomous rational moral agents, that fictive denomination into which many contemporary moral philosophers

38. Rom. 8:28.

seek to convert us all, were actualized, it too would share these characteristics.

If this theme is correct, the sustaining of a theological interpretation of man must take place in the context of a religious community, with its first-order religious language, its liturgies and symbols, and its procedures for transmitting a heritage. To be sure, the distinctive aspects of the views developed in this book are not completely at home in any particular Christian denomination, liturgy, or community. Yet they are grounded in some aspects of the rich and varied heritage of the Bible and of the Christian church and tradition. There are themes in the worship and religious life of the Christian tradition that do evoke and sustain the views I have espoused. In emphasizing some of them I am not merely attaching an idiosyncratic view onto a tradition; I am indicating various aspects of the tradition that evoke and sustain my views.

Those interpretations of prayer, for example, that claim that God will intervene particularly in the course of events to fulfill the self-referential requests of a petitioner are in error. But this does not mean that meditative prayers, expressed in a traditional language, are of no meaning. The traditional forms of Christian prayer are adoration, confession, supplication, thanksgiving, and intercession. All of these forms can both express and evoke an expansion of the human spirit in the presence of the powerful Other. Indeed, well-composed prayers, like great poetry, both affectively and intellectually become antidotes to the poison of the contractions of individuals and communities.

One example is a prayer of adoration, taken from a Reformed liturgy.

> Almighty God, most blessed and most holy, before the brightness of whose presence the angels veil their faces; with lowly reverence and adoring love we acknowledge Thine infinite glory, and worship Thee, Father, Son, and Holy Spirit. Blessing and honour, and glory and power be unto our God, for ever and ever. Amen.[39]

The words and metaphors in this prayer express and evoke a sense of the presence of the Deity. "Most blessed and most holy" and "Almighty God" suggest the powers of God. "Before the brightness of whose presence the angels veil their faces" images the mystery and the awesomeness of the Deity. The human responses are there, suggesting appropriate forms of piety: lowly reverence, adoring love, and the acknowledgment of God's infinite glory. The ascription at the end expresses a powerful theocentric focus of attention: "Blessing and honour, and glory and power be unto

---

39. *The Book of Common Order of The Church of Scotland* (Oxford: Oxford University Press, 1940), p. 18.

our God, for ever and ever." As the first prayer in a liturgy, this immediately and affectively orients the individuals and community away from themselves to the Other on whom all things ultimately depend, and to whom all things are ultimately related. Human life and "all things" are reoriented in the presence of One before whose brightness the angels veil their faces.

Prayers of confession of sin and of thanksgiving need little comment. Both express profound religious sensibilities: the sense of remorse and repentance, and the sense of gratitude. Both express and evoke, in whatever descriptive generality or detail they are composed, deep affectivities and sustain basic religious dispositions and attitudes. Both, properly, are theocentrically oriented; it is before God that the community confesses that "we have not loved our neighbor as ourselves. . . ."[40] It is before God that the community expresses gratitude for all that makes human life possible, all that sustains it, and all that creates conditions of human flourishing.

Intercession and supplication are theologically more problematic. Well-composed intercessory prayers enlarge both consciousness and affectivity; they call to attention a range of needs and concerns that are appropriate for a community that acknowledges the breadth of the divine governance: concerns for justice in particular places of oppression, for resolution of costly conflicts in particular times, for awakening of the slothful human spirit to debilitating poverty, and for challenge of complacent acceptance of unfairness. The efficacy of intercession is in the enlargement of affections and expansion of the vision of needs of the world. Supplications, like intercessions, can be extremely self-regarding; but they can also have deep spiritual and moral effects: "Strengthen us against temptation. Teach us to do Thy will. Cause us to abound more and more in faith and love, in holy desires, in kind and brotherly affections, in pure and peaceable dispositions, and in patient and humble service," reads a portion of a prayer of supplication from a Reformed liturgy.[41]

Prayers can, of course, be poorly composed, and they always reflect the implied or explicit theology of those who offer them. Prayers reflect the vision of God that a person has. Confessions of sin as well as thanksgivings can indicate this. To a "kitchen god," only household sins are confessed; to a god who makes persons feel psychologically good, persons confess the impediments they place in their own and others' paths to feeling good. To a moral god who acts in history, the consequences of historical injustices imbedded in social institutions are confessed; to a god of nature, ecological sins are confessed. To a powerful Other, all these

40. Ibid., p. 18.
41. *Book of Common Order*, p. 19.

and others can be confessed. The scope of confessions reveals the scope
of the activities we accept accountability for in the presence of the Divine.
The scope of thanksgivings reveals the scope of benefits we acknowledge
to be grounded in God. The scope of the Divine that is worshipped limits
or broadens the scope of the activities for which persons feel accountable
or thankful.

Prayers are part of the affective and imaging language that properly
is used in particular historical communities to evoke and sustain a deep
consciousness of the place of man in relation to the Deity. They are
essential to the historical community that bears a stream of piety and
morality, and that community is essential to the preservation and growth
of theocentric piety and theology. Piety, like any other aspects of human
experience and endeavor, has a language appropriate to it, and prayers
are part of that language. Prayer is evoked by the presence of God; it
expresses, awakens, and sustains piety.

A sense of remorse and repentance accompanies a sense of obligation to the divine governance. There is a consciousness of fault, not
only of natural limitations. The genesis of this is surely in interpersonal
relations, and is described and interpreted by various theories of personality. Just as it is important for persons in relation to each other to be
forgiven and to see that significant relations are not ruptured completely
by actions for which they are blameworthy, so also it is important that
in the expanded religious consciousness there be symbols of forgiveness
and of the possibilities of reconciliation and renewal. Highly anthropomorphic interpretations of God or the gods attribute to Deity such things
as anger, vengeance, and retributive punishment for particular actions
or states of character.[42] Thus the history of religions is replete with cultic
rites to placate the gods, or with interpretations of particular events such
as the crucifixion of Jesus as vicarious offerings on behalf of all mankind.
Penitential disciplines have been developed that make the believer bear
some of the cost of reconciliation, and induce the desire to avoid further
sins.

We know that in Christianity particularly the consciousness of sin
can be exaggerated beyond its due proportions, and that destructive consequences to human well-being sometimes ensue, but we also know that
Christianity can provide "cheap grace." God is sometimes described as
so gracious, so loving, and so indulgent, that with lightness of heart persons can "sin bravely." This theology is expressed in preaching, in some
hymns, and in pastoral counseling. Such theology and ecclesiastical activity is in part a reaction against the excessive consciousness of sin and
guilt that the tradition is charged with instilling in many persons.

42. On God's "emotions," see, for examples, Jonah 3:10 and Exodus 32:9–14.

Above, I argued with considerable care that the traditional language of God the Redeemer does disclose something about God's relation to man and the world. Corporate religious life, in its symbols and its liturgies as well as more private forms of piety, provides ways of expressing the powers of renewal and forgiveness, and expresses those powers. The efficient causes and the means of forgiving grace are other persons, or symbolizations of God. Narratives of historical experiences of particular persons, assurances of pardon, and declarations of absolution are all practical devices that awaken in the religious consciousness the sense of the possibilities of reconciliation with God and with others. They are ways that help to turn persons, from being curved in not only on their own interests but on their own guilt, toward others and toward God. Excessive preoccupation with one's own guilt is itself a contraction of the soul that fences it into a small space, that inhibits participation in the powers that make human life morally effective and give it a sense of proper well-being. Historic religious language and liturgies function to engender a consciousness of fault, to free persons to rectify the consequences of their misdeeds, and to participate in the service of the purposes of God.

Partly as the result of the beautiful exposition of love in 1 Corinthians 13, faith, hope, and love have become central terms in describing Christian affections or virtues. The historic Christian message evokes these affections, and these affections are fitting characteristics of persons who are related to God through this historically particular religious culture and community. The theology of this work requires some emendations of traditional Christian claims about these and other matters. But the necessity for particular communal and individual activities that sustain such affections is not thereby eliminated. The contemporary exponents of the importance of "the Christian story" are correct in their recognition that the story bears the particular meaning of the tradition, and that one internalizes the meaning of the tradition only by participating in the community that makes it the common story of its life.[43] The fact that one might be convinced that the story is not fully appropriate to human experience and to various things we now know about the world does not eliminate the need for language of piety and education that bears its proper meanings.

Abstract language seldom evokes deep affective responses. Human virtues are seldom nourished only by naming them and exhorting persons

43. A canonical text for current theological interest in story is H. Richard Niebuhr, "The Story of Our Life," in *The Meaning of Revelation,* pp. 43–90. On a justification for the use of story in ethics, see David B. Burrell and Stanley Hauerwas, "From System to Story: An Alternative Pattern for Rationality in Ethics," and Hauerwas, "Story and Theology," in Stanley Hauerwas, *Truthfulness and Tragedy* (Notre Dame, Ind.: University of Notre Dame Press, 1977), pp. 15–39, pp. 71–81.

to cultivate them. There is a language appropriate to the practical necessities required to effect the sorts of persons we ought to become. To
say that God is love, that persons related to God are empowered to be
more loving, and that they ought to love, may be more effective than to
say that love is an enlargement of the soul, a reordering of the heart, and
an expansion of vision. But both are less effective than narratives of
loving persons and deeds, or parables. To say that God is the ground of
hope, and that persons related to God are empowered and ought to hope,
may have more affective power than to say that the divine governance
provides conditions of possibilities for persons and for societies. Both are
less effective than those narratives of forgiven deeds and altered lives in
expanding vision and reordering the heart. To say that God enables trust
and loyalty, and that persons who trust in him are enabled to be trusting
and loyal persons, may be more effective than to claim that the divine
governance is the ultimate reality that sustains conditions appropriate to
human well-being. But both are weaker by far than the accounts of persons
who trusted in God, and have been loyal to him. To say that man ought
to be faithful to God and that the ordering of life for which man is accountable ought to be in accord with the ultimate ordering purposes of
the Deity does not move the human spirit as much as accounts of human
faithfulness and human consent to the purposes of the divine power. And
a focus on one who incarnates theocentric piety and fidelity, on the narratives of his life, and on the parables and teaching attributed to him, has
a communal evocative and sustaining power that is necessary to generate
the religious affections or virtues that are commended. First-order religious discourse is a practical necessity; religious communities with their
various activities are practical necessities. No sophisticated reinterpretation or alteration of the meanings of the first-order language and symbols
eliminates their necessity.

I have indicated that the charges leveled against "legalism" in religious moral life are often correct. Yet the symbol of the "law of God"
is of practical significance in religious morality. The law of God symbolizes
the ordering of things objective to ourselves, as well as the ordering of
ourselves. It indicates that persons are under an obligation to relate all
things in a manner appropriate to their relations to God. The theocentric
focus of morality and the religious dimensions of morality are both suggested by this ancient term. I have not claimed that all good morality
must be grounded in a conscious acknowledgment of an ordering grounded
in God. But within piety it is not only intellectually appropriate to speak
of the ordering of life as the law of God but also to speak about it in
language that expresses religious devotion. If God is the object of ultimate
devotion and fidelity, it is proper to find terms that affectively express
that devotion and fidelity. Intellectually, as Gordon Kaufman says, the

term "God" is an imaginative construct that the theologian believes provides a clue to man's relation to "The Real."[44] But the aspects of that relation are affective as well as intellectual in their significance. The ordering and empowering of life is not merely a hypothesis developed to bring some final and ultimate coherence to the multiplicity of things and experiences. God is the object of piety and devotion. The community that relates to the world in piety and seeks to discern what the object of piety requires must have a language that engages affections. Within the context of communal religious life, with its symbols and activities, the language of the law of God expresses not only the notion that there is such a law, such an ordering, but also that its source is worthy of ultimate respect and awe, and that such faithfulness as persons manage to show in their deeds and relations is fidelity to One worthy of devotion. The language can bear the evocative power to enable and sustain deep affective dimensions to human morality. The Old Testament tradition, with its strong hymnodic articulations of a love for the law, succeeds in expressing this much better than modern Protestantism. "Oh, how I love thy law. It is my meditation all the day," a psalmist writes.[45] The law of God is not merely an external constraint to be feared; it not only grounds requisites to be taken into account in the ordering of life: it is the object of love, devotion, and thanksgiving. The love of the law of God can enlarge the soul, expand vision, and turn persons and communities curved in on themselves to the service of a larger whole.[46] The moral principles and values that can be established to provide guidance of human conduct and relations are not merely the objects of obligations and duties but also of love and thanksgiving. The language of the law of God suggests the religious context within which moral life is conducted; it is affectively rich.

In an essay that is concerned with a somewhat different issue, Troeltsch makes some claims that bear upon the importance of the historical community.

> The Christian idea . . . will never become a powerful reality without community and cult. . . . So long as Christianity survives in any form it will always be connected with the central position of Christ in the cult. It will either exist in this form or not at all. That rests on social-psychological laws that have produced exactly the same phenomena in other religious areas and recur a thousand times over on a smaller scale up to the present. They render utopian the whole idea of a piety that simply springs from

44. Kaufman, *God The Problem*, p. 88.
45. Ps. 119:97. R.S.V.
46. Ps. 19:7–10. Calvin frequently refers to the praise of the law by the psalmists. See, for example, *Institutes* II, 7, 12; McNeill ed., 1:361. See also, *Calvin: Commentaries,* trans. and ed. Joseph Haroutunian (Philadelphia: Westminster Press, 1958), pp. 327–28.

every man's heart and nevertheless forms a harmony, that does not need reciprocity and yet remains a living power. . . . Lectures on religious philosophy will never produce or replace a real religion.[47]

This certainly does not imply, for Troeltsch, that the centrality of Christ in the cult takes historic Christianity outside the range of debate, change, and criticism from the sciences. It does not mean that the tradition has not developed in the course of its history, and does not need to continue to develop. "The argument I have produced is a matter of social psychology," he concluded.[48]

This social-psychological function is no mean contribution to evoking and sustaining affectively and intellectually a view of man in relation to God and the world. I agree with Troeltsch that "[i]t is . . . impossible either to affirm or to deny that Christianity will last forever and community and cult remain bound to the historical personality of Jesus."[49] Christianity is a historical movement, and thus is in interaction with other aspects of culture and society. It has changed, it will continue to change, and it may well disappear in some distant future. With its links to its charter document, and with a reliving of the events that brought it into being, however, it continues to provide the basis for the enlargement of vision, the alteration and expansion of the order of the heart, and the motivation to participate in the ordering of all things in a manner appropriate to their relations to God. The substance of its message, as I have argued previously, is itself distilled from historical experiences of a people whose piety was great and who sought to construe the world in the light of the presence of an ultimate ordering power. This substance, and the various combinations and permutations of its meanings that the tradition offers, is a source of contemporary understanding of the place of human beings in relation to God, and of the requirements of human activity. The point here, however, is not to defend a view of "revelation" in the particularity of the tradition. It is to claim the full dignity of the practical significance of a particular historic community with its symbols, cult, liturgies, and primary religious language. Religious affectivity is not nurtured by abstractions; and more general and abstract reflections are motivated and informed by religious affectivity. The maintenance of a community and its symbols is a necessary condition for the preservation and even reconstruction of the piety and theology that I have developed.

47. Troeltsch, "The Significance of the Historical Jesus for Faith," in Morgan and Pye, eds., *Troeltsch,* p. 196 and p. 197.
48. Ibid., p. 202.
49. Ibid., p. 205.

It now remains in this volume to indicate the general lines of the ethics that is based upon this theology and piety, that is coherent with the major principles of our understanding of God in relation to man and the world, and man in relation to God and the world. From the theocentric perspective that informs this and the previous chapter, what does theocentric ethics look like?

7

Moral Life in
Theocentric Perspective

The practical moral question in a theocentric construal of the world is, as I have noted, "What is God enabling and requiring us to be and to do?" The most general answer is that we are to relate ourselves and all things in a manner appropriate to their relations to God.

It is not the purpose of this chapter to work out a theological ethics in any detail; the second volume of this work will develop some of the principal concepts of traditional ethics and examine some specific moral issues in relation to the theology of this volume. Here I shall briefly explicate the moral life, both individual and corporate, by construing it to be a process of discernment.[1] It is in a process of discernment that we come to some certitude (but not always certainty) about what God is enabling and requiring, and about the appropriate relations of ourselves and all things to God.

The biblical text that best points to the moral life in this religious and moral perspective is Romans 12: 1–2. The Revised Standard Version translation is:

> I appeal to you therefore, brethren, by the mercies of God, to present your bodies as a living sacrifice, holy and acceptable to God, which is your spiritual worship. Do not be conformed to this world [or "age"] but be transformed by the renewal of your mind, that you may prove what is the will of God, what is good and acceptable and perfect [or "what is the good and acceptable and perfect will of God"].

The New English Bible renders the verses as follows:

> I implore you by God's mercy to offer your very selves to him: a living sacrifice, dedicated and fit for his acceptance, the worship offered by mind and heart. Adapt yourselves no longer to the pattern of this present world, but let your minds be remade and your whole nature be transformed. Then you will be able to discern the will of God, and to know what is good, acceptable, and perfect.

Amending the verses to fit the development of this book, one can say the following:

> Individually and collectively offer yourselves, your minds and hearts, your capacities and powers in piety, in devoted and faithful service to God. Do not be conformed to the immediate and apparent possibilities or requirements of either your desires or the circumstances in which you live and act. But be enlarged in your

1. See Gustafson, "Moral Discernment in the Christian Life," in Gene H. Outka and Paul Ramsey, eds., *Norm and Context in Christian Ethics* (New York: Scribner's, 1968), pp. 17–36. Also in Gustafson, *Theology and Christian Ethics* (Philadelphia: United Church Press, 1974), pp. 99–119.

vision and affections, so that you might better discern what the divine governance enables and requires you to be and to do, what are your appropriate relations to God, indeed, what are the appropriate relations of all things to God. Then you might discern the will of God.

The process of discernment, as I shall describe it, reasonably follows from what I have written. It coheres with the principal lines of my interpretation of persons and communities, of the possibilities and limitations of knowledge of the divine governance, and with what we can claim about that governance.

While to discern something sometimes means that we simply perceive what is difficult to behold, such as the profile of a human face in a natural rock formation, discerning normally bears a qualitative meaning. A discerning person is one who has a certain keenness of mind, hearing, sight, and so forth. The discerning critic of literature, art, or music is one who can describe, interpret, and evaluate things in such a way that their readers' perceptions, understandings, and evaluations become keener and more discriminating. To discern is not merely to see or to hear; it is to discriminate. Description of the process of discernment requires that attention be given to some of its facets, and this is best done with an example.

Think of different biographers, and their works. One expects every biographer to master the available information about his subject, about the times and events in which he or she lived, and so forth. If the subject was personally known to the author, one expects sound observations of the actions, relations, and events that are significant. The word "significant" begins to be one criterion by which we distinguish a discerning biographer from one who, in a positivistic way, simply gathers all available facts and arranges them chronologically. What is deemed significant is related to the author's sensitivity to the salient features of the subject's life: the important relationships, the critical events. Differences between biographers in part are differences in their sensitivities and their empathic capacities. The discerning author has insight into the important features of the subject; attention is not given to all available information but to that which sheds light on the subject's actions, character, and relationships. The interpretation, we say, is perceptive. It is subtle, and does not cram information into a simple general causal thesis about human life and activity. Yet its perceptiveness is in part due to the author's awareness of various factors that, if they do not determine life and action, establish certain conditions, explain certain desires and purposes of the subject, illuminate the subject's conflicts of motives, and so forth. A biographer who violates simple rules of accuracy for the sake of an explanatory thesis would not count as discerning. The determination of the salient features involves discrimination, a keenness of perception, subtlety, and imagination. It involves judgments about what is of greatest importance in understanding the life of the subject. Biography is not merely the collection of facts but the interpretation of a life: its motives, its decisions, its perceptions of the world of which it was a part, its responses to events, its conflicts and its aspirations, its effects on others and on events in which it participated. A discerning biographer gives the reader an understanding of the subject that is not only insightful but can be tested by others for its accuracy and explanatory power.

    Discerning what the divine governance enables and requires obviously is different in important respects from discerning the character and qualities of a human life. But there are some common elements in both processes. What does the person who discerns (in both a descriptive and evaluative sense) bring to the process? There is one's own nature; one's desires, appetites, and natural capacities. There is the particularity of one's life experiences and interests. A biographer of the last czar and his family who experiences hemophilia in his own family can shed insight on their actions that another biographer cannot.[2] Sensitivities, affectivities, capacities for empathy, and imagination are important. Imagining possibilities of motives, aspirations, and responses plays an important part. But what has been imagined must be tested; a biography is not a novel. There is a drive for the greatest possible degree of accuracy of knowledge; the biographer who believes that human character and action are explainable by a relatively single-minded theory casts the writing in ways coherent with such a belief. Principles of analysis are important; at least at some stages the fair-minded biographer is willing to test alternative principles of explanation of the life and actions of the subject. Synthetic principles or capacities are needed to bring some measure of coherence and wholeness to what is known and observed. Irrelevant principles of analysis and synthesis are discarded, yet there must be sufficient open-mindedness to avoid premature foreclosure: capacities for judgment are informed by all these and other elements. They go into establishing the perspective and the point of vision that bring the "reality" responded to and acted upon into a coherent and manageable whole. All of these go into making discerning choices and judgments, not only in the writing of biographies, but also in many other areas of human experience, including moral experience.

    Before describing the components of moral discernment, an account of some other ways of making moral choices is in order. One, often practiced in its worst form in medical ethics, is a checklist of "facts" to

2. See Robert K. Massie, *Nicholas and Alexandra* (New York: Dell, 1969).

be taken into account, a framework of analytical principles, and a few moral principles, all of which presumably lead to the correct moral choice or judgment. The relevant medical facts about the patient are listed in accurate scientific language; to this are added probabilities of prognosis, and other facts about the patient that are judged to be morally relevant, such as age, economic status, and home conditions. The moral principle of informed consent is applied, and the consequences of possible courses of action are assessed in terms of a risk/benefit ratio. To be sure, there are matters of judgment at every stage, and some are more readily agreed upon than others. Differences in judgment about the diagnosis may be conditioned by differences in judgment about the importance of relevant medical facts, but presumably this is a matter of scientific judgment. Prognosis involves predictions, and here differences occur over the weight to be given to the particular patient's conditions within a range of probabilities about which there is likely to be agreement. What constitutes adequate information for a patient and the patient's understanding of it, and what constitutes "free" consent, are matters of judgment within relatively standard limits. Assessment of possible beneficial and harmful consequences is on surer ground where there is long experience and where the "laws of cause and effect" are most stringently applicable. When benefits and harms go beyond the more strictly biological, the range and quality of probable consequences are more difficult to assess. The question of what other facts about the patient (age and home conditions, for example) ought to be taken into account as morally relevant is likely to evoke more disagreement. But there is an aspiration, I believe, on the part of many physicians and moralists to work out such a procedure so that the choice eliminates all moral ambiguity. The model is more like that of a scientific experimenter than of an experienced and perceptive clinician. The checklist and framework of procedures may well be rudimentary conditions in a process of moral discernment, but they do not fully capture an important element—how the parts are interrelated in a kind of whole. The choice, in the end, is about the whole with its parts in relation; an excessively "mechanical" way of making choices and judgments can be an impediment to seeing the "whole." The adding up of all the relevant facts, the application of relevant analytical principles and the application of one or a few prescriptive moral principles does not guarantee moral discernment. It can be important to engage in such a procedure, however, to make more certain that nothing important is left out of the reflective process that is more than the sum of the parts.

A second procedure is extremely intuitive, not of certain first moral principles judged to be self-evident, but of the proper response in the distinctive set of circumstances in which one is moved to act. There are "moral virtuosos" whose native talents, capacities for empathy and insight, and accumulated experience seem to enable them to make discerning moral choices without much or any self-conscious reflection or rational justification. They seem to have virtually a faculty one could call "moral sense," or at least capacities that have developed through a variety of moral experiences and that they can rely on in new and somewhat different circumstances. In contemporary Christian ethics one finds examples of this among persons who perceive what conditions are "dehumanizing" and what actions will enhance the "humanization" of life. To such persons an analysis of the elements of the "human" or an effort to determine a supreme principle of humanization are often academic impediments to trustworthy sensitive and perceptive intuitions. Among physicians one finds those who have confidence in their perceptions of the right course of action in a given case, but who have difficulty in giving the moral reasons, or at least sufficient moral reasons, to explain the rightness of the course of action. No doubt among such physicians there is a fund of assimilated scientific knowledge, and they undoubtedly use various procedures to determine the diagnosis of the patient's problem. The perception relies upon knowledge, assimilated principles of explanation, and experience with cases similar in the medical aspects of the decision. Where nonmedical factors enter in as morally relevant there is likely again to be reliance upon experience with similar cases. But the judgment is made on a kind of perception of the whole set of circumstances. Often it is a morally better judgment than the reasons that are given for it. It might be very discerning in a qualitative sense. But the question is whether, apart from some apparent capacities of moral genius, one can rely upon such judgments without the critical self-examination and self-consciousness that the more formal apparatus offers. The question is what constitutes an adequately informed and reflective process of discernment.

Moral dogmatists, with a single principle, or with a set of moral rules, are usually not discerning in their choices and judgments. One reason for this is that the rules often determine what is relevant about the particular persons or circumstances involved, and other features are excluded because they do not fit the rules. Aristotle long ago saw that whether a law is applicable to an act depends upon the "description" of the act, on the "label" that is put on it.[3] A rule prohibits an act: "Thou shalt not murder." Any act, then, that is described as murder is always morally wrong. A contemporary example of what, in my judgment, can be rather undiscerning moral judgments is the advocacy of an absolute prohibition of induced abortions. Induced abortions are said to come under the rule because they are acts of murder. What qualifies them as murder involves another judgment that embryonic and fetal life are human

3. Aristotle, *Rhetoric*, 1374, in *The Basic Works*, p. 1371.

life. The rule and the description, then, limit the aspects of the circumstances that are morally relevant. The rule and the description focus on what is believed to be *the* morally relevant feature of the case. The circumstances in which the pregnancy occurred, the motives of the woman seeking an abortion, and the probable consequences of the continuation of the pregnancy both for the mother and the child, are all deemed morally irrelevant. It takes no discrimination to determine the morally appropriate course of action in this way of thinking. The model for morality is a legal one, plain and simple. And, while certain general principles or laws require discrimination in their application precisely because of their generality, a moral rule with its particular prohibition of a particular act under a particular kind of description does not. There is no moral ambiguity because what is morally relevant is limited by the rule and the description. There is no moral tragedy, because the moral rightness of the act is determined by its conformity to the rule rather than by its consequences. There are no really serious conflicts of values, since a single value is supreme and overriding.

Among groups with common religious and moral interests, as well as among some groups concerned with public policy, one sometimes finds that the accumulation of information about a social or interpersonal moral problem is judged sufficient to lead to a moral conclusion. The ethical premise is suppressed. It is assumed that there is agreement about the major ethical premise or premises, and that they need not be lifted out for articulation and examination. The problem with this procedure is not that it always leads to morally wrong or inadequate conclusions; indeed, the conclusions are often morally defensible. Rather, the problem is that the suppressed ethical premises are not clearly stated and understood, and often are too simple to give the prescriptive guidance that a complicated social or moral situation requires. The information that is accumulated is often selective, and the selection is determined by the suppressed premises. The information is ordered in such a way that there appears to be only one possible moral conclusion to be drawn from it, and that conclusion is dictated by the suppressed premise that informs the ordering of the information. A good deal of "prophetic" moral discourse is of this sort. The evil of present social arrangements, detailed with examples and often quantified data, is vividly described. The description presumably is sufficient to lead to the conclusion that what is described is evil, and the necessity for change is prescribed. I am not suggesting that it is necessary to draw a sharp distinction between facts and values, as if the description of the "facts" can be morally neutral and values can then be used to evaluate the facts independently. One need not describe, for example, the processes of a torture in their physical or psychological terms and then independently ask why such processes and consequences are to be morally condemned. "Torture" is a description of processes that includes a moral evaluation. Medical descriptions of malnutrition and starvation need not be made independent of the value considerations which are applied to them. It is patently clear that malnutrition and famine have bad consequences for those who suffer from them. To see that such things are evil requires no sophisticated argument. But there is merit in understanding why such things are evil, what reasons one would give for their evil, and what moral theories can be adduced to make a strong moral argument in favor of doing something about them. Further, any actions that are to be recommended for rectifying such conditions require more than a moral indictment. Discernment of the available and appropriate means of action requires that, in the case of malnutrition, many other facts be taken into account. There is a weighing of various costs and benefits to be made. The question of justice is not resolved in the abstract, but must be asked in relation to the various interests that are necessarily involved in mitigating what is patently evil. If the moral indictment is clear as a result of the description, the actions to rectify it require the acquisition of different kinds of information and discerning judgments about policies that are feasible and adequate to respond to the problem. Often, and always in complex situations, there is no morally or socially perfect way to meet the needs described. Discernment is required not only in making a case for the existence of a wrong to be rectified but also in determining the effective response. Although this is the case, prophetic spirits who, for whatever reasons and experiences, have unusually acute antennae for indications of moral evil are an important ingredient in the human community, and religious moral sensitivities often sustain such acuteness.

Two questions remain to be answered more precisely. What goes into moral discernment as a process undertaken by agents? What can be discerned about the divine governance by this process? A general answer to the second will follow an answer to the first.

In the order of experience moral discernment begins with an evaluative description of the occasion or circumstances that come to our attention. Seldom do persons initiate the process of moral action; they seldom go out to seek an occasion or circumstances in which they can exercise their powers in accord with their moral convictions and principles. Generally events, occasions, and circumstances that come to attention provoke moral judgments and initiate processes of reflection and action. The response is not to "raw" events but to an understanding that I call an evaluative description, or a descriptive evaluation. Either consciously or intuitively we depict that to which we feel affectively moved to respond. In general human experience there is an affective aspect to our attentiveness to events. In the order of experience there are probably few persons who read the newspapers or observe what is occurring around them with, for example, a theory of justice in the forefront of their consciousness, ready to evaluate what is being made known to them in the light of it. Our "sense" of injustice more normally awakens our attention and motivates further reflection and action.

Evaluative descriptions have various elements. One is simply an awareness, or disciplined gathering, of pertinent information. Highly commendable moral discernment requires that effort be made to gather relevant information, test its accuracy, and not to avoid any that might alter our initial moral feelings about things. Moral judgments about the actions of others and moral reflection about our own proposed action require a discipline of "research." The variations of the depth and extent of such research, of course, are relative to the issues involved, the time constraints under which choices have to be made, and so forth. But research is essential, since inadequate or mistaken information can lead to serious moral errors. Also, in moral disputes sometimes the issues turn out to be factual matters.

An evaluative description develops on the basis of discernment of the salient information, or the salient aspects of an event. Information is in relation to attention and intention; not all possible information is taken into account. To respond to an event is to respond to an account of the salient features of the event, and to an ordering of those features in such a way that the event has a measure of coherence. There are different types of judgment about the saliency of particular features. One attends to the most significant causal factors in the event or circumstances. If we are engaged in making a moral judgment, the judgment is dependent upon ascertaining the important causal factors about which assessment of moral accountability can be made. An evaluative description involves an explanation of what has come to be. Descriptions differ, in part depending upon the time span one takes into account in explaining, and have effects upon the assessment of moral accountability. For example, there were several conflicting accounts of the war in Vietnam. The evaluative descriptions of that situation differed in part on the basis of the point in time chosen to begin an explanation of it, and the causal factors judged to have brought it about.

Another judgment is of what factors are morally relevant. Descriptions of the same "raw" events or circumstances differ in part on the basis of persons' perceptions and conceptions of what is morally at stake in them. And choices of what is morally significant in turn affect individuals' judgments about what is causally significant. For example, in the debates about the Vietnam War, differences of moral and other value judgments were critical and affected how persons construed the war. Whether it was a war of liberation from oppression by the poor and oppressed who had been subjected to generations of colonial imperialism or a war to restrain an evil political and military force made a difference in persons' assessments of the morally relevant features of the conflict, and even of the means that were justified in conducting it. If the motives of the formerly dominant powers were judged to be evil, the explanation of how the conflict came about differed from one in which the motives were deemed to be good. The differences were not resolvable simply by taking account of the same facts; different information was important depending on the moral and political perspectives of the participants in the debate.

The determination of a course of action in response to an event requires an analysis of the features that can be affected by the means of power available. In part such judgments are made in the light of what are deemed to be causally significant factors; to alter the direction of the powers that are being used is to affect the course of events. But there is no necessary symmetry between a causal analysis of what is occurring and an analysis of what powers are available to alter it. An impact on public opinion through the media, for example, might well have an indirect, but very important, effect on political and military choices. Persuasion or pressure on others who are not immediately involved but who have access to lines of influence on those who are is used in many circumstances to realize ends that persons believe to be morally or socially desirable.

The evaluative description is from a perspective, and the perspective has a critical significance for choices made about how events or circumstances are to be construed. Perspective widens or narrows the range of factors that are considered important. I have already indicated the importance of a time perspective. If one begins an interpretation of an act of theft with the particular act itself, it will be construed differently than if one examined possible motives for the act (e.g., some pathological condition of the agent) or certain social conditions which predisposed the person to engage in theft. The time-span that is judged to be relevant is a matter determined by one's perspective, and it has consequences for the evaluation. This is the case with reference not only to past time but also to possible future consequences. If the consequences to be considered in a moral discussion of abortion are limited to the time of the death of the fetus, one's interpretation will be different from one in which the probable consequences of the continuation of the pregnancy both for the fetus and for the mother are taken into account. The slogan "No unwanted child ought to be born" stems from the perspective of a different time-frame; such force as it has depends upon predictions about the quality of the subsequent life of the child.

Perspective also involves considerations of the range or "space" of relationships to be taken into account. We have seen how a fundamentally anthropocentric perspective tends to make the "interests" of nonhuman aspects of life instrumental to the human, how the natural world is construed to exist for the service of man, and how this limits what is judged to be relevant to policy and personal choices. In a traditional distinction, a perspective of egoism will construe the aspects of circumstances and events in a very different way from one of altruism. The "totality," as Roman Catholic moral theology calls it, to be taken into account has profound effects on the range of morally permissible acts. It has judged permissible, for example, the mutilation of the body by surgical removal of a diseased organ, because the relevant totality is the body as a whole with health as the end. It has judged it permissible to take the life of a criminal for due cause because the continued existence of the person may be a serious threat to the well-being of the society; the relevant totality is the particular society or community and the common good is the end. It has not deemed it permissible, however, to foster "artificial" means of conception control in the face of potential harmful consequences of overpopulation of the species in a nation or in the world as a whole. The species, it has claimed, is not an acceptable totality. This judgment arises from a perspective: the totality of the species is not a "finality" in the way that the totality of the individual body is, and its "common good" is not an approved end.

Moralists often determine the proper time- and space-limitations on the basis of how they distinguish between the moral and the nonmoral. The arguments about this need not be rehearsed here; their importance is apparent. If one has a very sharp, clear, and narrow conception of what constitutes the moral, and if moral discernment is confined within that, many considerations that would become relevant from broader perspectives of time and space are virtually eliminated by the stipulation of the definition. The benefit of this is to limit what must be taken into account from a distinctively moral perspective; its error is that events, circumstances, and actions cannot be so neatly divided in their aspects and consequences.

One's perspective affects one's analysis of the causes that are operative and of the powers available to affect the course of events. This perspective is shaped by inclination, training, and settled convictions. An illustration can be drawn from debates about international economics. Either on the basis of the restrictions of professional competence, or of a belief that purely economic factors are the most critical, economists define the problems and the prospects for prosperity in purely economic terms. A cultural anthropologist, however, with competence in the understanding not only of a particular culture but also of how various cultural factors affect choices and understandings of the good life, finds the economic analysis and prescriptions highly reductionistic. A moralist deeply committed to an egalitarian principle of distributive justice interprets the circumstances in the light of the vast discrepancies in standards of living between rich and poor nations, and between the rich and the poor within nations. This moral perspective leads to a different account both of the causes and solutions of problems. Greed, for example, becomes a cause of the problem; and the prescription is likely to be ready to enforce limitations on the liberties of people to produce and consume what they prefer for the sake of producing those things needed to raise the standard of living of the poor and oppressed. Each of these three perspectives is likely to be judged reductionist by the other two. One's inclination and training affect the depiction of the issue, and in turn affect the processes of moral discernment.

Obviously the human values and moral principles to which agents are committed affect their discernments. This has been noted in previous chapters. Persons dedicated to the principle that individual liberty is to be maximized and protected from as many intrusions as possible will assess the moral relationship between a patient and a physician or the relationship between the state and its citizens in a way that differs from that of a person who believes that there is a correct "paternalism" (a concern for the well-being of others that justifies overriding their self-determination in some circumstances), or who believes that the common good of the nation and of particular groups within it justifies state intervention. Persons who value flourishing of "nature" take environmental factors into account in a different way from persons who view nature as being exclusively in the service of man. The calculator of cost/benefit ratios, a kind of utility calculation, is appalled at the expenses required to make public transportation facilities accessible to all handicapped persons. Those for whom a severe handicap is not a morally relevant feature argue from a principle of justice that all citizens have an equal right of access to public facilities, and it is the obligation of justice to make them available. Individual reflection and public discussion are appropriate and necessary to determine which values and principles have priority, not only in general but in the constraining circumstances of the particular events in which choices have to be made.

More generalized beliefs about the world affect our valuations and moral discernment. These have been developed previously. If, as I have indicated, one believes that the rest of the natural world exists for the service of man, many things follow regarding the morally appropriate courses of action. If one believes that man is properly described by Hobbes and that self-interest motivates every action, human relations of contracts and restraints against egoism will flourish. If one believes that there is a timeless and changeless moral order in the universe that can be accurately known, the procedures for making moral choices is different from those that follow from other metaphysical beliefs. Certainly religious beliefs are among those that affect moral discernment.

Our affectivities and dispositions affect moral discernment. A person with a deep sense of duty and obligation to others is likely to come to different judgments in particular cases than a person dedicated to individual self-realization as the primary goal of life. From various causes some persons are more acutely sensitive to the sufferings of others and more willing to sacrifice something of their own for the sake of others in need. Perhaps hopeful persons envision possibilities for good in the course of events that "realists" and "pessimists" do not.

But moral discernment does not flow with an automatic ease and pleasure from all of these factors. Moral discernment is reflective; it is a rational activity. It is reflection on one's own motives and desires. These are examined and tested in the light of both formal and material principles. Persons and communities ought to be able to give good reasons for the choices they make, and they ought to be able to give good reasons for the values and substantive moral principles that decisively determine their choices. Sorting out the good and bad consequences and the better and worse means or courses of action is a reflective process. Ends are chosen; they do not merely flow from the sorts of persons we are becoming. In the interpretation of moral discernment given here, however, what is taken into account is expanded from the narrower limits that many religious and secular moralists suggest. The final discernment is an informed intuition; it is not the conclusion of a formally logical argument, a strict deduction from a single moral principle, or an absolutely certain result from the exercises of human "reason" alone. There is a final moment of perception that sees the parts in relation to a whole, expresses sensibilities as well as reasoning, and is made in the conditions of human finitude. In complex circumstances it is not without risk. To be sure, there are rules that fit cases so clearly that the discernment offers certainty and does not evoke critical ambivalence or ambiguity; the rule against murder is a case in point. There are general rules and principles that have strong presumptive authority. To be sure, in the normal course of events our socially and personally habitual discernments and responses are reliable. With social and cultural changes and with developments in technology and politics, however, many of the critical choices are morally fallible.

Our second large question is, What can be discerned about the divine governance? The second volume of my work will take up this question in greater detail. The divine governance can be known by a process of discernment. What can be discerned, and with what degree of certitude, follows from the discussion above. There, some possibilities were ruled out. What can be said about the divine governance when development in nature, history, culture, society, and self are taken into account rules out a timeless and changeless moral order. This does not imply that the human community is in a state of absolute relativism about its moral choices, or that in certain circumstances there is uncertainty about what course of action should be followed. It does imply, however, that ethics itself develops, and that as changes in the world objective to individual and corporate agents occur, traditional principles need to be extended in their applications, may need to be revised, and in some instances may need to be radically altered. The realities in which we experience the divine governance in nature and culture, for example, develop, and with them there must be development in ethics itself. In complex and difficult matters we often do not have freedom from the ambiguity of human and other values. We quite properly do not have the certainty that some Roman Catholic moral theologians and moral philosophers believe we can attain in many particular instances.

The divine governance is not revealed to us in its moral details in the Scriptures. The use of the Bible to gain insight into the law of God must be in accord with what I have said about its contributions to theology. We have there the record of a people of piety who, under their historical and natural conditions, did discern what was morally required of them. The changes that occurred in their perceptions and discernments are in the biblical record; the morality given in the Bible is not timeless and changeless. To be sure, there are commandments that one cannot foresee being broken without moral guilt (such as those condemning murder and adultery and attitudes such as covetousness). The Priestly Code prescribes both moral and cultic conduct in great detail, and some of the particular prescriptions and the principles that are implied by them have perduring force and authority. But within the Old Testament it is clear that a process of development of a moral tradition has taken place. The morality given in the Bible is distilled by a community of piety and faithfulness from their own perceptions and understandings of the divine governance through the course of their history.

In the second volume more attention will be given to what can be discerned about the divine governance, and how it can be discerned. What can be discerned, to put the matter abstractly, are the necessary conditions for life to be sustained and developed. There are fundamental requisites that can be perceived and must be taken into account not only for individual and interpersonal life but also for social institutional life and the life of the species; and not only for these but also for the proper relationships of human activity to the ordering of the natural world. A statement of these conditions or requisites emerges from reflection on the various arenas of human experience and activity, and from the knowledge that we have about nature and society. They are bound to be general, and quite formal in character. These requisites form the bases of ethics; they are not sufficient in themselves to determine the proper ordering of relationships and the proper courses of action in particular circumstances and events. And changes can occur not only in our perceptions of the requisites but in the requisites themselves, or at least in the substantive or material content that they take on in different times and places. As bases for ethics they not only establish the grounds of more particular and precise principles and general rules but also indicate the basic directions that more particular ordering and actions must take. The conditions or needs that they delineate can be met, at least in some cases, in a variety of ways which vary with natural, historical, cultural, and social conditions. Our knowledge of these conditions changes and develops in the course of changes in our understandings of the natural and social worlds. Not only does our knowledge change, but the worlds of which we are a part undergo changes; they are processes of ordering, not changeless and timeless orders. And our knowledge-conditions are relative to the cultures and periods of history of which any generation is a part. Because of the developments of science and technology, for example, certain courses of action are possible in our time that were not possible earlier. We understand the operations of the human body in ways we did not earlier, and this understanding makes a difference in ethics. Traditional Roman Catholic moral theology on medical matters was grounded in Aristotelian biology; modern biology, when taken into account, will alter those aspects of the medical ethics of the tradition that assumed an Aristotelian biology.

This does not lead to a radical relativism in ethics, nor does it deny that certain actions and certain relationships are always wrong. Most human choices are in areas in which certain absolute prohibitions can be assumed to set the outer limits of morally approvable actions and relations; many critical issues both for individuals and communities, however, are not resolved by them. Slavery and murder are always wrong fundamentally because they violate respect for persons, but that principle does not in itself resolve the question of how to deal with massive dependence of large numbers of people on the choices made by those who have power to determine national or international economic arrangements and developments. Those arrangements put masses at the mercy of others, but we do not call that slavery; they may lead to malnutrition and death, but we do not call that murder.

Radical relativism is limited in complex circumstances by both "objective" and "subjective" factors. Although in finitude we cannot know perfectly what the divine governance is, or precisely what is required by it in particular situations, there is an objective grounding and basis for our more particular ethical reflection in that ordering of life.

Subjectively, we have accumulated human experience: institutions, and other arrangements that have developed to provide many of the necessary conditions for human life; the vast body of reflection about these conditions, and about the institutions and proper ends of human activity that are recorded in the religious and ethical literatures of human cultures; narrations and evaluations of historical movements and events; the sciences that more accurately depict the operations of nature and society; factors of "ethos" that have sustained valued qualities of life; literature in dramatic, fictional, and poetic forms that disclose poignantly many aspects of human moral experience; and so forth.

What the view here espoused does limit is the certainty that would be ideally desirable in making moral choices in complex circumstances and in determining policies for collective action. We may come to a considerable degree of certitude about what relations are appropriate and what actions are right, but apart from relatively simple and extreme circumstances we do not have certainty. Limits of knowledge, foreknowledge, and the capacity to control many of the consequences of our interventions prohibit the achievement of absolute certainty. Conflicting values and claims, each of which can be ethically defended, cannot always be brought into harmony. Costs are involved in every complex choice: some properly valued ends cannot be achieved because others have been chosen and pursued; some proper interests cannot be met because others have been judged to be of greater merit; in many circumstances, some persons necessarily have to take risks, suffer, and even die because larger purposes require this. Tragedy, though not necessarily in an intense psychological form, is present in human moral and social life even as it seeks to consent to the divine governance. What is evil for some persons necessarily occurs in the pursuit of what is good for others—not only good for other persons but for social causes and for the sake of nature itself. As Augustine pointed out, the order of nature and the order of utility for the human community do not coincide.

The divine governance does not eliminate natural or moral evils, though persons have the capacities and responsibilities to avoid both insofar as possible. Persons and institutions might offer justifications for the infliction of evil on others. A just war might be a good reason for subjecting persons to suffering and death. But the evil remains evil; the loss of a soldier's life is no less an evil because it can be justified. One might be instructed that to take the life of a fetus is justified, but that does not eliminate the fact that the death ends a possibility for a person to develop who would have been of value and would have contributed values to others. One might be instructed that in combat one's intention is to incapacitate an enemy, and that if he is in fact killed that is accidental to the intention, but the rationalization does not remove the fact that one person has killed another. One might be instructed that third-world countries must accumulate sufficient capital to establish the degree of economic well-being which will provide for its citizens, but that does not eliminate the deprivations and suffering of many who are told, in effect, to wait patiently for a better day. One might have good reasons to honor the autonomy of a patient who refuses a medical procedure that could restore a good measure of health, but that does not eliminate the consequences of that death to persons dependent upon the patient for aspects of their own well-being. Ethics in the theocentric perspective developed in this book does not provide absolute moral certainty or eliminate tragedy.

Mary Midgley suggests that we need to get rid of the language of means and ends, and "use instead that of part and whole."[4] I believe she is incorrect to suggest we eliminate the language of means and ends but correct in suggesting that we need to take much more seriously the language of part and whole. Means and ends, and governing life according to moral principles, need to be seen in relation to a larger whole than individualistic and anthropocentric visions permit. Ethics in the theocentric perspective developed here both encourages and requires this. Ethics in theocentric perspective does not guarantee happiness, though it does not consign us to discontent. It requires consenting to the governance of the powers of God, and joining in those purposes that can be discerned. God does not exist simply for the service of man; man exists for the service of God.

Jonathan Edwards: "[T]he last end for which God has made moral agents must be the last end for which God has made all things."[5]

4. Midgley, *Beast and Man*, p. 359.
5. Edwards, *True Virtue*, p. 25.

Index

343